THE BIBLE IN MODERN CULTURE

Baruch Spinoza to Brevard Childs

• •

SECOND EDITION

Roy A. Harrisville

&

Walter Sundberg

WILLIAM B. EERDMANS PUBLISHING COMPANY
GRAND RAPIDS, MICHIGAN / CAMBRIDGE, U.K.

Wm. B. Eerdmans Publishing Co.

255 Jefferson Ave. S.E., Grand Rapids, Michigan 49503 /

P.O. Box 163, Cambridge CB3 9PU U.K.

Printed in the United States of America

07 06 05 04 03 02   7 6 5 4 3 2 1

Library of Congress Cataloging-in-Publication Data

Harrisville, Roy A.

The Bible in modern culture : Baruch Spinoza to Brevard Childs /

Roy A. Harrisville and Walter Sundberg. — 2nd ed.

p.   cm.

Includes bibliographical references and indexes.

ISBN 0-8028-3992-4 (alk. paper)

1. Bible — Criticism, interpretation, etc. —

History — Modern period, 1500-

I. Sundberg, Walter.   II. Title.

BS500 .H36 2002

220.6′092′2 — dc21

2002069680

www.eerdmans.com

THE BIBLE IN MODERN CULTURE

Contents

Contents

Contents

Acknowledgments

The first edition of this book, which appeared in 1995, had the invaluable help of colleagues at Luther Seminary: Librarian Bruce Eldevik, who shouldered the onerous task of checking birth and death dates of scores of persons cited; Old Testament scholar Mark Throntveit, who read the chapter on Rudolf Bultmann; and historian Todd Nichol, who examined the entire text and spared us many an error. The original edition could not have appeared without the Board of Directors of Luther Seminary and Lutheran Brotherhood Insurance Company of Minneapolis. The former granted sabbatical leaves; the latter helped with financing.

For this second edition Bruce Eldevik was kind enough to check dates for new figures cited, and Todd Nichol read added chapters on Adolf Schlatter, Paul Ricoeur, and Brevard Childs. A major portion of the chapter on Childs appeared in *Reclaiming the Bible for the Church,* ed. Carl E. Braaten and Robert W. Jenson (Grand Rapids: Wm. B. Eerdmans, 1995). Whatever fault remains is ours alone.

The basic theological frame of our argument has not changed in this second edition. The tests of the validity of our argument are two: first, the accuracy of the individual portraits; and second, the ability to place the figures studied in a context that illuminates their contribution to biblical scholarship.

To our students at Luther Seminary, who got this book going years back, this volume is dedicated with gratitude and affection.

ROY A. HARRISVILLE
WALTER SUNDBERG

Abbreviations

AW   Ferdinand Christian Baur, *Ausgewählte Werke in Einzelausgaben,* ed. Klaus Scholder, 5 vols. (Stuttgart: Friedrich Frommann, 1963-75)

GS   Ernst Troeltsch, *Gesammelte Schriften,* 4 vols. (Tübingen: J. C. B. Mohr, 1922-25; repr. Aalen: Scientia, 1962-77)

LW   *Luther's Works,* ed. Jaroslav Pelikan and Helmut Lehmann, 55 vols. (St. Louis: Concordia and Philadelphia: Fortress, 1955-86)

WA   *Weimarer Ausgabe, Martin Luthers Werke: Kritische Gesamtausgabe,* ed. J. D. F. Knaake et al. (Weimar: H. Böhlau, 1883ff.)

About This Book

I. The Subject of This Book

Historical-critical study of the Bible is a necessary component of responsible theology. To employ historical-critical method is to subject the putatively factual material and literary structure of the Bible to independent investigation in order to test their truthfulness and to discern their original historical meaning. This independent investigation assumes that the outcome of research will not be predetermined by a guarantee of the Bible's infallibility. The student of Scripture, using historical-critical method, is placed under the imperative of the historian who must seek the facts no matter where they lead.

The achievements of historical-critical study of the Bible are astounding. We know more now than the church has ever known about the historical backgrounds of both Testaments. Form criticism and tradition criticism have disclosed the process of text formation, and linguistic research has probed the meaning of the biblical vocabulary. We are more aware of the discrete theologies that make up the Bible and the ways they interrelate and differ. The volume of scholarly literature on the Bible, grounded in historical-critical method, is immense and, for the most part, unrestricted by confessional or national boundaries. Bibliographical research in this material operates efficiently at an international level. All major biblical scholars practice some form of historical-critical method. It is assumed widely among theologians. While hermeneutical proposals for doing theology continue to abound and conflict, historical-critical method appears to offer a common basis for dis-

1

cussion among even the most disparate parties. It is hard to imagine how the Christian intellectual community could live without historical-critical study of the Bible.

But can the church live with historical criticism? It is no secret that serious tension exists between historical criticism and the church. The problem goes much deeper than the issue of scholarly independence to pursue facts wherever they lead. The relationship of historical criticism and the church is characterized by deep-seated theological and doctrinal conflict over fundamental presuppositions of thought. A generation ago, Gerhard Ebeling made the following assertion: "[Historical criticism] is indeed all out to justify its existence as an independent theological discipline by discovering more and more new and increasingly radical theories of an anti-traditional kind. . . . [T]he impulses which lead to real advance in the development of this discipline are without question those which sharpen the tension with traditional dogmatics."[1] The same observation could be made today. Indeed, the problem appears more pronounced.

Conflict between historical criticism and church traditions has been apparent from the beginning. Historical criticism of the Bible originated in the opposition between church dogma and the new liberal political philosophy of emergent modern Europe in the seventeenth century. This in turn led to a concerted effort in the eighteenth century to uncover the original message of Jesus apart from church tradition. Historical criticism sought to measure the meaning of Jesus' message according to the standards of Enlightenment morality and rationality. Biblical critics eventually retreated from the claim that an historically pristine portrait of Jesus could be disclosed by scholarly investigation. But they never withdrew from the confident assumption that the historical discipline determines the standards of meaning and value that are used to interpret Scripture. This has resulted in the creation of complicated hermeneutical procedures in which the content of the Bible is separated from what stands behind it. What the Bible reports and what it means are conceived to be two different matters, the latter especially to be determined by scholarship operating under presuppositions of modern culture. The result has been to assess the Bible according to measures that scholars deem fit and to treat church tradition and its reading of biblical texts with a hermeneutic of suspicion. This situation propels historical criticism, and the academic culture out of which it comes, into a constant struggle to dominate the church and dogmatics.

Historical awareness, however, forces one to observe that the contem-

1. *Word and Faith*, tr. James W. Leitch (Philadelphia: Fortress, 1963), 88.

2

porary biblical scholar does not live in an ideal world of universal morality and scientific objectivity. The scholar brings the ideas of a specific intellectual milieu to bear on historical research and hermeneutical proposals. This milieu heavily influences the intellectual standards by which judgments about the Bible are made. The practitioners of historical criticism often ignore this fact. Each generation of biblical scholars has too easily assumed that it has achieved the consummate approach to biblical analysis when, in fact, what it has done is to equate cultural norms with eternal truth. Problems associated with these approaches have been revealed by succeeding generations of scholars. Few, however, have looked at the curious phenomena of advance, revision, and even rejection of analyses that are so much parts of the story of the development of historical-critical method. Nor has the spiritual impact of historical criticism on the church been a topic of sustained reflection.

We believe that what is needed is a confessionally critical history of modern biblical criticism. And by "confessionally critical" we mean an analysis that is historically aware of the influence of cultural contexts on the formulation of ideas while, at the same time, seeking to be responsible to the church and its dogmatic tradition.

We will attempt to trace historical criticism as an historical phenomenon that has undergone change and development over time to create the system of ideas with which so many operate today. This contextual approach allows the exploration of the philosophical presuppositions of the practitioners of the historical-critical method. We think this is important because we believe that the debate over historical criticism of the Bible is nothing less than a debate about primary theological principles in the life of the church. As Joseph Cardinal Ratzinger has stated: "At its core, the debate about modern exegesis is . . . a philosophical debate. Only in this way can it be carried on correctly. Otherwise it is a battle in a mist. The exegetical problem is identical in the main with the struggle for the foundations of our time."[2]

II. The Plan of This Book

We will proceed by means of an analysis of principal figures whose ideas represent major movements in the history of historical criticism. These figures, examined in terms of both their contextual cultural setting and their endur-

---

2. "Biblical Interpretation in Crisis: On the Question of the Foundations and Approaches of Exegesis Today," *This World* 22 (1988): 14.

ing significance, will provide us with the opportunity to explore the meaning of historical criticism of the Bible for our time.

We note the restrictions entailed by our method. The first is that persons whose works do not reflect a particular, discrete movement, whether in support of or in opposition to it, will not be given the attention they would have deserved had we proceeded by a method of encyclopedic description. For example, the great Tübingen scholar Johann Tobias Beck (1804-78) will receive some little attention, whereas his pupil, Adolf Schlatter (1852-1938), will be the subject of an entire chapter. The reason is that while Schlatter was greatly indebted to his teacher's freedom from orthodoxy and pietism as well as to his developed meditation on nature, a perspective at least part of which sets Beck among the precursors of the later "crisis," "neoorthodox," or "dialectical theology," the teacher did not share his pupil's historical sense. On the other hand, the advantage to the pursuit of movements is one that perennially attaches to classifications, that is, they enable the reader to identify motifs or currents of thought, thus "universals," by which to arrange the otherwise disparate, disconnected data of persons, influences, and perspectives. Further, since this volume is preeminently a survey of modern historical-critical study of the Bible, its primary task, as that of any survey, is to furnish definition, to outline horizons, and to fix contexts (in this instance, to fix the contexts of the use of historical-critical method), leaving it to further study to determine precisely where in those contexts a given datum, person, or perspective may belong — if, indeed, at all.

Second, our method very often involves the selection of a representative text or texts through which the figures chosen are evaluated. For example, although Friedrich Schleiermacher (1768-1834) was enormously productive, we have chosen his brief, dramatic dialogue *Christmas Eve* (1805) as our primary focus because it directly addresses the topic of historical-critical method, enunciates the rules for its application, and draws the theological consequences of its use. This procedure has the advantage of viewing the chief figure reflecting a given movement from the perspective of a strategic or signal work.

On the other hand, we have not limited ourselves to such selection. In our study of Adolf Schlatter, for example, it seemed most helpful to range over the whole of his work in order to make clear his position as the transition between a critical past and the new, fermenting scholarship. Similarly, we have attempted to position the two contemporary scholars Paul Ricoeur (1913-) and Brevard Childs (1926-) each within the total context of his work in order to point up its similarity or dissimilarity with a generation of scholarship grown exponentially.

Chapter 1 sets the scene for what follows by looking in more detail at what we have identified in this introduction as the theological and doctrinal conflict between historical criticism and the dogmatic tradition of the church. We consider this tension to be nothing less than a war between two worldviews of faith: the worldview of modern critical awareness originating in the Enlightenment and the inherited Augustinian worldview of the Western church. The reason we have chosen these two worldviews is that they and not others — such as Thomism or Orthodox sacramentalism — have had the greatest impact in shaping modern Protestantism. It is within the history of modern Protestantism that the discipline of historical criticism arose. We believe that philosophical and theological conflict between Augustinianism and modernity is the underlying reason for the ironic but unavoidable fact that while the church has been enriched by the knowledge that historical criticism provides, it nevertheless finds this preeminent scholarly discipline a hostile companion in the journey of faith.

Chapter 2 turns more specifically to the history of historical criticism. Our focus will be the rise of rationalist biblical criticism in the seventeenth century in the work of Baruch Spinoza (1632-77). Spinoza was suspicious of all claims of historical religion. The child of a Jewish family forced to emigrate from Portugal to Holland, Spinoza knew the burden of religious persecution firsthand. If that were not enough, he lived his life under the menacing shadow of the Wars of Religion (1550-1648) and their aftermath. In his *Theological-Political Treatise* (1670), Spinoza attacks the political power of religion by calling into question the legitimacy of religious authorities in matters of civil government. Since the Bible is central to religious authority, Spinoza undertakes a critical investigation of the claims of Scripture in order to subvert its role in European political life. This investigation is grounded in modern historical principles. The first such essay of its kind, the *Tractatus* is clear evidence that historical-critical method originated in politically engendered hostility to the claims of faith.

In Chapter 3 we turn to the eighteenth century. The one figure towering above all the rest in this period is Immanuel Kant (1724-1804). Although he took intriguing excursions into a "rational" interpretation of Scripture — as in "The Conflict of the Faculties" of 1798, occasioned by his distaste for the traditional custom of having theologians march in honored place at the head of the faculty in academic processions — Kant did not undertake any extended criticism. Such an effort was pursued by his older contemporary, the Wolfenbüttel orientologist Hermann Samuel Reimarus (1694-1768). The texts by which to view Enlightenment criticism through Reimarus's eyes are two "fragments" of his *Apology* published by Gotthold Ephraim Lessing (1729-81) in 1777 and 1778 respectively. The first is "On the Resurrection

Narratives"; the second, "On the Intentions of Jesus and His Disciples." It was these portions of Reimarus's four-thousand-page *Apology* that drew the heaviest fire from his critics and resulted in severe restrictions upon Lessing's publishing activity.

The subject of Chapter 4 is the movement according to which the divine revelation could not be grasped by thought but had to be apprehended through intuition, feeling, presentiment — the movement known as "romanticism." Yet, romanticism did not on that account abandon historical-critical study. On the contrary, since it viewed the individual not merely as the recipient of the revelation but also as the revealer, it was through the historical description of persons that the revelation was mediated. Without doubt, the most gifted and celebrated representative of this movement was Friedrich Ernst Daniel Schleiermacher. The text chosen to afford a glimpse at the romantic movement in theology and its use of critical method is from Schleiermacher's early years: his *Christmas Eve* of 1805. We have already mentioned the reasons for this choice. The piece is an oddity this side of the nineteenth century since it combines the scientific development of ideas with poetic description. It articulates standpoints inductively and imaginatively, and makes perspectives live as persons. It echoes the style of the Platonic dialogue and does so quite successfully. *Christmas Eve*, at least in the opinion of Schleiermacher's great interpreter Wilhelm Dilthey (1833-1911), furnishes the best introduction to the work of this theological giant's maturity. For all its brevity, *Christmas Eve* allows the connection between Schleiermacher's metaphysical worldview and his conception of the Bible to come to the clearest light, especially with regard to the complicated question of the relation of the "Jesus of history" to the "Christ of faith."

Idealism is the topic of Chapters 5 and 6. This movement is characterized by belief in a system, and on the basis of the assumption that the many have their home in the One, in an "Absolute" that is raptured beyond all division or differentiation between subject and object, the real and the unreal. In the area of historical-critical research, the two names most linked to this movement are those of David Friedrich Strauss (1808-74) and his teacher, Ferdinand Christian Baur (1792-1860). For Strauss the choice is obvious, his landmark work *The Life of Jesus* (1835). Because Strauss's approach to New Testament texts is repetitive and his conclusions so brief, we believe that insight into his method and presuppositions can be gleaned at any section of the *Life*. We will examine his discussion of the narrative of Jesus' baptism. For Baur we will range over more territory, although his *The Church History of the First Three Centuries* (2nd ed., 1863) is especially important. This mature work offers sufficient introduction to his method and interpretative principles.

In Chapter 7 we turn to Schleiermacher's one-time pupil, Johann Christian Konrad von Hofmann (1810-77), who, like his teacher, assigned to historical study the role of corroborating Christian experience, and thus came to represent a route out of Schleiermacher taken until this day, and by scholars to the right and left — the route known as "salvation history," or *Heilsgeschichte*. Von Hofmann thus has his proper place in any history of biblical criticism. We will explore several works, including his classic text, the posthumously published lectures entitled *Biblische Hermeneutik* (1880).[3]

Chapter 8 concentrates on historical-critical work within the movement of late-nineteenth-century liberalism. Within the larger stream of the liberal Protestant tradition, this particular and indeed culminating intellectual movement of the tradition may be described as that approach whose object is "faith" or that *by which* something is believed *(fides qua creditur)*, in contrast (or in opposition) to "the faith," or that which *is* believed *(fides quae creditur)*. Liberalism thus concentrates upon faith or "religion" as psychologically and philosophically explicable, for the reason that it is natural to the human species. The intent of such concentration is to liberate believers from the trammels of dogma and from all elitist attempts at creating division within the human family, and, as a consequence, from all attempts at removing theology from scientific investigation. Several essays of the prolific Ernst Troeltsch (1865-1923) will furnish the window to liberalism.

Chapter 9 will concentrate on the contribution of Adolf Schlatter. Poised between "left" and "right," affirming the necessity of a scholarship that momentarily tables the question of God only to take it up again in the requirement of a decision on behalf of the text, Schlatter belongs in the vanguard of those who radically challenged the assumptions of nineteenth-century interpretation and ushered in an era dominating the twentieth century.

The subject of Chapter 10 is American Fundamentalism. Originating in the late nineteenth century, this movement is that peculiarly American reaction to theological liberalism and to modern science as influenced by Darwinism. The movement will be viewed from the perspective of its ablest proponent among biblical scholars, J. Gresham Machen (1881-1937), whose work (unlike that of his predecessors) received attention here and on the continent, and elicited serious response from liberal scholars. Machen's *Christianity and Liberalism* (1923) has been chosen because it directly addresses the problem of scriptural inspiration and interpretation.

Chapter 11 will concentrate on the movement variously described ac-

3. This was translated into English as *Interpreting the Bible*, tr. Christian Preus (Minneapolis: Augsburg, 1959).

cording to its relation to its historical context ("theology of crisis"), its method ("dialectical theology"), or its principal concern ("theology of the word of God"). It is universally agreed that the impetus to an interpretation of Scripture in accord with this movement was provided by Karl Barth (1886-1968) in his commentaries on the Epistle to the Romans. Nevertheless, the name of Rudolf Bultmann (1884-1976) came to denote the biblical-critical component of that modern-thought revolt which followed the First and continued beyond the Second World War. Thus, Bultmann's "New Testament and Mythology" (1941), "The Problem of Hermeneutics" (1950), and the first volume of his *Theology of the New Testament* (1948), in addition to other essays, will be used in order to evaluate the contributions of this movement to biblical interpretation.

The subject of Chapter 12 is the "malaise" that subsequently set in among the followers of Bultmann, and its consequences for the historical-critical study of Scripture. In this era, no criticism of the old master proved to be as trenchant as that of his former pupil, Ernst Käsemann (1906-98), professor of New Testament at Tübingen University. Accordingly, a number of essays by Käsemann, including his "The Problem of the Historical Jesus" (1954), "'The Righteousness of God' in Paul" (1961), and "What I as a German Theologian Unlearned in Fifty Years," contained in his volume of published essays, *Kirchliche Konflikte* (1982), have been chosen as examples of the "post-Bultmannian" era of biblical criticism.

Chapters 13 and 14 are devoted to two contemporary scholars, Paul Ricoeur and Brevard Childs. Both attempt to return a scholarship become highly diffuse to the sanity of an arguable perspective. Ricoeur, the Frenchman, observes the circular relation between discourse apart from and within the Christian context, for which reason he justifies attention to both. Childs, the American, insists upon the preeminence of the present text functioning as the Christian canon in the face of a congeries of attempts at reducing it to its various levels. Neither scholar is without his critics, but neither scholar can be ignored.

Throughout these chapters of historical narrative and analysis, we will try to take the measure of the historic critics of the Bible in order to take the measure of historical criticism. Our procedure will be to keep in sight at all times the issue of the fundamental doctrinal conflict in modern theology that we see taking place between historical criticism and the tenets of the Augustinian worldview inherited in the dogmatic tradition of the Western church, especially Protestantism. In engaging this doctrinal debate, we seek to gain theological insight from the history we trace. As Protestants in the confessional Reformation tradition, we acknowledge our predisposition to Augustinianism. We recognize its difficulties for the much vaunted "modern mind." But we believe that it is that "better philosophy" which must be sought that allows both critical study of the Bible and the obedient hearing of its message as the word of God. In short, ours is a churchly stance, dependent on the heritage of the Augustinian tradition, and we make no apologies for it.

We also make no apologies for our heavy concentration on German figures. After Spinoza's pioneering work, it is largely German Protestant scholarship that advanced the discipline of historical-critical study. Upon this peculiar stream of intellectual thought the reading of the Bible in modern Christendom depends. A responsible survey of the discipline cannot, for the sake of originality or the desire for a "fresh" reading of the sources, ignore this fundamental fact. From Spinoza to Childs appears to us the way the story must be told at the present time. New directions in the field of biblical study will no doubt emerge. We think especially here of feminism. But more time is needed to make a judgment. In any case, the heritage from Spinoza to Childs will continue to exert enormous influence.

In light of our analysis, we will attempt in Chapter 15 to summarize our results. We will propose for consideration a faithful stance that a biblical interpreter might take that discloses, for the life of the church and its mission, the content of Scripture as the revelation of God.

The War of the Worldviews

I. The Agony of Historical Criticism

The use of historical-critical method, despite its necessity, opens huge questions that cannot be ignored. The exploration of these questions and their implications for the life of the church has been undertaken by scholars who are no strangers to the historical-critical enterprise. James Smart (1906-82), for example, in a study from three decades ago, examined the effect that historical study of Scripture has on preaching and religious education. His judgment remains valid: "The average scholar does not appreciate how devastating his critical analysis can be to the preacher."[1]

The brutal fact is that for a disturbing number of students and preachers, critical analysis fosters a tendency to treat the Bible as an atomized reality divided into a series of seemingly endless, discrete texts reflecting the points of view of particular authors, but not the sweep and grandeur of God's word. This is because the theological unity of the Bible — that is, the relation of the Old and New Testaments — is, in current scholarship, nearly impossible to argue, especially on the time-honored grounds of a traditional theology of revelation in which the Bible provides supporting texts for ecclesiastical articles of faith. Even within each Testament theological unity is a problem. The Old Testament is made up of a variety of traditions, and these often conflict. In the New Testament basic issues of soteriology, christology, and ecclesiology display no single red thread to unite them. As Ernst Käsemann puts it in a quota-

---

1. *The Strange Silence of the Bible in the Church* (Philadelphia: Westminster, 1970), 70.

tion familiar to two generations of biblical students: "the New Testament canon does not, as such, constitute the foundation of the unity of the Church. On the contrary, as such (that is, in its accessibility to the historian) it provides the basis for the multiplicity of the confessions."[2] Indeed, admits Käsemann, frankly and defiantly, "The one biblical theology, going from a single root and maintaining itself in unbroken continuity, is wish-fulfillment and fantasy."[3]

Awareness of the disunity of the biblical canon and the multiplicity of biblical theologies has led to the increasing tendency to shy away from confident use of the Bible as the principal source for theological judgment. Many have come to realize that what we have in theology is not the "use" of Scripture but, as David H. Kelsey points out, the "uses" of Scripture by various theologies.[4] These "uses" tend to neutralize each other.

Often another problem arises: the Bible is seen primarily as an ancient document under the control of specialists and therefore remote from the concerns of contemporary life. In this perspective, biblical interpretation tends to be treated as a forbiddingly difficult attempt to find a way to leap across the great chasm of time that separates the present from the biblical era. The enormous effort thought to be required for this dampens the traditional Christian habit of reading the Bible spontaneously and experiencing one's life directly mirrored in its pages. This can have a desolating effect on preaching. Classic Bible stories of patriarchs and kings that have guided generations of Christians tend to fade from the preacher's imagination as they are bombarded by scholars with questions of historical veracity, textual complexity, and obscurity of original intention. Preachers find themselves turning — some in desperation, some with eagerness — to the present cultural milieu to find a truth to speak.

While the mainline church offers no resistance to historical-critical method at seminaries and church colleges, knowledge of the content of the Scriptures among church school graduates and candidates for the ministry is woefully inadequate. This lack of knowledge cannot be explained solely by the decline in the respect for religion in liberal arts education. Historical-critical study of the Bible also plays its part as students expend energy on learning analytical techniques of research rather than concentrating on what the Bible says. Many biblical scholars are themselves uncomfortable with the theological task. In departments of religion at universities, they find their identity as "scientific" scholars but not as theologians.

2. *Essays on New Testament Themes*, tr. W. J. Montague (London: SCM, 1964), 103.
3. *New Testament Questions of Today*, tr. W. J. Montague (Philadelphia: Fortress, 1969), 18.
4. See *The Uses of Scripture in Recent Theology* (Philadelphia: Fortress, 1975).

As if this were not enough, historical-critical method can have a delete-rious impact on Protestant identity. Protestantism asserts that it bases its con-fession and theology directly on the Bible and that it is dedicated to placing the Bible in the hands of all believers who read it for the sake of the responsi-bility and joy of explicit faith. This is a classic teaching of the Reformation commonly known through its formulation in Protestant scholasticism as the doctrine of the perspicuity of Scripture. But few of the laity have had much contact with historical criticism. Leaders in the church are often afraid of the consequences of introducing historical-critical method into Bible study. In effect, modern knowledge of the Bible, demanded by the responsibility of ex-plicit faith, is withheld. This leaves church members exposed to the charge of practicing an antiquated approach to Bible study. This, in turn, reduces the legitimate authority of both Bible and laity in the church. Frequently the ap-peals that laypeople make to the Bible in study groups, church meetings, and the letters column of church magazines are abruptly dismissed by scholars and clergy eager to declare that the "historical context" of a passage is being misused.

All of this has produced, to use James Smart's phrase, "the strange si-lence of the Bible in the church." This silence threatens to create a fatal breach between the church of the present and the church of the past. It calls into question what the church has always assumed, that which gave the Reforma-tion its lifeblood: the conviction that it is the presence of the word of God that alone brings the church into existence and nourishes its daily life. As Smart observes: "Let the Scriptures cease to be heard and soon the remem-bered Christ becomes an imagined Christ, shaped by the religiosity and the unconscious desires of his worshipers."[5]

In these contemporary complaints history repeats itself. The costly ef-fects of historical criticism on the life of the church have long been recog-nized. For example, at the end of the last century, Ernst Troeltsch had this trenchant counsel to offer the church: "Historical method, once applied to biblical science and church history, is like a leaven that alters everything and finally bursts the entire structure of theological methods used up to now."[6] Martin Kähler (1835-1912) was even more direct. He declared that the "pure historical formulation" of the biblical writings "irresistibly leads to the disin-tegration of the independent discipline of biblical theology."[7] Neither of these

---

5. Smart, *The Strange Silence of the Bible in the Church*, 25.

6. GS 2:730.

7. *Realencyklopädie für protestantische Theologie und Kirche*, 3rd ed. (Leipzig: J. C. Hinrich, 1897), 3:195.

legendary figures can be accused of shying away from the consequences of critical thought. Their intent was to describe the situation of Christian faith in relation to historical-critical method as accurately as they could.

The renewal of theology at the beginning of this century was spurred on by dissatisfaction with the assumptions and effects of historical-critical study of the Bible at the time. Both Rudolf Bultmann and Karl Barth became acutely aware of the separation between critical scholarship and the life of the church at the point of the pastor's primary obligation to preach. They called into question the way in which the drive of critical study to uncover that which is "really historical" reduced Scripture to its purely human element and then elevated one or another aspect of human thought to absolute truth. This approach, they declared, dismissed the crucial factor that permeates every page of the Bible: the reality of God. From his pastor's study, Barth even raised the possibility of outright rejection of historical criticism:

> The historical-critical method of Biblical investigation has its rightful place: it is concerned with the preparation of the intelligence — and this can never be superfluous. But were I driven to choose between it and the venerable doctrine of Inspiration, I should without hesitation adopt the latter, which has a broader, deeper, more important justification. The doctrine of Inspiration is concerned with the labour of apprehending, without which no technical equipment, however complete, is of any use whatever.[8]

Barth did not finally reject historical criticism — although it is debatable how much he used it. Bultmann certainly did not reject it; he was indisputably one of its greatest proponents. The point here is that the nature and practice of historical criticism has been a serious and recurring problem in theology.

II. The Precritical Reading of the Bible

A. Basic Features

The intellectual and spiritual agony that the historical-critical method poses for the life of the church may be placed in broader perspective by recalling the basic features of the precritical reading of the Bible. Hans Frei (1929-88) has called this reading "strongly realistic." It was: "at once literal and histori-

---

8. *The Epistle to the Romans,* 6th ed., tr. Edwyn C. Hoskyns (London: Oxford University Press, 1933), 1.

cal, not only doctrinal or edifying. The words and sentences meant what they said, and because they did so they accurately described real events and real truths that were rightly put in those terms and no others."[9] The Bible was immediate to the reader, not a distant document. Its influence was intensely felt. At a given moment, any passage or combination of passages, even from widely divergent sources within the Scriptures, could disclose God's will.

This sense of the Bible's uncanny presence as literally containing "heaven on earth" was augmented by premodern notions of the nature of reality. Prior to the Enlightenment, theologians had at best only a dim awareness of the historical process of change and innovation. The common opinion was that the church represents directly "the faith once delivered to the saints" (Jude 3), "the holy commandment delivered to them" (2 Peter 2:21). Whatever differences specific Christian communities had with one another, their ontological framework for understanding was the same. The true church was one with the unchanging, pure teaching of its Lord passed on to all humanity by the authority of the apostles. In this regard, according to Gerhard Ebeling, the Bible was treated, especially after the fixing of the canon, as "a literary genius of a wholly peculiar kind": "Since [the Bible] is the sole way to approach revelation, it even came to take the place of revelation. As a communication of revelation it must be ontologically the same in kind as the event of revelation itself."[10] This ontological viewpoint allowed the church to witness to the peculiarity of its historical origins as transcendent and immediate to every age. Since the Bible records the origins of faith, its content — and even the act of reading its pages — was considered to be nothing less than a revelatory disclosure.

B. Martin Luther

At first glance it appears that the discriminating stance of Martin Luther (1483-1546) breaks this time-honored pattern of the precritical reading of the Bible. This is clear, first of all, in his dogmatic stance toward the Scriptures. The dynamic reality of his fundamental dogmatic principle of law and gospel holds greater authority in his theology than does strict exposition of biblical passages. The law is the moral imperatives given by the righteous God

9. *The Eclipse of the Biblical Narrative* (New Haven and London: Yale University Press, 1974), 1.

10. *Word and Faith*, tr. James W. Leitch (Philadelphia: Fortress, 1963), 31.

to order society and especially to expose the sinner as a fallen creature. The gospel is the gracious love of God in Christ that accepts the sinner even though fallen and unworthy. To read the Bible with the gospel as its heart is to "urge Christ" in each biblical text. "The Scriptures," assert Luther, "must be understood in favor of Christ, not against him. For that reason they must either refer to him or must not be held to be true Scriptures." And again: "If one of them had to be parted with, Christ or the law, the law would have to be let go, not Christ."[11]

Because of his fundamental dogmatic criterion of the gospel, Luther could be radically suspicious of certain elements within the Bible. The example of the Letter of James is well known. Luther referred to it as a "strawy epistle" because of its dependence on works. Luther made other candid observations. He asserted that Kings is more reliable than Chronicles. He questioned whether Esther should be in the canon given the fact that it does not mention God. He believed that Hebrews (Heb. 6:4) errs in denying a second repentance. Luther could even engage in biting sarcasm at Scripture's expense. In Acts 15:29 the Holy Spirit commands that Christians abstain "from blood and from what is strangled." In mock protest Luther appeals to the German stomach: "we must teach and insist that henceforth no prince, lord, burgher, or peasant eat geese, doe, stag, or pork cooked in blood. . . . And burghers and peasants must abstain especially from red sausage and blood sausage. . . ."[12] When the issue is sausage, the Holy Spirit must give way! Here Luther clearly anticipates the type of biting criticism that would later be commonly encountered in the Enlightenment.

Luther could take this apparently cavalier approach to the biblical text not only because of his dogmatic commitment to the gospel against the law but also because he never equated the gospel with the written Scriptures. On the contrary, he taught that the gospel is essentially oral in character; it is a "living voice." In oral form the gospel communicates best. In a famous passage from the *Church Postil* of 1522 Luther contrasts Moses as a writer of "doctrine" with Christ who commanded that his teaching "should be orally continued giving no command that it should be written." That the New Testament finally took written form is, for Luther, evidence of "a serious decline and a lack of the Spirit which necessity forced upon us. . . ."[13]

Luther's attitude toward Scripture was indicative of his willingness to recognize, at least to an extent, the essential historicity of existence. All hu-

11. *LW*, 34:112.
12. *LW*, 41:28.
13. *LW*, 52:205-6.

manity, all institutions are affected by the hurly-burly of events. This acknowledgment of history led Luther to refuse to identify the church as instituted by Christ with the church of the papacy. In taking this stance, he was far more radical than the late medieval criticism that preceded him. Luther was bold enough to assert that in the church itself Satan had begun to work, that error was being taught, and that the antichrist was allowed to reign. Against these demonic challenges, God's word alone is firm and unchanging. But God's word is mingled with and hidden under the forces of opposition that oppress the church at all times and places. That God's word is realized in the community of faith is only because the word itself forms a confessional response to divine grace from Adam to the present day. Knowledge of God's word is not a continuous, unbroken achievement of the church. That would make it the church's work. Rather, such knowledge is best understood as the spontaneous response of the Christian community to the gospel, a response created within the hearts of believers by the Holy Spirit. Certainly, insofar as the church adheres to its origin in Christ's sacrifice and to the articles of faith delivered in the Scriptures, a continuity in the witness of faith may be seen. But this is "the logic of the Holy Spirit, a logic which treats realities in their entirety rather than breaking them up."[14] God is able to provide faithfulness in the church and not theological conclusions or the legal succession of bishops. Therefore, under the guidance of the Spirit, responsible faith requires critical discernment of the text of Scripture as distinct from the tradition of the church.

This critical discernment demands a concentrated attention on the biblical text over against the "human traditions" of ecclesiastical interpretation. The artificial medieval system of allegorization, with its four senses of literal, allegorical, anagogical, and tropological interpretation, was largely although not entirely abandoned by Luther in favor of the right of the biblical text, literally interpreted, to speak for itself. Such a concentration on literal interpretation applied to the Bible not only provided what Frei calls "drastic relief" from exegetical custom,[15] but was vitally important in the reformer's struggle with church dogma and hierarchy. By means of literal exegesis, many ecclesiastical customs were exposed as being without biblical warrant.

Further, Luther sought to discern the meaning of biblical texts by paying close attention to the historical context of passages: "For before one learns the reason and the motive for what a man says, it is only letters, the shouts of choristers or the songs of nuns. . . . There are many passages in

14. *LW*, 41:139.
15. Frei, *The Eclipse of the Biblical Narrative*, 19.

Holy Scripture that are contradictory according to the letters; but when that which motivates them is pointed out, everything is all right."[16] This sense of context even extends to individual authors of Scripture and their differences. For example, commenting on Galatians 1:12 ("For I did not receive it from man, nor was I taught it, but it came through a revelation of Jesus Christ"), Luther declares:

> The histories in the Scriptures are often concise and confused so that they cannot be easily harmonized, as, for example, the denials of Peter and the history of Christ's Passion, etc. Thus Paul is not reciting the entire history here. Therefore I do not expend any labor or concern on harmonizing these things, but here pay attention only to Paul's purpose and intention.[17]

In these remarkable opinions, which go to the heart of the identity of the Reformation, the necessity of an historical criticism that candidly recognizes conflict among biblical texts — a necessity that we recognize as a hallmark of modern theology — is anticipated and affirmed. It is fair to say that the Reformation is an essential step in the formation of a theology that exercises its responsibility by employing historical criticism in its work.

It would be a serious mistake to push the intriguing insights of the reformer too far. While Luther represents a signpost on the road to modernity, he is no modern biblical critic. By no means did Luther reject a precritical viewpoint toward the reading of the Bible. Indeed, in a certain sense, he even exaggerated it as he practiced what Wolfhart Pannenberg calls a "Scripture-positivism" *(Schriftpositivismus),* inherited from late medieval nominalism.[18] Since the biblical text was his primary weapon against the power of the church, Luther relied on what he perceived to be the ability of Scripture to undergird his doctrinal formulations. His principles of exegesis and dogmatics were one. Standing against the might of the church and the weight of its hoary customs, Luther exalted the authority of Scripture in no uncertain terms. He considered the Bible to be *fons et judex* of the church's life. He asserted that the Bible alone is to be trusted because it is, "through itself most certain, most easily accessible, comprehensible, interpreting itself, proving, judging all the words of all."[19] Leaders of the church, regardless of rank, must subordinate themselves to its witness: "The Pope, Luther, Augustine, Paul, an

---

16. *LW,* 41:53-54.

17. *LW,* 26:62.

18. Wolfhart Pannenberg, *Basic Questions in Theology,* tr. George H. Kehm (Philadelphia: Fortress, 1970), 1:3.

19. *WA,* 7:97.

angel from heaven — these should not be masters, judges, or arbiters but only witnesses, disciples, and confessors of Scripture."[20]

This is Luther's doctrine of the clarity of Scripture. It has two important aspects. First, the literal sense of Scripture is identical with its historical content. There is no going behind the text in order to discover a different event than the event reported. Indeed, the question does not even arise. Second, the Bible has a universal and immediate sense, granted by the Holy Spirit and recognized by the eyes of faith, that transcends historical conditions and events. On the basis of these assumptions, especially the second, Luther attacked the theology of his time and the church of the papacy. He did so with the confidence that his doctrine was identical with the doctrine of Scripture, which is the doctrine of God. *"Doctrina est coelum, vita terra"*: "Doctrine is heaven; life is earth."[21]

While the reformer's theological vision of the sharp division between law and gospel and his concentration on literal or historical exegesis led him to practice a nascent form of historical criticism, he did not surrender essential premodern assumptions about reality that had guided the church from ancient times. According to Luther's view of revelation, history — or at least "true" history, the history that brings knowledge of God — is sure and certain. This is the *historia sacra* of Bible and church that is eternal, unchanging, and ever present. It is the word of God contained in the Scriptures and the community of those who respond to this word. It may be hidden because of the ways of the world and the power of the church or the papacy, but it is there for the eyes of faith.

Luther did not investigate the hermeneutical tension between what we would call modern and traditional elements in his understanding. The reformer was essentially an existential, imaginative, and spontaneous thinker not given to systematic exposition. His insights regarding the hiddenness of Christian truth and the need for critical discernment of the Scriptures stand side by side with assertions about the absoluteness of the word of God as a direct product of divine causality. The lack of thoroughgoing explication of his own position meant that Luther's most intriguing hermeneutical proposals, radical for their time, were unable to effect firm and immediate methodological consequences for the practice of theology as a whole.

---

20. *LW,* 26:56-57.
21. *WA,* 40:2, 51-52; *LW,* 27:41.

C. John Calvin

To turn from Luther to John Calvin (1509-63) is to enter a world that is similar theologically but different in temperament.[22] Calvin is one with Luther in affirming the right of Scripture to interpret itself over against the ecclesiastical ideology of allegorical exegesis. Indeed, if anything, Calvin is more disciplined than Luther in his rejection of allegory. Whereas Luther allows allegory insofar as it "embellishes and illustrates [the historical sense] as a witness," Calvin admonishes the biblical expositor that "there is nothing more profitable than to adhere strictly to the natural treatment of things."[23] Calvin's obedience to the historical sense can extend even to time-honored dogmatic traditions in the use of Scripture. Thus, even though he shares Luther's commitment to Christ-centered exposition of the Bible, Calvin can, at least on occasion, refuse to allow christology to violate the historical meaning of a text. In his examination of Genesis 3:15 ("I will put enmity between you and the woman, and between your seed [*zera'*] and her seed; he shall bruise your head, and you shall bruise his heel") he protests, unlike Luther, against identifying this verse as the *"protoevangelium"* that prophesies the incarnation: "I regard the word *seed* as too violently distorted by [other interpreters]; for who will concede that a *collective* noun is to be understood of one man *only?*"[24]

As a biblical interpreter, Calvin displayed a scholarly restraint that often eluded Luther. One reason for this restraint is that Calvin refused to conceive law and gospel in dialectical opposition the way Luther did. This allowed him to be more historically conscious in the treatment of texts than Luther, especially in the exposition of the Old Testament. But Calvin's restraint is also evident in his humanist training and commitment. Calvin was willing to draw on all fields of endeavor — language, classical studies, philosophy, even science — to explore the meaning of the biblical text. He did so in the confidence that God is the author of truth wherever it is to be found: "If we regard the Spirit of God as the sole fountain of truth, we shall neither reject the truth itself, nor despise it whenever it shall appear. . . ."[25] That an ancient jurist should establish the principles of civic order or a philosopher accurately describe the natural realm are not matters to be feared by Christians, nor are the

---

22. For what follows see especially Hans-Joachim Kraus, "Calvin's Exegetical Principles," *Interpretation* 31 (1977): 8-18; Frei, *The Eclipse of the Biblical Narrative*, 18-37.

23. *LW*, 6:125; John Calvin, *Commentaries on the First Book of Moses Called Genesis*, tr. John King (Grand Rapids: Baker, 1979), 257.

24. John Calvin, *Commentaries*, 170.

25. *Institutes of the Christian Religion*, ed. John T. McNeill, tr. Ford Lewis Battles (Philadelphia: Westminster, 1960), II.ii.15.

achievements of medicine and mathematics. We must admire these advances and give thanks to God for the knowledge we receive, no matter what its source. The divine Spirit dispenses benefits "to whomever he wills, for the common good of mankind."[26] In these insights, we have the kind of proposals that later would be called upon to support the modern quest for critical thought.

Calvin was also particularly effective in his description of how saving knowledge is received from Scripture. There is an existential clarity to his analysis, with which a modern Christian can readily identify and which focuses directly on the situation of the believer and the responsibility of explicit faith. Calvin had little patience with inessentials. In his view, we are not to quibble over the details of biblical passages or vacillate about fundamental content. We come to Scripture seeking saving knowledge. As we do so, we must come in faith. Faith is a gift; it is the inner testimony of the Holy Spirit that opens our hearts and minds. Without this faith we do not know what the Bible teaches about Christ. To think that some independent position can be obtained by the power of reason to disclose the content of the Bible is an illusion:

> The highest proof of Scripture derives in general from the fact that God in person speaks in it. The prophets and apostles do not boast either of their keenness or of anything that obtains for them as they speak; nor do they dwell upon rational proofs. Rather they bring forward God's holy name, that by it the whole world may be brought in obedience to him.[27]

There is no more eloquent statement of the Reformation position than this. Calvin sees the fundamental hermeneutical condition of faith and knowledge and describes it frankly. Either the Scriptures are about God or they are about nothing. Either we see this by faith or we see nothing. This is not a theory about the authority of the Bible relying on verbal inspiration or extrabiblical supports, but straightforward assertion.

Calvin's clarity about this fundamental matter was not entirely consistent. By no means did he reject what Hans-Joachim Kraus calls "a doctrinal mind-set that was oriented to the unity and inner harmony of Scripture."[28] At times, Calvin can act as a traditional biblicist not only in his dogmatic use of scriptural prooftexts but also in the confidence with which he speaks of the Bible's inherent superiority as a document:

26. *Ibid.*, II.ii.16.
27. *Ibid.*, I.vii.4.
28. Kraus, "Calvin's Exegetical Principles," 18.

20

What wonderful confirmation ensues when, with keener study, we ponder the economy of the divine wisdom so well ordered and disposed; the completely heavenly character of its doctrine, savoring of nothing earthly; the beautiful agreement of all the parts with one another — as well as such other qualities as can gain majesty for the writings.[29]

Here the text of Scripture itself is glorified in a generalized manner. It is praised for conforming to criteria that are essentially beyond the Genevan reformer's otherwise exclusive reliance on the transforming power of the gospel.

As in the case of Luther, so with Calvin, we find a confusing mixture of elements, at least from a modern viewpoint. On the one hand, there are insights that anticipate modern critical awareness; on the other hand, we find dogmatic assertions that ratify, and even intensify, the precritical tradition. The tension between these constituent factors of the reformer's theology did not come under the scrutiny of sustained analysis at the time.

III. The Precritical Reading under Threat

A. Protestant Scholasticism

The Reformation adopted its own form of scholasticism beginning in the following generation. The powerful urge to have Christian truth easily and publicly available returned as Protestant theologians, less confident than the original reformers in the independent power of the gospel, sought to link the presence of God to an enduring, visible structure that was both theological and metaphysical. Scholastic theology was taken over by the apologetic desire — ever present in the church — to secure the possession of philosophical truth for its cause. Those who came after Luther and Calvin claimed that the absolute truth ascribed to the divine could also be found to reside in a specific human form — in this case, the text of the canonical Scriptures. Protestant scholasticism refused to follow the reformers' often radical stance on the matter of biblical interpretation. Instead it gravitated toward a doctrine that emphasized the majesty of the biblical text: "We believe what the Holy Scriptures declare, simply because *they* declare it, and it is they that beget faith in us, and they are the only source from which we derive our faith."[30] Luther's free-

29. *Institutes,* I.viii.1.

30. Johann Wilhelm Baier quoted in Heinrich Schmid, *The Doctrinal Theology of the Evangelical Lutheran Church,* 3rd ed., tr. Charles A. Hay and Henry E. Jacobs (Minneapolis: Augsburg, 1899), 51.

wheeling approach to particular texts was interpreted to be peculiar to his volcanic personality; and Calvin's endorsement of humanistic openness to knowledge was ignored in favor of those elements that promoted a dogmatic biblicism. Rather than critical study of the content of the Bible, there was *"Theologia Biblica."* According to this approach, Scripture operated as an appendix to Protestant dogmatics, providing *dicta probantia* — that is, proof texts for individual *loci.* The method of using *dicta probantia* was complemented by the scholastic doctrine of the divine inspiration of Scripture that concentrated on securing the Bible as a whole from attack so that it could function in its chief role of providing the underpinning of divine sanction for the dogmatic enterprise. If Roman Catholics claimed infallibility for the Pope, Protestant scholastics claimed infallibility for the Bible.

The age of scholasticism had a dual relationship to the reformers, both positive and negative. Positively, it was one with them in affirming the principle of *sola scriptura.* This it did powerfully in its doctrine of the perspicuity of Scripture. "[T]hose things which are necessary to be believed and done by man in seeking to be saved," said Johann Wilhelm Baier (1647-95),

> are taught in Scripture in words and phrases so clear and conformed to the usage of speech, that any man acquainted with the language, possessed of a common judgment, and paying due attention to the words, may learn the true sense of the words, so far as those things are concerned which must be known, and may embrace these fundamental doctrines by the simple grasp of his mind; according as the mind of man is led, by the Scriptures themselves and their supernatural light. . . .[31]

The Reformed theologian Markus Friedrich Wendelin (1584-1652) spoke in similar terms. The perspicuity of the Bible is that attribute "by which the things necessary to be known for salvation are clearly unfolded in Scripture, that they may be understood even by unlearned believers who read with devotion and attention."[32] The Bible is open for all believers. It is not the property of an educated elite. The common person of common sense, under the guidance of the Holy Spirit, is able to discern Scripture's truth. Scripture is a gift given to the whole church and empowers all of its members.

Negatively, Protestant scholasticism differed from the reformers in its unwillingness to acknowledge the complexity of the relation of the gospel to the biblical text. This difference was a major obstacle in that it led Protestant

---

31. *Ibid.,* 70.

32. Quoted in Heinrich Heppe, ed., *Reformed Dogmatics,* rev. ed. Ernst Bizer, tr. G. T. Thomson (Grand Rapids: Baker, 1978), 32-33.

scholasticism ultimately to be motivated by a spirit alien to the original impulse of the Reformation. While the reformers were confident and assertive, scholasticism was defensive and dogmatic. Whereas Luther had written daringly of Christ against the law in the Bible, and whereas Calvin had refused to subject Scripture to rational proof and reasoning, scholasticism made of the Bible an impregnable fortress defended by a theological theory in which every verse was the truth from God's own mouth whispered into the ear of his scribes. In short, the Bible was inerrant. It contained:

> no lie, no falsehood, not even the smallest error either in words or in matter, but everything, together and singly, that is handed on in them is most true, whether it be a matter of dogma or of morals or of history or of chronology or of topography or of nomenclature; no want of knowledge, no thoughtlessness or forgetfulness, no lapse of memory. . . .[33]

B. Pietism

It was Lutheran pietism that first recognized the theological insufficiency of Protestant scholasticism as well as the contrast between scholasticism and the reformers. Pietists such as Philip Jacob Spener (1635-1705) complained that "the scholastic theology which Luther had thrown out the front door had been introduced by others through the back door."[34] They lamented the dry rationalism of scholastic theology and its penchant for defensive debate. They sought to concentrate attention on the fundamentals of the Christian's spiritual condition before God: "Let us remember that in the last judgment we shall not be asked how learned we were and whether we displayed our learning before the world. . . . Instead, we shall be asked how faithfully and with how childlike a heart we sought to further the kingdom of God. . . ."[35] Lutheran pietists appealed directly to the figure of Luther, who had "restored the bright light of the gospel"[36] by concentrating on the simple, clear word of God. What the church needed was not scholasticism, but "true biblical theology."[37]

---

33. Johann Andreas Quenstedt (1617-1688), *Theologia didactico-polemica* (Wittenberg: Johannes Ludolphus Quenstedt et Elerdi Schumacheri Haeredes [Matthaeus Henckel], 1685), 1:77; quoted and tr. in Arthur Carl Piepkorn, "What Does 'Inerrancy' Mean?" *Concordia Theological Monthly* 26 (1965): 578.
34. *Pia Desideria,* tr. Theodore G. Tappert (Philadelphia: Fortress, 1964), 54.
35. *Ibid.,* 36.
36. *Ibid.,* 78.
37. *Ibid.,* 55.

Pietism questioned the methodological presuppositions of scholastic theology. It was critical of scholasticism's defense of biblical inerrancy. Spener, for example, refused to proclaim the infallibility of Scripture in matters of history, geography, and chronology. He spoke of the inspiration of biblical authors rather than biblical words. The authority of Scripture flows from its center in Jesus Christ and the illumination of the Holy Spirit, not from strict allegiance to formal principle. Pietism helped to expose the Protestant scholastic movement as a self-conscious reactionary force and to turn the tide to new ways of thinking.[38]

C. Rationalist Biblical Criticism and Protestant Liberalism

Side by side with the reformers, Protestant scholastics, and pietists, an alternate tradition of Bible reading slowly began to make its way — haltingly in the sixteenth century, gaining impetus in the seventeenth century: rationalist biblical criticism. This movement, even more than pietism, was to have a profound impact on the nature of theological inquiry.

Rationalist biblical criticism originated in the cultural transition from a traditional conception of reality to a mode of understanding we recognize as distinctly modern. As Peter Berger points out, the premodern condition was essentially religious in temperament in that it referred all things to God. It viewed all of history as a realm of necessity and religious certainty. In the premodern understanding, "*what is experienced as necessary is also interpreted as necessary. . . . The world is what it is because the gods have so decreed it.*"[39] The premodern understanding posited a world of fate, not choice. Indeed, choice (*hairesis*) was condemned because it meant deviation; that is to say, choice by definition entailed heresy. This point of view — although it would not have been recognized as a point of view by those who held it at the time — produced confidence in enduring social structures, whether they be society as a whole, an institution, or a particular group. It created trust in the bonds that tie the social structure together. It invested these bonds with great meaning and distrusted any force that sought disruption by the assertion of individuality.

By contrast, modernization is "the universalization of heresy."[40] Choice, not fate, rules human reality. Modernity invests its identity in the expansion

---

38. See K. James Stein, *Philip Jacob Spener: Pietist Patriarch* (Chicago: Covenant, 1986), 149-58.

39. Peter Berger, *The Heretical Imperative* (Garden City, N.Y.: Doubleday, 1979), 14.

40. *Ibid.*, 1.

of choices. It is inherently pluralistic with regard to *"institutions and plausibility structures."*[41] Rather than trusting social bonds, it distrusts them. Instead of discouraging individuality, it literally forces individuality to emerge as it presses "individuals to become more reflective, to ask themselves the question of what they really know and what they only imagined themselves to know in the old days." By refusing to rely on inherited tradition, individuals are compelled "to turn to their own experience."[42] Thus "modernization has brought with it a strong accentuation of the subjective side of human existence; indeed, it may be said that modernization and subjectivization are cognate processes."[43]

The challenge of modernization was forced on the church by the emergence of liberal political philosophy in the seventeenth century. Figures such as Baruch Spinoza are among the first to practice what we recognize today as modern historical criticism of the Bible. The difficult task of accommodating their insights theologically to the ecclesiastical environment was undertaken by liberal Protestantism, which developed a body of specific ideas and attitudes that served both to herald the coming of modernity within the church and to alter fundamentally the conception of theological knowledge. To put the matter concisely, liberal Protestantism rejected the classic ontological interpretation of revelation assumed by the reformers and scholastic theologians in favor of what we recognize today as historical-critical method. How liberal theologians did this is, in large part, the subject of this book. For introductory purposes, three general observations may suffice.

First, liberal Protestants, following the heritage of rationalism, exalted free inquiry into the church's past. While they sought "the necessary truths of reason" in Christianity over "accidental truths of history,"[44] they did so less by uncovering a universal, metaphysical realm in the Bible (a task for which they had great hopes at first, but which was finally unsuccessful) than by intentionally and consistently employing what was, in effect, a reductionist hermeneutic in biblical interpretation. As the standard of truth, this hermeneutic relied on the perceived thought-world discovered and affirmed by the modern self. Liberal Protestants believed that modern individuals could exercise the unassailable authority of their own experience to choose between custom and truth. They believed they could recover Jesus of Nazareth as an authentic master of

41. *Ibid.*, 17.
42. *Ibid.*, 32.
43. *Ibid.*, 20.
44. These are the classic phrases of Gotthold Ephraim Lessing. See *Lessing's Theological Writings*, ed. and tr., with an intro. by Henry Chadwick (Stanford: Stanford University Press, 1957), 53.

rational and applicable insights free from the impediments of church dogma and ecclesiastical politics. They declared that the universal characteristics of the message of Jesus — those elements that transcend every age — are to be found in the constellation of ethical ideas acceptable to the modern mind.

Second, liberal Protestants exercised what Van Harvey has called "an almost Promethean will-to-truth"[45] that bore unmistakable kinship to the spirit of the Reformation. Certainly, their goal was different from that of the reformers. They were less interested in the gospel of justification than in uncovering what they believed to be the Jesus of history. They wanted "fact," not doctrine. Enamored with the achievements of the Enlightenment, they considered their work legitimate only insofar as it was "scientific," "descriptive," and "impartial." Their morality was that of the modern historian, not of the traditional dogmatician. Liberal Protestants rejected Protestant scholasticism out of hand. They were not afraid to criticize the Reformation for teachings they considered arcane. However, they found the reformers, and especially the colorful person of Luther himself, to be fascinating. In their view, Luther prefigured their own rebellion by his defiance of the institutional power of the Roman Church and its tradition. Luther followed the call of his conscience; he relied on himself. It is this that the liberal Protestants most admired about Luther. As Gotthold Ephraim Lessing put it: "The true Lutheran does not wish to be defended by Luther's writings but by Luther's spirit; and Luther's spirit absolutely requires that no man may be prevented from advancing in the knowledge of the truth according to his own judgment."[46] According to his own judgment — this is the key to the modern mind of the liberal Protestant.

IV. The War of the Worldviews

Third, liberal Protestants precipitated a doctrinal crisis in the church, the consequences of which persist to the present day. This crisis was caused by the attack of liberal Protestants on the Augustinian heritage of theology.

The inherited theological identity of the Western church — and especially the Protestantism of the Lutheran and Reformed traditions — was dependent upon the theology of Augustine of Hippo (354-430). The Augustinian tradition is characterized by certain basic assumptions. It takes a dark view of human nature. Humanity has been completely corrupted by the fall. Indeed, a human being may be accurately defined as a creature of God who is

---

45. *The Historian and the Believer* (New York: Macmillan, 1966), 4.
46. Chadwick, *Lessing's Theological Writings*, 23.

"not able not to sin" *(non posse non peccare)*. It follows that a human being cannot establish a right relationship to God by practicing any form of inherent virtue. To believe in such virtue is the heresy of "Pelagianism" — the arch heresy of the Western tradition. Human beings require divine grace to live. This grace does not reside in them as a quality. Nature and grace are opposed. To live rightly and to be forgiven necessitate the direct intervention of God. In this intervention, grace overcomes nature. The awareness that humanity lives under the direct intervention of God points to another basic feature of the Augustinian position: predestination. For Augustinians, election and predestination elucidate the sovereign attributes of the God of the Bible. They undergird the doctrine of justification and the explication of grace. Divine election determines those who are saved. Whether human beings are damned by predestination is a debatable question, but in the Augustinian tradition a crucial one. In this connection, the Augustinian tradition fosters a spirituality distrustful of the world. Human beings are pilgrims on this earth. They are travelers on a confusing, chaotic, and perilous journey. They are in a desperate search for their proper home. A Christian knows that there is no rest until one rests in God. Finally, the Augustinian tradition is essentially trust in the authority of the church over individual faith. Ultimate truth is Christian doctrine. It comes from God through the Bible and the church to the individual Christian. The Christian is invited to have confidence in that which is received from the ministry and the community of fellow Christians.

Augustinianism is the seedbed of the history of Western Christian thought. Its influence on biblical interpretation, doctrine, and piety is profound. It undergirds the ethos of Luther, Calvin, Protestant scholasticism, and pietism, running much deeper than any differences among them. In Catholicism Augustine is the great "doctor of the church," surpassed in importance only by Thomas Aquinas (1225?-74). In Jansenism Augustine finds his way into Catholic reform and protest. Even liberal Protestantism pays tribute to this tradition as evidenced by this classic description of Augustine's influence by the great nineteenth-century liberal Adolf von Harnack (1851-1930):

> If we western Christians . . . [have] the conviction that religion moves between the poles of sin and grace — nature and grace; if we subordinate morality to faith, in so far as we reject the thought of an independent morality, one indifferent to religion; if we believe that it is necessary to pay much greater heed to the essence of sin than to the forms in which it is manifested — fixing our attention on its roots, not on its degrees, or on sinful actions; if we are convinced that universal sinfulness is the presupposition of religion; if we expect nothing from our own powers; if we comprise all means

of salvation in thought of God's grace and of faith; if the preaching of faith and the love of God is substituted for that of fear, repentance, and hope; if, finally, we distinguish between law and gospel, gifts and tasks appointed by God — then we feel with the emotions, think in the thoughts, and speak with the words of Augustine.[47]

This is a description of an entire hermeneutical universe, indeed nothing less than a worldview — one that fits the premodern understanding of necessity and religious certainty hand-in-glove.

Beginning in the Enlightenment, this doctrinal heritage is subject to sustained assault. "Since the days of Leibnitz," says Harnack, "a powerful opponent has grown up, an enemy that seemed to have mastered [Augustinianism] during a whole century." This opposing vision that emerged under the new intellectual dispensation of choice and self-reliance is one of "cheerful optimism." It is "a mode of thought which removed the living God afar off, and subordinated the religious to the moral."[48]

No one has described the essential articles of this new vision — this alternate worldview — better than Carl Lotus Becker (1873-1945) in his classic study, *The Heavenly City of the Eighteenth-Century Philosophers*. Even though Becker does not have theology as his primary concern, he knows the religious instinct of the era he studies. The Enlightenment worldview that Becker defines makes the following basic assertions.[49] First, humanity is not depraved. The Christian doctrine of original sin is wrong. It was historically conditioned, and it has been superseded. When Luther, for example, calls a human being "a furious and untamed beast" requiring the "sword" and the "executioner" to keep the peace,[50] he speaks an unenlightened, primitive word. The progress of humanity disproves his assertion. Second, salvation must be redefined. Nature and grace are not opposed. Grace inheres in nature to the point that we know that the end of life is life itself, the good life on earth, the life of justice and peace and freedom from want, not the dream of life after death. Humanity is called into the world to transform it. A religion that directs its gaze from this world to another realm risks irrelevance and even inhumanity. Third, a human being is capable, by the light of reason and experience, of perfecting the good life on earth. Human beings are not subject to fate, but hold the future in their hands. Finally, there is an essential condition for human

47. *History of Dogma*, tr. Neil Buchanan (New York: Dover, 1961), 5:74-75.
48. *Ibid.*, 74.
49. Carl L. Becker, *The Heavenly City of the Eighteenth-Century Philosophers* (New Haven and London: Yale University Press, 1932), 102-3.
50. *LW*, 26:308.

progress: freedom — freedom from ignorance, superstition, and "the arbitrary oppression of the constituted social authorities."[51] Humanity must seek knowledge on its own. This is critical knowledge that begins by questioning all things. "What is Enlightenment?" asks Immanuel Kant. In one of the most often quoted passages of his work, he himself answers:

> Enlightenment is man's release from his self-incurred tutelage. Tutelage is man's inability to make use of his understanding without direction from another. Self-incurred is this tutelage when its cause lies not in lack of reason but in lack of resolution and courage to use it without direction from another. *Sapere aude!* "Have the courage to use your own reason!" — that is the motto of enlightenment.[52]

The doctrinal crisis of Western Christianity is the clash of Augustinianism with this new worldview. Where Augustinianism teaches that human nature is corrupted by the fall, the Enlightenment asserts boldly the innocence of human nature. Where Augustinianism professes that salvation requires the direct intervention of God to rescue humanity from the sorrows of the world, the Enlightenment declares that the end of existence is the good life on earth. For Augustinianism humanity stands under the sovereignty of God's election. In the view of the Enlightenment, humanity is capable of directing its own fate. Augustinianism affirms trust in the church and the Scriptures; they provide knowledge of the truth for individual life. The Enlightenment counters that truth is obtained by pursuing critical knowledge and obtaining freedom from superstition and oppressive institutions.

If most contemporary Christians look at these two worldviews honestly, they will find that an easy choice between them is nearly impossible to make. Most will find themselves divided in allegiance between these alternate visions on one article or another. What we are dealing with here is not a simple either/or, but a complex debate about the range of deeply held theological, philosophical, and political assumptions. Indeed, it is no exaggeration to say that the history of modern Protestant theology since the Enlightenment is the warfare between these two worldviews. This warfare has broken out again and again on many fronts. Historical-critical study of the Bible is only one of them; but it is perhaps the most important one. Peace does not appear at hand. In the chapters that follow we intend to recount the various phases of this warfare and to make our own effort to sue for peace.

51. Becker, *The Heavenly City,* 103.

52. *On History,* ed. Lewis White Beck, tr. Lewis White Beck, Robert E. Anchor, and Emil Fackenheim (Indianapolis: Bobbs-Merrill, 1963), 3.

2

BARUCH SPINOZA

The Emergence of Rationalist Biblical Criticism

I. From Dogma to Death

"How many questions, or rather squabbles, have arisen over the distinction of persons, the mode of generation, the distinction between filiation and procession; what a fuss has been raised in the world by the wrangle about the conception of the virgin as Theotokos!"[1] So wrote Desiderius Erasmus (1469-1534) in 1524, shocking the theological world by openly criticizing honored dogmatic traditions. According to the Dutch humanist, humanity now lives in a "carnal age." The confidence with which the church of the past proclaimed its articles of faith no longer holds. The easy traffic with God that characterized the work of the apostles is but a memory. The gift of the Spirit to discern the clarity of the Scriptures has ended: "I have the suspicion that just as the charismata of healings and tongues ceased, this charisma ceased also."[2] In this new age, Scripture reveals multiple meanings, even on an issue as dear to theologians as predestination. This dogmatic pillar of Augustinianism is little more than an "exaggerated view." Its primary significance is negative. When vigorously debated among theologians and ecclesiastical authorities, it serves only to destroy the civil peace: "It is from the conflict of such

1. E. Gordon Rupp and Philip S. Watson, eds., *Luther and Erasmus: Free Will and Salvation* (Philadelphia: Westminster, 1959), 40.
2. *Ibid.,* 44.

exaggerated views that have been born the thunders and lightnings which now shake the world. And if each side continues to defend bitterly its own exaggeration, I can see such a fight coming as was that between Achilles and Hector whom, since they were both equally ruthless, only death could divide."[3] If a choice must be made between dogma and death, dogma must give way.

In making these radical claims, Erasmus was the spokesman for what would become a new approach to the study of the Bible: the tradition of rationalist biblical criticism. Its arrival upon the scene occasioned fierce controversy. Luther could not abide Erasmus's reasoned approach: "These words of yours, devoid of Christ, devoid of the Spirit, are colder than ice itself."[4] In 1559 the Roman Church posthumously abandoned Erasmus by condemning his teaching. But the sort of thinking that Erasmus represents did not die. As the Wars of Religion engulfed Europe, Erasmus's warning about the danger of exaggerated views to the maintenance of civil peace became tragically prophetic.

The Wars of Religion involved Spain, the Netherlands, France, and the German states. Denmark, Sweden, and a host of lesser territories became embroiled in the conflict. England descended into civil war. The destructive force of battle was felt most heavily in Germany. Warfare was sustained for thirty years because neither Catholic nor Protestant could claim a majority of the populace. The German population of about 21 million was reduced to about 13.5 million. In some cities — Augsburg and Marburg are good examples — over half the population perished or abandoned their homes.[5] Among Protestants in Germany, the battle raged between Lutheran and Calvinist and even Lutheran and Lutheran. "Controversy over 'pure doctrine,'" writes James Hastings Nichols (1915-91), "played a larger role here perhaps than in any other period of church history."[6] Theological conflict penetrated all classes through sermons and pamphlet literature. It captured the imagination of those whose vocations had little to do with the fine points of dogmatics. For example, Elector Frederick III ("the Pious"; 1515-76) of the Palatinate expressed his Calvinist contempt for the doctrine of transubstantiation in the vulgar manner of a secular ruler for whom the exercise of power is the measure of thought. Tearing the Host in pieces, he boasted: "What a fine God you are! You think you are stronger than I? We shall see!"[7]

3. *Ibid.*, 95-96.
4. *Ibid.*, 140.
5. C. V. Wedgwood, *The Thirty Years' War* (London: Jonathan Cape, 1944), 512-16.
6. *History of Christianity: 1650-1950* (New York: Ronald, 1956), 43.
7. Wedgwood, *The Thirty Years' War*, 42.

International warfare was not the only way in which "exaggerated views" over doctrine wrought havoc. During the seventeenth century the great European witch craze reached its zenith and frenzied conclusion. The radical dislocation of beliefs, practices, and institutions that marked the Reformation unleashed dark forces of superstition and chaos. Estimating the total number of "witches" burned at the stake in Catholic and Protestant lands is a precarious business, but individual studies reveal startling statistics. In the Swiss Canton of Vaud 3,371 persons were tried and, without exception, put to death between 1591 and 1680. In the small town of Wiesenstieg in southwest Germany sixty-three women were executed in the year 1562 alone.[8] The extent of the suffering involved can only be imagined.

Steven Ozment has made the intriguing suggestion that the Reformation foundered as a reform movement and led to the nightmare of the seventeenth century because it asked too much of the common individual. It offered the privilege and responsibility of explicit faith grounded in a direct relation to the Bible and service to the neighbor. These simple challenges were beyond the average person. In Ozment's view, it was naive to expect "that the majority of people were capable of radical religious enlightenment and moral transformation." To ask that people "live simple, sober lives, prey not to presumption, superstition, or indulgence . . . proved a truly impossible ideal." The Reformation staggered before the intractable force of "men's indomitable credulity."[9]

A new way had to be found to overcome this "indomitable credulity." The failure of religious reform in the Wars of Religion opened the possibility of another approach to the challenge of religion. This approach echoed the humanist concern for political harmony that motivated Erasmus; only now it took more radical form. The demands of the churches for ultimate allegiance were treated with circumspection, even suspicion. A new vision of life surfaced that Joseph Cropsey has called "the great act of self-emancipation on the part of European mankind that was the opening of the modern age."[10]

This vision was grounded in the simple but revolutionary notion that earthly existence is its own end. The legitimacy of a political regime is not to be determined — as it was since the time of Constantine (288?-337) — by the propagation of true faith, but by the protection of property and by the provision for encouraging opportunity. A successful regime must be responsible to

8. Norman Cohn, *Europe's Inner Demons* (New York: Basic Books, 1975), 254.

9. *The Age of Reform: 1250-1550* (New Haven: Yale University Press, 1980), 437-38.

10. Joseph Cropsey, *Political Philosophy and the Issues of Politics* (Chicago: University of Chicago Press, 1977), 6.

the world that is, not the world to come. At the beginning of the sixteenth century, Nicolo Machiavelli (1469-1527) called on humanity to turn to earthly existence, to seize the naturalness of life and leave eternity to itself. He decried politics grounded in either divine sanction or utopian dream: "For how we live is so far removed from how we ought to live, that he who abandons what is done for what ought to be done, will rather learn to bring about his own ruin than his preservation."[11] In the chaos of the seventeenth century, there were those ready to heed this call to turn to the world. They had become convinced that the end of life was life itself.

For this modern movement of political thinking, religious passion was not a virtue but a danger. Religious obligations imposed upon the citizenry by law were judged to be an illegitimate means of oppressive authorities to control the freedom of thought. This was principally true when religion was particularized in an institutional ecclesiastical force motivated by clerical ambition that channeled the natural religious sensibility of the common individual into compulsory cultic practices and subscription to intolerant dogma. These criticisms of the church are the Enlightenment worldview aborning.

Among those in the forefront of this new movement was Baruch Spinoza. It is Spinoza who would carry on the rationalist tradition that Erasmus first championed. In doing so, he became the first to practice the fledgling "science" of historical criticism of the Bible.

II. Biography

As a Jew of Marrano background, Spinoza knew firsthand the danger of institutionalized religion. Between 1391 and 1492 Spanish Jewry had been persecuted, martyred, and deported. Many were forcibly converted to Christianity by Christian mobs and their rulers. Under Philip II (1527-98), "statutes of blood purity" *(limpieza de sangre)* were passed in the kingdom of Spain to discriminate against Jews even if they held to the Christian faith. Similar statutes became the law in Portugal as well. "For the first time in Jewish history, anti-Semitism stemmed not from opposition to the Jewish religion but from hostility to Jewish existence itself: it was existential anti-Semitism."[12] On the shoulders of the Jews was placed the blame for the breakup of Christendom.

---

11. *The Prince and the Discourses,* tr. Luigi Ricci, rev. E. R. P. Vincent (New York: Modern Library, 1950), 56.

12. Yirmiyahu Yovel, *Spinoza and Other Heretics* (Princeton: Princeton University Press, 1989), 1:189.

In 1556 Philip II declared: "All the heresies which have occurred in Germany and France have been sown by descendants of Jews, as we have seen daily in Spain."[13] Spinoza's family was among the many who emigrated to the Netherlands from Portugal in the early seventeenth century to escape persecution. They converted from Marrano Christianity back to strict orthodox Judaism and soon became part of the elite Jewish society of Sephardim in the city of Amsterdam.

The Dutch Republic was a port in the storm of the seventeenth century. Having declared independence from Spain in 1581, the Dutch emerged within two generations as masters of a world empire of trade. As this occurred, the Netherlands became the prototype of the modern state. It fashioned its political life more by knowing what it was against than what it was for. Calvinism was the ruling faith of the vast majority of the citizenry, but opposition to the Catholic absolutism of Spain and conflict within Calvinism between the orthodox and the Arminians made the Dutch wary of clerical presumption. Suspicious of the concentration of political power, relatively free from the excesses of superstition in the witch craze, and directing its passion to commerce rather than dogma, the Netherlands became home not only to its own fiercely independent populace of varied interests but also to dissenters and religious outsiders from abroad. Within this pluralistic state, the *Jodenbort* was a friendly environment where Jews could pursue the things of this world, as well as the next, in relative security. There was no enforced ghetto, no yellow "badge of shame" that Jews were made to wear in other parts of Europe, and no lockup at night behind gate and wall. After 1619 public worship was allowed.[14]

Spinoza was born in Amsterdam 24 November 1632 to Michael de Espinoza and his second wife, Hana Debora. His father did handsomely as an importer of fancy vegetables and other goods. The young Spinoza's intellectual promise was recognized early, and he received a rigorous education. His teachers included Rabbi Manasseh ben Israel (1604-57), the spiritual head of the Sephardim in Amsterdam. Manasseh had an international reputation among Christians because of his apologetic effort to stress what was common between Judaism and Christianity. It was under Manasseh's direction that Spinoza studied not only the Hebrew Scriptures but the New Testament as well. Manasseh may have been the first to introduce Spinoza to the new intel-

13. Quoted in Paul Johnson, *A History of Christianity* (New York: Atheneum, 1977), 307.

14. Simon Schama, *The Embarrassment of Riches* (Berkeley: University of California Press, 1988), 587.

lectual currents of the day in natural science and philosophy. Certainly he helped Spinoza to become familiar with both the great Jewish rationalist tradition of Maimonides (1135-1205) and the mystical tradition of the *cabala.*

Between 1649 and 1656 Spinoza participated in his father's import business and took over the management of the firm with his younger brother Gabriel after his father's death in 1654. On the Bourse in Amsterdam, Spinoza made lifelong friendships with Colligiant and Mennonite businessmen whose Christian commitment was marked by distrust of clergy, dogma, and ritual and who sought to live out their faith in practical, ethical service to the neighbor. His other acquaintances would eventually include Quaker evangelists to the Jews, to whom he was attracted for a time, and Johan de Witt (1625-72), councillor pensionary of Holland from 1653 to 1672. Spinoza's circle was antimonarchist, cosmopolitan, capitalist, and internationalist. "Spinoza," asserts Lewis Samuel Feuer, "is the early prototype of the European Jewish radical."[15]

In March 1656, two years to the month after his father's death, Spinoza began to retire from the business affairs of "Beato y Gabriel Despinoza." His contribution to the Jewish community, which had been considerable, was substantially reduced. Spinoza moved outside the *Jodenbort* to live with the family of Franciscus van den Ende (d. 1674), an ex-Jesuit who was typical of Spinoza's radical friends. Van den Ende would later be executed in France for involvement in a republican plot to overthrow Louis XIV. Spinoza's half-sister Rebeka, a brother-in-law, and perhaps his younger brother wrangled with him over the family's considerable estate. The family sought to discredit Spinoza for his radical ideas in politics and religion. Nevertheless, Jewish authorities offered Spinoza a yearly pension of 1,000 florins if he would return to the community. Spinoza refused. After public examination, Spinoza was condemned by the Ruling Council *(Ma'amed)* for what was determined to be his heretical opinions: "By decrees of the Angels and the words of the Saints we ban, cut off, curse and anathematize Baruch de Espinoza . . . with all the curses written in the Torah [*Ley*]: Cursed be he by day and cursed by night, cursed in his lying down and cursed in his waking up, cursed in his going forth and cursed in his coming in; and may the Lord's wrath and zeal burn upon him."[16]

Spinoza spurned his inheritance, latinized his name to Benedict, learned the trade of lens grinding (for which he would become internationally famous), and moved permanently into the gentile world to dedicate him-

15. *Spinoza and the Rise of Liberalism* (Boston: Beacon, 1958), 5.
16. Quoted in Yovel, *Spinoza and Other Heretics,* 1:3.

self to the intellectual life. Neither Christian nor Jew, Spinoza knew what it meant to be the hated object of religious passion. To curb the dangers of this passion and to find a new way to order society became Spinoza's goal. Pressure from the Jewish leadership eventually drove Spinoza out of Amsterdam in 1660. Spinoza found refuge in Rijnsburg near Leyden (a Colligiant center) and then in 1663 in Voorburg near the Hague. In 1663 he published the only essay in his lifetime under his name, *Descartes' Principles of Philosophy*, which established his reputation as a philosopher of note. In 1670 Spinoza took up lodgings in the Hague. Leading a frugal existence, which drew the admiration even of his detractors, Spinoza worked on his masterpiece, the *Ethics*.

Three notable events mark his last decade. First, in 1670 the *Theological-Political Treatise* appeared anonymously. Spinoza's authorship was quickly recognized. The work was harshly condemned. Second, on 20 August 1672, Johan de Witt, along with his brother Cornelius, was torn to pieces by an angry mob in the Hague. The mob was made of those who supported William of Orange (1650-1702) and feared the collapse of Dutch independence in the dark days following the sudden invasion of the United Provinces by the French. This event shocked Spinoza deeply. It reinforced his Marrano suspicion of the danger of the multitude. Third, in February 1673 Spinoza was offered a chair in philosophy at the University of Heidelberg. Spinoza turned it down because of the requirement that the occupant not disturb "the publicly established religion." Spinoza could not accept this condition in good conscience.

On 21 February 1677 Spinoza died of tuberculosis at the age of forty-four in his sparse upstairs room. At the entrance to the house in Rijnsburg, where he had briefly lived, Colligiant admirers of a later generation placed this plaque in his memory:

> O were all humans wise
> And would they also be well,
> The earth would be a paradise.
> Now it's mostly a hell.[17]

III. The *Theological-Political Treatise*

Spinoza's way out of hell is charted in the *Theological-Political Treatise*, a landmark work that stands as both the first theoretical defense of the idea of

---

17. Quoted in Joseph Dunner, *Baruch Spinoza and Western Democracy* (New York: Philosophical Library, 1955), 15.

liberal democracy and the first extended treatise on biblical criticism to employ recognizably modern methods of analysis. "In our time," writes Leo Strauss (1899-1973), "scholars generally study the Bible in the manner in which they study any other book. As is generally admitted, Spinoza more than any other man laid the foundation for this kind of Biblical study."[18] To understand Spinoza's views on the Bible, one must know his politics.

Spinoza begins his political analysis in the *Treatise*, like Machiavelli before him, and also like his contemporary Thomas Hobbes (1588-1679), by painting a bleak picture of the human condition. Humanity is driven by the passions. It lives in perpetual uncertainty, subject to the vacillation of fear and hope *(fluctuatio animi)*. This instability of the human condition breeds "superstition" — a central concept for Spinoza and the rationalist tradition generally — which is the belief that God "has written his decrees not in man's mind but in the entrails of beasts, or that by divine inspiration and instigation these decrees are foretold by fools, madmen or birds" (50).[19] The "unreason" of religious superstition, grounded in fear, serves only to worsen the inclinations of humanity toward cruelty, violence, and fanatical hatred.

All historical religions, including Christianity, exemplify superstition. Spinoza does not say this directly; he cannot. If the tragic fate of Marrano culture taught him anything, it taught him prudence and the ability to dissemble. The way he makes his radical claim is by defining true Christianity reductively. True Christianity is equivalent to the universal moral characteristics of "love, joy, peace, temperance, and honest dealing with all men" (52). True Christianity is contrasted with false Christianity, a *vana religio* of outward forms, credulity, prejudice, and the avarice of clerics. Since all historical forms of Christianity are open to these generalized criticisms, Spinoza's intent is clear, if indirect: false Christianity is dogmatic Christianity of any stripe. It is a child of unreason. For the sake of reason, dogmatic Christianity must be overcome.

To surmount the false religion of dogmatic Christianity, Christian faith must be placed under the control of reason. Such control is meant only for an elite who rule themselves by the rational faculties alone. The multitude will continue to be ruled by the passions. Unable to govern themselves by adequate ideas, they require the external authority of religion with its vulgar appeal to the human imagination. What is needed is something to direct the passion of the multitude from false religion to true religion *(religio catholica)*.

18. *Spinoza's Critique of Religion* (New York: Schocken, 1965), 35.
19. All page references in the text refer to Baruch Spinoza, *Tractatus Theologico-Politicus,* tr. Samuel Shirley, intro. Brad S. Gregory (Leiden: E. J. Brill, 1989).

Since the Christian Bible is the authoritative source for the Christian religion, its understanding must be reshaped by rational criticism. Spinoza's political program of reform, then, is established in the exercise of biblical criticism. Fifteen of the twenty-two chapters of the *Theological-Political Treatise* serve this purpose.[20] The opposition of reason and religion has the Bible as its battleground. According to Spinoza, biblical interpretation, as commonly practiced by believers and ecclesiastics, is an exercise in sin:

> We see nearly all men parade their own ideas as God's Word, their chief aim being to compel others to think as they do, while using religion as a pretext. We see, I say, that the chief concern of theologians on the whole has been to extort from Holy Scripture their own arbitrarily invented ideas, from which they claim divine authority. In no other field do they display less scruple . . . than in the interpretation of Scripture. . . . (141)

This judgment follows from Spinoza's subtle equation of dogmatic Christianity with superstition. A chief characteristic of superstition is that it "teaches men to despise reason and Nature, and to admire and venerate only that which is opposed to both" (140-41). Only a new form of biblical scholarship can free the Bible from this yoke of oppression. This new form of biblical criticism treats Scripture dispassionately. It places Scripture in historical context and takes from it only what human reason can know.

For much of the Bible, this means that "the point of issue is merely the meaning of the texts, not their truth" (143). The distinction between truth and meaning is crucial to Spinoza's argument. Truth refers to matters of universal significance that reason is able to discern regardless of time and place. Meaning refers to the cultural expressions and artifacts of specific peoples bound to time and place. Miracles — that is, "stories of unusual occurrences in Nature" — and revelations, which appear in the Bible in the form of prophecies, are phenomena of meaning, not truth. They arise in specific cultural contexts and are bound to those contexts (142). Their significance is the historical function they played for the culture of their time.

Miracles and prophecies are explained best by reference to what Spinoza believes is the most common characteristic of the Hebrew people: their penchant for referring all things immediately to divine causation:

> The Jews never make mention of intermediate or particular causes nor pay any heed to them, but to serve religion and piety or, as it is commonly

---

20. Stanley Rosen, "Benedict Spinoza," in *History of Political Philosophy*, ed. Leo Strauss and Joseph Cropsey (Chicago: Rand McNally, 1972), 445.

called, devoutness, they refer everything to God. For example, if they make money by some transaction, they say it has come to them from God; if it happens that they desire something, they say that God has so disposed their hearts; and if some thought enters their heads, they say that God has told them this. (60-61)

Such conduct is typical behavior of the multitude of humanity caught in the uncontrolled state of *fluctuatio animi* and ruled not by rational ideas but by vulgar creations of the imagination. Since, however, this conduct is typical of the people of the Bible, awareness of it is essential to the rational understanding of the hermeneutical context of Scripture. Hence what Spinoza disparages as the most common characteristic of the Hebrew people (and what he fears in the gentile world of his day) is used cunningly to subvert the Bible's truth: "By means of this principle Spinoza is able to undermine the authority of scripture as revelation or even as record of revelation; for obviously at any point where a divine decree or action seemed irrational, it could be claimed that Hebrew idiom was responsible for its attribution to God."[21]

In the pivotal seventh chapter of the *Treatise,* Spinoza offers three basic rules for critical study of the Bible (see 142-44). First, such study "should inform us of the nature and properties of the language in which the Bible was written and which its authors were accustomed to speak." Biblical study is based on language study. Second, the "pronouncements" of each book should be organized by subject matter for the purpose of comparison and contrast with special attention paid to those that are obscure or contradictory. Finally, the circumstances of each book and author must be set forth so that the various historical settings of Scripture are taken into account and clarified. Spinoza's method is one that the contemporary reader will readily recognize as common to scholarly literature on the Bible. The accent is on historical understanding; religious claims are studiously avoided.[22]

Spinoza reduces the rationality of Scripture — that is, its truth — to what agrees with the understanding of the autonomous biblical critic free of dogmatic commitments. The truth of Scripture is that which transcends its context and speaks directly to the reasonable mind: "The divinity of Scripture must be established solely from the fact that it teaches true virtue" (142). Spinoza defines this "true virtue" as "a simple conception of the divine mind as revealed to the prophets; and that is — to obey God with all one's heart by practicing justice and charity . . ." (55). To dogmatic Christians who might

21. Robert M. Grant and David Tracy, *A Short History of the Interpretation of the Bible,* 2nd rev. ed. (Philadelphia: Fortress, 1984), 106.
22. *Ibid.,* 108.

raise their voices in complaint over this reduction of biblical content, Spinoza's defense is clear. His definition of true virtue echoes nothing less than Christ's summary of faith upon which "depend all the law and the prophets" (Matt. 22:27-40). It also calls to mind the *Shema* (Deut. 6:4-5) and the injunction to serve the neighbor (Lev. 19:18), the latter passage being the most common summary of the Torah made by the rabbis. Hence, the truth of Scripture is common to Christian and Jew. As a student of the great Manasseh ben Israel, Spinoza had learned the most basic of lessons of seventeenth-century ecumenical Judaism.

On the basis of this powerful argument, Spinoza limits *religio catholica* to the sphere of piety (that is, the simple worship of God) and obedience to fundamental moral precepts. These matters are the proper subject of theology (232). The notion of *religio catholica* serves Spinoza's political concern. Reverence for God and consideration for the neighbor are both characteristics of good citizenship. In their simplicity and directness, neither is the seedbed of fanaticism. These "truths" of Scripture have been "revealed" by the free exercise of reason applied to the Bible. They contrast markedly with the type of truths that result from the application of dogmatic exegesis that, as the record of the seventeenth century attests, creates a citizenry torn by faction, strife, and extremism. By the free use of reason, Spinoza restricts the Bible and the Christian religion to their proper sphere where they can aid society instead of hindering it.

A final peg secures Spinoza's argument. For reason to be able to do its work in analyzing Scripture through historical-critical study, scholars must be free from ecclesiastical control. In a society where the political power of church and state are combined, this means that political freedom is an absolute necessity. "Everyone should be allowed freedom of judgment and the right to interpret the basic tenets of his faith as he thinks fit, and . . . the moral value of a man's creed should be judged only from his works" (55). It follows that the best political regime for the exercise of reason is one that allows unfettered access to the variety of institutions, activities, and opinions. Democracy is this best regime.

Spinoza's political philosophy complements his metaphysics. Democracy is the proper governing vehicle for recognizing the radical pluralism of the human condition. There is no standpoint beyond competing claims of individuals and factions striving to exist and exercise power. As such, democracy is a political articulation of the structure of reality because reality itself is characterized by a natural heterogeneity of individual attributes. These form one overall system or "substance" that Spinoza calls "God." God, for Spinoza, is identical with all there is. God, in other words, is the sum of immanent reality. Because of this claim, Spinoza is often tagged in philosophical textbooks as a "monist," a philosophical insult coined in the eighteenth century by Christian Wolff (1679-1754). This is misleading. Spinoza uses the concept of "God" to legitimate his radical vision of the multiplicity of truths in reality. In his view, it is the pluralistic condition of reality that is itself divine.

IV. Assessment

A. A New Method

In the *Theological-Political Treatise,* Spinoza introduces a new kind of exegetical method that may be broken down into four basic elements. First, the Bible is treated like any other text. It is shorn of *a priori* religious authority. The various books of the Bible are explained in relation to the mundane causes, historical conditions, and cultural presuppositions of the times in which they were written. Spinoza operates with what Peter Burke calls "the sense of anachronism." This is the realization that the past is different in being from the present and thus subject to conditions that no longer obtain in contemporary life.[23] It is basic to the rise of modern historical consciousness. Spinoza's sense of anachronism is more intense than that practiced by those in the rationalist tradition up to his time. The most dramatic and far-reaching example of this intensity is Spinoza's interpretation of the Hebrew people as engaging in the cultural habit of ascribing all things immediately to God's activity. That Spinoza judged this typically religious characteristic as anachronistic was a shock and an outrage to his contemporaries. His distinctive perception, so typically modern, follows from his radical philosophical demand that all meaning must be found immanent to reality.

Second, Spinoza rejects the dogmatic tradition of exegesis. The Bible must be understood in its own sphere apart from the use made of it by synagogue and church. The suspicion of the dogmatic tradition was a chief interpretive principle of the Reformation. It led to the qualification of the fourfold exegetical method in favor of an exacting commitment to literal interpretation of the text. Spinoza plants himself firmly in this Reformation tradition when he declares, "All knowledge of Scripture must be sought from Scripture alone" (142). But Spinoza carries this Reformation commitment to literal interpretation one step further. He identifies literal interpretation with temporal and profane understanding. Thus, if the text claims directly that "God

---

23. Peter Burke, *The Renaissance Sense of the Past* (New York: St. Martin's, 1969), 1.

41

speaks," then one is forced to go behind the text to explain it as human speech. In such a case, literal interpretation and the plain meaning of a text are not the same. Literal interpretation means going "in back of" a text to its human components. The assumption is that God never speaks "immediately" through any text. Research into biblical meaning is pursued *ut si Deus non daretur* — as if there were no God.

3   Third, the "truth" of Scripture is that which is recognizable to unaided human reason. The meaning of the Bible must fit the experience of reality as we know it. Its accessibility is determined by its correspondence to the "everyday" of human life, particularly its moral sensibility. Spinoza qualifies this notion of the "everyday" of life, however, by means of the fourth basic element of his exegetical method: the claim that it is only an educated elite that is fit to judge what is and what is not reasonable. The true exposition of the Bible is confined exclusively to the intellectual class in society, not the masses. The masses will continue to be driven by their passions. They will be unable to absorb the knowledge engendered by scientific study of the Bible. But the intellectuals of society can use this knowledge to interpret Scripture for socially beneficial ends — above all, the peaceful coexistence of differing religious sects. Historical exegesis, then, allows the public manipulation of Scripture for the purpose of enlightened culture.

In retrospect, Spinoza appears to be the trailblazer of a revolutionary position. In his work the Bible has become the object of historical science. This science is unalterably opposed to the proposition that the foundation of biblical study is revealed religion. The only proper foundation of religion is human reason.

The motivation for historical criticism of the Bible is clear. It is a primary means to free society from the destructive force of religious passion. That is to say, the purpose of this new exegesis is not proclamatory or dogmatic but political. The content of the Bible is investigated with an eye firmly fixed on its social effect. By undercutting religious passion, Spinoza encourages doubt. From doubt, Spinoza believes there will spring the social good of tolerance.

The kind of historical criticism that we meet in Spinoza, radical and destructive though it be, is not without its own historical rootage. It draws upon the wellsprings of ancient pagan tradition. Epicurus (341-270 B.C.) and Lucretius (94-55 B.C.) contended that the fear of the gods is a principal source of human unhappiness. Fear of the gods arises because human beings are anxious as to the causes of events and their evil effects on individual fortune. But to investigate the ultimate causes of events — which is the main responsibility of religion — is irrational. The ultimate causes of events must always remain indeterminate. Human beings must learn that the gods are indifferent to mortal concerns. True happiness consists in ridding oneself of the fear of the gods. In this life this is the best happiness that one can attain.

To reach this goal of happiness *(eudaimonia)*, science *(physica)* is crucially important. Science is the rational investigation of proximate causes in order to control brute nature and improve the human condition. It insures a rational quest for truth because knowledge of efficient causes is attainable. Science can bring about as much happiness as humanity may reasonably expect because it can alleviate the confusion and fear brought about by religion. This means that science and religion are opposed. The increase of the one is the decrease of the other.

"Epicurus' critique of religion," writes Leo Strauss, "is founded on the achievement of security divorced from the achievement of purity."[24] Radical intellectuals of the seventeenth century knew the insecurity and violence that result from the drive for purity. Against the power of religion, they placed their hope in the power of science. In the volatile context of warring Europe, the ancient Epicurean tradition spoke to them directly. Historical criticism of the Bible, then, took root as an Epicurean enterprise that engaged in the rational search for proximate causes of the scriptural narrative. The search for ultimate causes was rejected because it was seen as fruitless and the chief cause of social chaos.

B. Enduring Themes

Spinoza's legacy is a disquieting one in modern biblical studies. In turning from his method to the content of his investigation, we find that four of his basic themes are especially important to the subsequent history of the discipline. First, there is the tragic matter of Spinoza's hostility to his own people. It is clear from his contemptuous description of the Hebrew view of causation, which sees all things as coming directly from God, that Spinoza did not expect much in the way of intellectual achievement from the Jews. In his view, centuries of persecution had left them a shadow of their former selves: "The Hebrew nation has lost all its arts and embellishments (little wonder, in view of the disasters and persecutions it has suffered) and has retained only a few remnants of its language and of its books, few in number" (149). What has kept the Jews going is not their election as God's chosen people, but their unfortunate and obstinate self-separation through "external ritual" (especially

24. Strauss, *Spinoza's Critique of Religion*, 39.

circumcision) and "the hatred of other nations" (99). For Spinoza, the history of postbiblical Judaism is a history of depravation. This fundamental feature of his thought reinforced classical Christian teaching that the church supersedes the Jewish people. More significantly, it anticipated one of the most enduring and pernicious themes of modern biblical scholarship: what Jon D. Levenson calls the "degenerative model of ancient Israelite history."[25] According to this view, the Old Testament is the story of the decline of the people of Israel from an early ideal period of vigorous, primitive religiosity to a crippled state of existence ruled over by the irrational regulations of Jewish priests and legalists. From Christian times to the present, Jewish existence is nothing more than the fossilization of a corrupted state. Halakhic Judaism has no legitimate reason for being. The intellectual and social devastation of this thesis reached its frightening fulfillment in the twentieth century. That Baruch Spinoza, child of the Sephardim, is one of its most prestigious spokesmen, is sadly ironic.

Second, Spinoza is a prime example of the politicization of biblical exegesis. He comes to Scripture with a specific social agenda. He wants to liberate society from its religious restraints in order to secure the legitimacy of a democratic state grounded in pluralism and tolerance. His purpose is a noble one. But it issues in an "anti-theology" that construes God primarily as a function of an ancient social system. On the basis of this understanding, Spinoza reduces the election of Israel to no more than the desire for "a certain territory where [the Hebrews] might live in security and well-being." The Torah, that most sacred of Jewish realities, is discounted as "the laws of the Hebrew state alone, and . . . therefore binding on none but the Hebrews, and not even on them except while their state still stood" (54). Central theological claims are neutralized by social context. What motivates Spinoza is the belief that the Bible is an obstacle to progress that must be gotten around. To know Spinoza's politics is to know his theology. The same principle will apply again and again in the theologians of our study. The history of biblical criticism from Spinoza to contemporary liberationists is a story of the politicization of exegesis.

Third, Spinoza is the earliest example of the "Protestantization" of biblical studies being turned on its head. The essentially Protestant character of modern biblical studies is grounded in what James L. Kugel has described as the elemental desire of the modern biblical critic "to establish as direct and unmediated a link as possible between the modern reader/interpreter and the

---

25. "Theological Consensus or Historical Evasion? Jews and Christians in Biblical Studies," in *Hebrew Bible or Old Testament?* ed. Roger Brooks and John J. Collins (Notre Dame: University of Notre Dame Press, 1990), 123.

biblical author at the moment of his speaking his words."[26] Church and dogma must not get in the way of a direct encounter with God's word. The reason the Protestant reformers took this radical stance was their faith that the Bible is God's word, disclosed to the believer through the power of the Holy Spirit alone. The Bible does not share authority with any independent source. Nothing human stands above it.

Spinoza, like Protestants before him, also wanted an unmediated knowledge of the content of Scripture. In his view, however, the Bible is not unique in its authority, but passive historical material subject to the superior authority of the human mind. "The natural light of reason," asserts Spinoza, "has as much right as any other kind of knowledge to be called divine" (59). The meaning of Scripture can be discerned fully without specific religious commitment or connection. The Bible is just like any other book. And the "experts" who read it are obligated to conform to the canons of secular scholarship, not to creed. The momentous consequence of this fundamental supposition has been to turn the energy of biblical scholarship from the study of the message of the Bible to the theologically marginal matters of context and authorship.

Fourth and finally, as already indicated, Spinoza confines the understanding of Scripture to an intellectual elite. Only those few guided by the full light of reason, by virtue of their education and native talent, have the authority to interpret Scripture rightly. The mass of people lack this ability; indeed, to place the Bible in their hands is dangerous because it can unleash the forces of religious fanaticism. The Protestant tradition taught the perspicuity of Scripture, that is, the doctrine that the ordinary believer has the ability to discern the Bible's meaning. Spinoza seeks to take the Bible out of the hands of the people — a strategy that will have enormous consequences as theology becomes almost the exclusive province of the professorate over the course of the next two centuries.

---

26. "Biblical Studies and Jewish Studies," *Association for Jewish Studies Newsletter* 36 (1986): 22; cited in Levenson, "Theological Consensus," 112.

3

HERMANN SAMUEL REIMARUS

Pressing the Rationalist Attack

I. A Pattern of Warfare

"If what *Spinoza* affirms were true," writes Johannes Colerus (1647-1707), Lutheran pastor at the Hague and Spinoza's first biographer, "one might indeed very well say, that the Bible is a Wax-Nose, which may be turned and shaped at one's will; a Glass thro' which every Body may exactly see what pleases his fancy; a Fool's Cap, which may be turned and fitted at one's pleasure a hundred several ways." Colerus is here summarizing the opinion of the Augsburg divine and polyhistorian Gottlieb Spitzel (1639-91), who fulminated about the *Theological-Political Treatise* not long after its appearance. This negative reaction was typical. The publication of the *Theological-Political Treatise* brought a firestorm of criticism so vehement that the essay soon acquired the dubious honor of being, next to Hobbes's *Leviathan,* the most vilified intellectual work of the seventeenth century. The *Treatise,* said merchant and intellectual Wilhelm van Blyenburg of Dordrecht, "must needs have been fetched from Hell."[1] Agreeing with this judgment, the States-General in Holland condemned the *Treatise* in 1674.

In the decades that followed, various efforts were made to practice the infant science of historical criticism while seeking to reconcile critical work

---

1. Johannes Colerus, *The Life of Spinoza* (1706), quoted and tr. in Frederick Pollock, *Spinoza: His Life and Philosophy* (London: C. Kegan Paul, 1880), 427-28.

with faithful adherence to the church. These efforts not only failed, but they established a tragic pattern of warfare between historical criticism and the church that came to haunt the efforts of Christian intellectuals to make peace with emerging modern culture.

Richard Simon (1638-1712) published his *Critical History of the Old Testament* in 1678. Simon was among the first to dispute Mosaic authorship of the Pentateuch on textual-critical grounds. He also argued the novel theory that public scribes existed among the Hebrew people from early on in their culture. These scribes compiled significant portions of the Old Testament long after the original events by drawing on eyewitness accounts that had been preserved and passed on by tradition. Simon believed as a Roman Catholic that Scripture could be treated with the tools of historical science because the Roman Church had the security of tradition and did not rely on the Bible alone for the authority of faith. Neither the civil nor clerical authorities accepted his argument. The Parliament of Paris condemned Simon in 1689. He was hounded by Jacques Bénigne Bousset (1627-1704), Bishop of Mieux and great Catholic polemicist, with unrelenting venom.

Pierre Bayle (1647-1706), who converted from Reformed Protestantism to Roman Catholicism and then back again, attempted to allow reason to have its way in his *Historical and Critical Dictionary* (1697). Although Bayle knew that the exercise of reason often leads to skepticism, he believed that such skepticism could be understood as a test of the proper basis of faith: "God does not want [our minds] to find a standing ground too easily and sets traps for it on all sides."[2] Few accepted Bayle's fideistic defense. If anything was to be treated skeptically, it was the work of Pierre Bayle. In 1693 Bayle lost his professorial chair in history and philosophy at Rotterdam.

The most sustained early modern effort to reconcile reason and the Bible was made by the English in the deist controversy of the first half of the eighteenth century. John Locke (1632-1704) declared, "*Reason* is natural *Revelation*" and "*Revelation* is natural *Reason* enlarged." One cannot be without the other: "he that takes away *Reason*, to make way for *Revelation*, puts out the Light of both, and does much what the same, as if he would persuade a Man to put out his Eyes. . . ."[3] In *The Reasonableness of Christianity* (1696), Locke applied this thesis to an analysis of Scripture. He defended the need for Jesus Christ on the "reasonable" ground that the authority of the Savior is attested

---

2. *The Great Contest of Faith and Reason: Selections from the Writings of Pierre Bayle,* tr. and ed. with intro. Karl C. Sandberg (New York: Friedrich Ungar, 1963), 54.

3. *An Essay Concerning Human Understanding,* ed. with intro. Peter H. Nidditch (Oxford: Clarendon, 1975), 698 (IV.xix.4).

by his fulfillment of Old Testament prophecies and his performance of miracles. But these arguments, which show, in the judgment of I. T. Ramsey (1915-72), "empiricism at its crudest,"[4] did not long hold sway. John Toland (1670-1722), Matthew Tindal (1657-1733), and a host of others in what Leslie Stephan called "a ragged regiment"[5] of radical deist writers asserted that religious claims cannot rest on external authority of any kind, but must be fully contained by human reason exercised unfettered and without prejudice. According to Toland: "Since Religion is calculated for reasonable Creatures, 'tis Conviction and not Authority that should bear Weight with them."[6] For a religion to be true it must correspond to universal human experience. True religion is natural religion; it is the common thread of the human religious quest from culture to culture. On the basis of this assumption, Toland made the same assertion that Spinoza had made twenty-six years earlier: the Bible must be treated like any other book. "All Men," writes Toland, "will own the Verity I defend if they read the sacred Writings with that Equity and Attention that is due to meer Humane Works; Nor is there any different Rule to be follow'd in the Interpretation of *Scripture* from what is common to all other Books."[7]

While the deists confidently appealed to the common man, they had a hard time attracting him. The rationalistic reduction of faith to "universal principles" left the average believer cold and failed to produce an enduring style of ecclesial life. To make matters worse, the deists squabbled among themselves over the content of natural religion. Some deists believed in a future life while others denied it. Some thought that God rewards virtue while others claimed that virtue is its own reward. It was not long before deism itself came under attack, not only from the church but also from enlightened intellectuals whom the movement had hoped to attract. In the withering assault of David Hume (1711-76), the "natural history" of religion was shown not to be the ideal of humanizing, life-enhancing "natural religion," but rather the scandalous story of polytheism, fanaticism, and fear. "Men," he writes, "are much oftener thrown on their knees by the melancholy than by the agreeable passions."[8] The natural history of religion is the story of humanity's desperation.

4. John Locke, *The Reasonableness of Christianity,* ed. with intro. I. T. Ramsey (Stanford: Stanford University Press, 1958), 15.

5. *English Thought in the Eighteenth Century,* 2nd ed. (London: Smith, Elder, 1881), I: 87.

6. *Christianity Not Mysterious,* facsimile ed. (Stuttgart–Bad Cannstatt, 1964), xv.

7. *Ibid.,* 49.

8. *The Natural History of Religion,* ed. with intro. H. E. Root (Stanford: Stanford University Press, 1957), 31.

W. Neil is right when he claims that the result of the deist controversy was not the constructive engagement of modern reason and the Bible, but the reduction of biblical authority: "to bandy about the sacred texts in public dispute, and to make the Scriptures the small change of pamphleteers, was at once to unseat the Bible from the pedestal on which it had been placed. . . ."[9] The attacks on the Bible were serious. Thomas Woolston (1670-1733) questioned the literal meaning of Jesus' miracles, arguing instead that their significance is allegorical or "mystical." Peter Annet (1693-1769) rejected the veracity of Jesus' resurrection because of the numerous contradictions in the gospel accounts. Thomas Chubb (1679-1747) asserted that the apostles had altered Jesus' original message.

These criticisms of the Bible were no less shocking to the reading public than the ideas of Spinoza had been. They could, however, not be stifled. Spinoza, Simon, Bayle, and the radical deists may have lost battles, but they did not lose the war. In their struggle to be heard, they were able to plant their radical notions in the minds of influential leaders in the Church of England. Latitudinarian divines discussed them at weekly salons, argued them from book to book, and eventually passed them on to Germany where they were taken up in a thriving university culture.

What helped to make historical criticism of the Bible acceptable, or at least debatable, was a fundamental feature of Protestant intellectual culture. From the time of the Reformation, Protestants held the conviction that Roman Catholic Christianity was a false development of primitive Christian faith that distorted the clarity of the gospel. This simple but revolutionary idea — the assertion that the church itself betrayed the divine intention — was like the opening of Pandora's box. Once stated it could not be forgotten or repressed. When taken to heart as a formal principle, it could easily be turned on the Protestant ecclesiastical establishment itself and used to undermine Protestantism's own dogmatic heritage. Slowly but surely, the Bible came to be read by a Protestant elite of Christian theologians as Spinoza wanted it to be read: apart from all ecclesiastical entanglements. Scripture was divorced from the Augustinian worldview.

The German pioneer in these efforts, who is more responsible than anyone else for the introduction of historical criticism into the mainstream of Protestant theology, is Hermann Samuel Reimarus.

---

9. S. L. Greenslade, ed., *The Cambridge History of the Bible: The West from the Reformation to the Present Day* (Cambridge: Cambridge University Press, 1963), 243.

II. Biography[10]

Hermann Samuel Reimarus was born on 22 December 1694, in Hamburg, Germany, where his father was tutor and instructor at the Johanneum, a preparatory school established in 1528 by John Bugenhagen (1485-1558), friend and counselor of Martin Luther. The school's original purpose was to give instruction in Scripture and Reformation doctrine to persons for whom the costs of attending distant universities were prohibitive. Dedicated by devout parents to theology and the preaching office, Reimarus was introduced in his earliest years to the classical languages as well as to the *dicta probantia* or proof texts used in support of the regnant doctrinal system of Protestant scholasticism.

In 1710, following attendance at the Johanneum, Reimarus entered the Hamburg Gymnasium, established in 1613 for the purpose of providing a more scientific preparation for university study. Three years later Reimarus left home for the University of Jena, where he read with Johannes Franz Buddeus (1667-1729), an orthodox scholar attracted to the Enlightenment and advocate of the principle that nothing in revelation contradicted natural religion.

School bored Reimarus, and he began to read philosophy on his own. Restless, disaffected, he traveled in 1716 to Wittenberg, from which he earned a Master's degree in philosophy. In 1722, following tours of Holland and England, where he came into direct contact with the ideas of radical deists, and following the publication of a dissertation on the subject of "Machiavellianism" before Machiavelli, in which, for the first time, he revealed his interest in the disturbing question of the origins of modernity, Reimarus was offered a seat on the Wittenberg philosophical faculty as *Dozent,* or adjunct professor. One year later he left Wittenberg at the invitation of the citizens of Wismar, Sweden, to serve as rector of their city school.

The sea air at Wismar gave Reimarus catarrh. In 1725 the prospect of a professorship at Hamburg induced him to apply for the appointment. He was disappointed. Appealing to a former mentor to intercede for him with the Hamburg authorities, he was at last appointed professor of oriental languages in 1727. In November of the same year, Reimarus was married to Friederika, daughter of Johann Albert Fabricius (1668-1736), polyhistorian and rector of the Johanneum.

10. The biographical data throughout this chapter are taken from Carl Moenckeberg, *Hermann Samuel Reimarus und Johann Christian Edelmann* (Hamburg: Gustav Eduard Nolte, 1867), *passim.* See also *Reimarus: Fragments,* ed. with intro. Charles Talbert (Philadelphia: Fortress, 1970), 2-43.

Reimarus's lectures at the Hamburg Gymnasium included expositions of the gospel pericopes — preaching texts from the Gospels assigned to the various Sundays of the church year. His mastery of the classical languages was legendary. He was used and plundered by the best of his time, among them the Cicerone and theologian, Johann August Ernesti (1707-81). When his father-in-law, Fabricius, died, Reimarus completed Fabricius's work on the Roman historian Dio Cassius. He served seven times as rector of the Gymnasium. Reimarus died 1 March 1768.

The scholarly life of Reimarus has been variously characterized. Albert Schweitzer (1875-1965) refers to several of the writings published by Reimarus during his lifetime as "defending the rights of rational religion against churchly faith."[11] This is the unbending Reimarus, stalwart foe of orthodoxy. Peter Hanns Reill describes Reimarus as leading "a Jekyll-and-Hyde life of inward disbelief masked by outward orthodoxy."[12] This is the Janus-faced Reimarus, publicly conventional, privately biting the hand that fed him. Both of these familiar characterizations have merit and may be argued at length. But Peter Gay is probably closest to the mark when he draws a poignant picture of the celebrated orientologist as "tormented" because of the contradiction of reason and faith.[13]

Reimarus was a thinker caught between two sides. He illustrates the either-or quality that characterized many eighteenth-century rationalists in their confrontation with inherited belief. Either Christian orthodoxy was true in all particulars or it was a deception. No middle ground was possible. Reimarus, trained in the ways of Protestant scholasticism, found himself asking questions that went to the heart of the Augustinian tradition, and asking them with Aristotelian precision. If the Holy Scriptures are infallibly dictated, then why are they, in crucial matters, so recondite? If unbelievers are eternally damned, then why does the church proclaim Christ as the embodiment of universal love? Reimarus faced these questions grimly and with what Gay calls "fierce honesty." His ties to Protestant scholasticism ran so deep that he could only make his challenge on scholasticism's own terms of truth by examining the details of the biblical narrative with relentless logic. Reimarus was a man *in extremis;* he lived in the midst of the warfare of worldviews. Not surprisingly, his behavior could be unpredictable and even contradictory. He could defend the faith one moment and attack it the next. Most often he did

11. *The Quest of the Historical Jesus,* tr. W. Montgomery (London: A. & C. Black, 1922), 14.

12. *The German Enlightenment and the Rise of Historicism* (Berkeley: University of California Press, 1975), 162.

13. *The Enlightenment* (New York: Vintage, 1968), 1:61-62.

the former in public, the latter in private. But his actions probably had more to do with existential struggle than with hypocrisy.

The following anecdote illustrates Reimarus's contradictory nature. When, in 1735, Johann Lorenzo Schmidt (1702-49), devotee of the Enlightenment, student of Buddeus and Christian Wolff, produced his translation of the first five books of the Old Testament, the so-called Wertheim Bible, which substituted prosaic explanations for everything miraculous, Reimarus was among the many who attacked it vehemently. Behind Schmidt's attempt to rationalize Scripture, Reimarus saw the ubiquitous influence of the rationalist philosopher Christian Wolff at work. Although Reimarus himself drank deep of the Wolffian method, using it to nourish his own rebellious position, he nevertheless knew the danger of Wolff to Christianity and sought to warn the faithful away. At the same time, however, when, after the publication of his rationalist Bible, Schmidt was hounded by the authorities (he was, for a time, even under arrest), it was at Reimarus's home at Hamburg that Schmidt found sanctuary. While no martyr, Reimarus could nevertheless put himself rather jauntily in harm's way to help someone in need.

In his struggle over reason and faith, Reimarus found companionship, if not comfort, in reading Bayle and Spinoza. They helped to drive him forward to the point where, reluctantly, he gave up Christian faith. While Spinoza taught Reimarus much about historical-critical method, his philosophy of divine immanence left the orientalist cold: "The man builds a world in his brain totally different from that which actually exists. . . . If the concept of another Being outside the world is necessary in order to grasp that there are living creatures within the inanimate world . . . then the world is not the independent essence or, in Spinoza's language, the only substance; then it is not God!"[14] Reimarus's religious sensibility was still sufficiently beholden to inherited Augustinian orthodoxy that the identification of God and world was impossible for him to accept.

Amid all this confusion and personal anxiety, Reimarus slowly but surely created an intellectual monument that embodied his deepest and most private thoughts. Not even known to his wife, the work was to make him famous long after his death: the *Apology*.

14. Hermann Samuel Reimarus, *Abhandlungen von den vornehmsten Wahrheiten der natürlichen Religion*, 4th ed. (Hamburg: Johann Carl Bohn, 1772), 203.

III. The *Apology*

A. *Circumstances of Composition*

The story of the *Apology* has been told and retold. But seldom has the story included the events that furnished Reimarus the occasion for that vast work.

Despite Reimarus' inability to separate his philosophical from his theological views, with the resultant stumbling over every tenet of Christian faith, the man had a deep religious sensibility. It hurt him to read those pamphlets full of contempt for religion and Christianity that made their way across the border from France. He resolved to do something about it.

In a debate between the Ministry of Education and the Senate of Hamburg over the preparation of a new catechism for use in the schools, the Senate — to which Reimarus belonged — prevailed. Accordingly, Reimarus, with or without assistance, set to work preparing a text that would accommodate the tenets of "positive" religion to the principle that reason not merely possessed the power to grasp divine revelation, but itself contained divinely implanted truths. This was the public Reimarus at work, ready to argue that natural religion served as a preparation for Christianity.

At this point, the history is unclear and the connection between the initial attempts at a catechism and those portions of the *Apology* that Gotthold Ephraim Lessing finally brought to light after Reimarus's death is uncertain. When Reimarus's son delivered his father's manuscript to the Hamburg city library in 1813, he wrote that his father had entrusted it to a few friends. One of them, the poet Berthold Heinrich Brockes, died in 1747. In 1777, Lessing referred to the "thirty-year-old papers," writing that he did not know whether they were fragments of one work, or of a work completed but damaged, or of a work never yet come to light. Two years later, in 1779, Lessing wrote that he had never had the entire manuscript, only single essays that Reimarus had later used for his *Apology*. His daughter Elise admitted to giving several of her father's essays to a friend, and of these copies were made. Yet a granddaughter appears to have owned pages of the *Apology* as an heirloom. The list of manuscripts, their relation to each other, their eventual possessors, and the history of their publication is varied and confusing.[15] How much of this material contained portions originally pitched to the youth of Hamburg, and thus served as the core to which later drafts were attached, is a problem needing solution.

---

15. See Talbert, *Reimarus: Fragments,* 18-25. Talbert reviews the history of the *Apology*'s publication up to Voysey's 1879 translation, of which his own 1962 edition is a reprint. Ten years later a critical text of the *Apology* appeared in German; see below, n. 19.

However murky the history, the inference to be drawn is that Reimarus's hope in assisting the Hamburg youth to better instruction was not fulfilled. His attempt at writing a catechism was abandoned. Reimarus appeared with another work in 1754, the *Abhandlungen von den vornehmsten Wahrheiten der natürlichen Religion (Essays on the Chief Truths of Natural Religion)*. In this volume Reimarus pursues the link between natural religion and Christianity. He argues that religion is a humanizing force:

> When the atheist does not regard himself as better than a beast, a plant, or a machine, and regards his soul as a nothing, or at best as a medulla which took its origin from filth, muck, and manure; when he foresees that everything soon changes to muck again, no doubt he becomes downcast, base, and discontented with his delusion. But religion lets us see the nobility of our soul, and the image of deity it expresses . . . which, of course, can only be most pleasing to the most reasonable self-love, and rouses the heart to nobler intents and labors, giving the foretaste of greater blessings.[16]

From this volume, or at least from the ideas it contained, the Jewish rationalist Moses Mendelssohn (1729-86) acknowledged that he had borrowed his argument for immortality. Two years later Reimarus published his *Vernunftlehre (Instructions regarding Reason)*, and in 1760 he produced his last volume of size, *Allgemeine Betrachtungen über die Triebe der Thiere (General Observations concerning Animal Instincts)*.

But if Reimarus's attempt at writing a catechism was abandoned, his passion for his school and the youth of Hamburg had not diminished. He entered into combat with the rector of the Johanneum over the latter's furnishing the youth instruction that threatened decline in attendance at the Gymnasium. He led in the defense of a friend at the Johanneum accused of scorning religion, and took to print with his advocacy in the Easter class schedule. Not all whose part Reimarus had taken returned in kind. For example, a former pupil named Johann Bernhard Basedow (1724-90) authored an essay in which he advocated beginning with Jesus' humanity and from that point moving toward the ascriptions of deity. Drawing scorn from Lessing, but also removed from his teaching position by the orthodox, Basedow went on to publish another popular piece, praising but also attacking Reimarus's treatise on natural religion, in particular, for the weakness of its proofs. The similarity between Basedow's method and those of his former teacher only helped spotlight the irony of the situation.

At some time during the 1750s, Reimarus reexamined his earlier at-

---

16. Reimarus, *Abhandlungen*, 762-63.

tempt with a view to systematizing and publishing it. This was Reimarus on the attack:

> When I indicate, in a way absolutely clear and intelligible to all, that it is not frivolity or levity, but downright contradiction arising from every single piece of the supposed divine revelation which makes it impossible for us to believe, and forces us to hold strictly to natural religion, then the slander against our intentions and motives will fall away of itself. . . . One by one, I will examine the persons, deeds, teachings and writings of the Old and of the New Testament, indicating what and why each appears to contradict the pretense that through just such means a supernatural, divine revelation has been given us for our eternal bliss.[17]

The work, *Apologie oder Schutzschrift für die vernünftigen Verehrer Gottes* *(Apology or Defense for the Rational Worshipers of God)*, comprised two volumes, in excess of four thousand pages. Readied for the printer, not even a table of contents was lacking. Yet Reimarus had second thoughts:

> A time will come for a division between two groups: believers in revelation, and the despised advocates of reason. . . . This writing is and remains a true apology and defense against imposing a faith on us. Preserve it as a secret treasure . . . until it pleases God to give rational religion a path toward open, healthy freedom, and then draw you to responsibility for it![18]

Reimarus's prudence was warranted. The content of the *Apology* was unprecedented in its vehemence. Knowing full well the political persecution of rationalists from Erasmus through Spinoza to Wolff and Schmidt, Reimarus would have been a fool to let his work see the light of day.

In the *Apology* Reimarus treats with scorn any attempt to ground the authority of the Christian religion on proofs from miracle or prophecy. He argues the impossibility of a Christian exposition of the Old Testament. Indeed, the Old Testament in its entirety is dismissed for its religious inferiority:

> It is certain . . . no book, no history in the world were so full of contradictions, and therein the name of God so often and shamefully misused: Since all the persons who are cited here as men of God, their sum total, give sheer offense, annoyance and aversion to a soul which loves honor and virtue. In the whole series of this history one finds neither patriarchs, judges and

---

17. Quoted in Carl Moenckeberg, *Hermann Samuel Reimarus und Johann Christian Edelmann,* 120.

18. *Ibid.,* 123.

kings, nor priests and prophets, whose real and earnest purpose had been to disseminate a true knowledge of God, virtue and piety among men; to say nothing of the fact that one could encounter in it one single great, noble act useful to all. It consists of a weaving of sheer stupidities, shameful deeds, deceptions, and horrors, for which clearly selfishness and lust for power were the stimuli.[19]

Of the seven fragments of the *Apology* published by Lessing, the two most explosive were titled "On the Resurrection Narratives" and "On the Intentions of Jesus and His Disciples"; the first appeared in 1777, the second in 1778. In these fragments Reimarus discussed what he called the "system" of Jesus and that of his disciples.

B. *The System of Jesus and of His Disciples*

Of Jesus' "system," Reimarus, leaning on Matthew 4:17 and Mark 1:15, writes that Jesus only made use of simple religious ideas common to Judaism and his hearers. He never intended to reveal new articles of faith such as the Trinity or his own Godhead. His preaching, the gospel of the imminent kingdom of God, and the conviction attendant upon it that he was the Messiah and bringer of this kingdom contain nothing alien to Judaism. In fact, Jesus never left the soil of Jewish religion. He never intended that his gospel should extend beyond the Israelite-Jewish people but promised an earthly kingdom, deliverance from the yoke of Judaism's oppressors, and, in preparation for it, summoned his people to repentance. It was a pity, writes Reimarus, that Jesus did not make the work of converting his single purpose. It was only a means to an end. The triumphal entry into Jerusalem and the events of the last days were an attempt at a worldly-Messianic seizure of power. Jesus' goal was nakedly political; his vision finally as mundane as that of countless would-be rulers before or since. It had to fail.

The second "system" was developed by Jesus' disciples. Moved to follow Jesus from fleshly desires, once deceived — Jesus having intentionally spread a false system — they created a system matching those same desires. At the midpoint of their system lay the idea of spiritual redemption from sin and death. Naturally, the disciples had to admit that they understood Jesus differently in his lifetime, and since their second system was an interpretation of

19. Hermann Samuel Reimarus, *Apologie oder Schutzschrift für die vernünftigen Verehrer Gottes* (Frankfurt: Joachim-Jungius-Gesellschaft der Wissenschaften Hamburg, 1972), 671-74, 678-79.

the first, it had to lead to alterations. The contradictions in the Gospels are thus due to nothing else than the evangelists' attempts to adjust Jesus' teaching and life to their new system. Though Jesus' disciples clearly outdid him, they did not think their system through.

How did the change come about? With this question Reimarus believed he could solve the problem of the historical origin of the Christian religion and the alleged truth of Christianity. The change occurred with Jesus' resurrection, a story that Reimarus describes as either certain fact or deception — nothing lay between. Reimarus concludes that no honest or upright reader can assign to the gospel accounts of the resurrection any kind of credibility. The most suspicious among these accounts is that of the watchers at the tomb. If that story were true, it would have furnished a fixed, reliable starting point for the Christian witness to Easter. But if the tale is construed as mere fancy, as indeed it must be, then it leads to the suspicion that the very thing to be concluded from it — that is, the theft of Jesus' body by his disciples — actually occurred.

The disciples yielded to the temptation of employing fantasy to make of Jesus' followers a fellowship totally at their disposal. Thus emerged the church, which reshaped the teachings and usages, and reinterpreted the apostles' false prophecy of Christ's return, gradually setting it aside. And it was the church that attempted to shape a proof for the new system from the Old Testament — a development that sharpened opposition to Judaism.

Reimarus's critical reading of the Gospels is harsh and pointed. He claims that the careful reader can easily see the awkward conflation of Jesus' system and the apostles' system. Thus the apostles' fantasy of a merely spiritually suffering Savior has been woven into Jesus' life story with its program for an earthly kingdom. These two systems form an impossible and confusing alliance in the gospel narratives; indeed, they force the biblical account into blatant contradiction. So Reimarus charges:

> There is a clear contradiction between the disciples' constant hope for a temporal redemption, for an earthly empire, and such speeches of Jesus as indicate a spiritually suffering Redeemer. . . . If he had wanted to rid ideas of temporal honor and power totally from their minds, why then does he promise them they should have such a share in his kingdom? . . . The shattered hope in an earthly kingdom which no longer found nourishment after the crucifixion birthed the new system of the apostles. . . .[20]

20. *Ibid.,* 141-42.

Reimarus turns the doctrine of apostolic succession on its head. It is the apostles themselves who began the sad story of Christian corruption.

This is not to say that the Christian religion is without merit. One can see, here and there, evidences of moral virtue within it: "In the midst of this chaos of pure delusion and bad example, we encounter good insight and salutary teaching mixed in with it, especially respecting moral duties and virtues — less frequently in Moses and the prophets, of course, but more often in the glorious morality of Jesus and his apostles. . . ." But these insights are best uncovered by the autonomous biblical critic who is able to obtain the enduring kernels of wisdom from the historical husk of positive religion. Like Spinoza before him, Reimarus asserts that biblical criticism is the prerogative of a philosophical elite: "The true purified religion and unfeigned virtue is only . . . a preeminent share of a few wise persons by which they achieve a higher degree of perfection and happiness than others. . . . They would recognize in an eminently sound and serviceable fashion what is practical in the universal religion of Jesus and his disciples." Such people might even be willing to call themselves by the name of Christian if it were not for the dismal record of Christianity as the agent of fanatical religious passion. Thus, the wise: "observe with grief and sympathy, that among all peoples of the whole earth, precisely those who have pretended to know more of God and divine things than human nature allows, have planted and supported the crudest ignorance, the most contradictory errors, the most horrible practices in the name of divine revelation."[21]

It is clear that in the view of Reimarus, Augustinian Christianity with its electing God, atoning Lord, and salvation by imputed grace is alien to natural religion — the latter conceived to be a process of humanization and a struggle for political freedom.

IV. Assessment

A. The "Historical Head"

What could these devastating pieces have contributed to the interpretation of the New Testament?

To begin with, it was the first time a "historical head," as Schweitzer put it, undertook criticism of the biblical tradition. Schweitzer means that it was Reimarus who forced a breakthrough from the dogmatic to the historical

21. *Ibid.,* 583-85.

treatment of the Gospels — a breakthrough that went beyond Spinoza — because he was first to conceive Jesus' world of ideas in the context of his times, that is, as consisting of an eschatological worldview. To be sure, the perspective from which Reimarus eyed eschatology was faulty. He believed it was determined by the hope for the realization of the political-Davidic ideal of the Messiah that dominated Jesus' preaching, but it was nonetheless eschatology for all that.

Second, Reimarus was the first clearly to set forth the two main tasks of gospel research: the relation between Jesus' preaching and Judaism; and the relation between Jesus' preaching and that of his community. Did Jesus intend no more than a purification of Judaism, or did his teaching contain the seeds of the christology of primitive Christianity? And must not a creative element be assumed in the transmission of the Jesus tradition? Did the evangelists and apostles simply transmit the tradition of Jesus' sayings and doings in mechanical fashion? Is it not rather the case that scarcely a single element of that tradition was without the biblical authors' own flesh and blood? All of these important questions — questions that today are recognized as central to historical-critical work on the New Testament — are anticipated in Reimarus's analysis.

Third, since Reimarus derived the apostles' "system" from the collapse of their hopes at the crucifixion, albeit in bad faith, he raised the issue of theological innovation necessitated by the delay of the *parousia,* that is, the issue of the degree to which the documents of the New Testament or of the subsequent period reflect a struggle to come to terms with the non-appearance of Christ's second advent.

Fourth, by grouping all four Gospels together in his description of the intention of Jesus and of his disciples, Reimarus prompted the beginnings of a distinction between John and the synoptists (a name invented much later by Johann Jakob Griesbach [1745-1802]), as well as of the source criticism of the latter.

Fifth, Reimarus's comments respecting the Old Testament raised the question as to how it could be linked to the New in a Christian Bible. The differences between the Testaments were formulated in the sharpest possible terms. This too would become an important question for historical-critical scholarship, one that vexes the discipline to the present.

For most of his life, Reimarus participated in Christian worship and took communion. He could no more leave the Christian church than Moses Mendelssohn the synagogue, and when at last he gave up Christianity, he did so in misery. But in his difficult quest he had learned, like other rationalists before him, a simple truth: that the Bible is kin to all other literature. For the sake of its historically conditioned character, its having a home in languages people actually spoke, in places where people actually lived, its authorship by living, breathing human beings, and its destination among living, breathing human beings, the Bible cannot be cut off from the remainder of human history. It thus requires the use of the human mind for its exposition. This means, of course, that the interpretation of biblical texts is not confined to Christians. And once we assume the Bible's kinship with the rest of the human comedy — especially with all the political implications that such an assumption contains — it is inevitable that someone should lay cavalier hands on it.

B. Reason and Prejudice

In his book *The End of the Historical-Critical Method*, Gerhard Maier of Tübingen writes:

> The concept and development of the higher-critical method present an inner impossibility to the extent that one holds to the position that the witness of divine revelation is presented in the canonical Scriptures. The method cannot prove a "canon within a canon," nor can it offer any clarity on the subject of a "divine" and a "human" Bible. . . . But the most important objection is that historical criticism over against a possible divine revelation presents an inconclusive and false counterpart which basically maintains human arbitrariness and its standards in opposition to the demands of revelation. Therefore because this method is not suited to the subject, in fact even opposes its obvious tendency, we must reject it.[22]

After considering the origins of historical-critical method in the rationalist movement, one must give Maier his due. Historical-critical method is the child of enemies of Christianity and the Augustinian tradition. They are, to be sure, opponents whose bill of particulars against Christianity, especially as an established political force of the state, was, for the most part, entirely just. But these critics of the Bible were nonetheless engaged in unrelenting warfare, and they used historical criticism as their most devastating weapon.

In response to Maier and other critics, however, it ought to be argued that an approach to the Bible that assumes its connection with the rest of human endeavor, and on that basis requires the use of reason for its exposition, is a legitimate hermeneutical presupposition and something that can justifi-

---

22. *The End of the Historical-Critical Method*, tr. Edwin W. Leverenz and Rudolph F. Norden (St. Louis: Concordia: 1977), 25.

ably be taken for granted. Reason and logic have their place in the interpretation of the Bible.

But the believing Christian is also obligated to respond more specifically to Reimarus. The assumption that reason *alone,* or the use of historical-critical method *alone,* is sufficient for the interpretation of biblical texts is itself an article of faith. That is to say, a definite religion and piety are needed to sustain the idea that the rational or reasonable is not merely the essence of the human but also of the divine, that, in the words of the American Declaration of Independence, it is reflected in the "laws of nature and of nature's God," and that the only way by which to attain to the truly human and thus truly divine is to employ reason in the observation of those laws in which the divine is expressed.

If, as a modern American historian has put it, arguments that command assent depend "less upon the logic that conveys them than upon the climate of opinion in which they are sustained,"[23] or, according to the modern German thinker Hans-Georg Gadamer (1900-2002), if reason is always referred to data, to those realities of society prior to all experience, then the idea of an absolute reason with which every human who has ever lived has been suffused, and thus before which every thing under the sun must appear and be tried is a construction, a faith, a belief that the nineteenth century proved to be as void of proof or demonstration as Reimarus believed the resurrection of Jesus of Nazareth to be. It is a "prejudice" — to use a word to which the Enlightenment gave a pejorative sense. Prejudices indeed can be evil. They can derive from authorities that take the place of judgment. But prejudices or pre-judgments — and there is no movement of thought without them — can also be a source of truth. Reimarus sacrificed one "prejudice" for another that he believed was not a prejudice at all.

In his *Vernunftlehre,* Reimarus writes that evidence is not only the basis and rule of certainty, but also the mark of truth. He could not see that such evidence was lacking to his truths of natural religion. Or did he see it? In the *Vernunftlehre* he also writes: "Not even the soundest reason can assist against errors, if not always exercised and rendered skilful in most regular, intelligible fashion. . . . The use of reason depends upon the will, and the greatest errors rise through a will which is not filled with a zealous and pure desire for truth. . . . In the wisdom of the world one is not impartial!"[24]

23. Carl L. Becker, *The Heavenly City of the Eighteenth-Century Philosophers* (New Haven and London: Yale University Press, 1932), 5.

24. Moenckeberg, *Hermann Samuel Reimarus und Johann Christian Edelmann,* 103-104.

4

FRIEDRICH SCHLEIERMACHER

Formation of the
Liberal Protestant Position

I. Is Theology Still Possible?

In 1773 the young Johann Wolfgang von Goethe (1749-1832) composed "Prometheus," a startling attack on religion in the Epicurean tradition of radical criticism. "I know nothing more wretched/under the sun than you gods," rails the defiant mythical hero of the poem. Prometheus regrets that once he had raised "bewildered eyes" to the heavens. But that was when he was "a child." In his maturity, he realizes that whatever he has accomplished has been on his own. Worship is the futile exercise of fear. It is not divine guidance but time and fate that rule:

> I pay homage to you? For what?
> Have you ever relieved
> The burdened man's anguish?
> Have you ever assuaged
> The frightened man's tears?
> Was it not omnipotent Time
> That forged me into manhood,
> And eternal Fate,
> My masters and yours?

Prometheus vows to form humanity in his image. Humans will drink deeply of the cup of life, both good and bad, and pay no heed to the gods.[1]

Friedrich Heinrich Jacobi (1743-1819), celebrated controversialist of the later Enlightenment, reported that he showed Goethe's poem to Gotthold Ephraim Lessing in the summer of 1780, less than a year before the latter's death. Lessing told Jacobi that he was not at all shocked by what "Prometheus" contained, for he had learned it all from the study of Spinoza.[2] At the end of his life, Lessing had apparently given up on any effort to defend the truth of Christianity and to find a place for a transcendent God. Spinoza's philosophy of immanence became his final place of intellectual rest.

Before his death, however, Lessing tried mightily to salvage his Christian faith. In his later theological writings, stimulated by the challenge of Reimarus's fragments, Lessing made the effort to separate the truth of Christianity from its historical origins. He wanted to get around the "all or nothing" of Reimarus's position. To make his defense, Lessing drew upon his reading of Spinoza, Leibniz, and Wolff, using especially their distinction between absolute and contingent truth. Absolute truth is obtained through the serious reflection of reason; contingent truth is based on information derived from the senses, or, as Lessing sees it, on the facts of history. Absolute and contingent truth are antithetical: while the former is reliable because it comes from the logical necessity of the reasoning process, the latter is arbitrary because it is the product of the random flow of mundane events. On the basis of this distinction, Lessing makes his famous remark: *"accidental truths of history can never become the proof of necessary truths of reason."*[3] Lessing was thus ready to concede the scandalous facts of Reimarus's investigations. Historical Christianity is a story of confusion. But the truth of Christianity, says Lessing, can survive its historical context. The moral teaching of Jesus displays a universal import that speaks to the natural religious sensibility of humanity. Jesus' teaching qualifies as absolute truth and transcends the particulars of the biblical account. In "The Education of the Human Race" (1780), Lessing gives this apologetic argument a teleological rationale. The Bible provides nothing to humanity that it cannot get on its own. But humanity must be educated over time in the ways of God because human potential cannot be fulfilled all at once. Historical revelation is appropriate for the human race in its childhood. Truth is a developmental force that can employ external means for its realization.

1. *Goethe: Selected Poems,* ed. Christopher Middleton (Boston: Suhrkamp/Insel, 1983), 26-31.

2. *Lessing's Theological Writings,* ed., tr., with intro. Henry Chadwick (Stanford: Stanford University Press, 1957), 46.

3. *Ibid.,* 53.

At the end of the day, these apologetic arguments did not work, at least not for their author. Lessing succumbed, as Reimarus did, to the hostile effect of modern biblical criticism intended by Spinoza. The historical-critical approach to the Bible subverted religious authority. Christianity could not be rescued. Radical biblical criticism left him no choice.

In the latter half of the eighteenth century, the development of historical criticism continued apace with contributions from diverse figures. Jean Astruc (1684-1766) and Johann Gottfried Eichhorn (1752-1827) reconceived the character of Genesis with their discovery of discrete stylistic literary units within the biblical text related to the different names used for God. Johann Salomo Semler (1725-91) distinguished between Jewish-Christian and Gentile-Christian lines of development in the primitive Christian community. Johann David Michaelis (1717-1791) posed the thesis of an *Urevangelium* upon which the text of the Gospels is dependent and also conjectured that the Gospel of John contains an antignostic argument. Johann Gottfried Herder (1744-1803) examined the literary character of Hebrew poetry as a cultural expression of a people and an era.

Claude Welch is right to observe that these types of insight went "far beyond the questions of the detailed fulfillment of prophecy and the historicity of miracles."[4] They raised a more fundamental consideration. The increasingly widespread practice of biblical criticism, with its growing catalogue of impressive results, revealed Christianity to be firmly fixed in the historical context of all human endeavor. Johann Philip Gabler (1753-1826) went so far as to separate "biblical theology" from the enterprise of dogmatics:

> There is truly a biblical theology, of historical origin, conveying what the holy writers felt about divine matters; on the other hand there is a dogmatic theology of didactic origin, teaching what each theologian philosophises rationally about divine things, according to the measure of his ability or of the times, age, place, sect, school, and other similar factors.[5]

If this is true, if Christianity according to biblical theology is to be identified in its origin as the "feelings" of its ancient writers, then it is possible to conceive religion itself to be entirely a human endeavor. That is to say, historical consciousness carries with it the potential of placing the transcendent di-

---

4. *Protestant Thought in the Nineteenth: Century,* vol. 1: *1799-1870* (New Haven and London: Yale University Press, 1972), 41.

5. John Sandys-Wunsch and Laurence Eldredge, "J. P. Gabler and the Distinction between Biblical and Dogmatic Theology: Translation, Commentary, and Discussion of His Originality," *Scottish Journal of Theology* 33 (1980): 137.

mension of existence in doubt. By what authority, then, does theology operate as a discipline and claim privilege among the institutions of society? Is religious faith even possible?

It is within the intellectual sphere of the newly emergent romantic movement that the answers to these questions were sought. Franklin L. Baumer has described romanticism as a "counter-revolution" in European cultural history aimed against the scientific-rationalist ideals of the Enlightenment.[6] Jean-Jacques Rousseau (1712-88) taught a new generation of cultural critics to praise feeling and to explore the darker side of life. The shock and disappointment of the French Revolution, awash in the blood of the Terror, increased the impact of this new sensibility. The *Zeitgeist* that drove the romantics focused on experiences of wonder and introduced a mode of artistic expression that consciously rejected classical models. A new aesthetic ideal emerged in music and poetry, as these arts were thought to be the highest forms of human expression. The romantics claimed that they were the origin of human speech itself. The inexactness of meaning attached to music and poetry was not thought of as a liability, but an advantage to learning. Such forms, it was believed, are able to disclose the fundamental human yearning for an Infinite Other that determines existence and bestows upon it both beauty and unity.

These forms of human expression also disclose truth in an appropriate way. In romantic opinion, truth, including the truth of the sacred, is not a matter of exact definition or fixed proposition. Rather, it is known best when invoked by metaphor and emotional effect. The value and authority of a work of art, a text, or even a social institution reside in its ability to serve as a vehicle for contemplation and commitment to the deep and abiding mystery that stands at the center of life. As Friedrich Schlegel (1772-1834) put it in his "Lyceum Fragments," speaking specifically of the nature of truth in literature: "A classical text may never be fully comprehended. But those who are cultivated [*gebildet*] and who cultivate themselves must always be willing to learn more from it."[7]

The resistance of truth to fixed propositional form made subjectivity important for comprehension. In the romantic view, subjectivity is not the enemy of truth, but its companion. To know the truth of something, whether

6. *Modern European Thought* (New York: Macmillan, 1977), 268. See also M. H. Abrams, *Natural Supernaturalism: Tradition and Revolution in Romantic Literature* (New York: Norton, 1971).

7. "Lyceum Fragments," no. 20. See Friedrich Schlegel, *Dialogue on Poetry and Literary Aphorisms,* tr. with intro. Ernst Behler and Roman Struc (University Park and London: Pennsylvania State University Press, 1968), 122.

that something is artistic, social, or religious, is to enter into its mystery, to investigate it from all perspectives, learn what it means by becoming familiar with it. Hence it was typical for romantics to use subjective language when speaking of all sorts of subject matter. The German poet Novalis (1772-1801) is representative. "The object," he says, speaking in the most general terms of a work of art, "is allowed to be only the seed, the type, the fixed point. . . . Expressed differently: the object should determine us as the product of the self, not as sheer object."[8]

This analysis of the nature of truth had a profound influence on the configuration of philosophical and theological questions. Romanticism's philosophical partner, idealism, was determined by the same desire to grasp the wholeness and mystery of life by means of a mystical, intellectual vision. What Kant had lamented as a peculiar human fate — namely, that reason is burdened by questions of metaphysics that transcend its ability to answer[9] — was taken by the idealists to be not only attainable but the necessary goal of all knowledge. They believed firmly that humanity is blessed with faculties of knowing that allow it to explore the essence of life and apprehend reality in its totality. That is to say, they posited a metaphysical *"Vernunft"* (reason) beyond Kant's *"Verstand"* (understanding) that comprehends the disparate elements of experience and is able to organize these elements systematically into a true *"Wissenschaft"* (science) of knowledge. Particularly with regard to the historicity of human life, *Vernunft* was the means to penetrate the veil of accidental events, to interpret them as a purposeful, dialectical process of various forces to be intuitively grasped and reflectively reconstructed as a progressive "development" of ideas. Historical change is not arbitrary and meaningless, but rather the essential form of truth and being. History takes place at the behest of "Spirit."

It is these suggestive ideas that shaped the beginning of the nineteenth century and helped to restore confidence that theology was, indeed, still possible. The pioneering figure in the effort to reconceive the theological task according to romantic canons of truth was Friedrich Schleiermacher, rightly celebrated as the father of liberal Protestantism in the nineteenth century. Among his many contributions was a critical reassessment of rationalist biblical criticism that contributed to the revival of biblical theology.

---

8. *Novalis Werke,* ed. Gerhard Schulz (Munich: C. H. Beck, 1969), 314.
9. *Critique of Pure Reason,* tr. Norman Kemp Smith (New York: St. Martin's, 1965), 7.

II. Biography[10]

Friedrich Daniel Ernst Schleiermacher was born in Breslau in 1768, the son of a Reformed chaplain in the Prussian army. During his travels, the father had encountered and been attracted to the pietism of the Moravian Brethren. Accordingly, in 1783 Friedrich was sent to Gnadenfrei, a Moravian school at Niesky near Dresden, and in 1785 he entered the Herrnhuter Seminary at Barby. There he joined a group of independent youths whose activities led to inquiries, disciplining, and expulsions. In 1787 Schleiermacher left Barby for Halle, ostensibly to study the philosophy of Immanuel Kant, and took up residence at the home of his mother's brother. Two years later he accompanied his uncle to a parish charge in Drossen. In 1790 he successfully sustained examinations for ministry in the Reformed Church at Berlin, and began duties as tutor on a baronial estate in Schlobitten, East Prussia. In 1793 he left Schlobitten, and after brief service in a Berlin secondary school and a two-year assistantship in the parish of Landsberg, he returned in 1796 to Berlin as chaplain at Charité, a hospital for the poor. In Berlin he was warmly received into a circle of youths presided over by Friedrich Schlegel. The year 1799 saw his first edition of the *Speeches,* to which his previous preoccupation with ethical questions gave little clue.

In his *Speeches,* Schleiermacher shows himself ready to take on the problem that plagued Lessing: the rise of historical consciousness. Schleiermacher fully accepts the basic insight of historical-critical work, namely, that it is in history that the totality of human life in all of its reality and meaning is to be found. It is Schleiermacher's bedrock belief that it is ultimately God in the abundance of his creative energy who chooses to reveal himself through the multiplicity of the historical world.

Idle rumors of liaisons with female friends of his circle resulted in Schleiermacher's removal from Berlin in 1802, and in his "exile" to Stolpe in Pomerania. Two years later he published the first volume of his translation of Plato's works — planned with Schlegel but carried out alone — and accepted his first university appointment at Halle. Rich activity at Halle was interrupted by cataclysmic political events. Following Napoleon's defeat of the Prussians at Jena in 1806, the university was shut down. In the summer of 1807 Schleiermacher vacationed in Berlin, where he settled permanently the following December. Called by the king to the pastorate of Berlin's Trinity

---

10. Biographical details are for the most part taken from the first edition of *Religion in Geschichte und Gegenwart* (Tübingen: J. C. B. Mohr, 1913), 5:303-14. See also *Religion in Geschichte und Gegenwart,* 3rd ed. (Tübingen: J. C. B. Mohr, 1957-62), 5:1422-26.

Church in 1808, he married the widow of an old friend from Halle days, Henriette von Mühlenfels. In addition to two children from her previous marriage, Henriette gave birth to three daughters and a son, Nathaniel, who died in early childhood. In 1810 Schleiermacher succeeded to a chair at the University. In the period following the Vienna Congress, however, his independent attitude toward church and state provoked the authorities, resulting in trials, house searches, and threats of dismissal. Spending the remainder of his life pursuing the dual occupations of pastor and theologian, Schleiermacher succumbed to pneumonia on 12 February 1834, at the age of sixty-five.

III. *Christmas Eve:* A Dialogue

Schleiermacher's *Christmas Eve (Weihnachtsfeier)* is his only popular literary work. The entire piece was written and sent to the printer during the three weeks before Christmas of 1805, after its author had just published half of his six-volume translation of Plato's dialogues. *Christmas Eve* is the clearest introduction to Schleiermacher's attempt at linking the Christian confession to the results of biblical criticism. It also offers us the least complicated route to understanding Schleiermacher's christology, in particular his view of the relation between the Jesus of history and the Christ of faith, a central, neuralgic issue of the modern historical-critical enterprise.

Composed of three parts, the dialogue takes place in the bosom of a German, middle-class family, united with friends for Christmas. Eduard and Ernestine are the hosts; among their children a devout and musical little girl named Sofie. Next to these appear an engaged couple, Ernst and Friederike, a young woman named Agnes, a grown serving-girl named Karoline, and the lawyer Leonhardt, *advocatus diaboli* of the play. On the last two pages of the dialogue, Josef, an unidentified friend who arrives last at the party, concludes the piece.

The curtain rises in Part One as the hostess Ernestine appears, busy with Christmas preparations. Watching her, little Sofie says: "You might just as well be the happy mother of the divine babe!" (33).[11] Later, in Part Two, Ernestine will declare that "every mother has a child divine and eternal, and devoutly looks out for the stirrings of the higher spirit within it" (48).

All this comes to expression in three stories told by the women in Part

---

11. All page references in the text refer to Friedrich Schleiermacher, *Christmas Eve: Dialogue on the Incarnation,* tr. Terrence N. Tice (Richmond: John Knox, 1967).

Two. Ernestine relates her encounter with an unknown woman, "holding a small child to her bosom" (58). When she concludes, all sing two verses composed by Novalis: "I see thee in a thousand forms, O Mary,/lovingly expressed . . ." (59). Agnes, the young woman guest, tells the second story, its high point the moment at which a child is baptized by its father: "As we all then laid hands upon the child . . . it was as if the rays of heavenly love and joy converged upon the head and heart of the child in a new focus . . ." (62-63). Agnes's story concludes with stanzas from another Novalis composition:

> Through all things gleams his infant play;
> Such warm young love will ne'er decay;
> He twines himself, unconscious, blest,
> With endless power to every breast. . . . (64)

The third story, told by Karoline, the serving girl, is of her friend Charlotte, who gives up her dying child on Christmas eve. After drifting off to sleep, the mother wakes to find the child recovered and exclaims: "On the festival of the rebirth of the word, my precious child is born to a new life" (67).

The most famous part of the dialogue is the discussion among the men in Part Three. The women depicted the significance of the holy night in their three stories about children. The men now attempt to grasp in thought the significance of all that Christmas means. The lawyer Leonhardt is first to speak. He praises Christmas as the embodiment of festival. Through festival, he says, history is born, for which reason Jesus is not the occasion for the festival of Christmas; the festival is rather the occasion for the historical figure of the Christ.

Ernst, the happy bridegroom-to-be, is next to speak. He replies to Leonhardt: "While you only took the point of view that every festival is a commemoration of something, what concerns me is the question of *what* it commemorates" (77). This "what" Ernst defines as something "through the representation of which a certain mood and disposition can be aroused within men." The mood of Christmas is joy, "the fire, the rapid stirring, of a widespread, general feeling." "Some inner cause" must underlie it, says Ernst, and it cannot be other than "the appearance of the Redeemer as the source of all other joy" (78). The festival of Christmas, then, does not depend on the historical traces of Christ's life, but on the "necessity of a Redeemer, and hence upon the experience of a higher life" (80). With this "slight improvement" on Leonhardt's remarks, Ernst ends his discussion. In its essence, the festival is "true joy in finding the higher life. . . ."

Eduard the host is third to speak. Stating that he holds less to the "external biographers of Christ" than to the "mystical among the four evangelists," he quotes from John's prologue (81). The "flesh," says Eduard, is the finite nature; the word is the idea, "the original and divine wisdom." "Accordingly," Eduard adds, "what we celebrate is nothing other than ourselves . . . that is, human nature . . . viewed and known from the perspective of the divine" (82). Or, in a variation on the same theme, the object of celebration is "redemption," "man-in-himself," the union of being and becoming in the individual person, and for which the One who was already that unity furnished the starting point.

Finally, the late arriving Josef appears, and gently reproaches the men for their "goings on." He says, "just think what lovely music (the women) could have sung for you, in which all the piety of your discourse could have dwelt far more profoundly." For his part, says Josef, "all forms are too rigid, all speech-making too tedious and cold" (85). The dialogue ends with Josef's summons to "come . . . bring the child if she is not yet asleep, and let me see your glories, and let us be glad and sing something religious and joyful!" (86).

The year of the piece's composition was the last year of Prussian independence before its defeat at the hands of the French. More than two decades separated its author from his Moravian education. Yet, contact with Gnadenfrei and the Herrnhuter community was retained through a sister, Charlotte, and through a young pastor whose widow Schleiermacher would later marry. Behind the author lay also his attempt, in those early romantic years in Berlin, to conquer the rationalistic, moral conception of Christianity that had captured the imagination of intellectuals since the rise of deism. What appears to have emerged at Halle had now begun to ripen — new reflection on the nature of Christianity. Neither a speculative construction, such as urged by Friedrich Wilhelm Joseph von Schelling (1775-1854), nor the attempt to establish Christianity on an empirical basis would find room in that reflection. And as for the inquiry into the "nature" or "essence" of Christianity itself, it was perhaps under Plato's influence, whose work Schleiermacher was translating at the time, that such a question pressed for an answer.

IV. Assessment

A. The Fragment Hypothesis

In the dialogue, historical criticism finds its tongue in Leonhardt, the lawyer. Armed with his analytical skills, he advances to a definition of the primitive Christian tradition, contending that the festival of Christmas gave birth to the historical figure of the Christ. He thus functions as precursor of David Friedrich Strauss, who assigned the greater portion of the New Testament message to the myth-building capacity of the early Christian community.

But despite Leonhardt's unbridled pursuit of critical method, at one point at least Schleiermacher could have owned it. In his first discourse, Leonhardt says: "The life of Christ receded far to the background of early proclamation, and as most people now believe, was only told fragmentarily and by persons removed from the actual events . . ." (73-74). Twelve years later, in a "critical essay" on Luke, Schleiermacher would propose his "fragment" or *"Diegesen"* theory, according to which "many circumstantial memorials of detached incidents" underlay the portrait of Jesus in the written Gospels. In the public assemblies of Christians these fragments were told and heard, some of them written down by narrators, besieged with questions concerning particular occurrences, some by inquirers unable to consult eyewitnesses. Notes of this kind, writes Schleiermacher, were less frequent among Christians of Palestine, but became more so with the dispersion of the Christian community through persecution. Collectors thus emerged, one assembling accounts of miracles, another of discourses, a third gathering incidents relating to Christ's last days, and still another whatever had been handed down on good authority. Schleiermacher concludes:

> Many such collections then might have been in existence, greater and smaller, some simple, some composed of several others, not only before any one of them acquired public authority, that is, before it was made even in particular congregations the basis of public discourses as Holy Writ, but even before one of them assumed the character of a regular book with a beginning and conclusion.[12]

When Karl Ludwig Schmidt (1891-1956), pioneer in form criticism, declared that the oldest narrators of the stories of Jesus gave little or no attention to their linkage but focused exclusively on what was graphic and isolated, and thus of use in public worship, he was to that extent dependent upon a theory already over a hundred years old.[13] And when Rudolf Bultmann defined the form critic's task as reaching back of the written Gospels to the period in which the isolated pieces of the Jesus tradition circulated orally, he

12. *A Critical Essay on the Gospel of St. Luke*, n. tr. (London: John Taylor, 1825), 15; see also 10, 12-14.
13. *Der Rahmen der Geschichte Jesu* (Berlin: Trowitzsch & Sohn, 1919), vi.

was near to repeating Schleiermacher's attempt at "paying attention to the probable previous existence of detached narratives and collections."[14] Even the conclusion Schleiermacher drew from his fragment hypothesis — namely, that "it is undeniable that we cannot achieve a connected presentation" of Jesus' life[15] — would have its echo in the Jesus research of the twentieth century, whatever the methodology.

B. Universal Hermeneutics

For Leonhardt, confidence in the historicity of the biblical record did not constitute proof of its historicity. For Schleiermacher, confidence consisted of faith or trust. But this confidence was not to be construed as reliance on the biblical record itself, but rather on its recorders. Schleiermacher had no taste for the doctrine of verbal inspiration. In the first edition of his *Speeches,* published in 1799, he writes that all Scripture is a "mausoleum of religion," monument to a great spirit no longer present. This fact justifies splitting the hulls to obtain the kernel.[16] Of the orthodox doctrine itself, Schleiermacher states that the peculiar inspiration of the apostles did not belong exclusively to the books of the New Testament: "These books only share in it; and inspiration in this narrower sense, conditioned as it is by the purity and completeness of the apostolic grasp of Christianity, covers the whole of the official apostolic activity thence derived."[17] In other words, the biblical authors were not simply

14. See Rudolf Bultmann, *The History of the Synoptic Tradition,* tr. John Marsh (New York: Harper and Row, 1963), 3-4; and *Schleiermacher, A Critical Essay on the Gospel of St. Luke,* 17.

15. *The Life of Jesus,* ed. Jack C. Verheyden, tr. S. Maclean Gilmour (Philadelphia: Fortress, 1975), 43.

16. Friedrich Schleiermacher, *Über die Religion: Reden an den Gebildeten unter ihren Verächtern* (Hamburg: Felix Meiner, 1958), 27, 28, 68. See the English translation, *On Religion,* dependent on the second and third editions; tr. Terrence Tice (Richmond: John Knox, 1969), 75, 76, and 144.

17. *The Christian Faith,* tr. ed. H. R. Mackintosh and J. S. Stewart (Edinburgh: T&T Clark, 1928), 599. In the first edition of the *Glaubenslehre,* reprinted in 1980, Schleiermacher reinterprets the old orthodox terms used to describe the inspiration of Scripture: "If we do not regard the inspiration of the Spirit underlying the emergence of the sacred books as something particular, but as linked to the inspiration underlying the exercise of the apostolic office as such, then we are the more easily raised above all the merely apparently difficult questions concerning the extent of inspiration, whether it is to be sought only in the initial impulse [in the terms of Protestant scholasticism, *impulsus ad scribendum,* that is, the "impulse to write"], or also in the formation of individual ideas [*suggestio rerum,* that is, the suggestion of "fitting content"], and whether or not it extends to the words [*suggestio verbi,* that

moved by the Holy Spirit to write (see 2 Peter 1:21). They had already been "moved," and in this condition they spoke and wrote. Accordingly, their inspiration was a prior condition in which Scripture participated. More important, that "condition" was universal, to the extent that any book or person might serve as a point of contact with the infinite.[18] One consequence of this point of view would be the development of a methodology of interpreting texts at total variance with the view dominating orthodox biblical interpretation till Schleiermacher's time: that the Bible requires explication by entirely different rules than other products of the human spirit. According to Schleiermacher, the "doctrine of the art of understanding" is universally applicable, and whatever particular application the New Testament texts requires is merely a concrete conclusion drawn from it.[19] What Spinoza and Reimarus had taught before him, Schleiermacher receives into the dogmatics of liberal Protestantism: the Bible must be treated like all other books.

C. The Challenge of the Intellectual

It is customary to describe Schleiermacher as the first great synthesizer of modern theology. Portrayed as believing that the world of reason or the metaphysical view of the world and the Christian view are at bottom the same, he is represented as distinguishing the two merely in respect of form: in an ideal of humanity, reflected in science as a view of the world and in Christian experience as feeling. The position is, of course, close to caricature, in part due to the modern concept of "feeling." Ernst's proposal that the festival of Christmas is founded to commemorate "[what] through the representation of which a certain mood and disposition can be aroused within men," and Eduard's description of the union between being and becoming in the individual person as "redemption," as "man-in-himself," find their maturer form in Schleiermacher's *Christian Faith* and its description of the feeling of "absolute dependence." Schleiermacher writes that this feeling transcends the tension between freedom and passivity, which are two fundamental determinants of human self-consciousness. The feeling of absolute dependence

---

is, the suggestion of the "fitting word"], and whatever else is involved. For even the impulse is nothing by itself, and would not be inspired if the entire apostolic life had not been a life from out of inspiration." See *Der christliche Glaube* (New York: Walter de Gruyter, 1980), 234.

18. Schleiermacher, *On Religion*, 318.

19. See *Hermeneutics: The Handwritten Manuscripts*, ed. Heinz Kimmerle, tr. James Duke and Jack Forstman (Missoula: Scholars, 1977), 67, 107, 141, and *passim*. See also *The Christian Faith*, 609-11.

merges with these determinants in order to dominate self-consciousness and propel it toward a universal, moral goal, a merger Schleiermacher calls "affection." The distance between the self as subject and God as object is thus to be overcome in an experience of the power of the principle of identity. This experience does not consist in a subjective emotion, but in the impact of the universe upon us in the depths of our being, an impact transcending subject and object.

Schleiermacher was not an obscurantist. He refused to ignore the hostile intellectual elite of his day. This rapidly expanding class, with its materialism and practical atheism, furnished Schleiermacher the occasion for interpreting the biblical revelation. Tension between the "tradition" and the new currents of thought was present not merely in his contemporaries, but in his own heart and soul. The doubts that had afflicted him while at seminary, and over which he carried on agitated correspondence with his father, led to his setting out for the university. In modern parlance, the need for "translation" was existential. And, as with every "evangelist," the danger was real of accommodation to a program determined by neither the Bible nor the Christian community. The debate continues respecting the extent to which Schleiermacher capitulated before the questions of the "despisers" or surrendered to his own doubts. Most often ignored are its occasions. And what may be least known, due principally to an evaluation of Schleiermacher that has silenced every other, and for this reason has not even a capacity for being ignored, is that a few of Schleiermacher's contemporaries believed he was loathe to surrender anything.

In *Christmas Eve*, the romantic love of music comes to the fore when Schleiermacher asserts that it is in music that the "feeling of absolute dependence" as the impact of the universe within the depths of human existence is directly experienced. Thus the hymns of Novalis and music of all kinds pervade the work. Later, Schleiermacher would write: "Suddenly, one evening by the fire, the idea [for the Dialogue] came to me in a quite wonderful way, when we were coming from Duelon's flute concert, and less than three weeks after this first conception — I knew only some days later that it actually was one — it was done."[20]

In the expression of this feeling of dependence, the word, apparently, is no match for music. When Josef appears, he exclaims: "Think what lovely music [the women] could have sung for you" (86), and Eduard remarks: "every fine feeling comes completely to the fore only when we have found the

---

20. Quoted in Wilhelm Dilthey, *Leben Schleiermachers* (Berlin und Leipzig: Walter de Gruyter, 1922), 772.

right musical expression for it. Not the spoken word, for this can never be anything but indirect . . . but a real, uncluttered tone. And it is precisely to religious feeling that music is most closely related" (46).

If one were to ask with which of the human species that feeling of dependence is most compatible, the answer from *Christmas Eve* would be: *the feminine,* understood in its nineteenth-century romantic sense. The women with their stories, their variation on the mother-child theme, not the males with all their theologizing, appear to express what is truly substantial concerning Christmas. They are already what we celebrate — the union of the divine with the human, and, as Eduard adds, "by virtue of which no conversion is further needed" (55).

The reference to the communication of the divine in music and the eternally feminine suggests that Christmas represents a human possibility — the highest triumph of human nature. In *The Christian Faith* Schleiermacher writes:

> Along with the absolute dependence which characterizes not only man but all temporal existence, there is given to man also the immediate self-consciousness of it, which becomes a consciousness of God. . . . On the other hand, any possibility of God being in any way *given* is entirely excluded, because anything that is outwardly given must be given as an object exposed to our counter-influence, however slight this may be.[21]

These words lose their apparently paradoxical character when the stress is placed on the *awareness* of the divine as given, not on the divine as such. God is thus not an object over against which one stands as subject. The distance between subject and object is bridged in the experience or consciousness of the identity of the divine and human, the experience Schleiermacher calls "feeling."

D. Life-of-Jesus Research

This does not mean that the objective referent for Christian faith is entirely lost. The link between the concerns of faith and reason forms the background of *Christmas Eve.* The dialogue makes clear that the reflection on religion that in the *Speeches* seems to have appeared without antecedent, or that could be construed as an atonement for what Schleiermacher had long neglected, was, after all, prepared for in his earlier attempts at coming to grips with a basic

21. Schleiermacher, *The Christian Faith,* 17-18.

Enlightenment tenet — the moral consciousness as the basis for belief in God, freedom, and immortality. Principal advocates of the Enlightenment had assumed that the moral consciousness necessitated willing the good, whereas Schleiermacher argues that such willing requires developing. Schiller's popularization, "you can, because you should," in other words, had been too facile. *Christmas Eve* portrays what that development of will itself requires: the incarnation in a single individual of that moral consciousness that conquers competing impulses and results in unhindered achievement of the "highest good."

Arguing that the lawyer Leonhardt's purely historical understanding needs supplementing in experience, an experience that in turn necessitates an historical origin, despite the paucity of the record, Ernst says: "However unsatisfactory the historical traces of [Jesus'] life may be . . . even the smallest elements have sufficed to convince you that a trace was present. So it is actually Christ to whose powers of attraction this new world owes its formation" (79-80).

In *The Christian Faith*, Schleiermacher writes that in the case of Christ's immediate disciples the danger of influence from their previous thought forms was averted by virtue of the purifying influence of their living memory of Christ: "This holds good, in the first place, of their narratives of Christ's words and deeds. . . . But it also holds pre-eminently of all that the apostles taught and ordained for Christian churches, as acting in Christ's name."[22]

Throughout his life Schleiermacher contended that historical theology was incomplete and required philosophical theology as its partner. Still, Ernst's supplement and Eduard's insistence upon Jesus as the *starting point* of the formation of "man-in-himself," that is, the unity of being and becoming (or, better, of becoming *within* being), indicate the limit set to philosophical theology. Ultimately, the new life originates in a particular figure of space and time. This primal, original unity of being and becoming found in Jesus is what Eduard understands as a universal human possibility that he calls "self-knowledge." This definition of the meaning of Christ links the dialogue to what has come to be known in our time as the "New Quest of the Historical Jesus," in particular to those twentieth-century scholars who fix the material continuity between the Jesus of history and the Christ of faith in Jesus' own self-understanding, an understanding repeated by us through faith in the *kerygma*.[23]

---

22. *Ibid.*, 595.

23. See, e.g., James M. Robinson, *A New Quest of the Historical Jesus and Other Essays* (Philadelphia: Fortress, 1983).

E. Concrete Christ or Redeemer Idea?

In a 1924 analysis of *Christmas Eve,* Karl Barth writes: "Always Mary and always Christ, and, whether as Mary or Christ, always we ourselves. . . ."[24] At the end of his discourse, Eduard says: "Every mother sees Christ in her child. . . . And in like manner each of us sees in the birth of Christ his own higher birth, by which nothing else than devotion and love lives in him, and in him appears the eternal Son of God" (84).

Are Mary and Jesus merely paradigms? Ernst states that the content of the Christmas message is a mood or disposition, the universal experience of a higher life, of a "redemption." In the divine child we see this higher, exalted life raised above tension and contrast. In the second edition of *Christmas Eve,* the character of Eduard is made to juxtapose the *experience* of a higher life rooted in an historical beginning with the *idea* of a Redeemer. Barth claims that this juxtaposition makes Jesus nothing more than one figure in a series of great religious personalities that have dotted the religious landscape of humankind.

Barth takes this viewpoint because he reads *Christmas Eve* from the perspective of the *Speeches.* If this approach is adopted, then the reading of the dialogue is affected. For example, Agnes's word to Leonhardt that "all radiant, serene joy is religion" (63) or Eduard's statement that at Christmas we celebrate "ourselves as whole beings," that is, as "man-in-himself," can be interpreted in a way that recalls the famous passage in the fifth *Speech* where Schleiermacher writes: "A numerous party of Christians declare themselves ready to acknowledge everyone as a mediating and divine being who can prove, by a divine life or any impress of divinity, that he has been, for even a small circle, the first of quickening of the higher sense."[25] Accordingly, Barth asserts that in Schleiermacher's view whoever has experience of "redemption," of that union of being with becoming, has no objective referent upon which to draw,[26] that is, stands over against nothing and no one outside oneself. Experience *as such* is faith. It is Barth's opinion that Schleiermacher in *Christmas Eve* denies that one may possess God in doctrines to which the mind gives assent; that he construes God as given in feeling, thus interpreting Christian faith as a modification of a feeling given with consciousness.

---

24. *The Theology of Schleiermacher,* tr. Geoffrey W. Bromiley (Grand Rapids: Wm. B. Eerdmans, 1982), 61.

25. *On Religion,* 249-50 (*Über die Religion,* 170).

26. See *The Theology of Schleiermacher,* 66, 76.

We suggest a different reading. While it may be ill advised to argue that Schleiermacher makes a radically new departure in *Christmas Eve* from the *Speeches,* a departure of sorts, or at least an evolution in Schleiermacher's thought, cannot be denied.[27] *Christmas Eve* stands between the *Speeches* and the lectures on the life of Jesus, begun in 1819 and continuing until 1832. Contemporary scholarship tends to accent the continuity within Schleiermacher's thought throughout.[28] With this sense of evolution or continuity in mind, we think it is just as valid to read *Christmas Eve,* and especially its christological claims, with the life-of-Jesus lectures as a guide.

It was precisely this approach that two of Schleiermacher's most noted contemporaries, David Friedrich Strauss and Friedrich Wilhelm Joseph von Schelling, took. Schelling actually wrote a review of *Christmas Eve,* while Strauss directed his criticism at the life-of-Jesus lectures.

In his piece, Schelling constructs a fourth unnamed member of the dialogue, who asks: "How can you in fairness still call Christianity what merely binds you to your closest circle of friends?"[29] The accusation is that Schleiermacher had generalized on a particular, had allowed the mood within his circle of intimates to represent the universal. Commenting that apart from the universal and all-encompassing even the best is repulsive, Schelling's fourth speaker locates the most objectionable form of particularity in the idea of a church.[30] And, as for Ernst's notion that redemption consists in healing the division between being and becoming, Schelling's speaker contends that such only marks the birth, and not the *fulfillment* of Christianity. "Did He not himself," the speaker asks, "summon us to the positive, when He promised to send the Paraclete . . . knowing full well that He did not complete the work through

---

27. See Richard R. Niebuhr's explanation for the contrasts between the *Speeches* and *Christmas Eve:* (1) in the latter, Schleiermacher more insistently reflects his propensity toward systematic thought; (2) his thought is more closely allied with institutional Christianity; and (3) his interest increases in the historical unity of human nature. *Schleiermacher on Christ and Religion* (New York: Scribner's, 1964), 31-33.

28. See Stephen Sykes for a reflection of this same opinion: "The present writer . . . finds plenty of evidence of a basically consistent outlook, in which both development of views and divergences of emphasis must be allowed their natural place." *Friedrich Schleiermacher* (Richmond: John Knox, 1971), 17-18.

29. "Die Weihnachtsfeier: Ein Gespräch. Von Friedrich Schleiermacher. Halle, 1806," in *Friedrich Wilhelm Joseph von Schellings Sämmtliche Werke* (Stuttgart and Augsburg: J. G. Cotta, 1860), 7:501.

30. "The church is not the description and celebration of the original unity already established, but only the means to its establishment. . . . Far from depicting the original health of pure nature free of all contradiction, it is caught in the fragile and sinful; no longer an eternal idea, but a temporal means." *Ibid.,* 508.

the redemption . . . ?"[31] On the final page of his review, Schelling concedes that his own fictional speaker may not have addressed the author of the work, "for who knows what ideas he nourishes who himself does not appear?"[32]

Criticism of Schleiermacher's particularity is sharper in Strauss, since he addressed himself to the Berliner's lectures on the life of Jesus. Strauss writes that the idea of a personal Redeemer is among those "pious ideas" that Schleiermacher allows rational culture to sample but not consume, and that betrays his upbringing among the *Herrnhuter*.[33] These ideas are given a home in Schleiermacher's methodology of gospel criticism, according to which he assigns John to an eyewitness, in contrast to the first three that originated in "fragments" and have come down to us at second or third hand.[34] John thus yields the most important source for a life of Jesus. In what is clearly an interpretation, and not a literal quotation, though in essence correct, Strauss reports Schleiermacher as stating that if we were forced to regard John on a level with the Synoptic Gospels, "nothing would be reliable for us any longer."[35]

As to whether or not Schleiermacher's Jesus is merely first in a series of great religious personalities, Strauss is adamant on the point that he is not. Strauss was bemused and annoyed by what he terms a tenacious clinging to a personal Redeemer on the part of a man who otherwise displays such critical acumen, and who often betrays kinship with the great patriarch of rationalism himself, H. E. G. Paulus (1761-1851): "If the orthodox theologians before him were like the companions of Odysseus, who stopped their ears against the critics' siren voices, then he, of course, kept them open, but instead let himself be bound with ropes to the mast of faith in Christ, in order to pass by the perilous island unharmed."[36]

A Jesus who is merely first in a series would not have been removed from the tests that mark ordinary human existence. According to Strauss, the Jesus of Schleiermacher is in fact removed from those tests. In evidence, he cites Schleiermacher's admission that he could not believe Jesus first shared

---

31. "Once the Redeemer is born, and the redemption, occurred from all eternity, is revealed and realized in time, then it is not that beginning in division we merely attain to redemption, but rather that beginning from redemption we live immediately and first of all in eternity." *Ibid.*, 506; see 505.

32. *Ibid.*, 510.

33. *Der Christus des Glaubens und der Jesus der Geschichte: Eine Kritik des Schleiermacher'schen Lebens Jesu* (Berlin: Drucker, 1865), 25.

34. *Ibid.*, 28-31, 38, 52. See Schleiermacher, *The Life of Jesus*, 159, 223, and 262.

35. Strauss, *Der Christus des Glaubens*, 29; see 52.

36. *Ibid.*, 26, 100.

the common view that the Messiah would exercise civil power, then changed his mind; that this would reflect such a fundamental error that Christ would cease to be an object of reverence for him; that it is just as difficult for him to think of Christ's development in terms of formulating a plan for his activity, since it would "place him on the same level as other men."[37] Even in Schleiermacher's concession to the historicity of Jesus' healing miracles, easiest to concede by virtue of their analogy to our own experience, Strauss detects that penchant for distancing Jesus from all others. Such instances as are analogous to Christ's miracles, writes Schleiermacher, "are similar rather than identical cases."[38]

An interpretation of *Christmas Eve* in support of the contention that it has "redrawn" the figure of Jesus[39] must still reckon with the contrary, contemporary view that it has not. Ironically, this view was embraced by one whose reading of the young Schleiermacher current scholarship has in large part abandoned — Wilhelm Dilthey. But to the extent this view is held, to that extent the question remains: Have we in *Christmas Eve* a concrete Christ or only the idea of a Redeemer? It was, after all, Ernst who said: "However unsatisfactory the historical traces of [Jesus'] life may be when one examines it critically — in a lower sense — nevertheless the festival does not depend on this. It rests on the necessity of a Redeemer, and hence upon the experience of a heightened existence" (80-81). Ernst added that the festival could be derived "from no other beginning" than from Christ, but Dilthey appeared to place the accent on the words reading "experience of a heightened existence," for he writes: "In the end all this reflection sinks within the enjoyment of the exalted religious life itself."[40]

F. An Empty Gibbet

Strauss notes Schleiermacher's refusal to assign to Jesus any inner turmoil prior to or during his crucifixion.[41] And in fact, in the Jesus of Schleiermacher the conflicts of sensible human consciousness are so transcended by the unity of being with becoming that all conflict and struggle is relegated to the periphery. There are no sharp breaks, there is no inner conflict, no expec-

---

37. *Ibid.*, 42, 43. See Schleiermacher, *The Life of Jesus*, 108, 122.

38. Strauss, *Der Christus des Glaubens*, 54; Schleiermacher, *The Life of Jesus*, 204-5.

39. See Niebuhr, *Schleiermacher on Christ and Religion*, 35.

40. Dilthey, *Leben Schleiermachers*, 797-98.

41. Strauss, *Der Christus des Glaubens*, 71-72, 77. See Schleiermacher, *The Life of Jesus*, 395-96.

tation of an intervention of God heightened to an uncommon degree in the last hours of Jesus' life (an expectation all but smothered in English translation: "I have earnestly desired to eat this passover with you before I suffer"; Luke 22:14). There is no trembling ("He began to be greatly distressed and troubled" — another euphemism — "and he said to them, 'My soul is very sorrowful, even to death'"; Mark 14:33b-34). Finally, there is no cry of dereliction from the cross, "My God, my God, why hast thou forsaken me?" — the only word recorded in Mark and Matthew. According to Schleiermacher, these utterances, recorded in the first three Gospels, are in contrast to John at second or third hand. Of Jesus' last word in Matthew and Mark, Schleiermacher writes: "I cannot think of this saying as an expression of Christ's self-consciousness. I can think of no moment when the relationship between God and Christ could have changed. It must always have been the same . . . his cry of dereliction must have been a self-deception or an untruth."[42] Schleiermacher is reported to have registered his pleasure over the suggestion of one scholar that Jesus did not utter the cry of dereliction, but that it had been trajected back into his mouth by a later editor. At the moment of Jesus' "death," there was only a "Johannine" peace and serenity, more, an assumption of initiative: "Woman, behold your son! . . . Behold, your mother!" (John 19:26b-27), that is, an assumption of power ("It is finished!"; John 19:30).

Many critics have detected the thin air of docetism in claims such as these. The charge is well founded. Goethe, who treated with contempt the machinations of romantic theology, had once written: "An airy, decorative cross is always a cheerful object; the loathsome wood of the martyrs, the most repugnant object under the sun no man in his right mind should be concerned to excavate and erect."[43] Schleiermacher, it appears, found the Christ of the cross to be, at least on occasion, so frightening and repugnant that he was willing to deny the record of the Gospels.

But this said, we must not carry the charge of docetism too far. Schleiermacher was well aware of the threat of docetism. He believed that this heresy was characteristic of Protestant scholasticism, and he dedicated himself to its eradication. Schleiermacher also refused to accept Kant's notion, applauded by Strauss, that the idea of a humanity pleasing to God needed no concretization in an actual existence; that it was immaterial whether or not the historicity of a man answering to the idea of the good was demonstrable. For Strauss, this refusal spelled contradiction:

---

42. *Ibid.*, 423.

43. Quoted in Karl Löwith, *From Hegel to Nietzsche,* tr. David E. Green (Garden City, N.Y.: Doubleday, 1967), 15.

> This passion . . . for the Christ become personal, historical, is an anachronism in Schleiermacher's otherwise thoroughly modern spirit. . . . He himself senses the contradiction. . . . Thus the busy, one might almost say anxious, activity of his spirit . . . to establish peace between the two parts — to suit the Christ of faith to thought, and to suit thought to faith. . . . But his own Christ lacks real reality. He is still only a reminiscence from days long ago — as it were the light of some distant star which today still meets our eyes, while the body which emits it was extinguished years ago.[44]

Schleiermacher's portrayal of Christ may have been sentimental, but at least we must give him credit for refusing to break the tie between the Christ of faith and the Jesus of history. In his desire to keep the idea of Christ rooted in Jesus — imperfectly realized though it be in his theology — Schleiermacher was no docetist.

From these observations two facts appear to emerge. First, there is an alternative to the reading of Schleiermacher as substituting for the historical a religion merely of feeling. Schleiermacher did not abandon historical faith to subjectivity. The second is that for this reason the "feeling of absolute dependence" takes its origin, its occasion, and its content from Jesus of Nazareth. If this spelled contradiction in Schleiermacher, it also spelled the way of sorrows for the entire Life-of-Jesus Research to come, at least among such as Schleiermacher, for whom an intelligent-reflective attitude toward Christ could only be taken on the basis of a piety personally gripped by him.[45] It is such a piety that is expressed in Joseph's statement at the conclusion of *Christmas Eve:* "As Christ had no bride but the church, no children but his friends, no household but the temple and the world, and yet his heart was full of heavenly love and joy, so I too seem to be born to endeavor after such a life" (86).

44. Strauss, *Der Christus des Glaubens*, 104-5.
45. Wolfgang Sommer, *Schleiermacher und Novalis* (Bern: Herbert Lang, 1973), 128.

5

DAVID FRIEDRICH STRAUSS

The Bible as Myth

I. Faith under Siege

When Spinoza and Reimarus took up their pens to oppose Christianity and the Bible, they knew that they were waging war against a dominant cultural and political force. The church may already have been under challenge, but its privileged legal status and centuries of tradition continued to make it a formidable power. It is not surprising that Spinoza published the *Theological-Political Treatise* anonymously or that Reimarus hid the *Apology* from his wife. By the mid-nineteenth century, the situation had changed. Christianity lost its iron grip on the imagination of more than just the advanced forces of secularism. It now lost the allegiance of a significant portion of the European cultural elite. For the first time, "agnosticism" (a neologism coined by Thomas Huxley in 1869) and atheism became enduring cultural options to be openly held, discussed, and written about by educated people.[1]

The reasons for this state of affairs are not hard to find. First, there was the indisputable prestige of the sciences. From the emergence of physics and calculus at the turn of the eighteenth century, to steady advances thereafter in

---

1. On the emergence of atheism as a cultural force, see James Turner, *Without God, Without Creed: The Origins of Unbelief in America* (Baltimore and London: Johns Hopkins University Press, 1985). Despite the subtitle, Turner covers European as well as American developments.

botany, zoology, chemistry, and geology, the natural sciences had, by 1830, reached a level of prestige in Western culture that they have yet to relinquish. The damaging effect of natural science on theology was slow to emerge. Whereas Christian theologians found accommodation to Newton's universe to be, for the most part, a happy development, geology and biology were another matter. The benevolence of divine providence was hard to find when the record of earthly life revealed itself to have stretched across millennia, leaving whole species with a legacy of nothing more than fossilized imprints in layers of rock and shale. In *Principles of Geology* (1st ed., 1830-33), Sir Charles Lyell (1797-1875) conjured up a vision of a cold, unrelenting creation: "Species cannot be immortal, but must perish, one after another, like the individuals which compose them." Even the geological remains of species are subject to the ravages of time and natural events: "when they have been included in rocky strata . . . they must nevertheless eventually perish; for every year some portion of the earth's crust is shattered by earthquakes or melted by volcanic fire, or ground to dust by the moving waters on the surface."[2] Haunted by the untimely death of his close friend, Arthur Hallam, the young Alfred Tennyson (1809-92) found in Lyell's description the perfect metaphor for his grief: the indifference of nature.

> "So careful of the type?" but no.
>   From scarpèd cliff and quarried stone
>   She cries, "A thousand types are gone:
> I care for nothing, all shall go."
>
> "Thou makest thine appeal to me:
>   I bring to life, I bring to death;
>   The spirit but does mean the breath.
> I know no more."[3]

Tennyson read Lyell in 1837, twenty-two years before the publication of Darwin's *Origin of the Species.* In the way of great poets, he anticipated the spiritual shock of the next generation as he contemplated "Nature, red in tooth and claw" and its devastating effect on the security of religious faith.

The Industrial Revolution was a second factor in the continuing decline of religion. The growth of industry added to the prestige of science because industry was itself the result of science applied to the conditions of com-

---

2. *Principles of Geology,* 4th ed. (London: J. Murray, 1834-35), 3:155, 280. Quoted in Christopher Ricks, ed., *The Poems of Tennyson* (New York: Norton, 1972), 911.

3. "In Memoriam A.H.H." 16, Ricks, ed., *Tennyson,* 911.

merce. Scientific method thus had a direct impact on the lives of thousands of entrepreneurs and industrial workers. This helped to reshape the understanding of truth. Induction, observation, and experimentation, not tradition or deduction from general concepts, were the path to effective knowledge for daily life. In such a social environment, theological assumptions appeared increasingly irrelevant.[4] In 1843 Ludwig Feuerbach (1804-72) spoke with contempt about Christianity as a *"fixed idea"* that meant little in the brave new world of "our fire and life assurance companies, our railroads and steam-carriages, our picture and sculpture galleries, our military and industrial schools, our theaters and scientific museums."[5]

The third factor, and perhaps the most potent one on the continent of Europe, was the specter of political revolution. The French Revolution and the reorganization of national and territorial governments under the revolutionary imperialism of Napoleon had radically changed the political landscape of Europe. At the Congress of Vienna (1814-15), the aristocratic class reasserted governmental control. The legitimacy of this control, however, was tested in 1830 and, more seriously, in 1848 as cities from Copenhagen to Palermo, Paris to Prague and Vienna, erupted in revolutionary fervor. During this uncertain period, the institutional church aligned itself with reactionary forces. Against the repeal of the Test and Corporation Acts (1828), Catholic Emancipation (1829), and especially the Reform Bill of 1832 — all of which broadened the participation of the citizenry in Britain — the Oxford Movement, under the leadership of John Henry Newman (1801-90), cried "apostasy." It feared the emerging pluralism of English society and the power of non-Anglican members of Parliament to choose episcopal leadership and determine policy for the Church of England. In Prussia, Lutheran confessionalists, such as Frederick Julius Stahl (1802-61), identified revolutionary movements with opposition against the divinely instituted order of society. In 1864 Pope Pius IX (1792-1878) in the *Syllabus of Errors* declared his opposition to democratic reform and the separation of church and state, especially in matters of education. Intellectuals and political radicals responded to these developments by labeling Christianity, whether Protestant or Catholic, a backward social force dedicated to hierarchical rule. They identified "throne and altar" as co-conspirators in oppression and, like their predecessors in the Enlightenment, rejected the church.

One movement that tried to respond constructively to these cultural as-

---

4. Harold H. Hutson, "Some Factors in the Rise of Scientific New Testament Criticism," *The Journal of Religion* 22 (1942): 92.

5. *The Essence of Christianity,* tr. George Eliot (New York: Harper, 1957), xliv.

saults while yet retaining a place for the church was liberal Protestantism in Germany. In his *Speeches* of 1799, Schleiermacher had challenged the path taken by the "cultured despisers" of religion and had tried to defend the faith with a strategy of accommodation. Schleiermacher set a course that many would follow. As John Stroup describes it: "An openness to modern culture, joined to willingness to criticize finite expressions of the Christian tradition regarded as absolute, can be taken as characteristic of the German liberal Protestant tradition."[6] In the main, this meant attacking dogmatic Augustinian assertions concerning human corruption, divine election, and an otherworldly spirituality in favor of the Enlightenment's affirmation of self and world as enclosed in a universe of natural laws.

The front line for liberal Protestant apologetics was the German university system.[7] Unlike England, where the humanistic disciplines, including theology, were shielded from the effects of the new science and empiricism by the traditional pattern of university curricula, or France, where theological education fell under the control of the Roman Church, the situation in German lands was different. In the eighteenth century, German universities had largely separated themselves from the control of court and church. Objective research in the quest for truth became the academic ideal not only for the natural sciences but also for the humanities and theology. Science and humanities were studied together. The peripatetic habits of German students helped to unify university culture and spread the objectivist ideal across territorial boundaries. Philosophically, German romanticism and idealism encouraged the belief that sound historical research into the facts of history was the way to penetrate to the all-important ideas at the center of reality. Schleiermacher, for example, argued that Christianity is an "idea" that encompasses both change and identity. Its "essence" is not the product of biblical or dogmatic proof texts, but the subject of nondogmatic historical investigation.[8] Georg Friedrich Wilhelm Hegel (1770-1831) — Schleiermacher's colleague, if not his friend, at the University of Berlin — made a similar argument. The significance of Christianity for world history, according to Hegel, is the public record of its historical development. Christianity is meaningful because of its impact on historical existence as such. It reveals the purpose of human existence at a crucial stage of humanity's cultural evolution. A scholarly and

6. "The Idea of Theological Education at the University of Berlin: From Schleiermacher to Harnack," in *Schools of Thought in the Christian Tradition*, ed. Patrick Henry (Philadelphia: Fortress, 1984), 154.

7. Hutson, "Some Factors in the Rise of Scientific New Testament Criticism," 91.

8. *Brief Outline on the Study of Theology*, tr. Terrence N. Tice (Richmond: John Knox, 1966), 26 (para. 28); Stroup, "The Idea of Theological Education," 159-60.

philosophical account of Christian history is the proper defense of religion and the path to truth.

Both Schleiermacher and Hegel, and the liberal Protestants who followed them, made a crucial methodological distinction between "idea" and "temporal form." The former is the truth or concept that a phenomenon represents; the latter is the particular shape or image that a phenomenon takes in the historical arena. This distinction was enormously influential in the development of biblical criticism that, no longer a stepchild of the church as it had been in the eighteenth century, flowered in the German universities, becoming part of the normal educational process of the Protestant pastor. Historical criticism of the Bible operated under a simple but powerful assumption: "Impartial objective research was to solve the riddles of history. The facts might dissolve in source analysis; the all-important ideas would remain."[9]

There was in Germany an audience interested in the results of this analysis, although its size and stability remain a matter of dispute. Under attack by rigid ecclesiastics and, at times, governmental authorities on the one side and secularists on the other, this liberally spirited Christian elite believed that a vital role was to be played by "nonecclesiastical *Christentum*" in the cultivation *(Bildung)* of the German middle class.[10] In this view, Christianity was conceived as a necessary formative element of both German culture and the spirit of the German people. It was not Augustinian Christianity to be sure, but Christian humanism filtered through the lens of post-Enlightenment romanticism and idealism.

In summary, the liberal ideals of the German university, the philosophical commitments of romanticism and idealism, and a community of followers (however hard to define) persuaded liberal Protestants to take on the forces of secularization through a combination of concessions to cultural demands and reinterpretation of traditional dogmatics. The battleground was, as it had been since Spinoza's day, historical criticism of the Bible.

The two men most prominent in testing the limits of this approach after Schleiermacher were David Friedrich Strauss and Ferdinand Christian Baur. In Strauss, we see how tenuous the liberal Protestant enterprise was from the beginning. Strauss's effort to reinterpret the faith by means of historical-critical method quickly became an attack upon it. The key concept he employed was the notion of "myth."

9. Robert M. Grant and David Tracy, *A Short History of the Interpretation of the Bible,* 2nd ed. (Philadelphia: Fortress, 1984), 110.

10. Stroup, "The Idea of Theological Education," 159.

II. Biography

David Friedrich Strauss was born on 27 January 1808, in Ludwigsburg, Germany. Among his teachers at Tübingen were the supernaturalists Johann Christian Friedrich Steudel (1779-1837) and Ernst Gottlieb Bengel (1769-1826), grandson of the great Swabian pietist, Johann Albrecht Bengel (1687-1752). As a student Strauss was a fierce foe of rationalism. As a student colleague described it: "Wherever Strauss thought he detected the merest trace of rationalism in the discussion, he violently repudiated it. . . ."[11]

The first signal event in Strauss's spiritual pilgrimage occurred in 1828. He entered a competition arranged by members of the Tübingen Catholic faculty on the topic of the resurrection. "I proved the resurrection of the dead with full conviction," he wrote, "and when I made my last point, it was clear to me there was nothing to the entire story."[12] Strauss began to immerse himself in the study of Hegel's philosophy. In 1830 he passed his examinations and went as vicar to Kleiningersheim.

The next year, 1831, Strauss enrolled in the Master's program at the University of Berlin, hoping to study under Hegel. Two weeks after Strauss's arrival, Hegel died. Strauss attended the funeral, and wrote to an old friend of Blaubeuren days:

> We buried him yesterday. At about three o'clock in the hall of the university, Rector Marheineke gave a simple and heartfelt speech, totally pleasing to me. He described [Hegel] not only as a monarch in the realm of thought, but also as a true disciple of Christ in his life. Then he said what he would not have said at a church ceremony, that just as Jesus Christ, so he too has passed through bodily death to the resurrection of the spirit, a spirit bequeathed to his own. There followed a rather tumultuous procession from the house of mourning to the cemetery.[13]

"*We* buried him. . . ." The phrase seems presumptuous, but Strauss had laid claim to Hegel long since. Now the young scholar was left with what he considered to be second best: Schleiermacher and his lectures on the life of Jesus. Under Schleiermacher the critical spirit awoke. "Schleiermacher," wrote

---

11. Friedrich Theodor Vischer, "Dr. Strauss und die Wirtemberger," in *Kritische Gänge* (Tübingen: Osiander, 1844), 90.

12. *Ibid.*, 98.

13. From the letter to Christian Märklin, 17 November 1831, in Jörg Sandberger, *David Strauss als theologischer Hegelianer* (Göttingen: Vandenhoeck und Ruprecht, 1972), 192.

Strauss, "goes only half way. . . . I will write a life of Jesus according to my own idea."[14]

In 1832 Strauss returned to Tübingen as *Repetent* or tutor at the *Stift*. The connection between the university faculty and the *Stift* was such that in addition to receiving their theological education at the university, members of the *Stift* underwent examinations and participated in exercises conducted by the *Repetenten*, who were retained at the *Stift* and paid for their services by the individual students. Strauss began lecturing on the history of philosophy. He attracted students in droves, evoking envy from his fellow tutors whose audiences shrank, thus reducing their pay. In this period Strauss prepared his manuscript on the life of Jesus. As a result of intrigue by his colleagues, Strauss was relieved of his duties at the *Stift,* though he remained there to continue his work. In November of 1835, Strauss published the first volume of *The Life of Jesus*. The book unleashed a firestorm of controversy. Strauss left Tübingen for the bureaucratic post of administrator for the school council in Ludwigsburg. He soon surrendered his position and retreated to private life in nearby Stuttgart. Volume two of the *Life* appeared in 1836.

In 1839 Strauss was offered a theological professorship at the University of Zurich. Fearful of the reaction of conservatives incensed at his Jesus research and its political implications, the liberal government of Zurich reneged on the offer and furnished Strauss with a pension. The action culminated in the government's collapse in 1838, in a bloody event called the *Züriputsch.* The experience embittered Strauss, since in the period between 1836 and 1840 he had prepared to make concessions regarding his *Life of Jesus.* The year 1840 saw Strauss in a defiant mood, dismantling rather than reconstructing Christian theology in his *Glaubenslehre,* or dogmatics, as well as continuing to attack the faith in subsequent editions of *The Life of Jesus.* Never again would Strauss occupy a chair in philosophy or theology. In the years following, he spent time in Munich, Weimar, Heidelberg, Heilbronn, and Darmstadt.

In 1848 Strauss was a candidate for the first German National Assembly held at Frankfurt. On Easter Monday, 1848, between eight and ten thousand voters stood within the courtyard of the Ludwigsburg Castle to greet their nominee. Despite his popularity at home, opposition to Strauss's candidacy was fierce, and he clearly had not reckoned on it. The election results were a disaster, and the Ludwigsburg's black-red-gold flag flew at half mast. In the same year, Strauss was appointed to represent Ludwigsburg at the *Landtag,* or

---

14. Heinrich Benecke, *William Vatke in seinem Leben und seinen Schriften* (Bonn: E. Strauss, 1883), 75.

legislature, of the province of Württemberg. There he came into conflict with his supporters, due to his approval of the execution of Robert Blum, radical leader of the democratic left and participant in the bloody Vienna Revolution of 1848. Deeply shocked by the events of 1848, Strauss vacated his seat in the *Landtag* and devoted himself entirely to writing. During the Franco-Prussian war in 1870-71, Strauss carried on lively and much publicized correspondence with Ernst Renan (1823-92), French biographer of Jesus and political activist. Two years before his death, Strauss penned what he termed his "confession," *The Old Faith and the New,* recounting "the incredible and contradictory dogmas we left behind when we quit the church, and the crucifixion of reason and truthfulness which we escaped when we took that step."[15] He died in the city of his birth on 8 February 1874 and, on his own instruction, was buried without benefit of clergy.

III. *The Life of Jesus*

Soon after his arrival in Tübingen as *Repetent,* Strauss wrote a friend of his plan for lectures on the life of Jesus. The lectures would fall into three parts, a positive, a negative, and a third part in which the positive was restored. "In this way," Strauss wrote, "I would in part destroy, in part shake the infinite content faith has in this life — indeed, only in order to restore it in a higher way." The restoration, Strauss continued, would be threefold: first in the "crude" form of supernaturalism — later given greater subtlety by Schleiermacher — then in the "empty" form of rationalism as popularized by H. E. G. Paulus, and finally in the "true" form of science that viewed the life of Jesus as the consciousness of the church objectified by the human spirit as divine. To his friend's possible caveat that such a series might result in the lecture hall's being closed to him, Strauss replied that something of the sort was indeed possible.[16]

When the first volume of *The Life of Jesus* appeared in 1835, its purpose was clear: to penetrate what was historically conditioned or limited in the Jesus tradition to the true concept beneath. Strauss asserted that the limited character of the tradition derived from the fact that the Gospels of the New Testament originated in a process of "ornamentation." This ornamentation

---

15. *The Old Faith and the New: A Confession by David Friedrich Strauss,* tr. Mathilde Blind (New York: Henry Holt, 1873), xxxii.

16. From the letter to Christian Märklin, 6 February 1832, in Sandberger, *David Strauss,* 196-97.

consisted of "pure" or "philosophical" myths, that is, ideas in historicized form; "sagas," myths with particular, individual events at their base; and "poetic" myths or pure fiction. The causes of this ornamentation Strauss assigned to the person of Jesus himself, who occasioned the telling of his story in mythical narrative, as well as to mythical materials in extrabiblical, Jewish messianism and in extra-Jewish religious history. Strauss termed the means by which he sought to burrow beneath the historical representation to the concept it concealed the "mythical interpretation," and found precedent for it in Origen of Alexandria's (ca. 185–ca. 254) allegorical interpretation, that "mixture by which the lead and copper . . . of the biblical representations were transformed into the pure gold of rational concepts of religion."[17] The similarity in the two approaches lay in their holding fast to the absolute truth of what was narrated by "relinquishing the historical reality" (65).[18]

In applying his method to the entire Jesus tradition, Strauss began with the problem that a saying or narrative of Jesus posed for the contemporary reader, then proceeded to view its solution on the part of supernaturalist and rationalist, next demonstrated how the opposing views mutually excluded each other, and summed up the contents of both in preparation for his own results. For the supernaturalist's view, Strauss frequently referred to the comments of the Lutheran orthodox scholar Hermann Olshausen (1796-1839), and for the rationalist direction to the "classical" writings of Paulus. Clearly, the original intention to research the Jesus tradition by way of a positive, then negative, then final reconstructive approach had given way to a *Life* with only two sections, a critical-destructive and a dogmatic-restorative.

Any one of the gospel narratives treated by Strauss would suffice to illustrate the method pursued throughout *The Life of Jesus*. The illustration given here is from his discussion of the narrative of Jesus' baptism (239-42): "At the moment that John had completed his baptism of Jesus, the synoptical gospels tell us that the heavens were opened, the Holy Spirit descended on Jesus in the form of a dove, and a voice from heaven designated him Son of God, in whom the Father was well pleased" (239). At this point Strauss raises the question how any cultured person who reflected on the event could interpret it.

17. David Friedrich Strauss, *Die christliche Glaubenslehre in ihrer geschichtlichen Entwicklung und im Kampfe mit der modernen Wissenschaft dargestellt* (Tübingen: C. F. Osiander, 1840), 1:147-48.

18. All page references in the text refer to David Friedrich Strauss, *The Life of Jesus Critically Examined*, ed. Peter C. Hodgson (London: SCM, 1973). This edition reproduces the translation of the fourth edition by George Eliot (Mary Ann Cross, née Evans [1819-80]) in 1846.

First, that for the appearance of a divine being on earth, the visible heavens must divide themselves, to allow of his descent from his accustomed seat, is an idea that can have no objective reality. . . . How is it reconcilable with the true idea of the Holy Spirit as divine, as all-pervading Power, that he should move from one place to another, like a finite being, and embody himself in the form of a dove? Finally, that God should utter articulate tones in a national idiom, has been justly held extravagant. (240)

Next, Strauss refers to the way in which "cultured minds" — the supernaturalist, then the naturalist — answer these questions. The one tries to retain the divine origin of the event while modifying its apparent external absurdities: the crowd "saw and heard something," but the vision of a dove and the voice from heaven were sensed interiorly. Strauss comments: "Our understanding fails us in this pneumatology . . . wherein there are sensible realities transcending the senses; and we hasten out of this misty atmosphere into the clearer one of those who simply tell us that the appearance was an external incident, but one purely natural" (241). The naturalist interpretation, writes Strauss, asserts that Jesus and John, convinced of their identities, interpreted every event in terms of their mission. This type of interpretation retains the recorded event as actual, but has difficulty explaining how it could happen. "[Paulus] incurred the hard task of showing by a multitude of facts from natural history and other sources, that the dove might be tame enough to fly towards a man; how it could linger so long over one . . . he has not succeeded in explaining" (242). After recalling the scene of the baptism as the evangelists relate it, Strauss leads his reader to ask how long a well-trained dove could hover over someone's head. Strauss then proceeds to a more "intelligible" representation of the scene:

In the East, and especially in Syria, the dove is a sacred bird, and it is so for a reason which almost necessitated its association with the Spirit moving on the face of the primitive waters. . . . The brooding dove was a symbol of the quickening warmth of nature; it thus perfectly represented the function which, in the Mosaic cosmogony, is ascribed to the Spirit of God — the calling forth of the world of life from the chaos of the first creation. . . . Who then can wonder that in Jewish writings, the Spirit hovering over the primeval waters is expressly compared to a dove, and that, apart from the narrative under examination, the dove is taken as a symbol of the Holy Spirit? How near to this lay the association of the hovering dove with the Messiah, on whom the dove-like spirit was to descend. (245)

In effect, Strauss asks his readers: "Can't you see that those who believed Jesus to be the promised Messiah would inevitably imagine a dove descending upon him? In this case, they embellished an event that may have occurred — Jesus' baptism — with this image of the Messiah from their religious heritage." Thus, beginning with the presentation of the apparently historical reality narrated by the text, Strauss moves through a "revelation" of the implicit absurdity of such a reading to a resolution that recognizes what appears to be historical as a product of human consciousness.

To the question, What of the historical now remained in the Jesus tradition? Strauss gives the following answer: Jesus grew up in Nazareth, permitted himself to be baptized by John, assembled disciples, went about teaching in the land of the Jews, everywhere opposed Pharisaism, and invited people to the Messiah's kingdom, but in the end he was subject to the hate and envy of the Pharisaic party, and died on a cross. This was the "scaffold" that came to be festooned with the most varied and meaningful garlands of pious reflection and mythology.

Strauss had promised that the second section of *The Life of Jesus* would "re-establish dogmatically" what he had destroyed critically. In fact, the section is minuscule, containing a veritable compendium of orthodox doctrine concerning Christ, including vain attempts at its modernization by such as Schleiermacher, and the opposition to orthodox doctrine in thinkers such as Spinoza and Kant. Strauss's conclusion reads:

> As subject of the predicate which the church assigns to Christ, we place, instead of an individual, an idea; but an idea which has an existence in reality, not in the mind only. . . . In an individual, a God-man, the properties and functions which the church ascribes to Christ contradict themselves; in the idea of the race they perfectly agree. Humanity is the union of the two natures — God become man, the infinite manifesting itself in the finite, and the finite spirit remembering its infinitude. (780)

By faith in this Christ, writes Strauss, one is justified before God; that is, by kindling within the idea of humanity, the individual participates in the divinely human life of the species (780).

Reaction to Strauss's *Life* was sudden. He had already been removed from his position as *Repetent* at the Tübinger *Stift*. Now former instructors and colleagues, Steudel included, undertook to prevent the ruinous effects of his writing with pamphleteering. Strauss's former philosophy professor at Tübingen, C. A. Eschenmayer (1768-1852), attacked him in a brochure entitled "The Iscariotism of Our Days," a title that Strauss took as a high compliment, since it conjured up the image of Lessing, vilified as a second Judas for having received (or so it was said) one thousand ducats from Amsterdam

Jews for publishing the Wolfenbüttel fragments. The Heidelberg rationalist Paulus also objected to Strauss's method. He stated that the Ludwigsburger had no license to infer from the presence of myth within a given narrative that the entire narrative was to be classified as myth. Yet he entered the lists on Strauss's behalf. The celebrated theologian of mediation, August Neander (1789-1850), found fault with Strauss's work, but pleaded with government authorities not to kill it with prohibition. And it was Ernst Wilhelm Hengstenberg (1802-69), colleague of Neander at Berlin, neopietist and bitter foe of Hegelians, who called *The Life of Jesus* one of the happiest phenomena of the time, since it forced the decision for or against biblical criticism.

Strauss was totally unprepared for the political consequences of his work. He had supposed that the scientific diction of his manuscript would hinder nonspecialists from reading it. In this supposition he was dead wrong. *The Life of Jesus* would not be discussed merely as an academic treatise, but as a political symbol. Strauss's replacement of Jesus Christ by humanity implied radical democracy. For those on the political right, the idea of the incarnation as realized in a single person mirrored the state as realized in the person of the monarch. But for those on the political left, the incarnation as realized in humanity as such furnished an analogy to the state as realized in the populace, in the *demos*. To the "left," Strauss was a hero.

Still, the opposition troubled him. The period between the first two editions of *The Life of Jesus* (1835-36 and 1837) and the publication of *The Old Faith and the New* in 1872 saw him vacillating between retreat and advance. In the so-called *Streitschriften* or polemical pamphlets of 1837, written in defense of his *Life*, Strauss edged toward compromise with the official theology. The next year, 1838, saw the third edition of *The Life of Jesus*, in which Jesus appeared as genius or hero, as first in a series, providing its impulse. Years later, in his critique of Schleiermacher's *Life of Jesus*, Strauss would refer to a passage in which Jesus was compared with an artist and then remark: "It is the concept of creative genius which Schleiermacher here applies to Jesus, and in consequence of which he conceives of his activity as one which proceeded out of an inner constraint more or less instinctively."[19] Years before, while a student at Berlin, Strauss had heard Schleiermacher apply that concept to Jesus.

For those on the political left, this genius-hero was an aristocrat. Strauss had betrayed them and robbed them of a symbol by which to attack a political authority based on Christian orthodoxy. They would soon turn elsewhere. In 1840 Strauss published his dogmatics together with the fourth edition of

19. *The Christ of Faith and the Jesus of History*, tr. Leander E. Keck (Philadelphia: Fortress, 1977), 69.

his *Life,* and in it took again the position of his first edition. In the edition of 1864, Strauss conceded a historical kernel to the Jesus tradition, a kernel consisting of a personality that could not be judged as the source, but nevertheless as the means toward the fulfillment of human destiny. In *The Old Faith and the New,* Strauss returned to his earlier conclusions. In it he eschewed compromise between the old church faith and the negative results of its examination; asserted that reason not merely had the right to mediate the biblical content, but by virtue of its investigation of the Bible's origin, credibility, and value, displaced the Bible as the highest religious source of knowledge; referred to the modern view of the world as opposed to the worldview of Jesus; damned the orthodox dogma of vicarious substitution as barbaric; and concluded that the Jesus of history, of science, could not be the object of faith or a model for life. On the contrary, only the believer willing to put up with all the impossibilities and contradictions could still cling to the Christ of faith.

Karl Barth notes that Strauss's "retreats" in the third edition of the *Life* (1838-39) and in its popularized form of 1864 fell within the period of his negotiations with Zurich, and that his "advances" in the first edition of the *Life* and in *The Old Faith and the New* followed the rejection of his concessions, allowing the inference that Strauss was ruled less by reason than he advertised.[20] The inference is superficial. Initially, Strauss may have been totally unprepared for the political consequences of his *Life,* but he could scarcely have remained so. In fact, his hedging only mirrored the events of his time. In 1848 riots occurred in Berlin and Vienna. Strauss, patriot and increasingly conservative in his political opinions, was horrified to the point where he yearned for "the old police state." In the same year, 1848, the first National Assembly was established at Frankfurt. Strauss later admitted that he would as soon be Russian than ruled democratically.[21] His declining years were perforated with wars, with Denmark (1864), with Austria in the *Brüderkrieg* of 1866, and with France (1870).

There may have been a deeper reason for the vacillation: Strauss continued to struggle with the notion that when all was said and done religion and philosophy shared the same content. But once the struggle was over, it would be clear that Strauss had pulled down an entire school with him.

Friedrich Nietzsche (1844-1900) scorned *The Old Faith and the New:*

---

20. Karl Barth, *David Friedrich Strauss als Theologe,* Theologische Studien 6 (Zollikon-Zürich: Evangelischer, 1948), 29. Curiously enough, Barth begins his review of *The Life of Jesus* with the chastened "liberal" edition of 1864 rather than with the first edition of 1835 — no doubt his way of drawing the critic's teeth.

21. *Ibid.,* 12.

Once upon a time there lived a Strauss, a brave, severe, and stoutly equipped scholar, with whom we sympathized as wholly as with all those in Germany who seek to serve truth with earnestness and energy. . . . He, however, who is now publicly famous as David Strauss, is another person. The theologians may be to blame for this metamorphosis; but, at any rate, his present toying with the mask of genius inspires us with as much hatred and scorn as his former earnestness commanded respect and sympathy.[22]

The scorn was misplaced. It should have been reserved for the third edition of *The Life of Jesus,* not for the piece in which Strauss had returned to square one.

IV. Assessment

A. Strauss, Hegel, and Baur

Friedrich Nietzsche writes that Strauss showed signs of having "stammered Hegel's prose in youth."[23] Strauss's attempt to penetrate what was historically conditioned in the Jesus tradition to the concept beneath actually took its stimulus from the distinction between image or representation *(Vorstellung)* and concept *(Begriff)* in Hegel's *Phenomenology.* Strauss admits: "As early as in my university years, the most important point of [Hegel's] system appeared to me and my friends to be the distinction between *Vorstellung* and *Begriff* in religion."[24] Strauss further states that the most important question for him and his comrades was whether or not the historical character of the Bible belonged to content or was to be relegated to form. This question reveals the point of divergence from Hegel. While for Hegel the historical character of the Bible belonged essentially to the content of truth, for Strauss the Bible was separated from truth in a most radical fashion. Strauss identified image or *Vorstellung* with "mere" form, or the mythical, whereas the concept or *Begriff* comprised a content identical to the contemporary worldview. Next, according to Strauss, the relation between image and concept was undialectical. The form, or myth, was indifferent to the idea:

The pure distillate of religious ideas extracted from [the New Testament] is none other than the philosophy of our days still recognizes as true. . . . As to

22. *Thoughts out of Season,* tr. Anthony M. Ludovici (New York: Russell & Russell, 1964), 1:82-83.
23. *Ibid.,* 95.
24. *Streitschriften zur Vertheidigung meiner Schrift über das Leben Jesu und zur Charakteristik der gegenwärtigen Theologie* (Tübingen: C. F. Osiander, 1838), 1/3:57.

the form in which the New Testament author and in which the present-day theologian possess that content, there is the completest difference, since the entire worldview of our time is unlike that of the Jews in Jesus' and the apostles' times. . . . In this respect the exegete may not fear to extract from the biblical books ideas *(Vorstellungen)* which in this form present training cannot appropriate.[25]

For Hegel, the *Vorstellung* represented a deficient mode. It was a mixture of the sensuous with thought. It was necessary to stride past the *Vorstellung* toward the *Begriff*. But for all that, the way toward the *Begriff* lay through the *Vorstellung*, for which reason the *Vorstellung* was natural, true, and necessary. In other words, the "positive," as Hegel called it, did not, as with Strauss, simply veil or obscure the content: it unveiled it. The entire purpose of Hegel's distinction between *Vorstellung* and *Begriff* was to give philosophical justification to the content of Christian faith. It was a distinction that promised peace between Christianity and modern thought. Strauss rejected the very thing at which Hegel aimed. He did so by joining together what Hegel had put asunder: philosophy and historical criticism, a criticism for which Hegel nursed profound suspicion: "With us the so-called 'higher criticism' has taken possession not only of all philology but also of historical literature. This higher criticism has then served to justify the introduction of all kinds of unhistorical monstrosities of pure imagination."[26] Mere historical interest in religion, Hegel asserts, is such "in which the spirit has to do with the things of the past, with something one has set aside."[27]

But despite his demurrer at linking philosophy and historical criticism, Hegel himself may have prepared for it, at least negatively. He had asserted that the content of the idea and its representation were the same, but that the form of the idea and its representation were not the same. Where, then, did Hegel place the gospel stories: on the side of content, in which case their historicity would be given together with the truth of the idea? Or did he place them on the side of form, in which case those stories would be incidental to the truth of the idea? Strauss wrote that on this very point where he needed light Hegel and his pupils had left him in the dark.[28]

Did Hegel's philosophy of Absolute Spirit depend on the incarnation as

25. *Charakteristiken und Kritiken: Eine Sammlung zerstreuter Aufsätze aus den Gebieten der Theologie, Anthropologie und Aesthetik* (Leipzig: Otto Wigand, 1839), 296-97.

26. G. F. W. Hegel, *Reason in History,* tr. Robert S. Hartman (New York: Liberal Arts, 1953), 9.

27. Quoted in Sandberger, *David Strauss,* 155.

28. D. F. Strauss, *Streitschriften,* 1/3:57.

an actual fact? The Hegelians split over the question into right, left, and middle. For those on the right, the truth or historicity of *all* the gospel stories about Jesus could be deduced from the idea of the incarnation. For those in the middle, the truth of *some* of those stories could be deduced from that idea. For those on the right or in the middle, then, the gospel stories belonged on the side of content, essential to the truth of the idea of the God-man, since that idea could inhabit a single individual. For the Hegelians on the left, the truth of *none* of the gospel narratives could be deduced from the idea of the incarnation. Rather, those narratives belonged on the side of form, incidental to the truth of the idea, since the idea of the God-Man could never make its home in a solitary individual. Strauss took his place on the left:

> In making the assertion that the truth of the Gospel narrative cannot be proved . . . from philosophical considerations. . . . I should like to associate myself with the "left wing" of the Hegelian school, were it not that the Hegelians prefer to exclude me altogether from their borders, and to throw me into the arms of other systems of thought — only, it must be admitted, to have me tossed back to them like a ball.[29]

The statement is self-pitying. Strauss was not alone on the left. Extraordinarily comprehensive correspondence with a multitude of contemporaries is proof of it. But it is also true that no one stood next to him or behind him in public debate, not even his old mentor, Ferdinand Christian Baur.

In *The Life of Jesus,* Strauss quotes the Göttingen scholar Christian Gottlob Heyne (1729-1812) to the effect that "history and philosophy proceed from the myths of all the ancients" (52). The statement reveals commitment to a view of the development of human language and culture that would dominate the nineteenth and extend far into the twentieth century, which would beget a school whose influence reached around the globe and had its devotees not only among academics in lecture halls but among pith-helmeted missionaries in steaming rain forests, that is, the view that the mythical represents a stage at which humans had not yet succeeded to mature thought. Baur shared that view, and Strauss came to share it.

Alongside that view lay the conviction that the mythical — faith as not-yet-knowing — had to be raised to knowledge, to the *Begriff,* and in this way brought to its truth, the very action Strauss promised to undertake in the "dogmatic" or positive section of his *Life* (see 757). And the concept to which a particular myth would be lofted would be identical to the concept to which

---

29. Quoted in Albert Schweitzer, *The Quest of the Historical Jesus,* tr. W. Montgomery (New York: Macmillan, 1958), 115.

any one of a thousand other myths could be raised. A similarity in principle thus attaches to all occurrence — this was the axiom, and by it the distinction between the holy and profane was surrendered.

But if Hegel or the Hegel of the "right" could not satisfy, it was certain that Schleiermacher, with his attempt at a higher synthesis of supernaturalism and rationalism, could not. Baur, whom we will turn to next, had already seen to that. Whether or not Strauss read Baur's volume on gnosticism, published the same year as the first edition of *The Life of Jesus*, Strauss was in full agreement with its analysis of Schleiermacher's program. Of Schleiermacher's attempt to link Jesus of Nazareth to Christianity as the absolute religion, Baur writes:

> When Schleiermacher more closely defines Christianity as the absolute religion, stating that its essential difference from other monotheistic faiths is that everything in it is related to the redemption won by Jesus of Nazareth, then the question which directly follows is, By what right is the person of Jesus of Nazareth identified with the Redeemer, so that the same concepts by which the Redeemer must be viewed are also to be construed as attributes of Jesus of Nazareth? Once it is conceded that at this juncture dogmatics must take its support solely from the assumptions of apologetics, it is immediately clear that proof of Jesus of Nazareth as the Redeemer in the sense indicated can never be empirically adduced.[30]

The question is only whether or not Baur and his "mythical view" had stimulated Strauss's appetite for that Hegelian distinction between *Vorstellung* and *Begriff*, or vice versa. It is a fact that Strauss encountered Baur first and that he met Hegel's work later. It may be that for Strauss the lust for emancipation from the Christian theological tradition was first and strongest.

B. Focus on the Historical

Emanuel Hirsch (1888-1972) asserts that with Strauss occurred an event that could not have occurred in an earlier century: the location of the struggle over Christian teaching on the soil of historical research.[31] Strauss, of course, regarded that teaching as absolutely devoid of historical consciousness and

---

30. *Die christliche Gnosis* (Darmstadt: Wissenschaftliche Buchgesellschaft, 1967), 637-38.

31. *Geschichte der neueren evangelischen Theologie* (Gütersloh: C. Bertelsmann, 1954), 5:511-18.

conceived his task as assisting it toward an objectivity exclusive of the researcher's person or opinion. Had he been more cognizant of the place of pre-suppositions or pre-judgments in the sphere of science, he might not have concluded that science and faith had to part company. He might then have been able to link his historical research to theology. That he did not or could not was a fault, but the attention he gave to a question that later preoccupation with literary, rhetorical research and its auxiliaries have lain on the table — the question, "Did it really happen?" — this was a strength, since the question will never be downed.

Next, Strauss made clear that, whether possible or impossible, the mediation of critical, historical research and Christian faith had to begin with recourse to Jesus of Nazareth. No doubt there was little left of Jesus once Strauss had done with his *Life*. The negative work of dismantling the Jesus story left little to reconstruction. But Strauss's suspicion that to urge toward the center what is peripheral to the New Testament is merely a counsel of despair — or worse, an act of hypocrisy — was also a strength, since the person of Jesus lies at the heart and core of Christian teaching and history.

Finally, Strauss set the agenda for dogmatic discussion. He put the question concerning the finite as capable of the infinite in a new and provocative way. The regnant theology had conceived God as belonging to the world beyond, penetrating this world through occasional sorties upon the continuum of space and time. Only through miracles could the Almighty engage the world. Strauss disallowed the miraculous but insisted that a relation between God and humans is possible. How? That is the question that is still before us. Theology may not be closer to the answer, but it continues, for good or for ill, to pursue the matter under the terms Strauss laid down.

In sum, what Strauss wrote, stated, argued, asseverated, averred, or contended demanded response at the level of the historical and temporal. And however bankrupt may be the methods of biblical-historical research now become traditional, it was Strauss, and Strauss above all, who rendered them unavoidable.

C. Reason Is Divine

At the conclusion of *The Life of Jesus*, Strauss writes that one must use the *Vorstellung* with ordinary people, though, naturally, in such a fashion that the *Begriff* shines through (782). The remark contains more than a touch of the type of elitism that we first met in Spinoza. Humanity appears to be comprised of two classes: believers and philosophers. Believers require an actual, individual, historical God-man in order to ascend to the idea, whereas for the thinker that individual is merely one of a thousand representations of the idea to which he has already made ascent. But if elitism it is, it sprang from the one great tenet to which Strauss held throughout his career, despite whatever compromises he made or was ready to make for safety's sake. This tenet was his belief in reason as the link between the finite and the infinite, and thus belonging to both — his trust in rationality as the bar before which everything had to appear and be judged. At the least, Strauss would not have understood, and at best he would have dismissed the suggestion that the trust he reposed in reason was a faith. Whether or not there ever was or could be a science without presuppositions is a question he did not raise.

Reason, or, in his own words, "the philosophy of our days," moved Strauss to read a text, declare it unthinkable, eliminate the supernaturalist and rationalist explanation of it, then introduce the concept of myth to explain its origin. This "mythical view" was fired by yet another presupposition: that the myth conceived the narrative and did not merely explicate it. Because of this, Hegel's distinction between *Vorstellung* and *Begriff* was altered to the difference between form and content, content to which form was indifferent. The day was still ahead when the form-content category would be dismissed in the assertion that the "kerygma" was not expressed by the myth, but was encountered in it.

Strauss, to be sure, proceeded on the basis of assumptions neither he nor his age thought to question but which they made the criteria of their criticism. But what of his criticism, his historical study? The answer is that Strauss's interest in history was negative, that historical criticism was only a means toward emancipation. Rather than subjecting his texts to an analysis of their species, he inevitably plunged into the question of their historical accuracy to which, with the exception of a pitiful residue that could never in all the world account for the emergence of Christianity, he answered in the negative.

As for the theological orientation or "tendency" of a text — a term for which his old teacher, Baur, would earn everlasting fame — Strauss paid it mere lip service. For example, in illustrating the various incongruities and contradictions in the Bible, Strauss referred to Jesus' initial restriction of his mission to Israel, then to his applause for the Samaritan in the parable or among the ten lepers, to his disparagement of the Jew, to his prophecy in the Jerusalem temple of the rejection of the obdurate Jews, and to the calling of the gentiles. Not finding the contradiction "incredible," Strauss reached for the psychological explanation: "Between that prohibition and this prophecy . . . his circle of vision could have been widened as a result of his experiences." Strauss appears not to have noticed or cared that of the three events just cited, only the last is recorded in all three Synoptic Gospels, whereas the first appears only in Matthew (10:5-15), and the second only in Luke (10:29-37). Again, in adverting to contradictions Strauss notes that prior to Jesus' restriction of his mission to Israel he had promised help to the gentile centurion, though holding later to Jewish exclusivity "with the most extreme harshness," as witness his response to the Canaanite woman's plea. But again, the narrative of the centurion appears only in Luke (7:1-10), and the narrative of the Canaanite woman in Matthew (15:21-28) and Mark (7:24-30).[32]

To fault Strauss for neglecting to place his gospel sources in parallel would not be criticism "from a high horse," as the Germans put it. The Saxon pastor Christian Gottlob Wilke (1788-1854), later to recede into oblivion to the advantage of the philologist Karl Lachmann (1793-1851), had done that very thing thirty-four years prior to the date of *The Old Faith and the New,* from which the statements above are taken. Only in an incomplete way did Strauss allow the entirety of the Gospels to be viewed from out of their parts.

Ignorance of detail in interpretation creates dilettantes, but unless the details are seen in relation to an intelligible whole, the result is isolation. Let the fate of Strauss himself serve in illustration. He could not conceive the political implications of his work, could not set his work in relation to the life and experience of the community for which the object of his investigation functioned as norm. The advice he gives to Christian pastors who have taken his route is little short of cynical:

> It is an evidence of an uncultivated mind, to denounce as a hypocrite a theologian who preaches, for example, on the resurrection of Christ, since, though he may not believe in the reality of that event as a single sensible fact, he may, nevertheless, hold to be true the representation of the process of spiritual life, which the resurrection of Christ affords. (782)

In *The Old Faith and the New,* the piece written two years before his death, Strauss wrote: "My conviction, therefore, is, if we would not evade difficulties or put forced constructions upon them, if we would have our yea yea, and our nay nay — in short, if we would speak as honest, upright men, we must acknowledge we are no longer Christians."[33] Strauss, who at first sought to synthesize philosophy and theology, to link speculation and historical criticism, now wished only to prove the bankruptcy of theology. The impetus for change was supplied by a man who seems small when measured by the Leibnitzes or Kants, but who would function as theology's *bete noir* from the

---

32. *The Old Faith and the New,* 61-62.
33. *Ibid.,* 107.

day his *The Essence of Christianity* appeared till now — Ludwig Feuerbach. As early as in 1840, Feuerbach appeared to have furnished Strauss stimulus for his thought.[34] A quarter of a century later he would write that Feuerbach had broken "the double yoke" into which Hegel had forced religion and philosophy, and had proved that religion and philosophy did not at all share the same content only under different forms.[35] In what may have been the very last thing to come from his pen, Strauss wrote: "Since the concluding section on *The Life of Jesus,* chiefly through the influence of Feuerbach's earlier writings, my dogmatic standpoint . . . underwent that modification which I described in my *Halben und Ganzen;* I had given up the Hegelian identity of content between religion and philosophy."[36] There may have been something noble in that resignation of Strauss, in that final admission that what constituted the Christian community Christian would not yield to domestication, but required abandoning.

Legend has it that when George Eliot began her translation of *The Life of Jesus,* she kept her rosary nearby. When the work was completed, the rosary had disappeared. *Is historical criticism necessarily destructive of faith?* If Strauss was not the one to provide the answer, he was certainly the one to put the question, and by doing so, not merely rehearsed a tradition or mirrored his time, but altered both.

34. See Strauss, *Die christliche Glaubenslehre,* 4 n. 9; see also Sandberger, *David Strauss,* 138.

35. Strauss, *Gesammelte Schriften* (Bonn: Emil Strauss, 1876-77), 5:181-82.

36. *Ibid.,* 1:14.

6

FERDINAND CHRISTIAN BAUR

Historical Criticism in the Shadow of Idealism

I. Biography

Ferdinand Christian Baur was born 21 June 1792 in Schmiden, Württemberg, the son of Jakob Christian Baur (1755-1817), pastor and one-time dean of the evangelical theological seminary at the former Benedictine cloister in Blaubeuren. After attending the school at Blaubeuren and another in Maulbronn, Baur began his theological study at Tübingen. Upon completion of his academic work, Baur served as vicar at Rosswag and Mühlhausen, towns lying north- and southwest of Stuttgart. Following a year as teaching assistant at Schöntal, northeast of Stuttgart, as well as at Tübingen, Baur joined the faculty at Blaubeuren in 1817, lecturing on Greek and Latin prose writers, ancient history, and mythology. Upon the death of Ernst Gottlieb Bengel, Kantian, Socinian supernaturalist, and pillar of the "old Tübingen School," the Protestant theological faculty underwent drastic reform, and despite resistance from former teachers, Baur was called to the chair of historical disciplines in 1826, a post he held till his death in 1860.

Baur's literary activity fell into three periods. In the first he concentrated on the symbolism and mythology of the ancient world and its relation to Christianity. His first published work dealt with the "natural religion" of antiquity, and appeared in 1824. In 1827-28 followed a study of rationalism and supernaturalism, and in 1831 a volume on Manichaeanism.[1] In the second period Baur devoted himself to the history of dogma, releasing volumes on the chief tenets of Protestantism and Roman Catholicism (1st ed., 1834), on gnosticism (1835), on the atonement (1838), on the Trinity (1841-43), and on the history of dogma (1st ed., 1847), and prepared lectures on the history of dogma that were published after his death (1865-67).[2] In the third period, Baur, now sixty years old, proceeded to his life's task, the description of the origin and beginnings of Christianity. Preparatory work had been done earlier, on the Christ party at Corinth (1831), on the Pastoral Epistles (1835), on Paul (1st ed., 1845), and on the canonical Gospels (on John in 1844; on Luke in 1846, and on all in 1847).[3] A study of Christian historiography (1852) preceded Baur's *magnum opus,* a five-volume study of Christianity, *Geschichte der christlichen Kirche (Church History).* The first two volumes appeared in 1853 and 1859, published by Baur himself. The third appeared in 1861 and had been prepared by Baur before his death. The last two volumes were published posthumously in 1862 and 1863.[4]

In his *Church History,* Baur describes his task as conceiving the materials in their history "as they are objectively" (x).[5] He defines historical occur-

1. *Symbolik und Mythologie: oder, die Naturreligion des Altertums* (Stuttgart: Metzler, 1824); *Primae Rationalismi et Supranaturalismi historiae capita portiora* (Tübingen: Hopferi de l'Orme, 1827-28); *Das manichäische Religionssystem* (Tübingen: Osiander, 1831).

2. *Der Gegensatz des Katholizismus und Protestantismus, nach den Prinzipien und Hauptdogmen der beiden Lehrbegriffe* (Tübingen: L. F. Fues, 1834); *Die christliche Gnosis oder die christliche Religionsphilosophie in ihrer geschichtlichen Entwicklung* (Tübingen: Osiander, 1835); *Die christliche Lehre von der Versöhnung* (Tübingen: Osiander, 1838); *Die christliche Lehre von der Dreieinigkeit und Menschwerdung Gottes in ihrer geschichtlichen Entwicklung* (Tübingen: Osiander, 1841-43); *Lehrbuch der Dogmengeschichte* (Stuttgart: Becher, 1847); *Vorlesungen über die christliche Dogmengeschichte,* 3 vols. (Leipzig: L. F. Fues, 1865-67)

3. "Die Christuspartei in der korinthischen Gemeinde," *Tübinger Zeitscrift für Theologie* (1831): 61-206; *Die sogenannten Pastoralbriefe des Apostels Paulus aufs neue kritisch untersucht* (Stuttgart und Tübingen: J. G. Cotta, 1835); *Paulus, der Apostel Jesu Christi, sein Leben und Wirken* (Stuttgart: Becher und Müller, 1845); *Kritische Untersuchungen über die kanonischen Evangelien, ihr Verhältnis zueinander, ihrer Charakter und Ursprung* (Tübingen: L. F. Fues, 1847).

4. *Die Epochen der kirchlichen Geschichtsschreibung* (Tübingen: L. F. Fues, 1852; in English: *Ferdinand Christian Baur on the Writing of Church History,* tr. Peter C. Hodgson (London: Oxford University Press, 1968), 41-257; *Geschichte der christlichen Kirche,* 1st ed.; 5 vols. (Tübingen: L. F. Fues, 1853-63). The first two volumes were translated: *The Church History of the First Three Centuries,* 2 vols.; 3rd ed. tr. Allan Menzies (London: Williams and Norgate, 1878-79).

5. Citations in the body of the text are taken from the first volume of the Menzies translation, which corresponds to the third volume of Ferdinand Christian Baur, *Ausgewählte*

rence as the conjunction of the universal and the particular, by which the universal underlies the particular, makes itself known through it, and dominates it.[6] Specifically, this task involves inquiry into the essence of Christianity together with that of the period in which it emerged (6). Criticism is the means by which this task is to be achieved: criticism with its stimulus in the gospel message, in service to theological truth, and the building up of the Christian community.[7] The requirements for this criticism are threefold: first, to be bound by no dogmatic assumption that might disturb the impartiality of judgment; second, to validate nothing as historical truth that could not be demonstrated from the extant sources, and finally, never to lose sight of the universal.[8]

In an essay on New Testament theology, Baur assessed the work that preceded his own. Citing the penchant among predecessors for attacking the ecclesiastical system, he singled out Johann Philipp Gabler as the first to bring the historical task of biblical theology to consciousness, and to distinguish it from dogmatic or systematic theology. Rationalism, on the other hand, was unable to move from subjective reasoning to the "objectivity of history" and did not yet grasp the source of Christian history with a purely historical sense.[9] The same was true of interpretations that concentrated on the self-consciousness of the gospel writers and ignored the primacy of historical mediation. The result could only be the reduction of gospel history to a figment of the imagination. Such was the case with Bruno Bauer (1809-82), who abstracted the Gospels from all historical tradition, supposing that individual self-consciousness alone made history. In support of this notion Bruno Bauer had leaned on the hypothesis that Mark was the earliest written Gospel advanced by Christian Gottlob Wilke and Christian Hermann Weisse (1801-66), Mark's self-consciousness accordingly regarded as the ultimate source of gospel history. Till the end of his life, Ferdinand Christian Baur would oppose the hypothesis of Markan priority.[10]

Baur's research directly challenged the verbal inspiration of Scripture. Outspoken in attack, Baur asserts that there is no greater presupposition than that of the Bible's yielding an absolute doctrine of revelation. Such an assump-

Werke in Einzelausgaben, ed. Klaus Scholder, 5 vols. (Stuttgart–Bad Canstatt: Friedrich Frommann, 1963-75). The Scholder edition will be cited hereafter as *AW.*

6. *Die Tübinger Schule und ihre Stellung zur Gegenwart, AW,* 5:7.

7. See Ernst Käsemann's introduction, *AW,* 1:xv and xviii.

8. See *Die Tübinger Schule, AW,* 5:57-58.

9. Ferdinand Christian Baur, *Vorlesungen über neutestamentliche Theologie* (Gotha: Friedrich Andreas Perthes, 1892), 32-33, 35.

10. *Kirchengeschichte des neunzehnten Jahrhunderts, AW,* 4:386-88.

tion, in his view, spells the death of all historical observation.[11] Since the authority of Scripture as construed by the older Protestant theologians had now been pierced at so many points, he felt confident that such a doctrine could no longer be recognized as universally accepted teaching. To the anxiety resulting from the waning of the doctrine of verbal inspiration, Baur replies with the forthrightness of one who stands firmly in the liberal Protestant camp: "What kind of faith must it be that is eternally fearful and anxious that the foundation on which it rests . . . might be taken and forever removed from it, a faith that encounters . . . all critical doubts and investigations . . . with the constant alarm and apprehension that they might finally make a sorry end of it?"[12]

Baur himself drew his share of fire. Charged by his attackers with an "arbitrarily impudent, dizzying, intoxicated" critical skepticism,[13] he was often tarred with the same brush as had blackened Strauss. By implication Baur conceded responsibility for Strauss's "critical spirit," but objected to being portrayed as his twin. To begin with, Baur had commenced his investigation of earliest Christianity before Strauss' *The Life of Jesus* had seen the light of day. True, Baur had witnessed the emergence of Strauss's *Life,* and in close proximity. He had even discussed it with the author, but insisted that he could no more have appeared for as against it, since such required "deeper studies" not yet begun. Those deeper studies involved an investigation of the Johannine material in its relation to the first three Gospels. According to Baur, Strauss's tactic of striking at both the synoptists and John revealed a basic flaw in his method. The history of primitive Christianity required penetration from another point of view than the mythological, that is, from the viewpoint of "authorial tendency" or "party adherence," a proclivity lodged in the peculiar historical circumstances of the period in which the biblical authors wrote, and given expression in their modification of the gospel tradition. Baur believed that his standpoint was the only one on the basis of which Strauss' could be corrected or carried on, that it was more "methodological" than that of Strauss because it returned to the question with which Strauss should first have come to terms, that is, the question of the philosophical or religious perspective of a given biblical book — in Baur's terms, its "tendency," from which then derived that epithet applied to the later Tübingen school of which Baur was originator, that is, *Tendenzkritik,* or "tendency criticism."[14] "I believe I can be certain," says Baur, "that no view will succeed . . . in

11. Baur, *Vorlesungen über Neutestamentliche Theologie,* 61.
12. *Abgenötigte Erklärung gegen einen Artikel der Ev. Kirchen Zeitung, AW,* 1:296-97.
13. *Ibid.,* 287.
14. *Kirchengeschichte des neunzehnten Jahrhundert, AW,* 4:359, 395, 397-99; *Vorlesungen über Neutestamentliche Theologie,* 272-73.

gaining more universal recognition till mine . . . will be refuted."[15] His self-defense is passionate: "Where is . . . my criticism . . . supported on the mythical view? And where do I reject a purely historical fact . . . solely for the reason that it is a miracle, or, where do I argue solely and alone from the inner contradiction of content? . . . Does my research put the entire objective foundation of Christianity in doubt?"[16] Baur would be plagued all his life by his association with the notorious Strauss, his theology constantly placed under scrutiny.

II. *The Church History*

A. *The Question of Essence and Sources*

Baur gave classic expression to the results of his New Testament research in the first volume of *The Church History.* It is, perhaps, his most representative work and therefore the one upon which we concentrate the bulk of our attention.

The work opens with a provisional answer to the question regarding the essence of Christianity. Christianity spells universality because it was rooted in the universality of the Roman world. It was less in thrall to the external than any other religion; and was more deeply grounded in the innermost substance of human nature and the principles of moral consciousness. It did not emerge in a time of ruin or dissolution, nor was it unaffected by the series of causes and effects that preceded it. Stoicism, Epicureanism, Skepticism, and Eclecticism paved the way, as did Judaism with its purified concept of God (4, 9-11, 13-16, 17-22). At this point, Baur proceeds to the sources of the gospel history.

Baur asserts that the less we are permitted to regard the authors of the four Gospels as mere reporters, the more their writings gain in significance as sources. From these sources Baur excludes the Johannine writings, which are not at all on historical soil. In fact, the Gospel of John does not intend to furnish an historical account, but proceeds from a conception of the relation between the "divine idea" and history. The Synoptic Gospels, accordingly, furnish the basis for research, though they too require distinguishing. By virtue of dependence upon Matthew and Luke, Mark cannot be construed as an independent source, its authenticity and priority only "superficially grounded."

15. *Kirchengeschichte des neunzehnten Jahrhundert, AW,* 4:399.
16. *Abgenötigte Erklärung, AW,* 1:294, 295-96.

Luke, a late, "Paulinizing" work, has Matthew at its base. Matthew alone remains as the "relatively" most genuine and trustworthy source of the gospel story, though in its present form it is not original but rests on a foundational writing to which the "Judaizing portions" belong. Not even these portions, however, can be identified with Jesus' original teaching. Still, Baur regards the parables and the Sermon on the Mount as the most genuine and original portions of Jesus' teaching (25-27, 36).[17]

B. Jesus

Baur insists that the sources reveal the exclusively moral character of Jesus' self-consciousness. Jesus' stress on the inward as opposed to the outward, his disregard of the act in favor of intention as conferring moral value on the act, explains the apparent contradiction between his marginalizing of the Jewish law and his assertion that not one of its tiniest commandments would be cancelled. As to the point of contact between Jesus' self-consciousness and the world he encountered, it was furnished by the Jewish concept of the Messiah. Baur contends that nothing of higher significance on the soil of Jewish history could fail to be linked to the messianic idea. Jesus' appearance in Jerusalem, even apart from the entry scene, gives unequivocal proof of his messianic consciousness. Of the resurrection, Baur writes that historical research needs to hold merely to the fact that for the disciples Jesus' resurrection became the firmest and most irreversible certainty. Thus, not its factualness but rather faith in Jesus' resurrection serves as the object of research. The process by which this faith emerged lies beyond the reach of "psychological analysis" (30-32, 39-43), let alone historical verification.

Baur turns next to describe the conflict within earliest Christianity between different parties of believers. He declares that this conflict had its beginning in Jesus himself. In the "return to the interiority of intention" Jesus enunciated a principle that both affirms and opposes Mosaism; affirms it insofar as it requires the law's fulfillment, but opposes it insofar as it defines fulfillment far beyond the doing of the deed. In the acknowledgment of Jesus as Messiah and thus in the enunciation of this principle lay the seeds for the subsequent crisis in Christendom. To the question, Why Jesus did not pursue a single course as did Paul? Baur replies, "How would this have been possible without excluding those who had to be won?"[18]

17. See Baur, *Vorlesungen über Neutestamentliche Theologie*, 48-50.
18. See *Die Tübinger Schule*, AW, 5:28-29, 33, 35, 36.

C. The Antithesis

Stating that Jesus' disciples gathered in Jerusalem immediately after his death, Baur describes the Jerusalem company as comprised of two groups, Hebrews and Hellenists, the latter sympathizers of Stephen. These Hellenists formed the germ of the opposition later to be associated with Paul. Baur then goes on to describe Paul's conversion as a being "plunged, almost against his will, in a highly wrought and intense frame of spirit, into contemplation of [Jesus'] death" (44-48). For Baur, Jesus is above all the Crucified One who is known through the stark reality of the cross. Baur writes: "A death which ran so directly counter to all the facts and presuppositions of the Jewish national consciousness . . . must have a scope far transcending the particularism of Judaism. There can be no doubt that this was the thought in which the apostle first discerned the truth of Christianity" (48). This experience required interpreting; it needed a "theory" by which Paul could establish his equality with the other apostles as well as his entitlement to the same rights. The theory consisted of an identification of that "inward urge" or "inner sight of Christ" with the others' outward sight.[19]

Baur divides the conflict within earliest Christianity into three epochs. In the first epoch, beginning with the death of Jesus, chief representatives of the Jerusalem community extended the right hand of fellowship to Paul and his company. A twofold mission resulted, one Jewish, the other gentile, each independent of the other, though bound by care for the poor. Hostility between the groups broke out with Peter's equivocation at Antioch. There, Paul enunciated the principle that faith in Christ freed his followers from the law; that gentiles were thus not obliged to live as Jews (Acts 15; Galatians 2). This first epoch ended with Peter and Paul unreconciled, fated to remain thus till both had died. Attacks on Paul and his authority formed the second epoch in the strife, which extended from the destruction of Jerusalem up to the first decades of the second century. In these decades (the third epoch), the fronts were distinctly and decisively drawn between Jewish particularism and Pauline universalism. John the apostle and apocalypticist,[20] one of the pillar apostles in Jerusalem, had moved to Ephesus, the spot where Paul himself had sojourned, in order to defend the principles of Jewish Christianity against the inroads of Pauline Christianity (53-86).

19. See *ibid.*, 402.

20. Though challenged as early as in the third century, the Zebedean authorship of Revelation still enjoys popularity. See, e.g., the twelfth edition by Werner Georg Kümmel of Feine-Behm's *Einleitung in das Neue Testament* (Heidelberg: Quelle & Meyer, 1963), 341.

Turning to the reflection of the three epochs in the New Testament literature, Baur matches the "tendency" of each book to one or the other side of
the conflict. He regards the Jewish Christian side of the first epoch as reflected
in Revelation, and sets the date of its composition at A.D. 70, prior to Jerusalem's destruction, thus marking the *terminus ad quem* of the first period. Revelation, writes Baur, held to the "traditional opinion" that the Jews alone were
the elect; gentiles existed merely to be annihilated by God's wrath. Commenting on Revelation 2:2, in which John boasts of the Ephesians standing
fast against the spurious apostles, Baur asks, "To whom can the author be referring but to the apostle of the Gentiles and his apostolical assistants?" When
in Revelation 2:14 and 20 John attacks those who seduce the servants of
Christ to eat meat offered to idols, Baur describes his target as "that lax Pauline Christianity which was on such good terms with heathenism." In Baur's
opinion, the gulf fixed by the apostle between Jew and gentile is so wide that
virtually no trace of religious disposition or receptivity was conceded the
gentiles, to the point that with each plague upon them they became more
hostile and blasphemous (87).[21]

To the Pauline side of the first epoch Baur assigns the epistles to the
Galatians, Corinthians, and Romans. These four formed the antithesis to the
doctrinal concepts of the apocalypticist. The Corinthian correspondence,
above all, furnished the Archimedean lever by which to move the world of
early Christian history. The parties at Corinth (1 Corinthians 11–12) are
proof that at its very beginning Christianity was not a unity. The difficulty, of
course, was that no proper conclusion could be arrived at regarding the
"Christ" party. The choice of Christ as party leader is historically unthinkable,
writes Baur, but the riddle can be solved by interpreting the Christ party as an
extreme wing of the Petrine party. The Christ party, then, boasted immediate
connection with the earthly Messiah, and on it raised claims that set Paul in
the shade. To the other extreme stood the radical enthusiasts and adherents of
Apollos, who in opposition to Jewish Christianity linked Greek notions to the
Christian message, and thus out-Pauled Paul. The result was two chief, hostile
groups arrayed against each other at Corinth. Baur believed that Galatians
corroborated his thesis.

Baur attempts to interpret Romans from this perspective. He begins by
stating that Christian truth was not given to the apostles in its entirety, but
had to be deduced in the given instance. Romans was thus not the first Christian dogmatics, but a genuine letter addressed to an attack on the universal,

---

21. See Baur, *Vorlesungen über Neutestamentliche Theologie*, 67; *Die Tübinger Schule*,
AW, 5:40, 71.

law-free gospel of Paul on the part of Jewish-Christian particularism. Accordingly, Romans 9–11 was the midpoint of the epistle, and the key to its interpretation (66-74).

Baur assigns the Letter to the Hebrews to the Jewish side of the second epoch of the conflict, writing that whereas for Paul the law represented only a phase between promise and fulfillment, for the author of Hebrews the law inhered in a pattern of continuity, specifically, a continuity of priesthood. On the other hand, writes Baur, Hebrews does not reflect the sharp anti-Paulinism characteristic of Jewish-Christian literature of the first period. Rather, it leans toward the mediation eventually effected in the post-apostolic period.

To the other, "Pauline" side of the second epoch, Baur refers the briefer Pauline epistles, including 1 Thessalonians, Philemon, and Philippians.

From this point on, Baur's periodizing of the remainder of the New Testament documents is murky. In *The Church History* Baur refers Acts, Ephesians, Colossians, Philippians, the Pastorals, 1 and 2 Peter, and James to the period in which the antithesis had been or was about to be overcome (122, 127, 131-35, 149-51). In his lectures on New Testament theology, however, he refers the Synoptic Gospels, Acts, 1 Peter, and James to the second, and the Pastorals together with the Johannine writings to the third epoch of the conflict, but without setting up contrasts.[22] In *The Church History* Baur describes Luke as the "purest and most important source" of Paulinism after the letters of Paul, in sharp and open opposition to the Judaism of Matthew. Matthew and Luke, then, were clearly at odds, whereas Mark, an extract from both, was prepared with the intent of neutralizing the hostility between them (77-82).

Baur traces the conflict into the post-apostolic period and its literature, identifying the Shepherd of Hermas and the apologist Justin Martyr on the Jewish-Christian side, and Clement of Rome, Polycarp, Barnabas, and Pseudo-Ignatius on the Pauline side (138-44).

D. The Synthesis

Baur cautions against seeking the occasion for the reconciliation of the opposing groups in "abstract ideas, indifferently related to each other." The statement contains a barb hurled at Albrecht Ritschl (1822-89), a onetime protégé, who in his researches on the origin of the ancient church proceeded to deviate from the master respecting the origin of the conflict in earliest Christianity. In angry reply to Ritschl's contention that the two factions warred over the ques-

---

22. Baur, *Vorlesungen über Neutestamentliche Theologie*, 69-70.

tion whether Christianity could be conceived as law, whether the duty of ful-filling the law could be harmonized with the idea of rebirth, and whether hu-man moral behavior could be correlated to the religious sense as given with existence, Baur states that to construe the relations between the contending parties in such dogmatic terms necessarily skews the perspective from which those relations have to be conceived. The occasion rather exists in those con-trasts in which Christianity, set between the ruling powers of the age, had to fight for its life and create the forms necessary to its development (105-6).[23]

Continuing his argument respecting the reconciliation of the opposing groups, Baur writes that within Jewish Christianity, baptism began to enjoy a status analogous to that of circumcision. And once it was clear that this ritu-alistic means of achieving salvation was equal to circumcision, circumcision was surrendered. Baur suggests that baptism was of the Essene-Ebionite vari-ety, by which gentile converts came to be viewed as proselytes at the gate. Pe-ter, however, and not Paul, was made the author of this universalism. In fact, had Peter actually been its author, Jewish Christianity would have appropri-ated the Pauline universalism in its entirety. "This," Baur writes, "is the only possible reading of the fact that in the pseudo-Clementine writings Peter is the apostle of the Gentiles" (109-10). Gentile conversion to Christianity may have been an undeniable fact, but it could not be acknowledged to occur through an apostle without authority from Jerusalem.

If in all this Paul had won the ground, it was Jewish Christianity that erected the structure. Baur believed the influence of Jewish Christianity upon the shaping of the subsequent Christian church could not be estimated highly enough. From Judaism derived those theocratic institutions and aristocratic forms by which the church assumed the aspects of an organization meeting all the criteria of a world-conquering power (112-13). In a monograph on the Tübingen School, Baur states that no greater proof of the capacity of Judaism for development existed than the fact that it could surrender vigorously de-fended positions once it discovered other more successful means toward maintaining its ascendency over Paulinism. This capacity explains how bap-tism could appear so quickly in place of circumcision.[24] When, writes Baur, Jewish Christianity was about to intrude once more, this time in the post-apostolic period, when the church attached itself all the more firmly to an hi-erarchical episcopacy, Paulinism, with its doctrine of justification, was unable to appear with its old rigor.[25]

23. See Baur, *Die Tübinger Schule, AW*, 5:360-74.
24. *Ibid.*, 368.
25. *Ibid.*, 335-36.

As to the reflection of the synthesis in the literature, Baur refers chiefly to the Johannine writings and the Pastoral Epistles. But, as noted above, in *The Church History* he includes Acts, Ephesians, Colossians, and 2 Peter as marking the synthesis.

In Acts, Baur writes, everything about which Jewish and gentile Christians could unite was footed on the assumption that the relation existing between Peter and Paul had been intended by them, and established by mutual agreement. The immediate purpose of Acts was thus to set the two apostles in parallel, Peter appearing as Pauline and Paul as Petrine. The work, says Baur, was the peace proposal of a Paulinist who intended to purchase recognition of gentile Christianity through accessions to Judaism. Similarly, Baur describes Ephesians and Colossians as "Pauline" attempts at mediation, adding that the frequent reminiscences of gnosticism and its peculiar doctrines in Ephesians, Colossians, and Philippians automatically set them within the post-apostolic period. Baur likewise ranges 2 Peter on the Pauline side, its purpose to furnish Paul's letters with canonical authority (122, 127, 131-35, 149-51).[26]

The lion's share of synthesis Baur assigns to the Johannine literature. Conscious of his standpoint as new and peculiar, in essence different from both the Pauline and Jewish Christian perspective, this author, who assumed John's name for the purposes of his Gospel (154), sensed the requirement of bringing this new consciousness to genuinely apostolic expression. He did so through the idea of the *Logos*. Jewish unbelief in all its phases formed the obverse side of the *Logos* theme. Baur writes that the relation between Judaism and paganism in Revelation was reversed in the Johannine Gospel, for which Judaism itself now bore the character of a power hostile to God.[27] In this fashion, writes Baur, the Gospel celebrated Judaism's abolition, an abolition further reflected in the dating of Jesus' crucifixion on the fourteenth rather than on the fifteenth of Nisan — proof that the Gospel could not have been written by an apostle. As for the Gospel's principal protagonist and Peter's superior, "the beloved disciple," Baur believes that he was merely an ideal, not an historical person (154-56, 159-60, 173-74, 178).

In the post-apostolic period, writes Baur, Irenaeus (ca. 130–ca. 200) was the first to contend that the old and universally recognized Roman Church had been founded by the two most glorious apostles. For Irenaeus, as well as for Tertullian (ca. 160–ca. 225), Clement of Alexandria (c. 150–c. 215), and

26. In *Church History*, Baur can also speak of 1 Peter as reflecting the synthesis, writing that the author's amanuensis is Silvanus, companion of Paul (1 Peter 5:12), just as the Petrine Clement appears in the Pauline letter to the Philippians (4:3), and the same Mark whom Peter names as son (1 Peter 5:13) appears again in the company of Paul in Colossians 4:10; see 151.

27. *Die Tübinger Schule*, AW, 5:367.

Origen — in fact, adds Baur, for all the teachers of the church in this period — any trace of a division between Peter and Paul, or even of views shared between them, had completely disappeared (147-48).

III. Assessment

A. Legacy

Ferdinand Christian Baur was a giant of biblical scholarship. If it was Strauss in the nineteenth century who had raised the issue of historical criticism most sharply and fixed the battleground, it was Baur who gave a truer and deeper picture of the history of dogma and theology. It was Baur, more than any other before him, who put the question as to the meaning of the "historical-critical." It was Baur who saw his task as subordinating human subjectivity to an objectivity determined and ordered by God and thus prepared for a time when the Schlatters, Barths, and Bultmanns would require of the interpreter something more than an Olympian aloofness. It was Baur who yielded the negative result that a teleology of world history is beyond the historian's reach, that no dogmatism can immediately determine historical work, but that certain arenas of tension, centers of gravity in Christian history, can be recognized, thus that while the historian cannot know what only God can know, reality can be known, if only in a limited way.

A list of the anticipations of modern research in Baur's work would be very long. Suffice it to enumerate a few:

First, Baur's removal of Jesus' resurrection as an object of empirical research or demonstration would be repeated over and over by biblical interpreters of the twentieth century, whether or not they insisted upon viewing it together with the cross as a single event, or as an event consequent upon it. Second, in Pauline studies, the contention that the uniqueness of the Pauline theology lay in its concentration upon the cross of Christ would in great part merely mirror what Baur had written earlier: "From the moment of the revelation in which the Son of God was revealed in him, [Paul] lives only in contemplation of the Crucified One: he knows no other, he is crucified with him, his whole system of thought turns on this one fact" (47). Third, the prevailing opinion that from the outset the Christian community was beset by conflicts over theology and practice — a view developed more by Walter Bauer (1904-60) than anyone else in the twentieth century,[28] a study that still later gave

---

28. *Orthodoxy and Heresy in Earliest Christianity*, ed. Robert A. Kraft and Gerhard Krodel (Philadelphia: Fortress, 1971).

stimulus to Robinson's and Koester's argument for the cultural and religious pluralism of the Hellenistic and Roman eras[29] — that opinion had Ferdinand Christian Baur for its father. Fourth, however nuanced, the idea that structures developed outside of or prior to the emergence of Christianity, and Jewish structures in particular, underlay the organization of the Christian community once its eschatological passion had waned — an idea given classical form in the work of the Heidelberg historian Hans von Campenhausen (1903-89)[30] — also could be rightfully claimed by Baur as his bequest. Given the scholar's rage to prove the novelty of his cerebrations, neither Bauer nor von Campenhausen refers to Baur.

B. Identifying the Divine and the Human

Baur has often been described as an Hegelian. The similarity between the theologian and the philosopher is not accidental. Baur's conception of his task as tracing the movement of the universal beneath the particular is twin to Hegel's "biology of the Spirit." The difference between the two consists in the fact that whereas Baur gives greater emphasis to the concrete, to the history of Christianity, Hegel, ever the philosopher, gives greater attention to the process of which that history is only a specific moment. The difference is thus a difference only in respect of form, not of content. As to the warrant or competency for tracing this development of "Spirit" or the "Idea," for Baur — as for Hegel — it lies with the identification of the human and the divine consciousness. In his history of the nineteenth century, Baur cites Hegel with obvious approval:

> The "I" is aware of itself as universal. This universal is God, the Absolute Spirit. But it is the destiny of the Absolute Spirit to become finite, subjective spirit. In this finite spirit it recognizes that it is identical with itself, has consciousness of itself — which, in turn, is the finite spirit's consciousness of itself and its unity with God.[31]

It would be an error, however, to assume a philosophical sophistication in Baur beyond his appreciation for Hegel in broad outline. In response to an

---

29. See Helmut Koester and James M. Robinson, *Trajectories through Early Christianity* (Philadelphia: Fortress, 1971).

30. Hans von Campenhausen, *Ecclesiastical Authority and Spiritual Power in the Church of the First Three Centuries*, tr. J. A. Baker (Stanford: Stanford University Press, 1969).

31. *Kirchengeschichte des neunzehnten Jahrhunderts, AW*, 4:353.

attack on Hegel's "pantheism" as the "devil's doctrine" in the *Evangelische Kirchenzeitung*, founded by the celebrated conservative and polemicist Ernst Wilhelm Hengstenberg, Baur writes that he followed no philosophical system, since he knows what deception attaches to dependence upon human authority, but he is convinced that a great deal could be learned from Hegel if those who are so quick to slight him would read him with greater care.[32] In fact, Baur's yearning to chart the totality of the divine activity may have had different parentage than in Hegelianism, that is, in what his earlier preoccupation with the Graeco-Roman world had disclosed — the idea of *pneuma*, the Spirit, whose "work" is history. The attraction to Hegel may then have lain in the fact that both drew water from the same well of ancient Greece. If there was attraction to Hegel, there was also reaction to Schleiermacher, whom Baur believed had reduced the entire content of religion to consciousness, and thus mulcted the idea of God of any content.[33] At any rate, the theory is not farfetched that Baur read the New Testament "as a peculiar documentation of classical Greek," and related the concept of the *pneuma* to the divine, shunted to the Christian self-consciousness.[34]

Throughout his work, Baur assumes an identity of the human subject with its divine object. In a fashion associated with liberal Protestantism, he turns a blind eye to the Augustinian tradition with its dark view of human nature and capability. In Baur's world of thought, nature and grace cohere in the structure of reality. This assumption is his guarantee of objectivity in historical reconstruction. Because there is coherence in the world between the divine and the human, there is reason in the world; and whatever has come into existence through reason must be available to reason. Thus, it is possible to orient consciousness toward whatever it is in the world in which an object appears as it really is, possible to set oneself within the objective course of the matter, so as to pursue it in all its moments.[35] Accordingly, the task of "religious consciousness" is to recognize what has become objective reality through immanent historical development, to see in that reality a divine witness, and then to bow before it as a higher power. This is the work of "science" (*Wissenschaft*). And since the task was "spiritual," so also was the method. In reflecting on the scholar's task, Baur can even take up the biblical language of "spirit" and "flesh":

---

32. *Abgenötigte Erklärung, AW,* 1:313-18.

33. *Kirchengeschichte des neunzehnten Jahrhunderts, AW,* 5:350.

34. Käsemann in *AW,* 1:x.

35. See the preface to *Die christliche Lehre von der Dreieinigkeit und Menschenwerdung Gottes, AW,* 2:298.

To share in the living process of the unfolding of science . . . one must enter into it in such a way that one is prepared to offer science the sacrifice it demands. . . . Here too it is necessary to kill the natural man, to die to the flesh, that we may know not what is fleshly, but what is spiritual, that the old may pass away and all become new.[36]

The words are Pauline, but not the conceptuality. And the difference is not difficult to trace. In Baur's view, if it is possible to conceive the whole, to "track" the totality in idealistic fashion, then ambiguity, at least in the form of miracle or prodigy, must be excluded. And in fact, Baur contends that the "magical" or "teleological" view yields no *entre* to inner-worldly connections. Miracle annuls the "natural context"; it makes impossible the observation of one phenomenon as the natural result of another (7).[37] The self-realization of Christianity conceived as a process assumes in Baur's theology a continuity, uniformity, and coherence in which miracle has no place.

If Baur's Christianity lacks every trace of the prodigious or miraculous, then it follows that it should lack any trace of eschatology, at least according to the classical definition. And, indeed, if an eschatological aspect can be detected in Baur, it does not involve the "last things" outside of history but only within history. The *novum* cannot be without antecedent or consequence. The conviction of a later generation, voiced in the researches of Johannes Weiss (1863-1914) or Albert Schweitzer, seconded and qualified in the studies of Ernst Käsemann and others,[38] to the effect that imminent expectation of the visible appearance of God for judgment and salvation furnished the explanation to the self-consciousness and mission of a Jesus or a Paul, would have no hearing with Baur. It is excluded in the name of a piety drawing deeply on the Enlightenment worldview, the view of the divine activity as coterminous with the historical process. Call that conception an abbreviation of perspective veiling the distance between Christianity and the world or history, but for all that it is still a piety — the piety of modernist faith.

If miracle and eschatology are excluded in consequence of the critical task, dogma is by definition excluded. Baur asserts that just as with the history of dogma the question is not whether what is described is true and requires to be made an object of faith, but only what has been taught as such, so

---

36. *Abgenötigte Erklärung, AW,* 1:299.

37. See *Die Tübinger Schule, AW,* 5:308.

38. See Johannes Weiss, *Jesus' Proclamation of the Kingdom of God,* tr. R. H. Hiers and D. L. Holland (Philadelphia: Fortress, 1971); Albert Schweitzer, *The Quest of the Historical Jesus,* tr. Wm. Montgomery (New York: Macmillan, 1910); Ernst Käsemann, *New Testament Questions of Today,* tr. W. J. Montague (Philadelphia: Fortress, 1969).

the question for New Testament theology is not "what we ourselves should believe, but only what others have held or believed to be true."[39] Like Spinoza before him, Baur confines the specificity of religious claims to their meaning within a particular cultural context. After Baur, generations of works on the religion of Jesus, Paul, or the New Testament, as distinct from biblical theologies that explicated what was binding upon belief and action, would enshrine Baur's axiom within the bosom of the church.

Of course, the larger question is whether or not this union of the universal with the particular, the divine with the human, the finite with the Absolute Spirit did or could ever exist in a specific individual. To this question Baur's response was as equivocal as most thought Hegel's to be. Heinrich Georg August Ewald (1803-75), of the celebrated "Göttingen Seven," twice expelled from university professorship for political views, teacher of Julius Wellhausen (1844-1918), and arch-enemy of Baur's "tendency criticism," suggested that Jesus came to gradual consciousness of his messiahship. To Baur the suggestion screened the assumption that every individual possessed the requisite conditions for such consciousness, the difference with Jesus consisting merely in his realizing at one stroke what in others would occur successively or relatively. This type of reasoning does not deliver the subject from the dilemma that the highest in world history is either never fulfilled or fulfilled only in one with the qualifications for it. Thus, to bring the argument to its conclusion, one would have to prove that the highest could not remain unfulfilled, but was actually fulfilled in a specific individual. "But," Baur writes, "so long as this is not proved, the other assumption is just as possible, that it is never fulfilled. . . ."[40] Baur may have preferred neither assumption, though his perennial eagerness to draw or absorb or "dirempt" (the term shared with Hegel was *aufheben*) the particular into the universal allowed for expanding the person of Jesus into a universal world-consciousness.[41]

What if all this talk of absorbing, or the ease with which Baur appears to absorb the particular into the universal, is simply a distraction; a denial of the identity of both the particular and the universal; an ignoring of the particular as having conjured up or invented the universal? Baur was acquainted with the inversion of humankind's relation to God in the "historico-philosophical" analysis of Ludwig Feuerbach:

> If thou believest that God is for thee, thou believest that nothing is or can be against thee, that nothing contradicts thee. But if thou believest that

39. *Vorlesungen über neutestamentliche Theologie*, 59-60.
40. *Die Tübinger Schule, AW*, 5:433-34.
41. See Ulrich Wickert, "Einführung," *AW*, 3:33-34.

nothing is or can be against thee, thou believest — what? — nothing less than that thou art God. That God is another being is only illusion, only imagination. In declaring that God is for thee, thou declarest that he is thy own being. What then is faith but the infinite self-certainty of man, the undoubting certainty that his own subjective being is the objective, absolute being, the being of beings?[42]

Baur counters that one-sidedness has triumphed with Feuerbach; that whereas with Hegel everything has its objective as well as its subjective side, with Feuerbach everything has but the one, subjective aspect; that with him theology dissolves into anthropology, and everything universal and objective into the subjectivity of the individual. Thus, though assuming that truth and reality lie only in that of which one is immediately conscious, Baur contends that Feuerbach proceeds to make of Hegel's philosophy a transition to "communistic and other practical tendencies, whose principle is the most subjective egoism, denying whatever is universal and objective."[43]

This is all well and good. But the question remains: Does Baur escape Feuerbach's claim? The answer must be no.

William James (1842-1910) once wrote:

I have honestly tried to stretch my own imagination and to read the best possible meaning into the rationalist conception, but I have to confess that it still completely baffles me. The notion of a reality calling on us to "agree" with it, and that for no reason, but simply because its claim is "unconditional" or "transcendent," is one that I can make neither head nor tail of.[44]

What James means by the "rationalist conception" is a view of reality as uniform and indivisible. Baur not merely held that view, but in his investigation of earliest Christianity attempts to document it. The object of research is the Spirit's unfolding through the contrasts inherent in history, a research in which nothing, no individual detail, could be absolutized or negated.

It is at this point that Albrecht Ritschl broke with his old friend and teacher, Baur. According to Ritschl, the history of Christianity yields many tendencies. For this reason, the historian is forced to render judgments as to value, thus if not to absolutize or negate, at least to select what lay at the heart of Christian revelation. What for Baur, therefore, was natural to the unfolding

---

42. Ludwig Feuerbach, *The Essence of Christianity*, tr. George Eliot (New York: Harper and Row, 1957), 127.

43. *Kirchengeschichte des neunzehnten Jahrhunderts*, AW, 4:393-94.

44. *Pragmatism* (New York: Meridian, 1961), 152.

of Spirit, Ritschl could regard as alien and foreign, a deviation. To explain the transition of earliest Christianity to its catholic form, Ritschl assumes a "fall" from pure Pauline teaching as well as the disappearance of Jewish Christianity from the scene.[45] Baur never forgave Ritschl for his "apostasy."

His fealty to the idea of dialectical unfolding of the Spirit that he believed gave access to historical reality led to Baur's errors in historical reconstruction. For example, his commitment to the movement of Spirit through contrasts in distinct profile resulted in a portrait of the parties in 1 Corinthians that was not true to life. He identified a gentile Christianity influenced by the Old Testament, and more or less independent of Paul, with Jewish Christianity. His steely commitment to logic and order ruled out the possibility of a Paulinism that from the outset was only imperfectly understood, and was soon overwhelmed by other currents. Further, since the Paulinism that Baur opposed to Jewish Christianity was of a Greek sort, that is, was construed in terms of self-consciousness, the significance of primitive Christian eschatology was never understood by Baur.

Next, though Baur's contrast between Judaists and Paulinists was merely the application to primitive Christian history of the Reformation distinction between law and gospel, his "Protestant" criterion for distinguishing the one from the other had little to do with the Reformation. Commenting on Baur's view of Romans 9–11 as the epistle's hermeneutical center, championing Christian universalism against Jewish particularism, Ernst Käsemann states that in so resolutely raising the question of the letter's situation-in-life, Baur also set it within the relativity of all things historical, thus paving the way for removing the traditional Protestant doctrine of justification from its privileged place as the interpretive center of the Pauline corpus.[46] For the Reformation the gospel of justification served as the criterion, whereas for Baur it was the self-disclosure of Spirit by way of the immanent historical process.[47]

To illustrate yet again, Baur conceded that even the New Testament tradition is composed of fragments, that more cannot be gained from history than probability, but in that concession there is more clearly exposed the weakness of a method intent on apprehending the whole of history. If fragments are all we have, then how can we claim knowledge of total reality?

Despite these weaknesses, Baur's greatness cannot be denied. The discipline of New Testament studies owes him more than any of those who came

---

45. *Die Entstehung der altkatholischen Kirche* (Bonn: Adolph Marcus, 1857), 12.

46. Ernst Käsemann, *Commentary on Romans,* tr. Geoffrey W. Bromiley (Grand Rapids: Wm. B. Eerdmans, 1980).

47. Käsemann in *AW,* 1:xxiv.

before him. On the wall in Ernst Käsemann's living room study hung a copy of the University of Tübingen's portrait of Baur, a gift to the New Testament scholar upon his retirement. Once outside Baur's direct influence, the one-time pupil of Bultmann finally came to write of Baur as the true "progenitor" of a criticism at the root, a criticism conceived not merely as a scientific method but as a presupposition for the life of the spirit. One summer day he pointed to that portrait on his study wall and said, "greater even than Bultmann."

7

JOHANN CHRISTIAN KONRAD VON HOFMANN

The Bible as Salvation History

I. Pietist Protest against Historical-Critical Method

On 23 March 1819, the conservative journalist and playwright August von Kotzebue was assassinated by a twenty-four-year-old theology student from the University of Jena named Karl Ludwig Sand. Sand was a fanatical member of the German student movement *(Burschenschaft),* a loose-knit fraternity dedicated to German unity, independence, and republican government. In a letter of sympathy to Sand's mother, Wilhelm Martin Leberecht de Wette (1780-1849), professor of exegesis at Berlin and noted practitioner of the new methods in biblical criticism, called the assassination "a beautiful sign of the age."[1] The uproar that followed this shocking remark led to de Wette's dismissal. The political reverberations from Kotzebue's assassination finally resulted in a diplomatic summit in the city of Carlsbad at which the principal German states under the leadership of the Austrian Prince Nicolas von Metternich (1773-1859) decided to disband the *Burschenschaft* and place government officials at the universities, charged with the responsibility of guarding against any attempt to promote revolutionary teaching. The governments agreed to censor the contents of books, periodicals, and the press. A strict conservatism became the order of the day.

---

1. Quoted in Robert M. Bigler, *The Politics of German Protestantism* (Berkeley: University of California Press, 1972), 45.

At Berlin, de Wette's eventual replacement was Ernst Wilhelm Hengstenberg, part of a new generation of biblical scholars converted to the conservative cause. In his student years Hengstenberg had been a member of the *Burschenschaft*. His doctoral dissertation at Bonn (1823) argued that the science of philology rather than dogmatic theology discloses the meaning of the Scriptures. The following year he reversed his position and thereafter dedicated his career both to the defense of orthodox Lutheran doctrine and the battle against historical-critical method. "Philology, philosophy, and human reason [cannot] penetrate matters of religion."[2]

Hengstenberg's dramatic change of position came about when he was "awakened" to "true faith" after joining the neopietist circle of Baron Hans Ernst von Kottwitz (1757-1831). The purpose of this group of Prussian aristocrats and churchmen was to revitalize the Prussian people after the final defeat of Napoleon in 1813. For Kottwitz and his followers, including the Crown Prince Friedrich Wilhelm (1795-1861), this meant that the Prussian state must restore its commitment to the Reformation teaching of sin and grace as the primary experience of Christian life and reject "the ideas of 1789."

Hengstenberg was one of von Kottwitz's most effective disciples. During his tenure at Berlin as professor of exegesis from 1828 to 1869, Hengstenberg encouraged the reintroduction of traditional dogmatic study of the Scriptures. The student work that he sanctioned included arguments for the historical veracity of such passages as Numbers 22:28-29 (the witness of Balaam's ass) and Joshua 10:12-13 (Joshua's address to the sun), and a defense of the Mosaic origins of Deuteronomy.[3] Behind Hengstenberg's conservative exegetical practices lay an authoritarian and fideistic conception of revelation. In his *Christology of the Old Testament* (1st ed., 1829-35), Hengstenberg writes: "Who will prescribe for God the rules he is to follow in his revelation? Who will say that what he never does, as a rule, he may never do?"[4] In Hengstenberg's opinion, Old Testament prophecy pointed unambiguously, one might say even mechanically, to fulfillment in the New Testament. Despite his commitment to matters of historical veracity, Hengstenberg cared little for the question of historical context. He ruthlessly subordinated the Old Testament, especially the prophets, to the Christian dogmatic tradition.

---

2. Quoted in *ibid.*, 92.

3. John M. Stroup, "The Idea of Theological Education at the University of Berlin: From Schleiermacher to Harnack," in *Schools of Thought in the Christian Tradition*, ed. Patrick Henry (Philadelphia: Fortress, 1984), 161.

4. *Christologie des Alten Testaments* (Berlin: Ludwig Oehmigke, 1829), 1, part 2, 193. Quoted in Claude Welch, *Protestant Thought in the Nineteenth Century*, vol. 1: *1799-1870* (New Haven: Yale University Press, 1972), 196.

Kottwitz's circle was the most notable example of the *Erweckungs-bewegung* ("Awakening") of the early nineteenth century. The earlier pietism had originated in the seventeenth century as a protest movement against both the dry intellectualism of Protestant scholastic theology and the sacramental formalism of the territorial church. It taught that the beginning of genuine Christian life is spiritual transformation through Bible study and prayer. Especially important for the individual Christian was the fellowship of "circles of piety" *(collegia pietatis)* emphasizing the priesthood of all believers, moral behavior, and the development of a personal relationship to God. Throughout the eighteenth century, pietism was largely a privatistic and quietistic force within the church with a complex, even protean character. Its influence extended even to the emergence of the Enlightenment in Germany, which took from pietism an indifference to the vigorous pursuit of dogmatic argument, a suspicion of clerical authority, and a devotion to the autonomy of the individual believer as an able discerner of truth. Both Kant and Schleiermacher, for example, came from the bosom of pietism.

At the turn of the nineteenth century, a renewed pietism became a political force within the government of the Prussian territorial church. Rejecting the traditional pietistic suspicion of Protestant scholasticism, this neopietism embraced various forms of dogmatic confessionalism. It also became the chief ecclesiastical agent of protest against the cultural hegemony of Enlightenment ideas, especially as these were associated with revolutionary France. The subjection of Prussia and other German lands under Napoleon launched a period of deep soul searching among the German intellectual elite. It fired the passions of both Prussian and pan-German nationalism. Hatred of the French became, in turn, a convenient means for attacking all that was wrong with the eighteenth-century Enlightenment. The rationalist belief in the power of human reason, its willingness to subject inherited tradition to searching criticism, and, above all, its faith in liberty of conscience and democratic reform were treated with suspicion. Had these ideas not led to the chaos of the French Revolution? Better to recognize that human corruption is the driving force of history and that obedience to the God-given order of church and society is the most secure path to social tranquility.

In 1800, with Europe in the throes of conflict, the Lutheran court chaplain at Dresden, Francis V. Reinhart (1753-1812), criticized the rationalist quest for critical knowledge of the Scriptures. "I could not fail to perceive," he writes, "that . . . consistency of thought in religion could be acquired only by adhering entirely to reason or entirely to the Scriptures, and hence in reality only by the Rationalist or Supernaturalist." Reinhart defended the supernaturalist route to faith with a pietist testimony of personal need for a Savior:

I must give you a glance into my heart which will perhaps fill you with great surprise but which will completely solve for you the riddle of my unshaken adherence to the gospel in general and to the doctrines of our church in particular. To do so in a few words, in the relation in which I stand to God I need a Savior and Mediator, and just such an one as Christ is. After having paid long and close attention to my heart and its real condition, as well as to the language of my moral feelings, I find myself totally unable to comprehend how anyone can be bold enough to rely confidently upon his own virtue in the presence of God or even to expect the grace of God and the forgiveness of his sins without having received some express assurance from his Maker to this effect.[5]

Reinhart voiced a conviction shared by many. With the defeat of Napoleon, this conviction served as a catalyst for a conservative backlash against Enlightenment culture that had as its goal the revival of religion and protection of the monarchist tradition. The theological faculties of German universities, beholden as they were to the new methods of critical thought that developed in the eighteenth century, were the logical places to focus the attack.

The neopietist effort at conservative reform, supported by the legal authority of the Carlsbad Decrees, met with stiff resistance in German academia. The German dedication to science, the ideal of academic freedom, and the dominance of rationalism among professors and pastors insured a protracted struggle. As editor of the *Evangelische Kirchenzeitung* (1827-69), Hengstenberg was in the forefront of the struggle, representing the neopietist governmental party line on ecclesiastical issues. He regularly subjected Schleiermacher, Strauss, and Baur to fierce attack. Due to the association of his philosophy with those of Strauss and Baur, even Hegel, who had considered himself an enemy of rationalism, did not escape Hengstenberg's harsh judgment. "The Hegelian philosophy," writes Hengstenberg, has a "presuppositionless character" *(Voraussetzungslosigkeit)* that negates "all religious conviction and experiences."[6]

While the *Erweckungsbewegung* in Prussia was the most dramatic and influential form of pietist renewal in the nineteenth century, it was not the only one. In Bavaria and Swabia, pietism retained more of its traditional character as an inspiration for revival within the parish system of the territorial church. It was less identified with the authoritarian politics that characterized the Prussian neopietist movement. One did not need to be politically

---

5. Quoted in Theodore G. Tappert, ed., *Lutheran Confessional Theology in America, 1840-1880* (New York: Oxford University Press, 1972), 4.

6. "Die Zukunft unserer Theologie," *Evangelische Kirchenzeitung,* 4 May 1836, 283.

conservative to be sensitive to the limits of rationalism and the shortcomings of the historical-critical method.

Whatever form pietism took in the early decades of the nineteenth century, it found its reason for being in teaching that personal regeneration, grounded in the experience of sin and grace, is the heart of Christian faith. To understand revelation, as witnessed in the Scriptures, the exercise of human reason is not enough. One must be part of the community of faith and share in its experience of rebirth in the grace of Jesus Christ. Without rebirth, the knowledge that reason gains by its investigation of the Scriptures is inadequate to the advancement of Christian faith. One cannot practice genuine theology by confining intellectual analysis to the facts of the biblical story; to do so is to miss the inner truth and driving force of the gospel.

In the "Erlangen theology," associated with the names of Adolf von Harless (1806-79), Gottfried Thomasius (1802-75), and the subject of this chapter, Johann Christian Konrad von Hofmann, we see this basic pietist presupposition of the centrality of regeneration at work. At the same time, all three figures sought to define themselves over against Prussian neopietism. All three were pan-German nationalists with democratic sympathies. Thomasius and von Hofmann especially were influenced by Schleiermacher and idealism. But despite antipathy to Prussian neopietism and sympathy to liberal Protestant ideas, they nevertheless were sensitive to the limits of modern theological science. David Friedrich Strauss was as much their enemy as he was Hengstenberg's. Above all, they desired to remain obedient servants of the Augustinian tradition as they had received it from the study of Luther and the Lutheran Confessions, especially as these were refracted through the experience of personal conversion. As Thomasius put it, recalling his own conversion as a young theology student:

> The innermost root of our new life . . . was faith in Christ and the satisfying of our need for salvation through the forgiveness of sins. . . . This new evangelical life was from the start nourished, next to the Holy Scriptures, by the monuments of the Reformation. . . . *So we were Lutheran even before we knew it.* Without giving much thought to the confessional peculiarity of our church and the confessional differences that separate it from other churches, we were in fact Lutherans.[7]

They were indeed Lutherans grounded in the presuppositions of the Augustinian tradition. But they were also Lutherans reconciled to the liberal political spirit of the modern age. Their stance toward the historical criticism of

7. Quoted in Tappert, *Lutheran Confessional Theology*, 8.

the Scriptures was open, yet wary — an unusual combination of characteristics that appears most clearly in the work of von Hofmann.

II. Biography

Johann Christian Konrad von Hofmann was born in Nuremberg on 21 December 1810 to parents attracted to the German Awakening and shaped by the pietism of Bavaria and Swabia. Following the normal secondary school education, he studied at the University of Erlangen, where he came under the influence of the Reformed pastor and later professor Johann Christian Krafft (1784-1845), as well as of the natural scientist, pedagogue, and patriot Karl Georg von Raumer (1783-1865) — both advocates of the *Erweckungsbewegung*. Von Hofmann completed his studies at the University of Berlin, where, for a time at least, he came under the spell of the historian Leopold von Ranke (1795-1886). In 1832 he was appointed instructor in an Erlangen *Gymnasium,* and from 1835 to 1841 served as *Repetent, Privatdozent* (university instructor, non-salaried), and associate professor at Erlangen University. After three years as full professor at the University of Rostock, he returned to Erlangen in the same capacity. Between the years 1863 and 1869 he served as a Party of Progress representative to the Bavarian *Landestag,* or state legislature, vilified by his associates because of his commitment to parliamentary democracy at a time when Germany was increasingly drawn to nondemocratic power politics as a means to national unification. He died at Erlangen on 20 December 1877.

III. Interpreting the Bible

A. The Occasion

Two antithetical forces furnished von Hofmann the occasion for his work. The one was the new "science" that David Friedrich Strauss had come to represent; the other was Protestant scholasticism. Von Hofmann saw in Strauss an enemy of the Christian religion, "who maliciously drives nails into its living flesh to kill it, and thus adds the passion of Christianity to that of our Lord."[8] But it was Protestant scholasticism that evoked the greater bulk by far of von Hofmann's reaction. He opposed the legalism he believed

---

8. Quoted in Emanuel Hirsch, *Geschichte der neueren Evangelischen Theologie* (Gütersloh: C. Bertelsmann, 1954), 5:424.

was inherent in its structure, and inveighed against its doctrine of verbal inspiration — an erroneous conception, he contended, that obviated the understanding of the Bible's historical character.[9] In reaction to verbalists such as Hengstenberg, von Hofmann states that the manner in which a biblical figure was inspired, spoke, or acted in the given instance depended on that person's peculiarity, a peculiarity willed by God. He writes: "What is worked by the Spirit does not have its peculiarity from the Spirit, as the ancients stated, but rather from individual human nature. . . . Thus, wherever God intends to make use of someone, he effects the utterance of what is already in that person's nature."[10] Von Hofmann allows for differences, even contradictions, in the Bible, setting them down to authorial perspective. Because of the inescapability of authorial perspective, readers of the Bible are obliged to rely upon the form in which, for example, the words of Jesus had come to be Scripture, rather than upon the form in which they were originally uttered. Von Hofmann asserts that to make the Bible as word of God dependent upon the belief that it was without error, even regarding data available to natural knowledge, would be to assign it characteristics attributable only to God. On the other hand, von Hofmann eschews the popular definition of the Bible as "containing" the word of God, labeling it a mistake that results in distancing religious from nonreligious truth in the Bible. Conceding that the certainty derived from the Bible does not apply equally to what is to be believed and what is not; that one may not derive from the Bible the same certainty in matters of anthropology as in matters of faith, he nonetheless insists that the manner in which Scripture speaks of human existence is in harmony with "saving truth."[11]

Opposition to Protestant scholasticism as well as to the new science represented by Strauss had either its consequence or concomitant in von Hofmann's hermeneutical theory. Over against scholasticism he contends that biblical hermeneutics cannot be developed exclusively from theological premises or studied by itself. Rather, it is based upon the general principles of interpretation. How then, in employing such principles, can the peculiarity of the body of literature called Holy Scripture be given its due? In reply, von Hofmann writes of an "addition" to the general laws of interpretation that facilitates their application in harmony with the demands made by the Bible's

---

9. J. C. K. von Hofmann, *Interpreting the Bible,* tr. Christian Preus (Minneapolis: Augsburg, 1959), 14-16.

10. *Weissagung und Erfüllung im Alten und im Neuen Testament* (Nördlingen: C. H. Beck, 1841), 1:29; see also 28.

11. *Ibid.,* 1:70, 71, 206, 210.

peculiar subject matter. At any rate, it is the Bible's distinctive character, not the principles of its interpretation, that creates the hermeneutical task.[12]

Over against the new science, von Hofmann insists that the interpretation of Scripture requires faith or "spiritual understanding." He writes:

> A complete lack of presuppositions on the part of the interpreter would be unthinkable. It is impossible for the interpreter to be neither Christian nor non-Christian, neither religious nor irreligious, but merely interpreter. He approaches Scripture as a person with a definite character and nature and experience, not as a "blank sheet" upon which Scripture inscribes itself.[13]

The so-called "neutral interpreter" can more appropriately be called indifferent.

B. The "Fact" of Rebirth

That "addition" to the interpretative principles that neither the verbalist's unhistorical legalism nor the skeptic's radical historical criticism could supply von Hofmann believes he finds in what he calls a "fact." Upon this fact is built proof of the Bible's divinity and historicity. This fact, von Hofmann states, is "rebirth," the Christian experience of relation to God, an experience existing independently in its subject, independent of church or Bible, resting in itself, constituting immediate and certain truth. Von Hofmann writes:

> The relation between God and mankind existing in Christ is not merely available to the theologian in scripture and church. He also has it in himself by virtue of that experience. And though this experience has not come to him without the mediation of the church and scripture, insofar as it gives him real certainty of God, it is for that reason not dependent on scripture and church. It is rather the perception of the most immediate witness of God himself, thus of primary certainty. . . . The primary nature of that experience gives it an independence by which it has the right to set an expression and communication of its content alongside scripture and church.[14]

As the quotation makes clear, von Hofmann does not regard this "fact" of experience as self-generated, but rather as mediated through the church.

12. *Ibid.*, 1:13, 15.
13. *Ibid.*, 1:14.
14. Quoted in Karl Gerhard Steck, "Hofmann," in *Die Idee der Heilsgeschichte* (Zollikon: Evangelischer, 1959), 19-20.

He hastens to add, however, that the church itself did not arise through doctrinal statements but through "facts," that is, the sum of individual experiences of personal relationship to God. Further, since the Christian experience is communal, and since Scripture belongs to the community, von Hofmann refers to the necessary relationship between Bible and church. According to von Hofmann, this "fact" of Christian experience, independent, though mediated through Bible and church, guarantees a certainty in face of skepticism that no adducing of proofs by the orthodox could ever effect.

C. The Task and Method of Theology

Since, according to von Hofmann, the Christian community is obliged to learn the historical facts at the root of its existence, it is the task of theology to explicate the Christian experience, to give it scientific expression. Because this experience is mediated through the church to which the Bible also belongs, Christianity as an object amenable to scholarly research is given to theology in a threefold existence: (1) as a "fact" disclosed to the Christian; (2) as Scripture, and (3) as the actual church.[15]

The decisive scientific test of theology is the spontaneous coming together of the three totalities — experience, church, and Bible — in a harmonious unity. It is clear, however, that the point of departure, the normative source, remains the fact of rebirth. Thus, von Hofmann weds the practice of historical criticism to the pietist construal of faith. What is essential concerning church and Bible has to emerge beforehand, by way of introspection. For example, since certainty concerning the nature of Scripture is rooted in the Christian experience, the Bible offers exactly what is gleaned from that experience. "Evidence from Scripture" serves to indicate that the proper data had been lifted out on that path of introspection.[16] But if the experience of rebirth remains the point of departure, the movement between that experience and Bible or church is reciprocal. That is to say, when interpreted as a unified whole, Bible and church ratify experience, just as experience ratifies Bible and church. To this reciprocal movement among the three witnesses corresponds von Hofmann's method.

Von Hofmann called the method he believed would establish a new re-

15. Johannes Haussleiter, ed., *Grundlinien der Theologie Joh. Christ. K. v. Hofmanns, in seiner eigenen Darstellung* (Leipzig: A. Deichert, 1910), 27-28; Hirsch, *Geschichte*, 5:421.

16. Von Hofmann, *Interpreting the Bible*, 27; see also *Der Schriftbeweis: Ein Theologischer Versuch* (Nördlingen: C. H. Beck, 1857), 1:11.

lationship to the facts of revelation and a new approach to Scripture the "Two Ways." Since Christian experience of the relation to God remains the point of departure, the "First Way" is that experience. If von Hofmann is remembered for anything he said, it is no doubt this statement:

> Theology is a truly free science, free in God, only when precisely that which makes a Christian to be a Christian, his own independent relation to God, makes the theologian to be a theologian through disciplined self-knowledge and self-expression: when I the Christian am for me the theologian the essential material of my science.[17]

It is von Hofmann's boast that by this first way he can retrospectively deduce all of Christian dogmatics.[18]

The "Second Way" von Hofmann describes as the "historical way." This way sets forth the totality transmitted in the Bible. Together, these "Two Ways" lead to the scientific certainty of those facts without which there could be no theology.[19]

D. The "Historical Way"

To the elucidation of the Second Way von Hofmann devoted his life and energy. This is the way of *Heilsgeschichte* — "salvation history" or "holy history" of God's dealings with humanity — in contrast to the natural order of things also rooted in God. The Bible is the primary object of research in this "Second Way," not only because it is the record of salvation history but also because it shares in the "miracle of holy history," is a product of the history that establishes the life of the church. The Reformation, contends von Hofmann, gave legitimation to this second way, since it was the Reformation that restored the "historical" meaning of Scripture to its proper place.[20]

In his first great work, *Weissagung und Erfüllung im Alten und im Neuen Testament* (*Prophecy and Fulfillment in the Old and New Testament*, 1841) von Hofmann depicts the whole sweep of *Heilsgeschichte*, given here in broad outline:

In Act One of *Heilsgeschichte* occurred humanity's creation and thus the

---

17. *Ibid.*, 1:10, quoted in Gerhard O. Forde, *The Law-Gospel Debate* (Minneapolis: Augsburg, 1969), 15.

18. Hirsch, *Geschichte*, 5:423.

19. Haussleiter, *Grundlinien*, 29.

20. Hofmann, *Interpreting the Bible*, 9, 28-29, 47-48.

possibility of sinning. Sin, however, did not destroy humanity, but began an interim history between humanity's creation and perfection. The "how" of sin von Hofmann lodges in corporeality; or, more accurately, humanity's corporeality furnished the assumption for sin. Once God as Spirit, as the immanent life force, "indwelt" the created and natural world, that life force suffered division. Since the Spirit's indwelling was humanity's determining power, it established humanity's capacity for determining itself, even in contradictory fashion. But that indwelling of the Spirit also spelled humanity's redeemability: humanity could sin without forfeiting its destiny. Thus, those who were first created could remain alive when they sinned, though not without being punished, and they could die in punishment for their sin without humanity's being eliminated. To the question of "original sin" — the question as to how humanity came to such self-determination in perpetual conflict with God — von Hofmann replies that since God allowed the world to be also the site of Satan's activity, every individual was prey to that activity, thus to the reverse of life with God, and as a result possessed a nature that made it impossible to will anything else than Satan had determined one's ancestor should will.[21] But this willing was impossible only to the degree humanity was excluded from life with God, since existence still left open the reverse possibility.

The peculiar nature of humanity thus involved a contradiction, a contradiction that von Hofmann described as between outer and inner existence.[22] From this concept of the dialectic inherent in creation derived von Hofmann's statement that "where there is person, there I see freedom; and where there is nature, there I see unfreedom," or "man is unfree in everything which is not he, but merely his."[23]

The Second Act of *Heilsgeschichte* was marked by the assurance that the continuance of human life should be a means toward salvation, and the Third Act by the granting of grace to the righteous in contrast to the unrighteous, an act leading to the judgment of the great flood. In Act Four occurred the separation of a single family, the family of Israel, since constituting this family a nation was the first step toward the new way of God. In later acts of *Heils-*

---

21. For von Hofmann Satan is an actual spiritual being ("das widergöttliche Geistwesen"), for whom humanity's relation to the corporeal world furnishes occasion for reversing the work of God. His use of the term is not, as with Schleiermacher, "liturgical" or "poetic," calculated only to describe "the positive godlessness of evil itself." See von Hofmann, "Die wissenschaftliche Lehre von Christi Versöhnungswerk," in Haussleiter, *Grundlinien*, 34; and Friedrich Schleiermacher, *The Christian Faith*, tr. and ed. H. R. Mackintosh and J. S. Stewart (Edinburgh: T&T Clark, 1928), 169-170.

22. Von Hofmann, "Die wissenchaftliche Lehre," 33, 35-36.

23. *Ibid.*, 25-26.

geschichte, Israel received the law to assume the peculiarity of a nation. But, von Hofmann adds, the law was put in force only through the establishment of the sanctuary. Next, in order for the national community to become inwardly what it was outwardly, it had to be made aware of the insufficiency of its external, merely national fulfillment. This was accomplished, von Hofmann continues, through the destruction of temple, city, and land, whose subsequent restoration were the pledge of a perfect fulfillment and brought together a community of law and promise.

In the midst of this community Jesus appeared. Though hope of salvation rested on the propagation of the race, it was not enough that someone be born. A righteous man had to appear in whom the fellowship of love between God and humanity was complete. With Christ's birth the new nature was given, the history between God and humanity had come to its preliminary conclusion.[24] In other words, Christ's appearance was anticipatory of the goal of God's activity in creation.

Till Christ's death, writes von Hofmann, his relation to God was not yet complete. In fact, that relation was fraught with a twofold contradiction: first, sent from the Father, Christ was the object of his love, but as the one who entered sinful humanity he was also subject to the Father's wrath. Second, holy by virtue of his origin in God, once he had entered humanity Christ was obliged to be obedient in order to be holy. To remove this twofold contradiction one thing was needed — that God prove the eternity of the one who died through restoring him to life. It lay in the peculiarity of human nature that Christ as holy enjoyed an existence for which his nature was not suited. Precisely for this reason nature could become new.[25]

This interpretation of Christ's death could only result in von Hofmann's rejection of the traditional Anselmian view of atonement. According to von Hofmann, the theory of satisfaction as Anselm (c. 1033-1109) had set it forth cannot stand; Christ did not suffer "instead of man" what man should have suffered. The distinction between Christ as subject to God's wrath and Christ as subject to God's wrath against sinful humanity by virtue of the divine intention is crucial. By entering humanity as its redeemer, Christ became the object of the divine wrath against it. The distinction moves von Hofmann to the otherwise curious statement that it was not the triune God who required reconciling, but rather the Father, since the world's sin could only be atoned for by the Son's subjecting himself to the Father's wrath against it. Von

---

24. Von Hofmann, *Weissagung und Erfüllung*, 1:33, quoted in Steck, *Die Idee der Heilsgeschichte*, 25.

25. Haussleiter, *Grundlinien*, 38, 47.

Hofmann writes that it is an entirely different matter whether Christ had to suffer what we otherwise would have had to suffer because punishment had to be carried out on him or us, or whether Christ entered into everything to which we had fallen prey in order to free us from it by his obedience. In this sense, but only in this sense, could the death of Christ be called "vicarious." In fact, if the atonement for sin consisted in meting out its punishment on Christ instead of on humanity, the event would have been a mere transaction between God and Christ. In a series entitled *Schutzschriften für eine neue Weise, alte Wahrheit zu Lehren* (*Arguments for a New Way of Teaching Old Truth*, 1857), von Hofmann writes, "It is not the view of a legal procedure between God and Christ which meets us here."[26]

Our conception of the atonement, writes von Hofmann, must begin from the fact of God's originating love. An action of the triune God in its intention made it possible for humanity to be the object of that love, despite its sin. That is, God loved humanity on the basis of what he intended to do in Christ. So the atonement was a "satisfaction," but not something God would have needed had he not willed to need it, a "self-satisfaction of his love with its ground only in himself."[27] All the powers of contradiction shattered on the love with which Jesus was made to depend on the calling given him by the Father.

To support rejection of the atonement as vicarious, von Hofmann appeals to Luther and the Lutheran confessions. In the *Schutzschriften,* he asks precisely where or when the topic of Christ's death as vicarious has ever been discussed in the church. Acknowledging that the confessions or symbols spoke of Christ's death as redeeming from eternal death, von Hofmann denies that Christ's death was ever described as vicarious. Turning to Luther's exposition of the atonement in his explanation of the second article of the Apostles' Creed, preached in 1533, von Hofmann states that it contains no more of vicarious suffering and dying than of vicarious conception and birth. Rather, in Luther's exposition the law had sinned horribly against Christ, its Lord.[28] Thus, instead of urging the notion of Christ's death as substitution, Luther describes it as the imposition of a suffering in which Christ overcame the devil so as to win the victory he gives to us. Christ, subject to the power of the devil, experienced the devil's hellish power, but by means of his holiness he victoriously waged the war against him; this, contends von Hofmann, is Luther's view.

---

26. *Schutzschriften für eine neue Weise, alte Wahrheit zu Lehren* (Nördlingen: C. H. Beck, 1857), 2:83; see also 19, 73-74; Haussleiter, *Grundlinien,* 57; and Forde, *The Law-Gospel Debate,* 37.

27. Von Hofmann, *Schutzschriften,* 2:99.

28. *Ibid.,* 2:16, 20, 23-24, 31, 39, 49-50, 51.

Finally, at the end of von Hofmann's *heilsgeschichtlich* scheme stands Israel with its new Jerusalem, descended from heaven, intact throughout the transformation of the universe, to emerge after the "one thousand years" reign of Christ and his glorified church.

E. The "Eternal" Presupposition

According to von Hofmann, *Heilsgeschichte* reflects a disposition made within the Godhead from eternity. From eternity, God had not merely decided to enter into relationship with historical creatures, but in the deciding had willed for himself a process of self-realization, a movement from eternal identity to historical differentiation. However attracted to the great thinkers of his day, Von Hofmann was no philosopher, and throughout his writings he insists that the history of what occurred in God is not a part of *Heilsgeschichte* — only the salvation-historical aspect needs unfolding from the Christian experience. Still, there is evidence of a certain fascination for tracing *Heilsgeschichte* to a decision made within the Godhead before the world began. "The Trinity," he states, "assumed human nature into the relation within the Godhead as the nature of the eternal Son. . . ."[29] Again: "The Triune God assumed into the relation within the Godhead the contradiction between the living and holy God and a sinful humanity subject to death, in order to resolve that contradiction and redeem humanity from sin and death."[30]

F. The Relation between the Two Ways

If *Heilsgeschichte*, or the "Second Way," has its presupposition in life within the Godhead, this means that the "Second Way" presupposed the "First Way" that is the experience of faith. Or to consider the matter alternatively, the "historical fact" of Christian experience assumes previous "historical facts" that account for its existence. But with all his appeal to the experience of rebirth as starting point and normative source, von Hofmann, at least on occasion, assigns first place to an act of God occurring prior to and outside of faith. The accent thus lies on the insistence that the theologian "finds all the essential events of holy history summed up in the fact of the rebirth, and can reproduce the beginning and progress of that history from its anticipated

29. *Ibid.*, 2:101.
30. Haussleiter, *Grundlinien*, 38-39; see also Forde, *The Law-Gospel Debate*, 23, 25, 27.

end," anticipated, that is, in the rebirth.[31] Still, the "Second Way" recapitulates the "First," or more, is "authenticated" by recurring in the believer. In fact, the relation between the "Two Ways" is established by the necessity that all "essential events of holy history" have to be contained within the experience itself. This necessity of relation furnishes von Hofmann his vantage point from which to view the history of salvation.

IV. Assessment

A. *The Boehme Connection*

Human nature as the nature of the eternal Son; the contradiction between God and humanity taken up into the relation within the Godhead; events between the fall and the restoration as reflecting the relationship interior to the divine life — the "eternal" presupposition furnishes a clue to von Hofmann's spiritual ancestry.

Most European analysis of von Hofmann describes him as a spiritual descendant of Schleiermacher or a disciple of von Ranke. In his study of nineteenth-century theology, Karl Barth writes that von Hofmann learned his lessons thoroughly and directly from Schleiermacher. Von Hofmann's preoccupation with Christian experience as "starting point" or "normative source" obviously furnished Barth reason for this claim. Then Barth adds, however, that von Hofmann's understanding of the "text of history" reflects apprenticeship to von Ranke.[32] In his discussion of von Hofmann, the Göttingen historian-systematician Emanuel Hirsch allows the inference that Schleiermacher furnished impetus for the Erlangen scholar's preoccupation with history as establishing the truth of Christianity. While seconding the customary references to Schleiermacher and von Ranke, Hirsch adds the intriguing comment that in regard to the influence of speculative philosophy on von Hofmann — a factor his admirers would prefer to forget — "Jacob Boehme's system may have given him the most and the best."[33]

Von Hofmann's earliest encounter with Jacob Boehme (1575-1624), the great seventeenth-century German mystic and metaphysician, was through his chief nineteenth-century interpreter, Friedrich Schelling. Von Hofmann

31. Haussleiter, *Grundlinien*, 2; see Forde, *The Law-Gospel Debate*, 13-14.
32. *Protestant Theology in the Nineteenth Century*, tr. Brian Cozens and John Bowden (Valley Forge: Judson, 1973), 608-11, 613.
33. Hirsch, *Geschichte*, 5:420-21, 426; cf. Steck, *Die Idee von Heilsgeschichte*, 29-30.

confessed he had once lived with relish in Schelling's circle of ideas. According to Schelling, Scripture is a totality containing the order of successive divine revelations. Lecturing at Erlangen in the 1820s, Schelling outlined a method by which he could interpret the entire history of the world as the progressive self-revelation of God. For Schelling, the obvious starting point is the fact of the incarnation. Thus, what in rationalistic criticism had been denoted as myth is for Schelling the midpoint of history and starting point for an understanding of life. On the basis of this historical fact, Schelling asks: "Of what sort is the nature of God in its inmost self-activity, that it can be induced to become man?" The conclusion he draws is that Christ's incarnation and earthly life were not the whole of the tension suffered by the Godhead. The Trinity itself was disturbed by the incarnation of the Son. Employing this same notion, von Hofmann writes: "Since the triune God not merely establishes what is historical, but involves himself in it, the relation within the Trinity is necessarily involved in an inequality, which became greatest as the relation of the Father to the man Jesus living on earth."[34]

In his *Weissagung und Erfüllung,* von Hofmann writes that prophecy does not occur unmediated or accidentally, but at a specific point arrived at in history. The statement parallels Schelling's contention that mythology does not emerge from untamed, capricious fantasy, but in the "special feature of succession." History itself, then, is prophetic, or again, history itself is doctrine, the doctrinal contained in the historical. What von Hofmann has in mind in his reference to the Old Testament types is similar to Schelling's argument that if Old Testament events should lose their significance, what they prefigured does not lose its real meaning.[35]

But what of Boehme himself? Von Hofmann had encountered Boehme early through his study of Schelling. It is not known whether or not that encounter was refreshed in later years. One thing is certain — no modern Protestant theologian before or after von Hofmann has so accented corporeality as the historical medium of the life of God. And none before or after Boehme, with the exception of Hegel who owed a great debt to Boehme, had countered the deist separation of heaven from earth with the announcement that God had willed body, corporeality, the incarnation, from eternity. For this reason, Boehme said, the world had been created. But by getting a body, God — or "Spirit" — had introduced death into its being. All of Boehme's

---

34. *Encyclopädie der Theologie,* ed. H. J. Bestmann (Nördlingen: C. H. Beck, 1871), 61.

35. Ernst Benz, *Schelling: Werden und Wirken seines Denkens* (Zürich: Rhein-Verlag, 1955), 68, 69; Joseph Bracken, *Freiheit und Kausalität bei Schelling* (München: Karl Alber, 1972), 119; Karl Schlutter, *Schelling und die Christologie* (Göttingen: Dieterich, 1915), 103, 97, 104.

images were meant to explain the vast struggle between "Yes" and "No" within the world, the self, and God. To overcome the dialectic another birth, itself a birth in the body, was needed to spell the final removal of limitations.

With all this reflection on corporeality, there emerged still another idea. Boehme writes that if the hidden God, single in essence and will, had not willed creaturely life, and thus differentiation, that single hidden will of God would not have become known to itself. In short, the incarnation was a theogonic act — an idea that would find a home with more than one philosopher.

How could all this be known? Not by reason, writes Boehme. Reason serves to resolve antinomies and paradoxes. Nor could this be known by the letter of Scripture. Only a surrendered and humble understanding can know eternal nature; only the regenerate who has put on Christ's God-manhood as his own can know him. Although this Christ was present in everything, and lived within all as unchangeable love, in each person the word of promise had to become a "being." And this faith is the recapitulation of the Unconditioned's search for conditioned form, the repetition of the suffering of God and the overcoming of the dialectic, the inauguration of a new life cycle within a dialectic, straining toward a new birth in a new body:

> Beloved soul; Christ was tempted in the wilderness, and, if thou wilt put on him, thou must go through his whole process even from his incarnation to his ascension. Though thou art not able nor required to do that which he hath done, yet thou must enter wholly into his process and therein die continually from corruption.[36]

As for the atonement, Boehme had no more appetite for Anselmian views than did von Hofmann: Christ was the "tincture" transmuting God's wrath into love. Boehme can indeed speak of Christ's death as a sacrifice for sin.[37] But he pens a thought Hofmann could never use: distinguishing Christ as "the outer life" dwelling in Jesus, the "Holy Man," the "Creator of all things," he writes: "We are not to suppose that the Holy Man in Christ suffered death, for he does not die. The mortal one, the one from the kingdom of this world, cried on his cross: 'My God, my God, why hast thou forsaken me!'"[38]

---

36. *The Confessions of Jacob Boehme,* ed. W. Scott Palmer, 2nd ed. (New York: Harper, 1954), 171-72; see John Joseph Stoudt, *Sunrise to Eternity* (Philadelphia: University of Pennsylvania Press, 1957), 65, 86, 108-9, 231, 239, 285, 289, 304.

37. See K. W. Schiebler, ed., *Jacob Böhmes sämmtliche Werke* (Leipzig: Johann Ambrosius Barth, 1847), 7:159, 170.

38. *Ibid.,* 3:301; see also 7:159, 171. Stout, *Sunrise to Eternity,* 287.

B. The Unacknowledged Source

The ideas originating or introduced by von Hofmann have continued to influence theology to the present. Following more than a hundred years of separating theologies of the Old from theologies of the New Testament, scholars have once more taken up the problem of the relation of the two Testaments, due chiefly to the work of the Heidelberg Old Testament scholar Gerhard von Rad (1901-71). To assign von Hofmann the stimulus for contemporary return to the question of a total-biblical theology might strain credulity, but it was, after all, von Hofmann who, in face of the division of the Testaments from Georg Lorenz Bauer (1755-1806) in the eighteenth to Rudolf Bultmann in the twentieth century, insisted upon a theology of both.

In opposition to the scholastic view, which he believes ignores the difference in the presentation of salvation in Old and New Testaments, von Hofmann writes that what is recorded in the Old Testament is a history proceeding toward its realization. Its record is thus to be interpreted teleologically, aiming at a final goal. Further, von Hofmann contends there can be no correct "spiritual" understanding of the Old Testament if historical interpretation is omitted, and attacks Hengstenberg for transposing all the individual features of the Old Testament directly into those of the New. Von Hofmann nonetheless opposes the purely historical approach, according to which Jewish religion serves only as one among many antecedents of Christianity. Each Old Testament detail must be oriented to the conclusion that in Jesus Christ the history of God with humanity comes to preliminary completion.

From this perspective von Hofmann draws two conclusions for Old Testament interpretation. First, events in the life of Jesus and events occurring in Israel are typologically related. Second, interpretation proceeds by way of a prophecy-fulfillment scheme. It is not sufficient to indicate an event at only one stage of Old Testament history. The event must be pursued throughout all its stages, whether as prophecy or fulfillment. What is prophetic thus depends upon the necessity with which it assumes its place in the *Heilsgeschichte* — hence the axiom of prophecy that deed must keep pace with word and vice versa.[39] Viewed "teleologically," the Old Testament simply mirrors the same divine will to love as does the New, a will intent on realizing itself despite all opposition, an intention marking the whole sweep of *Heilsgeschichte* from beginning to end.

---

39. Von Hofmann, *Interpreting the Bible*, 135, 166, 145, 193; Haussleiter, *Grundlinien*, 11, 14, 29; von Hofmann, *Weissagung und Erfüllung*, 1:3, quoted in Steck, *Die Idee der Heilsgeschichte*, 25.

Contemporary biblical scholars will hardly miss the similarity with those "models of thought"[40] by which Gerhard von Rad attempts to establish the unity of the Testaments. Of the Old Testament as a history straining toward realization, von Rad writes: "The Old Testament can only be read as a book of ever increasing anticipation . . . as a book in which expectation keeps mounting up to vast proportions."[41] Von Rad, like von Hofmann, concedes the necessity of historical-critical interpretation, but, like von Hofmann, opposes the purely historical approach: "Does not the way in which comparative religion takes the Old Testament in abstraction, as an object which can be adequately interpreted without reference to the New Testament, turn out to be fictitious from a Christian point of view?"[42] Thus, von Rad concludes that "the coming of Jesus Christ as a historical reality leaves the exegete no choice at all; he must interpret the Old Testament as pointing to Christ, whom he must understand in its light."[43] For this reason, typological exegesis assumes significance, a method von Rad redefines in terms of "correspondences and analogies" between the Testaments.[44] These analogies indicate that the chief consideration in Christian interpretation of the Old Testament "does not lie primarily in the field of religious terminology, but in that of saving history, for in Jesus Christ we meet once again — and in a more intensified form — with that same interconnexion between divine word and historical acts with which we are already so familiar in the Old Testament."[45] Due to this *heilsgeschichtlich* connection, "re-telling," as von Rad labels it, remains the most legitimate form of theological discourse on the Old Testament.[46]

A host of students in the United States were weaned from the verbalism of orthodoxy through introduction to *Heilsgeschichte*. Otto A. Piper's (1891-1982) *God in History* (1939), John Bright's (1911-89) *The Kingdom of God* (1953), G. Ernest Wright's (1909-74) *The Book of the Acts of God* (1957), and Oscar Cullmann's *Christ and Time* (English translation, 1962) were all part of a flood of literature described by one scholar as having reduced German twentieth-century theology to a "jungle." Von Hofmann was the ancestor of them all. Christian Preus's translation of von Hofmann's *Interpreting the Bible*

40. Manfred Oeming, *Gesamtbiblische Theologien der Gegenwart* (Stuttgart: W. Kohlhammer, 1987), 21-32.

41. *Old Testament Theology*, tr. D. M. G. Stalker, 2 vols. (New York: Harper and Row, 1962 and 1965), 2:319, 321.

42. *Ibid.*, 2:321.

43. *Ibid.*, 2:374.

44. *Ibid.*, 2:369.

45. *Ibid.*, 2:382.

46. *Ibid.*, 1:121.

was a chief factor in effecting a radical change in perspective toward Scripture inspiration on the part of an entire Lutheran denomination in this country. In the foreword to that volume, Piper of Princeton Theological Seminary writes of von Hofmann: "He had not only defined the starting point of Protestant exegesis, but also discovered with ingenious certainty what the basic attitude and the guiding perspective are that are consonant with the Christian faith without in any way hampering the legitimate scholarly treatment of the Biblical books."[47]

Another idea important to Protestant theology was the rejection of the interpretation of Christ's death as vicarious substitution — later to be given classical formulation in Albrecht Ritschl's three-volume work on justification and reconciliation.[48] The second, untranslated volume of Ritschl's work is perforated with such statements as these:

> It would be a grave error to refer the mercy-seat of the Israelites . . . to protection from the divine wrath. It is not the wrath but the grace of God on which the existing covenant relationship is based. . . . The links between sacrifice and vicarious punishment, sacrifice and the working of the divine wrath, sacrifice and the covering of human sin, have proven to be in error. . . . One may not translate [1 John 2:2; 4:10][49] to read that Christ is the atonement, that is, the object of punishment for the sins of the world.[50]

From such stimulus as von Hofmann furnished and to which such as Ritschl responded derived a new period of Luther research. Given new impetus in the Erlangen edition of Luther's works (1826-57), and continued in the work of Theodosius Harnack (1817-89), Ernst Troeltsch, and others, Luther research achieved what we recognize as its modern maturity with the Weimar edition (1883-) and the remarkable studies of Karl Holl (1866-1926).[51] From this

---

47. *Interpreting the Bible,* Foreword, ix.

48. Albrecht Ritschl, *The Christian Doctrine of Justification and Reconciliation,* tr. H. R. Mackintosh and A. B. Macaulay (Edinburgh: T&T Clark, 1902).

49. 1 John 2:2: "And he is the expiation for our sins, and not for ours only but also for the sins of the whole world"; 4:10: "In this is love, not that we loved God but that he loved us and sent his Son to be the expiation for our sins."

50. *Die christliche Lehre von der Rechtfertigung und Versöhnung* (Bonn: A. Marcus und E. Weber, 1900), 2:209, 212-13.

51. See Julius Köstlin, *Luthers Theologie in ihrer geschichtlicher Entwicklung und inneren Zusammenhänge dargestellt* (Stuttgart: J. F. Steinkopf, 1863); Theodosius Harnack, *Luthers Theologie mit besonderer Beziehung auf seine Versöhnungs- und Erlösungslehre* (Munich: Chr. Kaiser, 1927 [first published in 1868]); Ernst Troeltsch, *The Social Teachings of the Christian Churches,* tr. Olive Wyon (New York: Harper and Row, 1960 [first published 1911]); Karl Holl, *Gesammelte Aufsätze zur Kirchengeschichte,* 6th ed. (Tübingen: J. C. B. Mohr,

time forward, the Reformer could no longer be simply identified with the denomination that bears his name.

When von Hofmann rejects the view of Christ's death as substitution or propitiation and appeals to Luther's description of it as a victory over sin, death, and the devil, readers will scarcely miss in these statements the antecedents of a view now long since popularized as the "classic" or *Christus victor* idea of the atonement, with particular reference to Luther as its greatest exponent. The existence of this idea, writes the Lundensian systematician Gustav Aulén (1879-1978), had been all but overlooked and its typical features unnoticed. Aulén concludes his study of the main types that the idea of the atonement has assumed throughout the centuries with this statement:

> No form of Christian teaching has any future before it except such as can keep steadily in view the reality of the evil in the world, and go to meet the evil with a battle-song of triumph. Therefore I believe that the classic idea . . . is coming back — that is to say, the genuine, authentic Christian faith.[52]

C. Loose Ends

The criticisms of von Hofmann are legion. From one quarter has come the attack upon his wedding of faith and criticism in the "Two Ways" as inconsistent. From another has come the reproach for his "stacking the deck," for first lifting out from Bible and church what he allegedly derived from experience. Barth writes:

> It is a banal question but one that cannot be avoided, whether something has not happened here which according to the programme should only happen later, whether Hofmann the Christian, who claims to know all this, is not already Hofmann the theologian, who knows the history of the Bible and the Church.[53]

Banal or not, von Hofmann's point of departure in the Christian's experience of the relation to God has earned him the reproach of anthropocentrism, of describing the human without restriction as subject of the entire theological enterprise. However great a debt the young Barth may have ac-

---

1932); Heinrich Böhmer, *Luther and the Reformation in Light of Modern Research,* tr. E. S. G. Potter (New York: Dial, 1930).

52. Gustav Aulén, *Christus Victor,* tr. A. G. Hebert (New York: Macmillan, 1961), 159.

53. Barth, *Protestant Theology,* 613.

knowledged to von Hofmann, in the end he came under the same judgment as all the rest:

> The Gospel is not one thing in the midst of other things, to be directly ap-prehended and comprehended. . . . The Gospel is therefore not an event, nor an experience, nor an emotion — however delicate! Rather, it is the clear and objective perception of what eye hath not seen nor ear heard.[54]

Von Hofmann's definition of faith has been dubbed reminiscence. Gerhard von Rad's allegiance to an understanding of faith as trust in the word of contemporary proclamation led him to include in his *heilsgeschichtlich* scheme what von Hofmann had omitted: the mark of the saving event as hid-den, not empirically demonstrable, thus as promise to be believed. Von Hofmann has been attacked for leaving no room for what alone is amenable to empirical investigation, namely, the history of sin — that history of the breach of fellowship with God paralleling those progressive prefigurements of Christ — and thus of embracing two mutually exclusive views of history, the one historical, the other a priori.

As to *Heilsgeschichte* itself, von Hofmann has been perennially blamed for lack of clarity regarding its relation to the remainder of human history — although he did make an attempt at synthesis. In the first thesis of his theo-logical dissertation, he writes that no other difference exists between univer-sal and ecclesiastical history but the difference between gentiles to be gath-ered to the church, and the church to be extended among the gentiles.[55]

Finally, the assumption that all of history is evident to the eye of faith may lead to an idea that von Hofmann would have never embraced, the idea that the course of history *as such* is evident. Decades later, this idea would re-sult in the notion of the signal role of a single nation in *Heilsgeschichte,* would climax in the awful night of the Third Reich, which plunged an entire genera-tion of scholars into war, and where it did not reduce their number, then robbed them of their youth, and in the end left *Heilsgeschichte* of any variety with few defenders. Conversely, the notion of a course of history as evident per se may result in the identification of *Heilsgeschichte* with a poorly theologized socialism or even capitalism. Attention to "salvation history" as theocentric (that is, which allows that God is free to act or even to reverse

---

54. Karl Barth, *The Epistle to the Romans,* tr. Edwyn C. Hoskyns (London: Oxford Uni-versity Press, 1933), 7, 28.

55. "Inter historiam universalem et historiam ecclesiasticam nihil aliud differt nisi quod differt inter gentes ad ecclesiam congregendam et ecclesiam inter gentes propagandam," quoted in Steck, *Grundlinien,* 22.

what he has begun), as "inclusive" (that is, in which humans are not simply observers of the "mighty acts of God" but part and parcel of those acts themselves), and in which Old Testament prophecy is viewed as situational, can furnish effective resistance to such perversions.[56]

56. Oeming, *Gesamtbiblische Theologien der Gegenwart*, 161-62.

8

ERNST TROELTSCH

The Power of Historical Consciousness

I. Historicism

"In the discovery of history," writes Hajo Holborn, "the Germany of the first half of the nineteenth century made its most original intellectual contribution to the modern world."[1] German historiography owed its uniqueness to the quality of its professionalism. We have highlighted the steady advance of discoveries in historical biblical scholarship, a field dominated by German figures since the mid-eighteenth century. The same holds true for secular studies after 1800. Barthold Georg Niebuhr (1776-1831) and Leopold von Ranke, both of the University of Berlin, led the way in establishing history as a prestigious university discipline. In Niebuhr's investigation of the origins of Rome and in von Ranke's voluminous output covering the whole range of European history, modern, secular, historical method developed. Great advances were made in philology, the employment of archival sources, the assessment of documentary evidence, and the establishment of critical standards for historical research. The discipline of history took its place as part of the romantic revolt against Enlightenment rationalism. Learning much from the celebration of historical and cultural diversity in the thought of Johann Gottfried Herder, Niebuhr, von Ranke, and their students found fulfillment in describing the panorama of human life in all of its particularity *wie es eigentlich gewesen* — as it actually was.

---

1. *A History of Modern Germany: 1648-1840* (New York: Alfred A. Knopf, 1964), 527.

A second factor accounting for the prominence of German historians in the nineteenth century was the fact that they were "consciously guided in their practice by a conception of history."[2] This conception has come to be called *historicism*, which may be defined as the assertion that human life displays in history an infinite variety of manifestations that must be investigated by any observer with complete and open empathy. It is in history that the totality of human life in all of its reality and meaning is to be found. "The world of man is in a state of incessant flux. . . . There is no constant human nature; rather the character of each man reveals itself only in his development."[3]

The historian, argued the Germans, must avoid the temptation to impose rational generalizations on the intractable stuff of history. "There are really only two ways of acquiring knowledge of human affairs," writes von Ranke, "through the perception of the particular, or through abstraction; the latter is the method of philosophy, the former of history."[4] History is made up as much by irrational behavior and accidental events as it is by intention, plan, and order. In the examination of history, intuition *(Ahnung)* and contemplation *(Anschauung)* are as useful to the historian as logic in discerning the complex secrets of historical truth. Despite the variety of phenomena that can effect history and the varied means by which it comes to be known, the historian must concentrate scholarly attention on conscious human willing and action. It is from these that the web of history is finally woven. Historical science is much different from natural science. The natural scientist investigates recurring patterns of natural phenomena that are experimentally repeatable. The historian is the custodian of the unrepeatable. History is the enemy of nature. History began only when humans escaped nature's grasp by conquering the limitations of unreflective animal existence.

Ethically, the historian is obligated to follow historical subject matter wherever it leads and to appreciate its own inherent values, even if those values clash with the value system of the historian. Historicism means the acceptance of the relativity of human life. It is the insight that humanity lives not at the behest of static being and absolute truth, but rather forges itself in a constant process of becoming in which individuals and institutions struggle over competing truths, each vying for its place in the sun.

This is not to say that German historians lacked faith in the ability to

2. George G. Iggers, *The German Conception of History*, rev. ed. (Middletown, Conn.: Wesleyan University Press, 1983), 3.

3. *Ibid.*, 5.

4. Fritz Stern, ed., *The Varieties of History* (Cleveland: Meridian, 1956), 58-59.

organize historical knowledge and make generalizations about history's course and character. Certainly the historian must avoid abstraction and the imposition of alien ideas. But history can reveal its secrets to the patient, obedient observer. Von Ranke writes, "I believe . . . that the discipline of history — at its highest — is itself called upon, and is able, to lift itself in its own fashion from the investigation and observation of particulars to a universal view of events, to a knowledge of the objectively existing relatedness."[5]

Indeed, history has, in von Ranke's opinion, a guiding theme, a dramatic plot. Its fundamental character and destiny are shaped by the struggle of nation-states for identity and power. Through this struggle, human life discovers its potential and forms its very self. The struggle of nation-states is the ultimate historical subject; it bears the imprint of the hand of God. In its War of Liberation from France (1813), Germany entered into this grand struggle for nationhood in its modern form. In the formation of its religious and cultural life, Germany, asserts von Ranke, engaged in the quest for human identity. The drive to nationhood is the fulfillment of the universal instinct for power. In this understanding of Germany's role in history, von Ranke — who taught until 1871, when he retired at the age of seventy-five — had many followers: Johann Gustav Droysen (1808-84), Heinrich von Sybel (1817-95), Ludwig Häusser (1818-67), and Heinrich von Treitschke (1834-96), to name the most prominent.

Von Ranke was not alone in conceiving history as the struggle of nation-states. Behind him stands idealism, and particularly the work of Hegel, who taught the peculiar combination of radical historical relativism and fervent nationalism that came to typify nineteenth-century German historiography. Hegel's philosophy of history is a dark but compelling interpretation of human affairs that centers in the nation-state as the vehicle of the Absolute Spirit. Within the constant fluctuation of historical life, human beings are subject to forces beyond their control. The nation-state is a center of stability for the realization of larger purposes. It provides meaning for individuals who dedicate themselves to its goals. To achieve its aims, the nation-state must exercise power. It engages in activities (for example, the making and breaking of alliances, the practice of war) that go beyond the bounds of individual morality. Self-interest, not selflessness, motivates it and shapes its ideals. Nation-states are not confined by the rules of natural law. The natural law tradition is for Hegel a naive illusion of abstract reasoning that has no realistic consequence in politics. This rejection of natural law is a significant development. It separates German thought in the nineteenth century from the

5. *Ibid.*, 59.

shared values of Western political philosophy. In the German view, it is not the securing of the "rights of man" or the defense of "inalienable truths" but the exercise of power that is the path to the corporate freedom of a society. The nation-state is ultimately a *Machtstaat* (power state). History contains experiences of great agony and exaltation. It will never issue in lasting peace. The struggle of history will continue to the end of time. When struggle ceases, history ends.

The political predicament of Germany in the first half of the nineteenth century provided the cultural context for these reflections on history by the intellectual elite. The German people were divided between the "competing truths" of Catholic Austria and Protestant Prussia. They were fragmented by ethnic strife as the former "Holy Roman Empire" contained within its fluid borders not only Germans but a host of Slavic peoples. The upheaval caused by the Revolution of 1848 confirmed Hegel's analysis regarding the primacy of power politics. Western liberalism, in the form of democratic parliamentary reform, failed to achieve the dream of German nationhood. If rational deliberation on constitutional rights could not create a viable state, then it must be formed by force and will. "To rule means to exercise power," wrote August Ludwig von Rochau (1810-73) in his widely read *Principles of Realpolitik* (1853). "This direct connection of power and rule forms the fundamental truth of all politics and the key to all history."[6] The success of Otto von Bismarck (1815-98) as Prussian Chancellor under Wilhelm I (1797-1888) appeared to ratify Rochau's dictum. In 1871 Bismarck achieved the establishment of the German Empire by Machiavellian diplomacy and force of arms. That Germany defeated its onetime conqueror, France, on the field of battle not only sweetened the final triumph but had the effect of sanctioning Germany's unique path, its *Sonderweg*, into modernity.

This dramatic interplay of ideas and events understandably captured the imagination of the *Bildungsbürgertum* or educated middle class in the latter half of the nineteenth century. Germany was powerful, prosperous, cultured. Its academics — who, it must never be forgotten, were civil servants in the employ of the state — allied themselves with the benevolent *Zeitgeist* of German achievement. They included the theological professorate, which readily adapted itself to the historicist worldview. The neopietism that dominated the regime of Friedrich Wilhelm IV eventually fell into disrepute, and theology embraced the historicist vision. In the work of Albrecht Ritschl, for example — whose importance lies precisely in "the representative character

---

6. Quoted in Hajo Holborn, *A History of Modern Germany,* vol. 3: *1840-1945* (New York: Alfred A. Knopf, 1969), 117.

of his thought"[7] — the church was conceived analogously to a struggling nation-state that creates itself in the crucible of contending historical forces. History is the story of striving, willing humanity. Jesus is the founder of a community that is the vehicle of freedom and purpose for those who belong to it. Knowledge of God and his kingdom comes not by abstract reasoning. (Both traditional metaphysics and dogmatics, according to Ritschl, do more to obscure God than to reveal him.) God is not discovered in the nebulousness of ecstasy or the warmth of religious feeling. (Ritschl treats mysticism and pietism with deep suspicion.) God is known by practical engagement in human affairs. Knowledge of the divine is moral knowledge. The meaning of faith is the mastery of the natural environment so that one may enter the course of history and engage in the exercise of power through the divine calling of one's vocation: "Religion springs up as faith in superhuman spiritual powers, by whose help the power which man possesses of himself is in some way supplemented, and elevated into a unity of its own kind which is a match for the pressure of the natural world."[8] On the basis of this fundamental interpretation, Ritschl conceived Christianity both as a relative phenomenon of history, ever changing the particular forms of its faith, and as a transcendent reality that perseveres in its identity through history in the battle against contrary forces. Christianity is a varied story, but has a single, dramatic plot.

Ritschl was the teacher of a generation of theologians and church historians. His students were many and varied: Adolf von Harnack, Wilhelm Herrmann (1846-1922), Martin Kähler, and many more. But it was Ernst Troeltsch, more than any other, who was willing to confront, in methodological terms, the full power of the historicist vision of German historiography and explore its implications for the understanding of Bible and modern culture. The question of faith's relation to history was Troeltsch's primary religious and theological question throughout his productive life. It is needless to put or answer the question of Troeltsch's relevance to our time. Current reference to him as offering a "thus far unexcelled explanation of the structure of historical criticism" reflects dependence among the majority of biblical interpreters, whatever their demurrer.[9] It is indeed arguable that none before him,

---

7. Claude Welch, *Protestant Thought in the Nineteenth Century,* vol. 2: *1870-1914* (New Haven: Yale University Press, 1985), 1.

8. *The Christian Doctrine of Justification and Reconciliation,* tr. H. R. Mackintosh and A. B. Macaulay (Edinburgh: T&T Clark, 1900), 3:199.

9. Peter Stuhlmacher, *Historical Criticism and Theological Interpretation of Scripture,* tr. Roy A. Harrisville (Philadelphia: Fortress, 1977), 45. Stuhlmacher's own attempt at overcoming the dilemma created by historical criticism of the Bible does not involve departing from, but supplementing the principles enunciated by Troeltsch. See 11, 44-46, 48, etc.

and none since, has given such prominence to the question of the degree to which critical, historical science requires rereading of Christian faith.

Troeltsch's birth and death dates agree with his place in theological history. Born in the nineteenth century, researching the past, he marked what Karl Barth once called the end of the "good old days" for evangelical theology.[10] Working and dying in the twentieth, seeking a way into the future, Troeltsch not only furnished the occasion for the emergence of a new, "dialectical" theology following the First World War, but, insofar as discussion of the relation of history to faith is still alive, he dominates that discussion — at least from its "historical" side.

II. Biography

Ernst Peter Troeltsch was born 17 February 1865, at Haunstetten near Augsburg, Germany, oldest child of the physician Ernst Troeltsch and his wife Eugenie. His family traced its ancestry to ancient burghers who had lived for centuries in the hilly country between Swabia and Bavaria (in the Lausitz, between the Elbe and the Oder), but who later had settled at Nuremberg and Augsburg. Completing his secondary education with "good" and very good" grades, Troeltsch entered the Augsburg Lyceum in 1883, and a year later began military service as a one-year volunteer. In 1884 he began his university studies in theology, first at Erlangen, then at Berlin and Göttingen, again at Erlangen, concluding them at Göttingen in 1891 with the licentiate of theology degree, along with permission to teach for two years in the department of history. While at Göttingen Troeltsch came under the influence of Ritschl and Rudolf Hermann Lotze (1817-81). In those same university years, Troeltsch had burned the midnight oil reading Kant and Schleiermacher.

In 1892, following a year in Göttingen as instructor without salary or stipend — the Ministry having rejected the faculty's appeal on his behalf due to lack of funds — Troeltsch was called to an associate professorship in systematic theology at the University of Bonn. In 1893 he received the invitation to full professorship at Heidelberg, where he remained for the next twenty years. At Heidelberg Troeltsch came into contact with Max Weber (1864-1920). In an obituary notice for Weber, he wrote that he had been in daily conversation with the great sociologist, to whom he owed a goodly portion of

10. *The Humanity of God*, tr. Thomas Wieser (Richmond: John Knox, 1960), 14. Barth's reference to Troeltsch's symptomatic move from theology to philosophy in 1914 is inaccurate. Prior to the 1914 Berlin appointment, Troeltsch had already occupied twin posts in philosophy and theology at Heidelberg since 1910.

his learning and understanding.[11] Finally, in 1914, Troeltsch was called to a professorship in philosophy at the University of Berlin, where he resided till his death on 1 February 1923.

Troeltsch was politically active, through pamphleteering — an avocation shared with academics of his time — but also through actual service to the state. At the outbreak of the First World War, he enthusiastically defended the German conception of history, opposing "the ideas of 1914" to the hated French "ideas of 1789." Germany, argued Troeltsch, had rightly traveled its own path to nationhood apart from the course of Western nations. Germany roots itself in "Prussian power *(Machtwesen)*, Kantian duty consciousness and the German-Idealistic cosmopolitan content of our culture." Germany, unlike the individualistic West, knows "the essence of genuine political ethics." It alone realizes that freedom is "not equality but service by the individual at his proper place" within the social order. The meaning of individual life is found in obligation to the state.[12]

Troeltsch was not an uncritical observer of Prussian policy. In 1915 he signed a petition urging the German Chancellor, Theobald Bethmann-Hollweg (1856-1921), to disavow the annexation of sovereign states. He later wrote that history's most hideous insult was that Bethmann-Hollweg, victimized by a reckless, posturing Kaiser and a disastrous military policy, should be billed for the "German crime."[13] In 1917, in apparent contradiction to his publicly stated views on the German conception of corporate "freedom," Troeltsch joined in the demand for immediate introduction of a universal, equal, direct, and secret voting right. In the same year he participated in the "National Confederation for Freedom and Fatherland," which opposed notions of peace through victory for the sake of peace with understanding. In 1919 Troeltsch participated in the second Extraordinary Party Day of the left-wing, liberal German Democratic Party. From 1919 to 1921 he served in the auxiliary position of Undersecretary of State for Evangelical Concerns at the Prussian Ministry of Culture. In his Jewish friend Walther Rathenau (1867-1922), minister of the Weimar Republic murdered by fanatics on the right, Troeltsch, an ardent foe of anti-Semitism, saw an analogy to England's Benjamin Disraeli (1804-1881), passionate for the spiritual and moral rebirth of his country. He spoke of Rathenau's awareness of the fascist peril, and of his fearless death "at

11. Ernst Troeltsch, *Deutscher Geist und Westeuropa,* ed. Hans Baron (Aalen: Scientia Verlag, 1966), 249.

12. See the essays: "Privat Moral und Staatsmoral" and "Die deutsche Idee von Freiheit," in *Deutsche Zukunft* (Berlin, 1916), quoted and tr. in Iggers, *The German Conception of History,* 187.

13. Troeltsch, *Deutscher Geist und Westeuropa,* 255.

the barricades."[14] By 1922, less than a year from death, Troeltsch was ready to make this sober reassessment of the course of German politics:

> The conception of the abundance of national spirits was transformed into a feeling of contempt for the idea of Universal Humanity. The pantheistic idolization of the state turned into blind respect, devoid of all ideas, for success and power. The Romantic Revolution sank into a complacent contentment with things as they are. From the idea of a particular law and right for a given time and place, men proceeded to a purely positivistic acceptance of the state. The conception of a morality of a higher spiritual order which transcends bourgeois conventions passed into moral scepticism. From the urge of the German spirit to find embodiment in a state there arose the same kind of imperialism as anywhere else in the world.[15]

In Troeltsch's tumultuous political journey from "right" to "left," the basic insight of the historicist vision was ironically confirmed. The individual self is indeed a constantly developing entity who finds identity in relation to the fate of the nation-state. The agony of Germany was the agony of Troeltsch's last decade.

III. The Power of Historical Consciousness

A. The Task

According to Troeltsch's own testimony, the historical studies that had formed him soon collided with the theological-philosophical work in which he had become immersed. In his introduction to the series of essays for which he is best known, Troeltsch acknowledges his debt to Ritschl, who had attempted to adjust traditional Protestant dogma to the modern intellectual and religious situation. The synthesis was too facile for Troeltsch's taste. He contends that it did justice neither to the tradition's actual historical setting nor to the present situation.[16] Analysis of early Protestantism and analysis of the modern world will never be abandoned; nor will the attempt at synthesis of the two. Troeltsch never denies this heritage from Ritschl. But the nature of the analysis and the nature of the attempt at synthesis are different from that of the old master.

---

14. *Ibid.*, 258.

15. *Ibid.*, 17-18; quoted and tr. in Iggers, *The German Conception of History,* 188.

16. *The Social Teaching of the Christian Churches,* tr. Olive Wyon (New York: Harper and Row, 1960), 1:19.

The task, as Troeltsch sees it, is to undertake a new and rigorous historical analysis of the dogmatic tradition and the modern situation, and to arrive at their possible synthesis. The historical task is thus twofold: "To make clear . . . both the ecclesiastical dogmatic tradition of Protestantism in its own historical sense, and the intellectual and practical situation of the present day in its true fundamental tendencies."[17] The task of synthesizing takes specific shape in an attempt to relate Protestantism to the religious character of the modern spirit. But the decision as to whatever it is in Protestantism that will not simply survive but will also enrich modernity involves the decision as to precisely which "Protestantism" should survive; and with that the now famous distinction between "old" and "new" is born.

Lest he appear to fall prey to indiscriminate relativism in the discharge of the historical task, Troeltsch turns to metaphysics in order to establish the guarantee of an independent, universal, religious consciousness. Troeltsch is convinced that theologians have ignored or been unconscious of this "basic, religious-scientific idea." What is needed is investigation into the place, origin, and meaning of religion in human consciousness, followed by research into the law and context of that idea within the particularities of historical life. "We want to see," Troeltsch writes, "whether or not religion, according to what it says of itself, has a place among the immediate . . . contents of the life of the soul."[18] The move inevitably led to preoccupation with ethics, that "higher and most principled science," a concern pursued to the end of his life.

While it is easy to understand what led Troeltsch in Ritschl's direction — Ritschl was, after all, the teacher of the age — it is much more difficult to discern what led Troeltsch away from Ritschl toward new territory of increasingly frank secularism. The suggestion that a single theme underlay all Troeltsch ever did — namely, the encounter with German historicism and its challenge to the normative claims of Christian faith — is as valid an explanation of the combination of historian, philosopher, and ethicist in him as any other. In the words of one biographer, Troeltsch's question read: "In view of the anarchy of values, prevailing since the shattering of the Christian world of ideas, in view of the secret, fundamental temper of the time, how does one arrive at a new world order?"[19]

---

17. *Ibid.*, 1:19. See also Troeltsch, *Protestantism and Progress* (Philadelphia: Fortress, 1986), 13-14, 88-89.

18. "Die Selbständigkeit der Religion," *Zeitschrift für Theologie und Kirche* 5 (1895): 386; see also 364, 369-70.

19. H. Benckert, "Troeltsch," in *Die Religion in Geschichte und Gegenwart,* ed. Kurt Galling, 3rd ed. (Tübingen: J. C. B. Mohr, 1957-62), 6:1044.

B. The Method

In a treatise unrivaled in its explanation of the structure of historical criticism, Troeltsch proceeds to describe the authentic method of historical analysis — *Über historische und dogmatische Methode (Concerning Historical and Dogmatic Method)* — the point at which the Christian world of ideas begins to shatter.[20] From now on, writes Troeltsch, Protestant ideas of faith will require the scientific means of historical research and psychology for their explanation. In fact, to decide questions of faith merely from the reasons faith supplies robs Christian conviction of its universal validity. This means that dogmatic method of whatever stripe, not just traditional dogmatics, needs surrendering; only the historical method is appropriate to theology. Once this method is applied, Troeltsch argues, it will transform everything like a leaven and finally burst every previous form.[21]

This said by way of introduction, Troeltsch now sets forth what he believes to be the "three essential pieces" or axioms of the historical method. The first axiom requires acclimatization in historical criticism (the principle of criticism); the second, knowledge of the significance of analogy (the principle of analogy); and the third, knowledge of the correlation occurring among all historical events (the principle of correlation).

According to the principle of criticism, the historical disciplines yield only judgments of probability, and of vastly different grades. For this reason each tradition has to be investigated for the degree of probability attaching to it. Further, each tradition has to be incorporated within the nature and character of all traditions waiting to be researched. Such investigation, Troeltsch adds, spells a principal alteration in our relation to the "monstrous" amount of tradition adhering to Western civilization.

The principle of analogy prescribes the means for facilitating such criticism: "The analogy of what is occurring before our eyes or taking place within us is the key to criticism." This "omnipotence" of analogy spells the principal similarity *(Gleichartigkeit)* of all historical occurrence that, while acknowledging the uniqueness of historical events, asserts that they are also analogous to events drawn from life today. Through analogies, Troeltsch states, we arrive at the causal explanation of past events. In particular, this means the incorporation of Jewish-Christian history within the analogy of all other historical occurrence.

Respecting the principle of correlation, Troeltsch writes that the con-

20. *GS*, 2:729-53.
21. *Ibid.*, 729-31.

strual of analogy on the basis of the similarity of the human spirit and its historical activities assumes the alternation of all the phenomena of human existence. No change can occur without precursor or follower; all occurrence consists of a continual flux in which everything relates to everything else.[22] Thus, the area of what can be exempted or removed from analogy has shrunk; the "naked difference" between true and false, natural and revealed religion disappears.

Troeltsch accepts the full implications of historicist relativism.[23] He claims that whoever concedes even the least to an historical study based on such axioms is required to surrender everything to it. From a purely orthodox standpoint, therefore, it bears "a certain similarity to the devil."[24] Troeltsch insists that his personal religious views have been carefully excluded from his historical analysis, that his inquiry has not aimed at providing a basis for any judgment of value, although he does admit to the "generally idealistic basic view" that underlies his research.[25]

The enemy of historical criticism and its application is inherited dogmatic Augustinianism, or "old Protestantism," with its "supernaturalism," its despairing sense of sin, its great world-suffering imposed on the race for its purification and punishment, and its notion of miraculous redemption from a corrupted and God-abandoned, natural state of things. Orthodoxy, Troeltsch states, proceeds from a fixed point of departure totally removed from history and its relativity. Miracle thus lies at the basis of its metaphysics, the supernatural proof of an authority that excludes all analogy. The result, Troeltsch contends, is a division of human existence into two parts — one requiring an extraordinary activity of God, the other subject to the ordinary tests of life. By contrast, Troeltsch's method is truly "Protestant," since it has emerged from criticism of the old Roman Catholic notion of authority, a criticism prepared for by the Enlightenment.[26] For Troeltsch, true Protestantism in its historical development is both companion and contributor to the emergence of modernity.

Troeltsch does not restrict his criticism to orthodoxy. Ritschlians, contemporaries in the train of his old teacher, are also the object of his attack. Their advocacy of the independence of the religious sense — a conviction shared with Troeltsch — seems merely to be a ruse for isolating Christianity

22. *Ibid.*, 731-34.

23. Troeltsch, "Die Selbständigkeit der Religion," 371.

24. *GS*, 2:734.

25. Troeltsch, *Protestantism and Progress*, 14, 100; "Die Selbständigkeit der Religion," 415.

26. *GS*, 2:737, 739-45; see also *Protestantism and Progress*, 27, 50.

from philosophy, as though in isolation it could be scientifically proved to be absolute truth. Troeltsch concedes that the harnessing of religion to philosophy or speculation may lead to submerging the peculiarity of an individual religion in the abyss of metaphysical generality, but stoutly resists the suggestion that his application of method necessitates such a result.[27]

C. The Results

The general results to which Troeltsch's method brought him are twofold. First, the method renders every individual datum uncertain. What is certain is merely its effect, together with its historical context. In respect of religious faith, this means that the context of faith is loosed from its individual details. It means that it is impossible to establish faith upon any single datum since the link between faith and its historical details is mediated through its context. Of this result, and in terms of the relation between faith and probability, Troeltsch writes:

> It is possible for us to live from a purely religiously based certainty, but we are still infinitely more subject to the anxious fear of self-deception than when we allow for that increment of probability. Human science as such cannot achieve more than probability. Certainty is always a matter of faith.[28]

Second, the method sets a particular religious faith within a wider religious-historical context. This results in evaluating Christian faith from the perspective of "religion" as a unified phenomenon, operating according to its own laws, enjoying relative independence from other aspects of life, and revealing its content by way of historical movement.[29] Opposed to all attempts at portraying Christian faith as the highest expression of this unity, or of conceiving that unity in metaphysical, monistic fashion, Troeltsch writes: "Religions are first of all pure facts, and are scornful of all theories. Only these religions themselves yield essential information about themselves. All else is secondary."[30] Troeltsch exhorts his reader to live within his own "complex," undisturbed by questions concerning the absolute, whether philosophical or religious: "One has only to resolve to let each complex go untroubled on its

27. Troeltsch, "Die Selbständigkeit der Religion," 373-75, 378.
28. *Ibid.,* 436.
29. *Ibid.,* 368, 370.
30. *Ibid.,* 379.

way, and to live in each according to its own special demands, without elevating any one of them monistically into a universal basis or a single all-determining accent."[31] Use of the historical method thus demonstrates the relative uncertainty of all historical knowledge, the link between faith and fact as mediate and relative, and the necessity for weaving a given religious faith within universal history.[32]

The specific results to which Troeltsch's method carries him are four-fold. First, the historical investigation of Christianity demonstrates that it is but one phenomenon, be it ever so sublime, alongside others with similar claims.[33] Later in life, Troeltsch would assign Christianity highest rank only within the European-American cultural sphere. Writing that the evidence for Christianity as a manifestation of the Divine Life lies in a "profound, inner experience," and that this experience yields the criterion for Christianity's validity, he insists that it retains such validity only "for us." Other racial groups, living under entirely different conditions, might experience contact with the Divine in a radically different way.[34]

Second, of Christianity's founder, Troeltsch concludes that criticism has returned him to history "where all is finite and conditioned." Yet for the Christian community and cult, the position of Jesus is central. Troeltsch opens his essay on the historical Jesus by attacking the radical assertion that Jesus never lived, or that the main lines of his teaching cannot be known. Next, he outlines the modern conception of faith, which dispenses with an historical Christ, since the idea of humanity's redemption through a miracle has been exchanged for its redemption through practical knowledge of God's true and innermost essence as will. This conception, writes Troeltsch, harks back to the early mystics who found Christianity in "the eternally advancing operation of God upon the soul," without linking it to the historical personality of Jesus. Troeltsch concedes that it is quite impossible to treat Christian faith as something absolutely separate: "Christocentrism" belongs to that "idyllic small and narrow world picture of the ancients and the Middle Ages." In the third portion of his essay, Troeltsch admits to membership in the group that recognizes modern thought but also sees in Christianity religious powers that should not be given up. In a reference to Schleiermacher, Ritschl, and Wilhelm Herrmann, for whom, in modern parlance, "continuity" between the historical Jesus and the Christ of faith consisted in the former's setting the

---

31. *Christianity: Its History and Application*, tr. F. von Hügel (London: University of London Press, 1923), 121.
32. *GS*, 2:736-38.
33. See "Die Selbständigkeit der Religion," 372.
34. Troeltsch, *Christianity*, 26.

latter in motion, thus rendering the power of Christianity inexplicable apart from the impression of Jesus' person, Troeltsch writes that it is but a weaker form of the old idea of original sin and redemption. What remains, then, is the merely symbolical significance of Jesus for the Christian idea. But it is precisely this position that lacks "all forms of community" and constitutes the "real sickness" of modern Christianity.

Troeltsch proceeds to the argument that in "religions of the spirit" the prophets and founder personalities serve as rallying points, that individuals with merely parallel thoughts and experiences can never simply coexist for long without establishing communities with a concrete focus. Lessing's "third kingdom," in which religious faith would live from its own power without the support of history, will probably never arrive. As long as Christianity survives, it will always be connected with the central position of Christ in the cult. "Social psychology" and the demand of history for concrete embodiment thus yield the locus within which continuity should be fixed. Though a personal relationship with Jesus is not possible, he nevertheless remains indispensable. Since religion or "a view of God" does not occur in isolation but originates in the "medium" of a reality surrounding and acting upon us, and since Jesus is so intimately connected with the content of Christian faith as its "enduring medium," he has been "incorporated" as the indispensable symbol of its language and portrayal.[35] For this reason, Troeltsch concludes, whoever belongs to the world of Christian experience will never be able to see a mere myth at its center.

Troeltsch concedes the similarity of his "quest" to that of the Schleiermacher-Ritschl-Herrmann school, but with the demurrer that his argument is a matter of social psychology:

> The manner in which I represent [the view of God] here, differs from most attempts named only in the fact that I do not set out from any particular philosophical or other system, but on the basis of a generally idealistic view attempt to analyze the psychological and historical phenomena of religion as such.[36]

Again, he recites the favorite religious opinons of the day, their relation to idealisms without cult or history, and their inability to make anything of community, church, cult, or preaching. And once more he declares bankruptcy on the orthodox notion of the absolute uniqueness of the Redeemer or his church, though speaking of Jesus as the center about which all the prepa-

35. "Die Selbständigkeit der Religion," 386, 417.
36. *Ibid.*, 415.

rations and effects of the Christian and prophetic type of belief cluster, stating that as long as the Christian-prophetic religion continues, "all possibilities of a community and cult, and so all real power and the extension of belief, will be tied to the central position of Christ for faith."[37]

The third result of Troeltsch's application of historical method concerns the beginnings of the modern world. Troeltsch concludes that there is no direct road leading from "Protestant church-civilization" to modern civilization independent of the church. On the contrary, the Protestant Reformation is merely a transitional element, a vigorous "second blooming" of the Middle Ages. It is the great struggle for freedom at the end of the seventeenth and in the eighteenth century that actually brings the Middle Ages to an end. It is the Enlightenment that first paves the way for an historical mode of thought.[38] Proof of Protestantism as transitional, as standing with one foot in the old and the other in the new, lies in its elevation of the Bible above tradition, thus above all analogy with "natural productions." Protestantism, and not Catholicism, first closes the biblical canon and holds it aloof from all other human literature.[39] Further proof lies with one of the two great divisions within Protestantism, that is, with Lutheranism, characterized, in Troeltsch's chastened postwar view, by its "anti-democratic and absolutistic disposition toward the state; its non-resistance and glorification of obedience; its traditionalist attitude toward economics, and its glorification of the inherited system of dividing professions into estates."[40] This passivity, writes Troeltsch, this affirmation of the state's omnipotence resulting in the relinquishing of all political-social activity to the state, derives from a biblical-religious idea of seclusion over against the world, and ultimately leads to those problems of theodicy still burdening Lutheranism, inducing it to make salvation dependent upon the attitude of the creature, in order to save God's righteousness and love. Calvinism — because of its active involvement from the beginning in the cities in which it took root — is better suited for entry into the modern age.[41]

37. Troeltsch, *Writings on Theology and Religion*, tr. Robert Morgan and Michael Pye (Atlanta: John Knox, 1977), 182-206.

38. Troeltsch, *Protestantism and Progress*, 9, 52; *GS*, 2:745.

39. *Ibid.*, 81.

40. *GS*, 4:255.

41. *Ibid.*, 4:256, 258. Earlier, and in the prewar context, Troeltsch took a much more accommodating stance with regard to the relation of Lutheranism to the state. The significance of Lutheranism's attempts to hold to the "simpler conditions" obtaining in the Middle Ages was not due, said Troeltsch, to subjection or accommodation to the status quo, but rather to the search for a situation in which it would be easier "to carry the Gospel ethic into practice with less compromise"; *The Social Teaching of the Christian Churches*, 87.

Finally, there are consequences for ethics accruing to Troeltsch's application of historical method. In the brief volume of lectures intended for delivery at London University but never realized, Troeltsch first adverts to the relation between the "endless movement of the stream of historical life" and the need of the human mind to limit and shape it through fixed standards. Despite that need, present existence leaves no hope for realizing humanity's ethical ideal by damming up or canalizing historical life with a timelessly valid morality that transcends history. Historicist reality will not permit fixation of human character and its rules of behavior; there is no natural law. Troeltsch concedes that while this contemporary mode of thought initially promised release from religious confessions, state, and education, in its final stages it appears to be the tragic end of liberalism and to lead to "dissolution, decomposition, and spiritual anarchy." How could historicist relativism be mastered by an ethic that is "conceptually assured and clarified"? Troeltsch's answer is in terms of "the ethic of cultural values." Harnessing existence by fixed standards, by "the morality of conscience," leads away from history into the sphere of the timelessly valid. The ethic of cultural values leads into history and development. And it does so, Troeltsch states, through its concentration upon the individual, through its accenting the attainment and defense of a free personality, its foundations in itself, possessing a unity of its own. In this, Troeltsch writes, lies the "end of moral action." Thus, while he rejected natural law, it appears that, at the end, Troeltsch had found his way to a political doctrine of natural rights that was reflected in his courageous support, unlike that of other German academics, for the doomed effort of the Weimar government at parliamentary democracy.

The results of Troeltsch's use of historical method, general and concrete, and viewed from the perspective of the historical, philosophical, or the ethical, are amply summarized in an article written for the first edition of a product of the school for which he would be celebrated as chief thinker. The school was the History of Religions, and the product *Die Religion in Geschichte und Gegenwart*, still the greatest of its kind:

> Christianity is not the only revelation and redemption, but the climax of revelations and redemptions working to lift humankind to God. . . . Its revelation is . . . a religious heightening and elevating of personal life. . . . As any other, its revelation is an interpenetration of the divine and human. . . . Every identification of the divine within that revelation involves an ever new task of personal surrender and thorough study, in which each must first determine for himself what is divine. . . . This constitutes a continual call to struggle against raw nature and sin. . . . The degree of distance between the Christian revelation and non-Christian revelations will . . . be evaluated in very differ-

ent ways. In a few . . . we will detect more or less closely related revelations. . . . But the distance between Christianity and all non-Christian religions will . . . to a large extent always be shown to be extraordinarily great.[42]

D. The Guarantee

In his essay on historical and dogmatic method, Troeltsch asserts that, by definition, his position opposes the full, secular consequences of historical relativism.[43] In response to the atheistic or "illusionist" description of religion as "anthropomorphic eudaimonism," as sprung from wish or need, Troeltsch insists that the analysis of religious need clearly reveals an antecedent object. Viewed pyschologically, the atheistic position expresses a "monstrous tenet." It assumes that a phenomenon, originating in an idea, originally gave birth to that idea, an assumption that would eliminate consciousness. No serious thinker, writes Troeltsch, would imagine that religion arises purely and exclusively from desire. Not even John Stuart Mill (1806-73), Auguste Comte (1798-1857), or Feuerbach dispensed with religion in terms of the necessity of a meaning or goal for human striving. To argue that the idea of God is in direct proportion to religious benefit is as much as to say that the benefit has been aroused by the idea of God.[44] "The very curse and torment of the modern world," writes Troeltsch, "seems to be that it only knows the directive forces of the mind as particular realities at play by the side of one another."[45]

What is it that guarantees independence and universality to religion? The answer, writes Troeltsch — and it may be found in almost all of his work — is "religious intuition," an involuntary relation to the infinite, a nonderivable and immediate relation to God, a contact with the supersensuous world, an ideal perception or experience of deity through an unconscious activity of soul. This intuition or "revelation" — Troeltsch does not hesitate to identify it — is linked to all spiritual life, but proceeds according to its own laws. It is in possession of its own inner dialectic and power for development. It utilizes the collapse of human hopes in order to fill the abandoned space with its own ideas and sentiments.[46] From the psychological perspective, says Troeltsch,

---

42. Troeltsch, "Offenbarung, dogmatisch," in *Die Religion in Geschichte und Gegenwart* (Tübingen: J. C. B. Mohr, 1913), 4:921-22.

43. *GS*, 2:747.

44. Troeltsch, "Die Selbständigkeit der Religion," 385, 399, 402-3, 405, 409, 412.

45. Troeltsch, *Christianity*, 107.

46. *GS*, 2:739; "Die Selbständigkeit der Religion," 368, 396, 413, 431; *The Social Teaching of the Christian Churches*, 48.

this intuition consists of a linkage of ideas with accompanying feelings, from which emerge stimuli to the will. The ideas can be incredibly varied, so that the accompanying feelings or impulses to the will can take on the most varied coloration. The point, however, is that this "content of soul" is universal, based on the supposed similarity of human nature.[47]

Since this intuition belongs to a sphere other than that of sense, it lacks the similarity and clarity of sense perception. For this reason, it makes appeal to the feelings of value and impulses of the will. For this reason also, it has to grow by stages within the race and the individual. "The image of the tree," writes Troeltsch, "is subject to much less development than the idea of love or truthfulness." Further, Troeltsch describes this "faith" or "relation to an infinite," in Ritschlian fashion, as ultimately ethical in nature, as including the striving toward a highest good. The ethical a priori is comparable to the religious a priori, and is nourished from two great historical streams. The one flows by way of the Sermon on the Mount, Stoicism, and Kant into a morality of personality and conscience. The other, sprung from antiquity, flows by way of Schleiermacher into an ethics of cultural values, develops historically in marriage and the family, the economy, law and the state, art, science, and religion — the independence of these values corresponding to the independence of the religious a priori.[48]

In outlining the development of the religious sense, Troeltsch contrasts a stage of "naivete" with that of the "culture of reflection," assigning superiority to the former, in which prophetic Old Testament religion and the religion of Jesus first broke through the limitation of the human spirit's original tie to nature. Since, he writes, in all higher religions the subjective experience of God requires supplementing in a religious object, conceptual marks and representations of the deity inevitably result — for which reason the personality of Jesus has become the abiding medium for Christianity. Similarly, it is at the highest stages of religious development that the indissoluble link between religious and ethical faith purely and sharply emerges. On the other hand, this experience or "Divine Life" within history does not tend toward unity or universality, but rather toward the "fulfilment of the highest potentialities of each separate department of life." Christianity is thus not the reconciliation and goal of all the forces of history. Rather, that goal lies in the development of the autonomous self.[49]

Protestantism, Troeltsch maintains, and Luther above all, gives to the

47. Troeltsch, "Die Selbständigkeit der Religion," 380, 381; *GS*, 2:745.
48. Troeltsch, "Die Selbständigkeit der Religion," 391, 396; *GS*, 2:745.
49. *GS*, 2:748; "Die Selbständigkeit der Religion," 396-97, 417, 421; *Christianity*, 14.

world this "metaphysic of absolute personality," according to which it is humanity's destiny to acquire perfection through ascent to God as the source of personal life. There is nothing new in Luther's goal — assurance of deliverance from condemnation incurred through original sin. What is new is Luther's introduction of the means by which to achieve it — a personal, subjective conviction, seizing the inner self at its core, bringing it into closest touch with the divine activity. And the way comes to overshadow the goal, ultimately giving free rein to the establishment of faith on a purely subjective, inward foundation.

Finally, since it is left to the individual to orient existence by choosing a central value that will function as the "pivot of organization," and since that choice rests on the individual, personal experience of that "towering power in whose hands lies our salvation or damnation," it is faith that ultimately decides, faith that justifies.[50]

In this concept of an independent, universal, and necessary religious sense in tandem with a moral sense equally independent, universal, and necessary lies Troeltsch's answer to relativism. That this concept derives from purely historical investigation, from what religion has to say of itself and with nothing added, of this Troeltsch is absolutely convinced. "Religions," he writes in an echo of von Ranke, "are first of all pure facts, and scorn all theories. Only they themselves give the essential information about themselves."[51]

IV. Assessment

In his history of nineteenth-century theology, Barth traces Troeltsch's lineage from Johann Gottfried Herder to Novalis, to Schleiermacher, to Wilhelm Martin Leberecht de Wette, and Richard Rothe (1799-1867) — in other words, to the romantic movement in theology.[52] Troeltsch would have agreed with the assessment. With others in his genealogy whom Barth describes as "circumventing Kant," Troeltsch could assert that the total isolation of nature and the surrender of phenomena to a mechanical law of causation have led to ignoring the witness of the immeasurable reality surrounding us. He is an advocate of feeling as arousing the will, that ground of being and becoming.[53]

---

50. Troeltsch, *Protestantism and Progress*, 11, 30; "Die Selbständigkeit der Religion," 397; *Christianity*, 95-98.

51. Troeltsch, "Die Selbständigkeit der Religion," 379; see also 370, 385.

52. Karl Barth, *Protestant Theology in the Nineteenth Century*, tr. Brian Cozens and John Bowden (Valley Forge: Judson, 1973), 316, 343, 361, 597.

53. Troeltsch, "Die Selbständigkeit der Religion," 380-81, 389-90; see also *Protestant-*

Barth's further description is harsher: the lifework of this "last great Romantic in theology" consists chiefly in "the proclamation and ever-renewed proclamation of programmes." In contrast to Schleiermacher, who took the trouble to safeguard the "specifically theological quality of theology," Troeltsch's theology is a "thorough distraction."[54]

But if, as Barth assumes, romanticism is pure "as yearning," there is more to Troeltsch than yearning, thus more than romanticism. There is Idealism, Hegelianism. In his essay on dogmatic and historical method, Troeltsch acknowledges his debt to Hegel:

> In essence my view flatly opposes the historical relativism which is the result of historical method only for the atheistic or religiously skeptical position. And, it seeks to annul this relativism by means of the concept of history as an unfolding of the divine reason. Here lie the inalienable merits of Hegelian doctrine, which need only be freed of its metaphysic of the absolute, its dialectic of opposites, and its specifically logical notion of religion.[55]

The word here translated "annul" is Hegel's favorite *(Aufhebung)*, and the identification of the "religious intuition," that ideal perception or experience of deity through an unconscious activity of soul, with revelation — more, with the "Divine Reason" or the "Divine Life" — clearly has Hegel for its father.

And there is more than Idealism in Troeltsch. The argument in "Die Selbständigkeit der Religion" ("The Independence of Religion") concerning the apparent lack of clarity within the sphere of ideas, in contrast to the world of sense — as a result of which the sphere of ideas must make appeal to feelings of value and impulses of the will, and for which reason the moral development of the race or individual occurs by degrees, an argument illustrated in the contrast between the growth of the tree and that of love[56] — reads like a paraphrase of Aristotle's *Nicomachean Ethics*:

> The moral virtues, then, are produced in us neither *by* Nature nor *against* Nature. Nature, indeed, prepares in us the ground for their reception, but their complete formation is the production of habit. . . . The moral virtues we do acquire by first exercising them. . . . We become just by performing

---

ism and Progress, 98; and "The Ideas of Natural Law and Humanity in World Politics," Appendix I in Otto Gierke, *Natural Law and the Theory of Society 1500 to 1800*, tr. Ernest Barker (Cambridge: Cambridge University Press, 1950), 210.

54. Barth, *Protestant Theology in the Nineteenth Century*, 347, 431.

55. *GS*, 2:747.

56. "Die Selbständigkeit der Religion," 391.

just actions, temperate by performing temperate actions, brave by performing brave actions.[57]

This eclecticism irritated the monists among Troeltsch's contemporaries, who
found his philosophizing puzzling and confusing. One author thought he saw
Søren Kierkegaard (1813-55) reflected in Troeltsch's emphasis upon the necessity of the individual's deciding upon a "pivot of organization," but could
not be certain.[58]

The Anglo-Saxons, or those who had trafficked among them, appeared
to have clearer appreciation. For example, the appraisal of Friedrich von
Hügel (1852-1925), displaced Catholic lay theologian, active in the modernist
struggle, and responsible for preparing the posthumous publication of
Troeltsch's London lectures, is conciliatory. Remarking the change in
Troeltsch during the First World War, von Hügel writes that the wonder is
that Troeltsch's conclusion is not thinner than it actually appears. "But then,"
he adds, "we have to do with a soul of the rarest richness which, in spite of every logical self-entrapment, does partly have its way . . . and retains certain
grand convictions . . . from pre-individualistic days."[59] Von Hügel's criticism
of Troeltsch is that this soul of "rarest richness" ultimately ignored the role of
the Christian community in favor of the notion that the cognition of faith's
benefits lies solely with the individual cognizer.[60]

It is one thing to assert that certain spiritual facts exist and are
apprehendable prior to the movement of faith, but quite another to assign the
criterion for truth to individual experience, and thus to relegate the function
of "organized" religion to the mere disclosure of its origins. Or did the one
thing lead to the other? If, according to Troeltsch, the "assurance of grace" —
in the Augustinian parlance of "old Protestantism" — belongs to those facts
that are apprehendable prior to faith, then the gravity of the human condition and the necessity for repentance and renewal had approached Troeltsch
on his blind side.[61] Troeltsch himself finally admitted in his last days that
modern society presents the picture of "calculating coldness and soulless-
ness," of an "agonising lust of victory" and "blatant satisfaction in the tyran-
nical power of the merchant class." He agreed that deductions had been
drawn from romantic aestheticism and romantic ideas of individuality to
"foster the cause of scepticism, of amoralism, of pessimism, of belief in the

57. Aristotle, *Ethics,* tr. J. A. K. Thomson (London: Penguin Books, 1953), 55-56.
58. Benckert, "Troeltsch," 1047.
59. Von Hügel, Introduction to Troeltsch, *Christianity,* xv, xxiii-xxiv.
60. *Ibid.,* xxvii-xxix.
61. Benckert, "Troeltsch," 1045.

policy of force, of simple cynicism." But despite all, he remained convinced that the "universal-historical" way of thinking and feeling about life he embraced would check the current. He celebrated, as we have seen, what he termed the "total and fundamental dissolution of the idea of a universal Natural Law" in favor of a morality that was altogether a matter of the "inner self." The impulse to humaneness forever lies, he believed, in "super-personal forces, radiating from individuals who laid the foundations of social life."[62] Each, if not already climbing, was yet capable of climbing Jacob's ladder, where "every rung goes higher, higher." In spite of the damage done its credibility by the bloodiest conflict in the history of the West, by some as yet undiscovered law the "theory of progress" persisted up to and beyond the second half of this century. A book produced by a celebrated historian of the ancient world, and hailed during the 1932 Chicago World's Fair, in which the idea of progress is declared to be incompatible, even inimical to the notion of providence, was a secular, more vulgar variation on Troeltsch's theme, yet not unrelated to it for all of that.[63] Contemporary events would inflict the theory of progress with a mortal wound, but it would die hard.

Troeltsch had put a flea in the ear of the historians through his identification of the Reformation with the late Middle Ages. Paul Althaus (1888-1966) and Werner Elert (1885-1954) of Erlangen, Emanuel Hirsch of Göttingen, and Karl Holl of Berlin presented the strongest opposition. In volume one of his collected essays, Holl states that one of the most glaring errors in Troeltsch's description of the church's social teaching is his identification of Luther with Philipp Melanchthon (1497-1560) and Protestant scholasticism, assigning their concepts to him. In such fashion, Holl contends, Luther is robbed of his peculiar greatness; what in Luther towers above what came after him does not get its due. Holl adverts to Troeltsch's fear of "modernizing" Luther — a laudable concern, but which ought not lead to characterizing Luther as more medieval than he actually is. This criticism is but the first of twenty-six in Holl's volume.[64] Additionally, the Luther researchers accuse Troeltsch of having misunderstood the social-ethical effects of Lutheranism. But with the exception of Holl, who died too early for the experience, none of the others named above would be celebrated for proving Troeltsch wrong in the holocaust to come.

Three years after Troeltsch's death, Friedrich Gogarten (1887-1968) of Göttingen responded to Troeltsch's denial of Christianity's claim to absolute-

---

62. Troeltsch, *Protestantism and Progress,* 74; "The Ideas of Natural Law and Humanity in World Politics," 211-12, 217-18, 221.

63. John Bagnell Bury, *The Idea of Progress: An Inquiry into Its Origin and Growth* (London: Macmillan, 1924).

64. *Gesammelte Aufsätze zur Kirchengeschichte* (Tübingen: J. C. B. Mohr, 1932), 106n.

ness and on behalf of all that restless tribe of revived Augustianians, soon to be identified with what the journalists learned to call "dialectical theology":

> For us, only the finite event can be beyond history, an event that eludes all absorption in infinite movement. . . . When this one finite event is opposed to the infinity of relations belonging to an infinite historical context, it finds its end in them. Then this one event and it alone is the end-time. There is no sense in speaking of another. For this end is not only one in an infinite series, but is the one end in which the infinite series ceases to be infinite and becomes finite. For this reason, then, it is also origin. For if it has brought infinite relations to a standstill . . . then new relations have already begun, that move everything toward a new order determined by this one finite event. And this beginning is not merely a beginning within the infinite series. It is the one origin than which there is no other, which can find its end nowhere else than in this one finite event from which it began.[65]

Troeltsch's idealism, his romanticism stuck in Gogarten's craw. The denial of absoluteness to anything finite; the description of one faith's claim to validity over against any other as "naive" — though a proper object of research as a universal phenomenon, since every variety of religion, sophisticated or primitive, raises an identical claim — all resulted in the absorption of the finite in the infinite, in that "idea," "view of God," or "direction toward the absolute." A new conjuror from Endor had summoned up an old ghost with the denial that the "accidents of history" could yield the universal truths of reason. And "not all the king's horses," nor "all the king's men," not all the Barths and von Hügels, Althauses and Elerts, Hirsches and Holls or Gogartens, could *aufheben* Ernst Troeltsch. His definition of the task and method of criticism, but above all his conclusions and his guarantee, spawn of eclecticism, would outlive their assailants into the end of the twentieth century. There are signs everywhere that it may be Troeltsch, the romantic historicist, who speaks for religion in the years to come.

65. *Illusionen* (Jena: Eugen Diederich, 1926), 13-17.

9

ADOLF SCHLATTER

Biblical Criticism and the Act of Faith

I. Attack upon Christendom

In the last year of his contentious life, Søren Kierkegaard wrote a bitter and ironic meditation on biblical scholarship that reads like a parable:

> Imagine that it says in the New Testament that it is God's will that every human being is to have 100,000 dollars [*Rigsdalere*] (we can surely imagine it!) — do you think there would be any question about a commentary? I wonder if everyone would not say: This is easy enough to understand; no commentary is needed; let us for God's sake stay away from commentaries — they might make the whole matter ambiguous. We prefer to have it as it stands — therefore, out, out with all commentaries.
>
> But what stands in the New Testament (about the narrow way, about dying to the world, and so on) is no more difficult than this matter of 100,000 dollars. The difficulty lies somewhere else, in its not pleasing us — and therefore, therefore, therefore we must have commentaries and professors and commentaries. We are not "running the risk" of its becoming ambiguous — no, that is precisely what we want, and we hope that little by little, with the cooperation of commentaries, it will become ambiguous.
>
> Is not, then, scholarship of evil? Is it not something we humans have invented because we do not want to understand what is only too easy to understand? Is it not an invention whereby we are strengthened in evil, in sneakery and hypocritical shirking?

We have invented scholarship in order to evade doing God's will. This much we certainly do understand — that face to face with God and his obviously understood will to say "This I will not do" — this no one dares to do. We do not dare do it that way, so we protect ourselves by making it seem as if it were very difficult to understand and that therefore we — he must indeed be flattered by this and regard it as praiseworthy in us — study and investigate etc., that is, we protect ourselves by hiding behind big books.[1]

Kierkegaard belonged to no recognizable school of biblical interpretation. But he was fully conversant with the range of academic debate in his day. In his mind the problem was not confusion over the meaning of Christianity in the face of modern historical consciousness. History is not in itself an impediment to the knowledge of true Christianity. The real problem is moral. Ecclesiastical leaders, both academic and bureaucratic, want to protect the constituencies that pay for their keep from the rigorous claims that Jesus makes in the New Testament.[2] This protection is accomplished in two ways, both of which exploit the phenomenon of historical consciousness.

The first way is academic. Kierkegaard calls it "speculative thought."[3] He has the figure of Hegel especially in mind. According to this approach, "Christianity is viewed as a historical document," the understanding of which at any given time can only be "an approximation."[4] If one can know the object of belief only at an intellectual distance, then one can hardly be expected to make a passionate commitment that involves personal risk and sacrifice. Speculative thought produces spectators: detached observers adept at schematizing and criticizing reality but little affected in their actual behavior. At most, speculative thought engenders a mild allegiance to Christianity that finds pleasure in intellectual curiosity.

The second way that protects ecclesiastics and their followers from the harsh claims of the New Testament is what Kierkegaard calls "the Church theory."[5] Here the individual is absolved of all responsibility to make a decision for faith. This is because the church theory assumes that everyone is a Christian already, membership being guaranteed by the prestige of an historic institution, enduring across time, that possesses orthodox creeds and confes-

---

1. *Søren Kierkegaard's Journals and Papers,* vol. 3: *L-R,* ed. and tr. Howard V. Hong and Edna H. Hong (Bloomington and London: Indiana University Press, 1975), 657.

2. Thomas C. Oden, *Agenda for Theology* (San Francisco: Harper & Row, 1979), 111.

3. *Concluding Unscientific Postscript to Philosophical Fragments,* ed. and tr. Howard V. Hong and Edna H. Hong (Princeton: Princeton University Press, 1982), 1:31.

4. *Ibid.,* 1:23.

5. *Ibid.,* 1:40, 43, 608.

sions, divinely mandated liturgy, and, above all, the sacrament of infant baptism conceived "as something magical to hold on to" apart from personal faith.[6] Kierkegaard satirizes this as "a Danish idea." His specific object of derision is Nikolai Grundtvig (1783-1872).[7] But what he is after generally is the conventionality of nominal faith that is the curse of the European territorial church. The church theory is an ideology of "sheer estheticism."[8] It offers an appealing cultural vision of religion as a blend of sacramental theology, piety, and patriotism. This may be Christendom, but it is not Christianity.

True Christianity involves what Kierkegaard calls "the Socratic secret," that is, a personal appropriation of the content of faith that entails a painful examination of the self and a "subjective transformation" of one's entire way of being in the world.[9] This is a risky and unattractive business. It is the very opposite of nominal church membership: "remember that the higher the religious is taken, the more rigorous it becomes, but it does not necessarily follow that you are able to bear it."[10]

Although Kierkegaard called into question the legitimacy of the Lutheran state church, he did not break his ties with the Lutheran theological tradition. Indeed, there is a deep affinity between Kierkegaard and Luther. Like Kierkegaard, Martin Luther turned a cold shoulder toward any idea of Christianity as "Christendom" that appeals to the lowest common denominator and reduces personal faith to participation in the liturgical and sacramental life of the state church. To the people of such a church, Luther gave fair warning: "It behooves everyone to search his heart and examine himself. Let no one bank on thoughts like these: 'I am baptized and am called a Christian. I hear God's Word and go to the Sacrament.' For here Christ Himself separates the false 'Christians from those who are genuine.'"[11] Luther places believers before the privilege and duty of explicit faith *(fides explicata)*. One is called by the word of God out of custom, lethargy, obedience to a priestly hierarchy, and outward participation in sacramental life *(ex opere operato)* into the fullness of an individual relation to Jesus as Lord, Master, and Savior. This is personal faith. Nothing can substitute for it. Reflecting on the First Commandment, Luther asks: "What is it to have a god? What is God? . . . A god is that to which we look for all good and in which we find refuge in every time

6. *Ibid.,* 1:44.

7. *Ibid.,* 1:36.

8. *Ibid.,* 1:608.

9. *Ibid.,* 1:38. See also *For Self-Examination/Judge for Yourself!* ed. and tr. Howard V. Hong and Edna H. Hong (Princeton: Princeton University Press, 1990), 10-11.

10. *Ibid.,* 11.

11. *LW,* 24:250.

of need. To have a god is nothing else than to trust and believe with our whole heart."[12] God has made us to be worshiping creatures. Giving our whole heart to a god (whoever or whatever that god might be) is what we do. It is the very essence of our being. Everyone has a god. The only question is, Who is our god? Is it money, security, power? Or is it the God of the Bible. This is the religious question *in nuce*. To avoid this question or to substitute a less personal, less invasive question is not to engage in religion.

It is in the context of these basic elements of the Lutheran confessional tradition that Kierkegaard wages his attack upon Christendom. How can one be truly "religious" in the territorial church where conventional allegiance is the lowest common denominator? The religious level of existence, if it is to be authentic, cannot be content with mere conventionality. Rather, it involves an intense form of commitment demanded by one's private and unique relationship to God. It necessitates an absolute relation to the Absolute and a relative relationship to all things relative in this life. Kierkegaard's favorite scriptural passage is "Seek ye first the kingdom of God" (Matt. 6:33). One must be transformed, and this cannot be done alone. It means suffering — the suffering of a change wrought against the grain of basic inclinations.[13]

It took a while for Kierkegaard's work to be known outside of intellectual circles in Denmark. The first German translation of any of his material appeared in 1861, six years after his death. Published by a Baptist press, it consisted of some of his most bitter occasional essays from the last year of his life. This reinforced the impression that Kierkegaard was nothing more than a sectarian "interested in subverting the ecclesiastical order."[14] But a translation into German of *For Self-Examination* the following year offered at least the beginnings of a more balanced picture of Kierkegaard's larger theological project. Among the very few who were receptive to Kierkegaard's ideas was the Swabian biblical scholar and protégé of Ferdinand Christian Baur at Tübingen, Johann Tobias Beck. Kierkegaard, said Beck, "looked beyond the transitory horizon of the Church, the mission and other communities to the horizon of the kingdom of God and bore witness from his watchtower."[15]

12. Theodore G. Tappert, tr. and ed., *The Book of Concord* (Philadelphia: Fortress, 1959), 365.

13. We are grateful to Charles C. West, late of Princeton Theological Seminary, for this understanding of the "religious level" of personal existence.

14. Habib C. Malik, *Receiving Søren Kierkegaard: The Early Impact and Transmission of His Thought* (Washington, D.C.: Catholic University Press of America, 1997), 219.

15. *Gedanken aus und nach der Schrift*, 4th ed. (Gütersloh: C. Bertelsmann, 1900), 169; quoted and tr. in Karl Barth, *Protestant Theology in the Nineteenth Century*, tr. Brian Couzins and John Bowen (Valley Forge: Judson, 1973), 618.

Like Kierkegaard, Beck belonged to no school. But his thought is generally characterized by what Claude Welch calls, "a rigorous objectivism with respect to Christian doctrine, Scripture, and to the divine reality that works in Christian existence."[16] Scripture is the "original representation" of revelation that by the power of the Holy Spirit creates a "living unity" enduring across the ages that brings about the renewal of believers: "You have been born anew, not of perishable but of imperishable seed, through the living and enduring word of God" (1 Peter 1:23).[17] Renewal is the focus of the Bible. In light of this, justification is to be understood as "no mere forensic act, but an act of divine creative power" that remakes the world.[18] Christianity is never meant to be part of a conventional cultural establishment, a sort of polite religious gloss on the obligations of citizenship. Rather, Christianity is a divine breaking into the world as "Spirit and life . . . dynamically and substantially." Beginning with Christ, and continuing with born-again individuals responding to him, the church is a new community that is destined by Providence to grow and spread.[19] For this community to conform to the will of God, it is not enough that people are intellectually conversant with Christian truth. Revelation is received properly only when God becomes the central principle of one's entire existence. To live in faith is to take part in "an infinite spiritual economy of life to which our natural thought-patterns have to be subject, and which extends them beyond their normal limitations." Thus, "there cannot be a separation between dogmatics and ethics."[20] Christianity is the obedient life or it is nothing.

Inspired by Kierkegaard, Beck sought to break Christian theology out of its captivity to the bourgeois mores of the church of his day, a church that one commentator has described as a version of Christianity "so tamed and domesticated that its demand for radical and decisive choice was completely concealed."[21] The contemporary challenge to biblical interpretation and dogmatic theology, according to Beck, was to uncover this concealed choice and challenge people to confront it. Christian faith has at its very heart an existen-

---

16. Claude Welch, *Protestant Thought in the Nineteenth Century,* vol. 1: *1799-1870* (New Haven: Yale University Press, 1972), 198-99.

17. J. T. Beck, *Einleitung in das System der Christlichen Lehre* (Stuttgart: J. F. Steinkopf, 1870), 246.

18. Welch, *Protestant Thought,* 200.

19. *Ibid.* See J. T. Beck, *Vorlesungen über Christliche Glaubenslehre,* ed. H. Lindenmeyer (Gütersloh: C. Bertelsmann, 1887), 383ff.

20. Barth, *Protestant Theology,* 619.

21. Diogenes Allen, *Three Outsiders: Pascal, Kierkegaard, Simone Weil* (Cambridge: Cowley, 1983), 53-54.

tial imperative that neither speculative theology nor ecclesiastical practice can disguise. Responding to Beck's vision of theology was his most distinguished student, Adolf Schlatter. Through Schlatter, two generations of significant figures in German theology learned that biblical interpretation and theology cannot be separated from living a life obedient to Christ.

II. Biography

Adolf Schlatter was born on 16 August 1852, in St. Gallen, Switzerland, the seventh of eight children. His father Stephan, due to suspicions regarding sacramental practice in the Reformed Church, was re-baptized a member of the free evangelical community in St. Gallen. His mother Wilhelmine, unable to follow her husband, remained a member of the Reformed Church all her life. His paternal grandmother Anna, a woman of renowned piety and intellect, had entertained Friedrich Ernst Daniel Schleiermacher and Martin Leberecht de Wette in her home, and included among her descendants six missionaries and sixty-six theologians, among them Schlatter's cousin, the Lutheran conservative Theodor Zahn (1838-1933).

After his years at elementary school, begun in 1858, Schlatter entered the local gymnasium with its requirement of six hours in Latin and five in Greek per week. Of his teacher Misteli's instruction in Greek at the St. Gallen gymnasium, he wrote that it dominated his "entire interior life." His introduction to the origins of language urged on him an "exact observation and disciplined interpretation of processes which arise from meditating on the physical world."[22] In this period, wrote Schlatter, he learned never to separate thought from love. It was his first step toward a theology that would not neglect the world, and toward the practice of a form of historical observation that would not neglect God. At the same time, Schlatter's years at the gymnasium raised questions concerning the intellectual carrying capacity of his biblical faith.[23]

Following the completion of his studies at the gymnasium, Schlatter matriculated at the University of Basel, where he heard the renowned historians Jacob Burckhardt (1818-97) and Franz Overbeck (1837-1905), as well as the philosopher Karl Steffensen (1816-88) — a "great discovery" — who rescued him from a period of inner conflict due to a period of gorging himself

---

22. *Rückblick auf meine Lebensarbeit* (Stuttgart: Calwer, 1977), 32.

23. Werner Neuer, *Adolf Schlatter: Ein Leben für Theologie und Kirche* (Stuttgart: Calwer, 1996), 46.

on philosophy. For one semester Schlatter attended lectures on Plato by Friedrich Nietzsche, whose lasting impression on his memory he described as the "cruel insolence by which he treated his audience as a contemptible rabble."[24] By chaining himself to Nietzsche, Schlatter wrote, Overbeck had put his "glorious knowledge" to death.[25] At Basel, Schlatter read Johann Friedrich Herbart (1776-1841), philosopher, psychologist, and ethicist, who resisted pigeonholing the various activities of the mind, and whose analysis of Spinozism freed the young scholar from the "superstition" of paying homage to abstraction. In the lecture hall Burckhardt and Steffensen reinforced Schlatter's distaste for the abstract. The one demonstrated how the historian's perspective shines through and shapes and interprets his material, and the other signaled the death of "pure reason" through uncovering the historical processes that gave it birth.[26] According to Schlatter, it was the historians at Basel who helped determine his life's history; no dogmatician could have moved him.[27]

Following a pattern pursued by most European students, Schlatter did not complete his university studies at Basel, but set out for Tübingen in Germany, where he came under the spell of Beck. Schlatter attended Beck's lectures from the spring of 1873 until the fall of 1874. Now, he wrote, he found himself in an auditorium in which godlessness was not regarded as a condition for scientific work.[28] Beck's lectures on Romans contained a criticism of the Reformation that loosed Schlatter from the Reformed and Lutheran traditions. He wrote: "We could not wander back into old Tübingen, in which everyone possessed the true, pure faith, while at the same time a violent man sat in the house of the chief official, and a thief in the house of the lower city, both, however, indubitably orthodox and Lutheran."[29]

Toward Protestant scholasticism and pietism Beck maintained a refreshing freedom, alongside which the atmosphere of a Hegelian lecture hall was "gloomy and oppressive." Further, Beck brought to his work a "second armament," a lively, developed meditation on nature, a resolute affirmation of the divine leading in the natural process. As a general rule for all theological work Beck formulated the *gnomon:* "The eye of the wise man sees what is there; the brain of the idler invents hypotheses." But while Beck observed with devotion what had come about through nature, he assumed, in Schlatter's view, an almost exclusively negative stance toward what had come about

---

24. Schlatter, *Rückblick,* 41; Neuer, *Adolf Schlatter,* 64.
25. Schlatter, *Rückblick,* 50.
26. *Ibid.,* 39-41.
27. *Ibid.,* 51.
28. *Ibid.,* 45-46.
29. Adolf Schlatter, *Erlebtes,* 4th ed. (Berlin: Furche Verlag, n.d.), 76.

through history.[30] Beck's attack upon Christendom meant that the communal dimension of Christian existence and action was decidedly lacking. Here work needed to be done.

Resolved to enter the service of the church, Schlatter was commissioned by the Zürich authorities in 1875 to assume temporary oversight of a congregation at Kilchberg on the Zürich See, followed by a term as intern at Neumünster. During his internship at Neumünster, Schlatter was befriended by Edmund Fröhlich, pastor of the chapel of St. Anna in Zürich, a critic of pietism's moral achievements, and leery of adorning "clumsiness and stupidity with a Christian aura."[31] Fröhlich introduced Schlatter to the works of Franz Xaver Baader (1765-1841), Catholic mystic and opponent of Kant's ethic of obedience to an inner moral law. From Baader Schlatter received an impulse to master the Reformation "deficit" in a more comprehensive appropriation of the biblical message. In addition, Baader's plea for a "reason which perceives," that is, for a knowledge totally dependent on the reality to be known, would become the point of departure for Schlatter's own epistemology with its accent on an "objective" knowledge of reality in contrast to the skepticism at home in Protestantism.[32]

Ordained in St. Gallen in 1875, Schlatter preached a trial sermon a year later at Kesswil-Utwil on the Bodensee, was subsequently called as its pastor, and served from 1877 to 1880. Scarcely a half year following his arrival in Kesswil, Schlatter began courting Susanna Schoop, a young woman from the neighboring village of Dozwil. After a two weeks' acquaintance, and after four months' correspondence, they were married on 15 January 1878.

In the city of Berne, churchly-pietistic circles were anxious for representation on a university faculty dominated by liberals, and accordingly urged Schlatter to apply for the *Lizentiatur* and adjoining *Habilitation* — the first an equivalent of current doctoral work, and the second a study culminating in permission to teach. Since Schlatter was suspect as a pietist whose faith in the Bible rendered him unfit for scientific work, the Berne faculty in a move never again repeated required that he submit to oral examinations in five main subjects together with eight written examinations, and that he be allowed to teach only on condition of achieving the *magna cum laude* distinction. Schlatter passed the tests, produced dissertations on John the Baptist as well as on the relation between history and knowledge of God, and lectured

30. Adolf Schlatter, "J. T. Becks theologischer Arbeit," in *Beiträge zur Förderung christlicher Theologie* (Gütersloh: C. Bertelsmann, 1904), 29, 30-32, 39, and 40-41.
31. Neuer, *Adolf Schlatter*, 102-3.
32. *Ibid.*, 103-5.

as *Privatdozent* or instructor (unsalaried by the university) at Berne from 1880 to 1888.

At Bern Schlatter was close to Samuel Oettli (1846-1911), pietist and professor of Old Testament at the university, who had first approached Schlatter to join forces with him through a position on the university faculty. According to Schlatter's most recent biographer, his closest companion at Bern was the historian of law Johannes Schnell, who introduced him to the writings of Johann Georg Hamann (1750-88), "celebrated antipode" of Immanuel Kant, author of that stinging article on the Enlightenment.[33] It was Hamann of whom Baader's work had been a reminder and Hamann to whom Schlatter appeared "spiritually related."[34]

In the winter semester of 1885-86, at the urging of clergy and laity, he held "Bible hours" on Romans, attended by seventy to eighty men, from which grew his *Erläuterungen zum Neuen Testament,* a series of commentaries on the New Testament for ordinary readers. To supplement his income, Schlatter gave instruction in religion and Hebrew at the local, independent gymnasium, whose founder, a certain Theoderich von Lerber, was suspicious of a young theologian educated at Swiss and German faculties who questioned the verbal inerrancy of the Bible and advocated biblical criticism. Schlatter thus spent his years at Berne dodging the blows of both liberals and fundamentalists. During this period faculties of the universities of Halle, Kiel, Heidelberg, Marburg, and Bonn all applied to their respective authorities to grant Schlatter a teaching position. Refusing invitations from Halle and Kiel, Schlatter accepted a call to the University of Greifswald.

At Greifswald Hermann Cremer (1834-1903), the Lutheran scholar who was preacher at St. Marien's Kirche and "grandfather" of the *Theological Dictionary of the New Testament,* applied to the university of Berne to grant Schlatter an honorary doctorate, a degree that in this period was required for a tenured post. The University of Berne responded that it was not ready to grant the needed degree. Halle, on the other hand, awarded Schlatter the degree, and two days before his thirty-sixth birthday he left Switzerland for Greifswald.

Schlatter lectured at Greifswald from 1888 to 1893. Prior to his call to Greifswald, Schlatter's contact with Lutherans usually evoked distaste for their doctrine and behavior. In Hermann Cremer he encountered a type of Lutheran whose piety and theology wrung from him high regard. Of Cremer he wrote:

---

33. Johann Georg Hamann, "Brief an Christian Jacob Kraus," in *Was ist Aufklärung?* (Stuttgart: Philipp Reclam, 1974), 18-22.

34. Neuer, *Adolf Schlatter,* 105, 202.

We were together because we longed for a theology of faith; not an ignorant faith, without a basis, but a faith conscious of its truth and thus capable of giving a reason for it; no longer a godless theology having its impulse in conflict with God and a struggle against Jesus, but a research with its basis and directing in the faith given us by Jesus.[35]

For Schlatter, Cremer's Sunday celebration of Holy Communion at St. Marien's Kirche underscored the proclamation of the free grace of God, despite a certain narrowness that Schlatter detected in his colleague's preaching.[36]

During these years he toured the Holy Land on horseback and founded the *Beiträge zur Förderung christlicher Theologie.* The majority of its essays were authored by Schlatter himself, and, as he wrote, it would scarcely have appeared had any scientific journal been available to him.[37]

In 1893 Schlatter received an invitation from Berlin University to lecture as *Ordinarius,* or full professor. Contrary to custom, the call was arranged by state authorities against the express wish of the Berlin faculty. Among the faculty, the celebrated interpreter and author Bernard Weiss (1827-1918) sensed unhealthy competition in Schlatter's intent to lecture on New Testament exegesis. Schlatter accepted the invitation, and described the decision to leave Greifswald for Berlin as the most painful of his life.[38] Cremer, with whom he had formed a bond against Ritschlians resolved to get the upper hand in church and university circles, was bereft.

Schlatter lectured at Berlin from the fall of 1893 until the spring of 1898 and shared the chancel of the *Kaiser-Friedrich-Gedächtniskirche* on second festival days. During this period he became a fast friend of Friedrich Bodelschwing the elder (1831-1910), with whom Schlatter joined to found the *Theologische Woche* at Bethel in Bielefeld, as well as of Adolf Stöcker (1835-1909), court preacher and founder of the Christian Socialist Party, whose friendship he described as the greatest thing Berlin gave him.[39] Schlatter read dogmatics and ethics with Julius Kaftan (1846-1926) and Otto Pfleiderer (1839-1908), but in the Berlin faculty he formed a friendship only with Adolf von Harnack.

In the spring of 1898 Schlatter assumed the newly founded sixth theological professorship at Tübingen. With wife and children, he settled into his

35. *Ibid.,* 230.
36. *Ibid.,* 237.
37. Schlatter, *Rückblick,* 158.
38. Neuer, *Adolf Schlatter,* 295.
39. Schlatter, *Rückblick,* 187.

new home above the Neckar on the Osterberg, the spot at which old Swabians believed Christ would appear on the last day. Initially, Schlatter had considerable difficulty establishing contact with the Swabian students, due not only to his habits of speech and dress (following a haircut he would be met with roaring applause), but also to their theological orientation, in great part determined by the History of Religions School.[40] Ultimately, in order to accommodate his listeners, the number of which clearly exceeded that of all his Tübingen colleagues, Schlatter had to hold his lectures in the *Neue Aula* or festival hall of the university. Among his hearers were those who would dominate the course of exegesis and theology not merely in Germany but in all of Europe and abroad: Paul Althaus; Karl Barth; Dietrich Bonhoeffer (1906-45); Rudolf Bultmann; Ernst Fuchs (1903-83); Ernst Käsemann; Walter von Lowenich (1903-92); Ernst Lohmeyer (1867-1946); Wilhelm Lütgert (1867-1938); Otto Michel (1903-93); Karl-Heinrich Rengstorf (1903-92); Erich Seeberg (1888-1945), Paul Tillich (1886-1965), Karl Heim (1874-1958), and Hans Lilje (1899-1977), who stated that whoever was not attracted by Karl Barth at Basel went to Schlatter. After a visit to Schlatter's lecture hall, Martin Heidegger (1889-1976) is said to have remarked: "That is theology!" Barth, however, whose father had sent him to Tübingen to learn "something good from positive theology," heard Schlatter "with the greatest reluctance," and faulted him for his "totally paradoxical concept of 'history'" and for "elegantly somersaulting over difficulties without basically getting at them."[41]

In addition to his university lectures, Schlatter had regular preaching duties at the Stiftskirche each month. He was active in the "German Christian Student Union" *(Deutsche Christliche Studentenvereinigung),* and its house on the Osterberg still bears his name. He joined the "Young Men's Christian Association" *(Christlicher Verein Junger Männer),* and served as its president throughout the entire period of the war. In the late 1920s he enlisted in the "Christian National Service" *(Die Christlicher Volksdienst),* an organization occupied with the preservation of the Weimar Republic on the basis of Christian values.

Among the happiest experiences of Schlatter's Tübingen period was his friendship with the young historian Karl Holl , a native of Tübingen, at first a *Repetent* or lecturer at the Tübinger Stift, then associate professor in church history. Prior to and following his departure from Tübingen in 1915 for a full

---

40. Neuer, *Adolf Schlatter,* 386.

41. Werner Neuer, "Der Briefwechsel zwischen Karl Barth und Adolf Schlatter," *Theologische Beiträge* 17 (1986): 87, 92.

professorship in Berlin, Holl wrote thirty-nine extensive letters to his old friend Schlatter and was godfather of his daughter Elly. Schlatter experienced two of the worst events in his life at Tübingen — first, the death of his wife on 9 July 1907, and then the death of his youngest son, Paul, mortally wounded by a grenade on the Western Front. The father accompanied the son's coffin from Germersheim, north of Karlsruhe, home to Tübingen, writing on his cross: "None of us lives to himself." Paul's death plunged Schlatter into a severe depression from which friends and acquaintances doubted he would recover.

Initially hopeful of change following the collapse of the Weimar Republic, Schlatter ultimately dissociated himself from the National Socialist Movement prior to Hitler's seizure of power in January of 1933. The decision of his colleagues Karl Fezer (1891-1960), Gerhard Kittel (1888-1948), Hans Rückert (1901-74), and Artur Weiser (1893-1978) to join the *Deutsche Christen*, Protestant spawn of the Nazi party led by Hitler's toady, Ludwig Müller (1883-1945), distressed him.

Retired in August 1922, Schlatter continued to lecture and to hold "open evenings" at his residence, and in 1929 he began the composition and publication of scientific commentaries on the New Testament — all this one year after stating his belief that he had come to the limit of his power.[42] Schlatter delivered his last lecture toward the end of February, 1930, but he did not breathe his last till noon on 19 May 1938. He was buried 23 May 1938, in the old Tübingen cemetery. From his deathbed, according to the report, Schlatter wrote out these words from John's Gospel for the inscription on the cross above his grave: "If any one thirst, let him come to me and drink." To the quotation he appended an incorrect reference to chapter and verse, which none thought to challenge, due to his celebrated powers of recall.

III. Getting Free

Since his student days at Tübingen, Schlatter, like his father, was eager to dissociate himself from Protestant scholasticism, but in his case, from the Lutheran variety. His teacher Beck had insisted that theology required ethics for its completion, a position distancing the Swabian scholar from the conventional perception of the Reformation tradition,[43] a tradition that all but alienated Schlatter from the Christian fellowship.[44] The Reformed tradition, he

42. Neuer, *Adolf Schlatter*, 621.
43. Schlatter, "J. T. Becks theologische Arbeit," 40.
44. Schlatter, *Rückblick*, 196.

thought, was reductionist. It limited the gospel in Melanchthonian fashion to a "doctrine concerning faith,"[45] while in the area of ethics it offered nothing but a pre-Christian declaration of war on nature.[46] Whatever the Reformation had gained it had subsumed under the old Greek formulas.[47] Schlatter reserved biting criticism for the reemergence of scholasticism in the Ritschlian School:

> What had remained narrow and ailing in Lutheranism — the egoistic use of faith to coddle the "I"; the suspicioning of love and love's work dedicated to God; the despising of nature; the flight from community felt to be merely a burden; a clericalism unable to show the "third estate" any service of God beyond natural labor; support of the church by the might of the state; the erection of a scholastic and imperious orthodoxy — all this was not merely retained in Ritschl, but further shaped and sharpened.[48]

Of Luther himself Schlatter could write that he "gloriously set forth the indissoluble connection between faith and love."[49] He could answer the question regarding his own personal faith in the words of the explanation to the Second Article in Luther's Small Catechism.[50] In fact, like von Hofmann, Schlatter could chart the difference between Luther and the Protestant form of scholasticism that followed.[51] Most often, however, he faulted Luther for his preoccupation with the origin of faith rather than with its goal.

On the occasion of the quadricentennial of the Reformation, Schlatter criticized Luther's exposition of Romans. He charged that the Reformer engaged in Aristotelian syllogistic reasoning from the existence of sin to the necessity for faith, stating that if faith arose by such means it was merely the product of our thinking process,[52] a product that in the last analysis remained an unattainable, "dreamy" goal.[53] In reducing justification to forgiveness

---

45. Adolf Schlatter, "Luthers Deutung des Römerbriefs: Ein Beitrag zur vierten Säkularfeier der Reformation," in *Beiträge zur Förderung christlicher Theologie* (Gütersloh: C. Bertelsmann, 1917), 19.

46. *Ibid.*, 84-85; Adolf Schlatter, *Die Korintherbriefe* (Stuttgart: Calwer, 1962), 176; Neuer, *Adolf Schlatter*, 717.

47. Adolf Schlatter, *Die Gründe der christlichen Gewissheit* (Stuttgart: Calwer, 1917), 21.

48. Schlatter, *Rückblick*, 141-42.

49. *Ibid.*, 175.

50. Neuer, *Adolf Schlatter*, 137.

51. See *ibid.*, 547 n. 106.

52. Schlatter, "Luthers Deutung des Römerbriefs," 24, 38-39; Neuer, *Adolf Schlatter*, 788.

53. Schlatter, *Rückblick*, 58-59.

from sin — that is, in assigning it a purely defensive or negative purpose — Luther had contradicted Paul's conception of it as conquest of sin.[54] This one-sidedness in interpretation that spawned a passive, quietistic ethic required correction in an orientation of faith to thinking, willing, and acting.[55] In a sentence later echoed by Ernst Käsemann, Schlatter described Paul as looking toward the universal goal of Christ, "in whom the work of divine grace achieves its greatness in spanning the world."[56] Undoubtedly, Luther's experience, wrote Schlatter, accounted for this narrowing in interpretation. Luther spoke of what moved him, "not of what he did not understand."[57] Schlatter would make the same argument in his own commentary on Romans,[58] for which he raised hackles among members of the guild. For example, Georg Merz (1892-1959) wrote that it never occurred to Schlatter to read anything about Luther and that the Tübingen scholar assumed a scriptural theologian had to exercise criticism not only of German idealism but of the Reformation as well.[59] Eduard Ellwein (1898-1974) also contended that Luther had never distanced the founding or awakening of faith from the proof of its necessity in such fashion as Schlatter had argued.[60]

Schlatter was similarly suspicious of pietism. For example, during a lecture at Barmen in 1889 he irritated his hearers by saying that he was "definitely opposed to identifying our rebirth with some sort of individual feeling, with this or that experience."[61] Pietism, however, was never a threat equal to Protestant scholasticism. After all, it was the pietists or "positive theologians" at Berne who had first launched Schlatter on his scholarly career. More important, he shared with them, as he shared with Beck and Kierkegaard, the conviction that faith cannot be reduced to a matter of intellectual assent but involves the total thinking, willing, and feeling person, a posture requiring activity for its fulfillment.

The reason for Schlatter's animus toward Protestant scholasticism lay deep. He was convinced that Protestantism, principally through its clergy,

---

54. Schlatter, "Luthers Deutung des Römerbriefs," 52, 60; Neuer, *Adolf Schlatter*, 548; Schlatter, *Erlebtes*, 39; see also Schlatter, *Die Korintherbriefe*, 27.

55. Neuer, *Adolf Schlatter*, 191.

56. Schlatter, "Luthers Deutung des Römerbriefs," 55-56; Neuer, *Adolf Schlatter*, 786; see also 784.

57. *Ibid.*, 41-42.

58. Adolf Schlatter, *Gottes Gerechtigkeit* (Stuttgart: Calwer, 1952), esp. 37-45.

59. "Schlatters Kritik an Luthers Römerbriefvorlesung," *Zwischen den Zeiten* 5 (1927): 527.

60. "Schlatters Kritik an Luthers Römerbriefvorlesung," 536.

61. Neuer, *ibid.*, 261.

had been infected with an originally Greek disregard for perception, resulting in alienation from nature and history and in assigning value solely to the self.[62] Carrier of the infection was the Enlightenment, and its principal virus, Immanuel Kant. Schlatter was, however, no dilettante at this point. He could never have addressed the representatives of all disciplines at Tübingen on the subject of philosophy since René Descartes (1596-1650) had he not been at home in the subject, or been expected to discourse on it. This piece, preceded by another published in 1883[63] and followed by still another lately retrieved,[64] displays his capacity for dealing with the uses of philosophy in theology.

Schlatter hints at botany, at his knowledge of flora and fauna, as first sparing him any inclination toward a Kantian epistemology.[65] It was Kant who asserted that we can never get beyond our consciousness to the point of setting something objective alongside its construct. It was Kant who replaced the eye for reality with the abstraction; Kant whose denial of all feeling in knowing lay "heavy as lead" on German thought; Kant, "tied intimately to Hellenism," who evoked an epistemological skepticism rendering the certainty of the reality of God and the world questionable or impossible; Kant whose exclusion of God from knowledge prepared for that dualism of the "heathenish head and the pious heart," the "atheistic science and the religious mood," that peculiar tendency in Protestantism to divide nature and spirit, thus setting history aside.[66]

Schlatter was certain: faith had its place within the context of nature and history.[67] Jesus was "at home" in nature because it was the possession of his Father.[68] The tension between our understanding of nature and our certainty of God, aided and abetted by a Protestantism "ensouled by the spirit of German Idealism," did not emerge from any real contrast between them, but was purely a concoction of the mind.[69] Lodged between a biblicistic-pietistic-pious parental home and a nineteenth-century Protestantism driven by "Hellenic-Kantian" Idealism, Schlatter struggled to get free.

---

62. Adolf Schlatter, *Die philosophische Arbeit seit Cartesius* (Gütersloh: C. Bertelsmann, 1906), 86; *Die Furcht vor dem Denken: Eine Zugabe zu Hiltys "Glück"* (Gütersloh: C. Bertelsmann, 1900), 32; *Die Gründe*, 46, 74.

63. Neuer, *Adolf Schlatter*, 173.

64. Adolf Schlatter, "Metaphysik," *Zeitschrift für Theologie und Kirche* 7 (1987): 1-88.

65. Neuer, *Adolf Schlatter*, 21.

66. Schlatter, *Die Gründe*, 42, 107; *Die philosophische Arbeit*, 110, 147; *Die Furcht*, 10; Neuer, *Adolf Schlatter*, 415.

67. Schlatter, *Die Gründe*, 108.

68. *Ibid.*, 100, 108.

69. *Ibid.*, 81; cf. Merz, "Schlatters Kritik," 526.

IV. Historical Research

Insistent on perception as the basis of all knowledge, thus on the content of theology as traceable to observable facts recognizable as founding faith, Schlatter proceeded to the interpretive task. In a rejoinder to the Baden cleric who had urged a tabling of the question of God in scientific work, Schlatter stated that there is "no movement toward God which would separate us from what is shown to be God's work,"[70] and described science as "first of all seeing, and second seeing, and third seeing, and seeing yet again."[71]

For his pains Schlatter drew fire from the liberals. The Berne faculty thought his book on faith *(Der Glaube im Neuen Testament)* void of scientific value. Emil Schürer (1844-1910), founder of the study of Judaism, wrote that "Schlatter can form no proper conclusion and is incapable of scientific work." Rudolf Knopf (1874-1920) contended that "Schlatter will not see" — obviously adverting to that summons to see, see, see, and see again. As to Schlatter's series of New Testament commentaries composed for lay readers *(Erläuterungen zum Neuen Testament)*, another wrote that "Schlatter writes explanations to the New Testament, but doesn't understand it." Paul Feine (1859-1933) admitted he could not come to terms with Schlatter, and following the publication of his first book Bernard Weiss wanted to hustle him off to Kiel.[72]

To the liberal Ritschlians, Schlatter responded that despite their concentration on God's revelation in Christ and conscious return to Reformation theology, they exercised such radical criticism of the biblical and dogmatic tradition that they undermined the biblical truth's objective claim to validity. Specifically, the liberals' "pale rationalism" saw nothing in the Old Testament but the make-work of Jewish priests, and created a religious movement calculated to lead beyond Jesus Christ. The result, said Schlatter, was disastrous for preaching and church life. For one thing, at worship it became impossible to detach preoccupation with self from the divine activity. For another, the liberal-minded preacher had constantly to veil the contrast between himself and the church's tradition, thus ridding his talk of all content.[73]

Schlatter drew fire from the conservatives. While the liberal-minded on the Berne faculty declared him incapable of genuinely scientific work, the "positive" camp of the community was bemused by his refusal to share its

70. Schlatter, *Rückblick*, 224.

71. *Atheistische Methoden in der Theologie, Theologie und Dienst*, ed. Helmut Burkhardt und Gerhard Maier (Wuppertal: Brockhaus, 1985), 13.

72. Schlatter, *Erlebtes*, 84-85.

73. See Neuer, *Adolf Schlatter*, 57, 93, 158, 231-33, 258, 316, and 467-68; Schlatter, *Rückblick*, 229.

conviction of the Bible as an entirely reliable and inerrant book, even regarding historical questions. To the "positive" theologians Schlatter responded, "if we are too cowardly to think then we must honorably shut our mouth. . . . Fear of thought cannot be united with faith in divine guidance."[74] Since Jesus himself took his place in history, setting his work in its historical context was not antithetical to the gospel but essential to it. To note connections between, for example, the gospel of Paul and his Greek-Jerusalemite learning was an important "perception." In fact, in certain instances the contemporary view of history was sharper, more complete, and more correct than that of Jesus' own contemporaries.[75] According to his latest biographer, the nine editions and 35,000 copies of Schlatter's commentary on Romans reflected debate not only with Luther and orthodoxy, but also with the holiness movement of his time.[76]

Thus, in face of the "positive" use of the Bible and its liberal denial,[77] Schlatter confessed that he could never separate the two movements of thought and love, that he had neither a theology that forgot the world nor an observation of history that forgot God.[78] It was the "link to Jesus" that gave the critical faculty its positive power.[79] As he said:

> For me, the two activities — faith and criticism — were never mutually opposed, so that at one time I would have thought in Bible-believing fashion, and at another critically. Rather, I thought in critical fashion because I believed in the Bible, and I believed in it because I read it critically.[80]

Or again: "If I had been unable to place scripture above everything else . . . I would have lost Christ. . . . But if the capacity for judgment had left me . . . I would have rejected him and been alienated from the history prepared for us by God's grace."[81] This idea of the indissoluble connection between the question of truth and the question of God led Schlatter to concede that "profane," contemporary science could perform a valuable service, that every contribution to the knowledge of reality that does justice to the facts must be welcome

74. Schlatter, *Die Furcht*, 19, 20.

75. *Ibid.*, 19, 20, 22; Adolf Schlatter, "Christus und Christentum, Person und Prinzip," in *Beiträge zur Förderung christlicher Theologie*, 21-22, 23.

76. Neuer, *Adolf Schlatter*, 152, 216.

77. *Ibid.*, 167; Schlatter, *Rückblick*, 123.

78. Neuer, *Adolf Schlatter*, 32; See also Schlatter, "J. T. Becks theologische Arbeit," 236; *Die philosophische Arbeit*, 253.

79. Schlatter, "Christus und Christentum, Person und Prinzip," 17.

80. Schlatter, *Rückblick*, 83.

81. *Ibid.*

to Christian faith.[82] For him there was no "loathsome ditch" between histori-cal-contingent and rational-necessary truths. The historicizing of theology could not be solved by a platonizing separation of the essential revelatory wit-ness from the nonessential witness of history. What was essential in the reve-lation consisted in the witness to the divine activity within human history.[83]

V. Presuppositions

Schlatter's interpretive work had its presuppositions. Until the emergence of Rudolf Bultmann, none before and few after Schlatter would so clearly out-line the conceptuality driving his exegesis. For a scholar devoted to interpre-tation, it may appear strange to cite his lectures on philosophy as the key to his interpretation of the biblical revelation. It is necessary to recall, however, that at the outset of his career Schlatter had applied for a licentiate and the concomitant "habilitation" in both the history of dogma and New Testament exegesis; that throughout his life he was occupied with dogmatics while at the same time immersed in the exegetical task. In fact, Schlatter's interest in phi-losophy was sufficient to raise in Bernard Weiss the hope that upon his arrival in Berlin he would entirely dispense with the New Testament.[84]

Again, Kantianism was the enemy — by way of Greek, Platonic meta-physic — with its notion of consciousness as constituting the world, its denial of objective reality, cutting itself off from nature and history.[85] Kantianism concealed the connection between the idea of truth and the idea of God.[86] It rendered the entire content of life religiously worthless[87] since it denied the possibility of establishing the idea of God.[88] And it was no accident that it should have lingering effect on Lutheran soil, with its half- or totally misun-derstood *sola fide*.[89] And while Hegel widened the field of observation and did not deny value to appearances, in fact, could affirm that God disclosed himself in them, he found logic revealed only in history — "an impossible, fantastic thesis."[90] In Hegel, wrote Schlatter,

---

82. Neuer, *Adolf Schlatter*, 55.
83. *Ibid.*, 647.
84. *Ibid.*, 147, 296.
85. Schlatter, "Metaphysik," 11, 36, 43, 50.
86. Schlatter, *Die philosophische Arbeit*, 120.
87. *Ibid.*, 117.
88. *Ibid.*, 118-19, 135.
89. *Ibid.*, 128.
90. *Ibid.*, 176, 182.

the observer gains nothing from history, but remains empty. He may never seize on what has occurred with a faith to determine him; never attach to it a love by which to acquire a will; never have in it a source of power that could enable him to act.[91]

At the same time, reaction to the Kantian "deformity" was excessive, wrote Schlatter.[92] When reason began to suspect that its world was more than appearance, the solution was not to assign priority to yet another function, that is, feeling. Beyond the reference to Schleiermacher's service as consisting in the "simple idea" that theology is the formation of religious language, Schlatter seldom or almost never mentioned Schleiermacher.[93] To a greater degree than did his friends Hermann Cremer and Martin Kähler, he ignored the inventor of "the feeling of absolute dependence."

Schlatter insisted that in the individual act of life, thinking, feeling, willing, and acting were so intimately connected that neither could appear without the other.[94] Reducing these various capacities to one spelled abandonment of a great part of philosophical tradition.[95] Schlatter insisted that the first, unconditionally necessary function of thought is perception. Perception thus precedes explanation, for the reason that it yields whatever is to be explained.[96] It is perception, receptivity, "experience," that mediates to us the activity of the world around us.[97] From this relation to the world derives our consciousness of the difference between ourselves and the world. From it also derives our connection with the world.[98] Because of our connection with the world, what we see is always given us as part of our consciousness. Space, for example, is a persistent part of consciousness.[99] Schlatter could have said the same of time, thus of historical occurrence. From this same relation to the world derive feeling, willing, and acting. When, for example, our perceptions move us with particular force, feelings seize hold of us.[100]

Clearly, Schlatter's quarrel was not with Hellenic philosophy as such but only with that idealistic portion of it which regarded the senses or the link of self to the world and its natural processes as a weakening and degrading of

91. *Ibid.,* 188.
92. *Ibid.,* 115.
93. *Ibid.,* 202; cf. Merz, "Schlatters Kritik," 525-26.
94. Schlatter, "Metaphysik," 56.
95. *Ibid.,* 32.
96. *Ibid.,* 22; see Schlatter, *Die Gründe,* 48-49.
97. Schlatter, *Die philosophische Arbeit,* 100.
98. *Ibid.;* Schlatter, "Metaphysik," 73.
99. *Ibid.,* 70, 71.
100. *Ibid.,* 27.

genuine life, the portion he dubbed "Platonic."[101] From his student days onward Schlatter shared an "Aristotelian" notion of the reality and objectivity of perception as the basis of knowledge.[102] That notion underlay his accent on nature and history as determinative of human life. In fact, throughout his life he cited no ancient thinker as often as Aristotle.

But if perception mediates an activity of the world from which derives our consciousness of connection with it; in other words, if what we think is connected to what exists prior to and alongside our thought — nature and history — then a causal relation exists between our consciousness and the world.[103] Then everything in and about us is worked, produced, effected (gewirkt) by God.[104]

Why or how it comes about that perception, that receptivity yields such knowing, and not the other way around, Schlatter left to what he called an "event independent of our decision."[105] Given to us with seeing is the perception that we see; given to us with knowing is the knowledge that we know. It is enough that we perceive what encounters us within the "illumined space of our consciousness."[106] Or again, our task is to "affirm the image in which an existing thing makes itself visible to us, even when it gives no information respecting its origins."[107] To that world, to that "existing thing" belonged Christianity, the sending of Jesus Christ, and the status of his fellowship. These too, Schlatter contended, were "facts" requiring pure observation and unfalsified description.[108] From this perspective the interpreter of Scripture was summoned to "see, see, and see again."

Interestingly enough, Schlatter saw in the emergence of Darwinism a challenge to idealistic veneration of the abstract. Darwinism, he said, had developed a new method of interpreting nature by which the Enlightenment notion of the relation between nature and the idea was reversed. Now, nature was no longer the child but the mother of the idea.[109] And how could this widening of nature's area, how could giving its entire life coherent movement, end in the denial of God? Schlatter wrote: "The mystery which we require in order to bow before nature and see its Maker over us remains true and great

---

101. *Ibid.,* 11, 32.
102. Neuer, *Adolf Schlatter,* 65.
103. Schlatter, *Die philosophische Arbeit,* 96.
104. Schlatter, "Metaphysik," 59.
105. *Ibid.,* 79; see also 60.
106. Schlatter, *Die Gründe,* 33.
107. Schlatter, "Metaphysik," 61.
108. Schlatter, *Die philosophische Arbeit,* 251.
109. *Ibid.,* 240, 241.

enough precisely in the most brilliant execution of the doctrine of development."[110] Among the ethical values won through Darwinism Schlatter named the concept of struggle: "We do not achieve the conditions requisite to life without struggle. . . . To bury that slack idea of happiness dominating us, it had to be shown how firmly our life is tied to nature."[111]

VI. The Great Qualifier

Insisting on revelation as observable fact requiring only "pure observation" or "unfalsified description,"[112] had Schlatter reduced faith to what for all intents and purposes was merely "intellectual assent," and thus fallen into that "Lutheran" pit he had struggled to avoid? Martin Kähler entertained considerable doubt regarding his old friend's ability to derive the necessity of the idea of God from his analysis.[113] Later, his Tübingen colleague Karl Heim would declare Schlatter's attempt at an "apologetic founding of faith" to be faulty, a "radical voluntarism" that traced Christian faith to human decision.[114] And, "apologetic" aside, where was the discrete methodology on which this "critical realism" or "philosophy of perception" was presumably based? Agreed, Schlatter had gotten free of an Idealism alienated from nature and history, but had he forgotten God or faith in the process?

The confusion of Schlatter's friends and detractors was to some degree due to his unfashionable view of individual life as a totality of knowing, feeling, and willing, for which reason he could speak of faith as embracing that totality, and further confound his critics by speaking of faith as "founded in knowledge," or of the "will to believe" as residing in thought, or, better, could state that "we must know in order to believe, and believe in order to know."[115] The evidence is everywhere: Schlatter insisted that in the struggle to "perceive," the error arose from one's own "interior life,"[116] that what was needed to determine that life for the sake of a true perception was faith. "In one's own experience of faith in Jesus," he wrote, "lies the possibility, the motive, and the preparation for a truly historically faithful understanding of the New Testament."[117]

---

110. *Ibid.,* 242.

111. *Ibid.,* 244.

112. *Ibid.,* 251; Adolf Schlatter, *Das christliche Dogma* (Stuttgart: Calwer, 1911), 12.

113. Neuer, *Adolf Schlatter,* 495.

114. *Ibid.,* 710.

115. Schlatter, *Das christliche Dogma,* 120; see also *Die Furcht,* 26.

116. Schlatter, "Metaphysik," 82.

117. Neuer, *Adolf Schlatter,* 190.

On the other hand, Schlatter insisted that a word that could not be understood had no power to create faith;[118] that when the act of thinking was damaged, faith did not emerge unharmed since it required a content accessible to perception. Compelled for epistemological reasons to found Christian dogmatics on the perception of reality, Schlatter viewed that perception as founded, not on Christian dogmatics, obviously, but on faith.

In an address honoring his old teacher, Johann Tobias Beck, delivered at Tübingen in 1904, Schlatter gave eloquent voice to this harnessing of perception to faith or union of historical-philological analysis with theological-pneumatic interpretation — a curiosity to his contemporaries but intelligible to at least some of his successors. In the address Schlatter quoted Beck's inaugural lecture of 1843:

> Criticism of biblical Christianity is not merely conceptual. It involves all of life *(Lebenskritik)*. It penetrates to the very core and driving force of one's way of thinking. Even opposition to biblical Christianity, to the extent it is conscious, cannot remain merely scientific, but becomes an opposition involving all of life. . . . No one arrives at biblical Christianity by way of mere thought, for good or ill. Thought is taken captive by life, refuted by life and ultimately ruined by life. Adherence to rules of performance yields no virtue; adherence to rules of thought yields no truth.[119]

VII. Assessment

For Schlatter, obedience to the summons to "see, see, and see again" required concentrating on the influence of Judaism on Jesus and the apostolic witness. None since the eighteenth-century heterodox scholar Johann Jakob Wettstein (1693-1754) had been so intensively occupied with rabbinic parallels to the New Testament, a study commencing in his Berne period and reflected in the 1882 volume on New Testament faith. In face of the History of Religions School's habit of citing parallels from non-Jewish religions, Schlatter's preoccupation with Judaism made of him an outsider. His legacy nevertheless remains with the school of "Judaists" that continues to advocate Judaism as the matrix of New Testament faith. Schlatter seldom tired of emphasizing that Jesus was a Jew, not merely by virtue of genealogy but in thinking and willing. The Gospel writers were likewise Palestinian in language and conceptuality. In his commentary on Matthew, for example, Schlatter wrote that the author was

---

118. Adolf Schlatter, *Der Brief an die Römer* (Stuttgart: Calwer, 1948), 192.
119. Schlatter, "J. T. Becks theologische Arbeit," 44 n. 5.

at home in two languages, and proceeded to translate all the rabbinic data into Greek. Or behind Luke's special material he thought he detected a narrator who had been among the first disciples of Jesus to go over from Jerusalem to Syrian Christianity. Schlatter's work on the Third Gospel contains a wealth of linguistic parallels from Josephus. In *Die Geschichte der ersten Christenheit* (1926), translated almost thirty years later later by the Jewish Christian Paul Levertoff, Schlatter wrote that it was in Judaism that Christianity first emerged as a living entity.[120] Seventy years later the Göttingen scholar Joachim Jeremias (1900-79) would speak of the pioneering significance of Schlatter's study, an occupation that yielded contact with the Talmudic scholar, Hayyim Saul Horovitz (1859-1921) as well as with Martin Buber (1878-1965).[121] References in contemporary New Testament studies to Schlatter's pioneering work in Jewish research are rare. The reason, however, may not lie in the absence of his influence, but in the penchant among academics to eschew dependence.

In a conversation with Rudolf Bultmann during the summer of 1962, and to the question why his celebrated pupil, Ernst Käsemann, punctuated his lectures with such frequent reference to Adolf Schlatter, the Marburger replied that the university where Käsemann was now lecturing furnished the explanation: "look where he's at, in Tübingen." The answer lies deeper. Schlatter shared one powerful conviction with his erstwhile, disaffected pupils, Barth and Bultmann, that to the interpretation of the New Testament belonged the stance of the total person, since its message was calculated to evoke either faith or unbelief, and nothing between; that the mere pursuit of the interpretive "steps" developed over the last century and a half could not automatically unlock the meaning of a text. For that reason Schlatter deserved referring to. But if Barth and Bultmann left Schlatter's lecture hall disaffected, they earned disaffection from the side of their old teacher, despite his concession to their theology as a needed corrective to pietism's concentration on the self. Toward Barth's commentary on Romans Schlatter entertained three misgivings: first, it displayed a decidedly nonhistorical character issuing in a poorly represented or even violated biblical text. Second, its emphasis on the "infinite qualitative difference between time and eternity" ignored Paul's concept of the redemptive work of God manifest in human-historical reality. In 1925 Schlatter would ask, "[A]re there really no 'works of God' . . . no 'work of Christ' in the New Testament? And what else are works than history, than what is happening?"[122] Third, Barth's concept of faith was irrational. The

120. *The Church in the New Testament,* tr. Paul Levertoff (London: SPCK, 1955).
121. Neuer, *Adolf Schlatter,* 180, 387, 410, 473, 631-32, 635, 696, 704, and 748-49.
122. Neuer, "Der Briefwechsel zwischen Karl Barth und Adolf Schlatter," 92 n. 32.

"No!" which he had set over our life-situation struck at the act of thought with ruinous force. As for Bultmann, Schlatter faulted him for his historical skepticism, for the disappearance from history attaching to his description of Jesus' preaching and activity. In Bultmann's Jesus book Schlatter found only the speaking, not the creating God, only the commanding, not the giving God. As he put it in a 1934 essay on the Talmud, "the law is neither the only nor the first word of God which Israel received."[123]

To the extent that the "Barthian" (at least initially) exclusive concentration on divine sovereignty has now run its course, and to the extent that the "Bultmannian" allowing for methodological skepticism in historical study has been challenged, Schlatter's criticism of his two disaffected pupils remains intact. But his insistence upon the requirement of faith in interpretation, however sanguine the confidence in method, intimately links him with those two latter-day giants. In addition, Schlatter's insistence that a word that cannot be understood has no power to create faith leaned him more toward the one candidate for disappointment than the other — something that perhaps not even a Bultmann, though indeed a Käsemann, would remember.

As to the philosophical context of his interpretive work, Schlatter's was especially beholden to Georg Hamann. The so-called "Magus of the North," long unread except by Soren Kierkegaard and a few others, had been a bitter opponent of Immanuel Kant, especially what he believed to be Kant's cold prejudice in favor of mathematics, his "gnostic" hatred of matter, and his almost mystical love of form. Hamann opposed the division of the human animal into separate functions. Only the whole person, with all its passions, emotions, desires, and physiological reactions, could approach the truth. Therefore, whatever a person intended to accomplish required all its powers. The weapon with which Hamann proceeded to attack the Enlightenment and its theology was, ironically, David Hume, the very philosopher who had awakened Kant from his "dogmatic slumbers." What attracted Hamann was Hume's argument that all knowledge rests on belief, on faith. It is not reason that generates faith, but the other way around.

Schlatter followed where Hamann led. It was, as Schlatter saw it, faith that generated reason and therefore was present in every act of consciousness, every act of perception. Like Hamann, Schlatter resisted the splitting of the individual into ingredients, or elevating the one ingredient over the other. Like Hamann, he insisted upon belief in or the conception of a material world as correlative or concomitant with perception, with sensation. And,

---

123. "Das Alte Testament und der Talmud," in *Bekennende Kirche,* 2nd ed., no. 7 (München: Chr. Kaiser Verlag, 1934).

like Hamann, he advocated a "critical reason" that allowed room for the idea of God.

From the Anglo-American perspective, Schlatter's position during the two world wars was unfortunate. He explained Germany's entry into the First World War as occasioned by Bismarck's politics with its support of the Hapsburgs. Vienna was thus the "dark place" from which ruin had come on Germany.[124] On the other hand, Schlatter believed that Germany's declaration of war was ethically justified in light of English and French plans for annexation, and together with ninety-three other intellectuals he signed the famous appeal to the "cultural world," published in Frankfurt, October 1914, later described by Karl Barth as his *dies ater,* or "black day." At the war's conclusion, Schlatter insisted Germany had no guilt in the war, and that the peace of Versailles was a crime. His political naivete would allow him to embrace the notion of Germany's surrender as a "stab in the back," a legend *(Dolchstosslegende)* exalted to gospel truth in the generation following.

Schlatter's opposition to Nazism was not unambiguous. He could speak of the Germans as suffering from a "fantastic Führer politics," he could declare that an evangelical pastor "is forbidden to wear the brown shirt," and he could give earnest warning against the anti-Christian acts of the Third Reich.[125] But two years later he could not bring himself to protest the discrimination against Jews.[126] In fact, he went so far as to compare National Socialist race-ideology to Jewish hostility to Christianity, and spoke of the threat of the ideological "victory of the Jew" in Nazism's anti-Christian struggle.[127] Schlatter's 1934 essay on the Talmud described the precursor to that ideological victory in the rabbinic setting of the law between God and humans.[128]

In the discussion evoked by the Aryan Paragraph, which excluded all Jews from responsibilities of state, Schlatter agreed with the Marburg theologians that Jewishness did not have to do with race but with community and history,[129] but he still refused to sign it because he denied any judicial claim to the spiritual office.[130] When Hermann Sasse (1895-1976) and others drafted the "Bethel Confession"[131] and mailed it to Schlatter, he could not sign it be-

---

124. Schlatter, *Erlebtes,* 18.

125. Neuer, *Adolf Schlatter,* 681, 740, and 779.

126. *Ibid.,* 761.

127. *Ibid.,* 758, 760-61.

128. Schlatter, "Das Alte Testament und der Talmud," 29, 32, 33, 34, 35, and 36.

129. Neuer, *Adolf Schlatter,* 748.

130. *Ibid.,* 751-52.

131. A statement of faith designed to challenge the "German Christians" (Protestants

cause he could not agree with the statement that Christians ought to endure persecution rather than surrender unity with their Jewish Christian brothers. Finally, he refused to subscribe to the Barmen Declaration accepted in 1934 at a synod of the Confessing Church *(Bekennende Kirche),* which naturally set him in proximity to the infamous German Christians.[132] He was suspicious of the Declaration's "Barthian" denial of divine revelation prior to or outside of Christ,[133] and vehemently opposed Barth's thesis that the doctrine of revelation in creation was the spiritual culture for German Christian theology. As his biographer states, in historical retrospect the fact that in 1935 Schlatter could not achieve public protest against discrimination of the Jews can only be regretted; a shadow remains over his otherwise so clear-sighted judgment of Nazism's race-ideology.[134]

Many a theologian has insisted that his point of view cannot be subsumed under any known persuasion, and has exhausted time and energy defending his singularity. Schlatter had no need to spend time advertising his uniqueness. The struggle to sail his sometimes frail craft between the reefs of reductionist nineteenth-century theology and conservative, "positive" theology, hostile to criticism; his belief in an objective world as part and parcel of perception and which allowed for the idea of God; his refusal wholeheartedly to embrace any current project however great his affection for its advocates — all of this made Adolf Schlatter an outsider. The statement of Karl Barth, his onetime pupil and critic, to the effect that Schlatter may not have been "at the front," but in his time and beyond would come to stand "in the inmost line of defense,"[135] has about it the air of faint praise. Schlatter's conviction that, though it may be temporally postponed, affirmation of the biblical witness is for all that ultimately essential to its interpretation set him in the vanguard of a movement with representatives in virtually every school of theology here or in Europe, in spite of attempts at viewing the interpretive task as merely another exercise in mathematics or logic.

---

in support of Hitler), and which denounced Aryanism and the attempt to rid the church of any Jewish taint or influence.

132. Adolf Schlatter, *Jesus — Der Christus,* ed. with intro. Rainer Riesner (Giessen: Brunnen, 1979), 12-13.

133. Neuer, *Adolf Schlatter,* 765.

134. *Ibid.,* 761.

135. Neuer, "Der Briefwechsel zwischen Karl Barth und Adolf Schlatter, 94; Schlatter, "Das Alte Testament und der Talmud," 26-36 n. 9.

10

J. GRESHAM MACHEN

The Fundamentalist Defense

I. "We Have No Strauss"

For ten days in October of 1873, the Sixth General Conference of the Evangelical Alliance met in New York City to assess the state of the church. The greatest ecumenical enterprise of the nineteenth century, the Alliance represented a broad range of international evangelical opinion and fostered cooperation and theological exchange across national and denominational lines for over half a century. Prominent among the topics discussed at the 1873 meeting was the damaging effect of modern biblical criticism. The work of Ferdinand Christian Baur and David Friedrich Strauss garnered the lion's share of attention.

M. Cohen Stuart, delegate from Rotterdam, sounded an alarmist note. The school of Baur, he declared, has won increasing numbers of disciples among clergy and laity in Holland and counts among its adherents "well-armed, gifted, learned, serious men." The fundamental teaching of this formidable "enemy" is opposed to all that Christians hold dear: "it acknowledges an all-reigning law of continuous causality and development, which consistently must lead to the denial of an Almighty and free-willing God, to the rejection of miracle, of the Divine character of Revelation . . . and even of the character of sin as guilt toward God. . . ."[1] The "rationalistic and materialistic

---

1. *History, Essays, Orations, and Other Documents of the Sixth General Conference of the Evangelical Alliance,* ed. Philip Schaff and S. Irenaeus Prime (New York: Harper & Brothers,

spirit" that Baur and his disciples represent is part of "the combustible mass of sundry brooding social questions" facing modern society. Its success puts the church on notice that many "are estranged from Gospel truth and faith."[2]

The Reverend Hermann Krummacher of Brandenburg agreed with this pessimistic assessment in his survey, "Christian Life in Germany." "Thousands upon thousands," he opined, "are alienated from any kind of worship, especially in large cities." The masses have turned from Christ to "Socialism," and "the lust after riches" motivates even "the highest classes."[3] Krummacher concentrated his invective on David Friedrich Strauss, whose *Der alte und der neue Glaube* had been published in Germany the previous year. An English translation, *The Old Faith and the New,* appearing in 1873, made Strauss's final testament very much *au courant* for English-speaking delegates. Strauss, said Krummacher, "sets before us without reserve the final results of miracle-denying criticism." His theology is the ultimate example of immanentism: "Laplace and Darwin are his apostles, who teach him the knowledge of the universe, his God; self-creation of the world, natural selection, and descent of man from the ape are the mysteries of his religion; the amusements of the theater and the concert room, his worship."[4]

That Darwin and Strauss were lumped together in the mind of many evangelicals at the 1873 conference is hardly surprising. The unsettling effect of *The Origin of Species,* published in 1859, continued to embroil the church in debate. Strauss himself spoke in glowing terms of Darwin as one who "has opened the door by which a happier coming race will finally cast out miracles"[5] — a sentiment hardly calculated to win the endorsement of evangelical Christians. James McCosh (1811-94), president of the College of New Jersey (Princeton), made the effort to reconcile the purpose of religion with the new science of evolution: "Development is a law of successive nature, and secures a connection between the past and the present, and I may add the future. . . . It is merely an exhibition of order running through successive ages. . . ."[6] But after his presentation, others rose to debate his irenical conclusions, including the aged Charles Hodge (1797-1878) of Princeton Seminary. Hodge, whose essay *What Is Darwinism?* would be published the following year, made his opposition to the new science plain. He asked the

---

1874), 93. On the significance of the meeting, see George M. Marsden, *Fundamentalism and American Culture* (New York: Oxford University Press, 1980), 11-21.

2. *Evangelical Alliance,* 94.

3. *Ibid.,* 80.

4. *Ibid.,* 83.

5. *The Old Faith and the New,* tr. Mathilde Blind (New York: Henry Holt, 1873), 205.

6. *Evangelical Alliance,* 267.

delegates rhetorically: "Is development an intellectual process guided by God, or is it a blind process of unintelligible, unconscious force, which knows no end and adopts no means?"[7] The answer to this question separates the theist from the atheist.

Most evangelical leaders shared Hodge's opinion. They believed that the science of evolution, like the science of biblical criticism, reduced all events to mundane causality. Both enterprises allow no place for the sovereign God of biblical faith and Augustinian heritage to work his almighty will. What the church faces, said Theodore Gottlieb, professor of theology at Bonn, is a new "materialism" that has Western Christendom in its iron grip. Materialism is a modern form of "infidelity" that denies "special Divine Providence" and "takes the innermost nerve out of all moral and religious action. . . ."[8]

A strong sense of anxiety pervaded the reports from the European delegates. They felt the force of advancing secularization and conveyed their consternation to their American brethren. A number of Europeans looked wistfully to America as the new bastion of Christian civilization. "The voluntary exertions for the furtherance of Christ's Gospel in Germany," confessed Krummacher, "can not, of course, be compared to those of America. . . ."[9]

William Fairfield Warren (1833-1929), staunch Methodist and the first president of Boston University, was only too willing to ratify this impression of American superiority. He expressed unswerving confidence that America would hold its own against atheistic forces from abroad. Certainly, there have been "successive waves of opposition to the kingdom of Christ."[10] "But we have no Strauss," that is, no infidel "of cosmopolitan, national reputation" who comes out of the bosom of the church and turns against the Christian faith. Infidelity in America, asserts Warren, has always had an "extra-ecclesiastical position." Deists like Jefferson, transcendentalists like Emerson, and socialists like Robert Owen have brought their ideas from abroad and made their opposition to orthodoxy plain. This has helped American Christians recognize that unbelief is "the natural, and in a sense normal characteristic of unawakened and unregenerate souls."[11] America is an evangelical land. The Great Awakening of the eighteenth century formed the nation by giving its people a shared experience of conversion that broke down "intercolonial jealousy, isolation, and repellency."[12]

7. *Ibid.*, 318.
8. *Ibid.*, 209.
9. *Ibid.*, 81.
10. *Ibid.*, 252.
11. *Ibid.*, 253.
12. *Ibid.*, 249.

Evangelicalism is the mother of America. It will protect the nation from the scourge of heterodoxy whenever it arises. No doubt "infidels and errorists" will continue to raise their heads. But the means to combat them are at hand: "We expect to abolish infidelity only by bringing all natural men into the experience of a spiritual life, whose supernatural facts will admit of no explanation short of that given in the supernatural Word and in the holy Catholic Church."[13]

Warren's reference to "supernatural facts" and his confidence that "natural men" will accept the "explanation" of them is a characteristically American apologetic formulation in the nineteenth century. Its philosophical lineage is Scottish commonsense realism, the dominant philosophy of American evangelicalism since the latter third of the eighteenth century. This philosophical school, founded by the Scotsman Thomas Reid (1710-86), taught that our perceptions of the world reveal the reality of the world — that is to say, what we see and sense is what is. This simple notion, "common to men with whom we can converse and transact business,"[14] contradicted the representative theory of perception argued by René Descartes and John Locke which maintained that "ideas," or initial constructs of the human mind, control human understanding. In David Hume, this representative theory led to an extreme skepticism that questioned the reliability of even our most fundamental impressions and intuitions and called into question the existence of God. Reid would have none of this. "It is a bold philosophy," he declares, "that rejects, without ceremony, principles which irresistibly govern the belief and the conduct of all mankind in the common concerns of life."[15] The general principles by which our forebears learned that cold freezes water and heat turns it to steam are the same ones that governed the work of Isaac Newton (1642-1727) when he examined the heavens and discovered their universal laws.[16] Our empirical knowledge, whether concerning the characteristics of water or the movement of planets, can be trusted. It is reliable — objectively true. It is "fact" discovered by "science." Extolling Francis Bacon (1561-1626) as his model, Reid contends that nature's works yield their mysteries through observation and experiment, the basic methodological pillars of all true scientific procedure.[17] The knowledge of nature achieved through science reveals the design of an Intelligent Power. Religiously, commonsense realism as-

---

13. *Ibid.*, 254.

14. *Essays on the Intellectual Powers of Man*, ed. James Walker (Boston: Philips, Sampson, 1855), 350-51.

15. *An Inquiry into the Human Mind* (Edinburgh: Bell & Bradfute, 1810), 24.

16. *Ibid.*, 3.

17. *Ibid.*, 2-3.

serted "a wise and good Author of Nature"[18] whose shaping hand may be inferred from his works.

Commonsense realism was not only an epistemology but a moral philosophy defending the enduring qualities of civilization and its written record. It taught that humanity could readily discern true from false by the natural faculty of intuition and act with prudence in the conduct of affairs. It defended the credibility of human testimony across time grounded in the continuity of human character and the stability of the conventions of language. The words we use are satisfactory representations of reality. Whether from the past or the present, they signify the same objective world that defines universal human experience. Knowledge involves a community of discourse that spans the generations — a philosophical point of view that readily lent itself to the defense of Scripture.

Here was a philosophy in which "faith, science, the Bible, morality, and civilization" all found affirmation.[19] It was practical and anti-elitist, tailor-made for the democratic ideal that celebrates the common man and asserts that human existence can be shaped anew in a "large commercial republic." No wonder that after its introduction to the colonies, which began with the election of John Witherspoon (1723-94) to the presidency of the College of New Jersey in 1768, it quickly spread to Harvard, the College of Philadelphia (University of Pennsylvania), and William and Mary. It even established its influence at Yale where Lockean ideas were dominant.

Commonsense realism proved to be a friendly companion to Calvinistic Protestantism. It was employed by Archibald Alexander (1772-1851), founder of Princeton Seminary and student of Witherspoon, by Timothy Dwight (1752-1817), Nathaniel William Taylor (1786-1858), and Charles Hodge, among others. The reason for the philosophy's attraction was that Calvinism in America, whether orthodox or evangelical, rested on the Reformed doctrine of Scripture's perspicuity which asserted that all matters related to salvation are "plainly and clearly unfolded in Scripture" so that "unlearned believers who read with devotion and attention" will understand them.[20] In the American context, this meant that the propagation of Christian faith needed neither establishment nor hierarchy, but only the proclamation of the biblical word to the believing individual in the free marketplace of ideas. Truth is represented objectively in the biblical word. The

18. *Ibid.*, 428.

19. Marsden, *Fundamentalism and American Culture*, 17.

20. Heinrich Heppe, *Reformed Dogmatics*, rev. Ernst Bizer, tr. G. T. Thomson (Grand Rapids: Baker, 1978), 32-33, quoting Markus Friedrich Wendelin (1584-1652).

common man of common sense, empowered in faith by the Holy Spirit, is capable of understanding this objective word or "plain fact" that the Bible delivers. To facilitate this process of delivery, the theologian is obligated, like the scientist of nature, to obey the clear rules of his discipline. As Hodge states the case:

> We cannot put the roots of a tree in the place of the branches or the teeth of an animal in the place of its feet. . . . So the facts of science arrange themselves. . . . The same is obviously true with regard to the facts or truths of the Bible. They cannot be held in violation, nor will they admit of any and every arrangement the theologian may choose to assign them. . . . [The theologian] can no more construct a system of theology to suit his fancy, than the astronomer can adjust the mechanism of the heavens according to his own general pleasure.[21]

The conjunction of commonsense realism and Calvinism in nineteenth-century America is routinely criticized by commentators. Diogenes Allen, for example, charges that "What in fact often resulted was a static view of Christian doctrine and morals with no sense of historic development, a defense of biblical inerrancy, and a rationalistic style of apologetics."[22] While this point of view is not without merit, it fails to appreciate the constructive social role that commonsense realism played in the nineteenth century as a conceptual framework for articulating the essentials of Calvinist faith. For three generations, commonsense realism helped to negotiate the thorny paradox of teaching divine election and human depravity while at the same time affirming American optimism in the great experiment of a new nation founded on Enlightenment ideals. It did so by aiding theology in teaching that the common man, listening to the preaching of the church, is capable by the use of reason of assessing the full scope of his moral predicament as a lost creature under the judgment of God who has nowhere to turn but to the love of Christ. Commonsense realism thus helped to accommodate Augustinian faith to the peculiarities of the American mission field, thereby making the heritage of the Reformation accessible to a broad public. Doctrinal rigorists might argue the differences between "consistent" Calvinism and "Arminian" tendencies in the rhetoric of conversion, but such conflicts pale in comparison to the pervasive consensus of American evangelicalism that minimized denominational differences, preached the sovereignty of God, shared in the exuberance of the revivalist tradition, and held to the conviction that Amer-

---

21. *Systematic Theology* (Grand Rapids: Eerdmans, 1989), 1:18-19.
22. *Philosophy for Understanding Theology* (Atlanta: John Knox, 1985), 193.

ica was a chosen nation. Protestant evangelicalism in America was willing to confront an individual with the "facts" of heaven and hell. It trusted that an individual could discern the difference between good and evil, God and the devil. It offered to the converted the glorious expectation of spiritual satisfaction to follow from the adoption of a changed life. In the fall of 1873, President Warren of Boston had ample reason to declare that there was no Strauss to darken the prospects of mission and that the "supernatural facts" of faith would reach "all natural men."

Within two decades, however, the situation in America changed as a "New Theology" spread rapidly in major Protestant centers of learning. The intellectual climate fostered by the successive influence of European romanticism, idealism, and historicism developed a parallel on American soil that won widespread influence, particularly among the affluent and educated of the East. This theology called into question the basic Augustinian avowal of both the electing God and human corruption. It was suspicious of bald assertions of biblical "facts" and inherited creeds. Instead, it expended considerable energy separating the "idea" of faith from the historical particularities of its human expression. If God is to make sense, it declared, then he must be explained in interpersonal and subjective terms. The relevance of the divine to the human had to be argued on the principle of analogy or it meant nothing. The New Theology went out of its way to emphasize human participation in the process of redemption.

Henry Ward Beecher (1813-87) of Plymouth Congregational Church in Brooklyn, New York, exemplified the approach of the New Theology and did more than any other figure to popularize it for the American public. Beecher spoke against "the Dogmatic school of Preachers" who rely "upon a pre-existing system of truth, which has been founded before their day and handed down from generation to generation. . . ." Addressing divinity students at Yale Divinity School in 1871, Beecher claimed to represent "a *Life School*" that cares less for the "ordinances" of the church than for "such portions of the truth as are required by the special needs of man." The way to God's nature is through human nature, and "the facts of the past" are relevant only insofar as they become "factors of the life that now is."[23] According to Beecher, emphasis upon the judgment of a righteous God and the effort to convert people by threat do not win human hearts but make them recoil in horror. He shunned the "barbarous doctrines" of Calvinism as out of step with the progress of humanity. In a sermon from 1874 on "The Universal Heart of God," Beecher gives an account of the knowledge of God in relation to human capacity that

---

23. William R. Hutchison, *American Protestant Thought* (New York: Harper, 1968), 38.

echoes Lessing's argument in "The Education of the Human Race." In the "lowest physical estate" of primitive humanity, God governed "with power, with imperiousness, compelling obedience." These were the fitting means by which humanity could be educated in the ways of salvation. But in this age of progress and maturity, it is different: "We whip children; but we do not whip men."[24] What is required is a view of God "which shall satisfy the highest reason" and meet "the wants of the world."[25]

The New Theology had its own historical antecedents in American religious thought upon which to draw. Its roots may be traced to the non-evangelical, non-revivalist faction of the New England churches at the beginning of the nineteenth century where the explicit effort was made to accommodate Christian doctrine to modern culture in such a way that traditional divisions of sacred and secular were softened and the reality and inspiration of the divine were located within the immanence of human cultural formation.[26] The most drastic revision was made by Universalists and Unitarians. Writing against the traditional understanding of the atonement as the satisfaction of divine "honor," which dominated the Edwardsean School, the Universalist Hosea Ballou (1771-1852) declared in 1805, "It is profane to attribute a disposition to the Almighty which we can justly condemn in ourselves."[27] In 1819 the Unitarian leader William Ellery Channing (1780-1842) stated boldly that God and humanity share an "essential sameness" so that all virtue must be sought in the analysis of human nature. He maintained that Scripture must be investigated like any other book.[28] The Congregationalist Horace Bushnell (1802-76), who inspired an entire generation of liberal preachers and theologians, called into question the confidence in the notion that words denote unchanging facts. Words are but "faded metaphors." Christian truth in the Bible has an inexactness of meaning that cannot be gotten around. "The scriptures of God, in providing a clothing for religious truth, have little to do with mere dialectics, much to do with the freer creations of poetry. . . ." The same is true of the language of creed and dogma: "Considering the infirmities of language . . . all formulas of doctrine should be

24. Henry Ward Beecher, *Plymouth Pulpit* (New York: Fords, Howard, & Hulbert, 1890) 2:370.

25. *Ibid.*, 2:381.

26. See William R. Hutchison, *The Modernist Impulse in American Protestantism* (New York: Oxford, 1982), 1-11.

27. *Treatise on Atonement* (Boston: A. Tompkins, 1860), 88; quoted in Ann Douglas, *The Feminization of American Culture* (New York: Alfred A. Knopf, 1988), 125.

28. H. Shelton Smith, Robert T. Handy, and Lefferts A. Loetscher, *American Christianity* (New York: Scribner's, 1960), 1:493-502.

held in a spirit of accommodation. They cannot be pressed to the letter, for the very sufficient reason that the letter is never true." The context in which they are spoken and the needs of the speakers and hearers have a decisive determination on their meaning.[29]

The clash between evangelicals and liberals did not take long to surface. The heresy trial of the liberal Presbyterian preacher David Swing (1830-94) in 1874 received national attention, as did the resignation of Henry Ward Beecher from the Congregational Association of New York in October of 1882. The heresy trials of Charles A. Briggs (1841-1913) in 1891 and of Henry Preserved Smith (1847-1927) in 1892 and the attack on Arthur Cushman McGiffert (1861-1933) in 1900 indicate both the influence the New Theology exercised in the academic establishment and the corresponding fear it engendered among evangelicals.

Conservatives in the Presbyterian General Assembly responded to the challenge of the New Theology by passing a five-point resolution in 1910 defining the basics of orthodox belief. To be a Christian meant that one must unambiguously affirm: (1) the inerrancy of Scripture, (2) the virgin birth of Christ, (3) a substitutionary doctrine of atonement, (4) the bodily resurrection of Christ, and (5) the veracity of biblical miracles. Between 1910 and 1915, twelve paperback volumes entitled *The Fundamentals* argued against historical criticism and liberal theology. Their impact was enormous, in part because they were sent free of charge to pastors and church leaders across the land, courtesy of two conservative businessmen from Southern California. With over three million copies in distribution, *The Fundamentals* became "a symbolic point of reference" for evangelicals in the church.[30] In 1920 the label "fundamentalism" was coined by Curtis Lee Laws (1868-1946) of the *Watchman-Examiner* and taken up by the national press.[31] It helped to solidify the interdenominational consciousness of the conservative cause.

The New Theology, however, overcame this stiff resistance and prospered. William R. Hutchison estimates that by 1920 liberal ideas had captured a third of the pulpits of American Protestantism and half of its literary production.[32] Frank Chamberlain Porter (1859-1946), prominent New Testament scholar at Yale Divinity School and pioneer in the use of modern historical criticism in the American context, could even entertain the notion, at least privately, that if Jesus never lived, the thinking Christian could neverthe-

---

29. Horace Bushnell, *God in Christ* (Hartford: Brown and Parsons, 1849), 77, 81.
30. Marsden, *Fundamentalism and American Culture,* 119.
31. *Ibid.,* 107.
32. *The Modernist Impulse in American Protestantism,* 3.

less assent to the gospel "as poetic truth embodied in imagined historical form."[33] In such an assertion, unimaginable in the days of Dwight and Taylor, the triumph of the Ideal over the Real appeared complete.

There is no doubt that the great evangelical consensus of the nineteenth century had lost its hegemony. No longer would any church leader dare to boast that "we have no Strauss." The American church found itself in the same crisis of belief that European evangelicals had warned about a half century before. The postwar period of intellectual and spiritual malaise as well as the failure of projects such as the Interchurch World Movement contributed to a sense of foreboding that the great evangelical Protestant tradition — which had carried the spiritual life of the nation for two centuries — had lost its impetus. Living through this crisis, and seeking to make sense of it, was J. Gresham Machen of Princeton Seminary.

II. Biography[34]

John Gresham Machen was born 28 July 1881, the second of three sons of a prominent and prosperous Baltimore lawyer, Arthur Webster Machen, and his wife Mary Jones Gresham Machen. The young Machen was reared in an "Old School" Presbyterian home with deep Southern traditions, where he was profoundly influenced by the piety of his mother, who catechized him in the faith. From his father, the youth developed his love for classical culture. At Johns Hopkins University, he studied under the great philologist and classics scholar Basil Lanneau Gildersleeve (1831-1924). Graduating in 1901 with the highest honors, Machen stayed for a year of graduate study at Johns Hopkins before enrolling in the fall of 1902 in Princeton Seminary, where he enjoyed the tutelage of Benjamin Breckenridge Warfield (1851-1921), another "Old School" Presbyterian with Southern roots. He received a master's degree in philosophy in 1904 from Princeton University and his Bachelor of Divinity degree from the Seminary the following year. While successful at scholarship, Machen was unsure as to the vocation of ministry.

Winning a fellowship in New Testament studies persuaded Machen to explore biblical scholarship abroad. He left for Germany in the fall of 1905 to study at Göttingen and Marburg. At Marburg he encountered Adolf Jülicher

33. This from an unpublished essay, "The Place of the New Testament in the Christian Religion." See Roy A. Harrisville, *Frank Chamberlain Porter: Pioneer in American Biblical Interpretation* (Missoula: Scholars, 1976), 66.

34. See Ned B. Stonehouse, *J. Gresham Machen* (Grand Rapids: Wm. B. Eerdmans, 1954); W. Masselink, *Professor J. Gresham Machen* (privately published).

(1857-1938), famous for his work on the parables; Johannes Weiss; and Wilhelm Herrmann — the same teachers under whom Rudolf Bultmann and Karl Barth, Machen's German contemporaries, studied. It was Herrmann who had the greatest impact on the young Machen.

At the height of his career, Wilhelm Herrmann was a brilliant representative of the Ritschlian School of Protestant liberalism. The center of his theology was a radically revised christology. The meaning of Jesus for contemporary faith, said Herrmann, is not to be found in the accounts of his virgin birth or resurrection. It is not to be located in the "historical Jesus" understood in terms of the "events" of his life recorded in the Gospels. Nor can we discern the significance of Jesus by uncovering the nature of his impact on the early disciples. Neither mysticism, dogmatism, nor metaphysics can recover the experience of the early church in such a way as to make it ours. Rather, the relevance of the gospel record to the modern age centers in the fact that it conveys the "personality" of Jesus. The enduring authority of Jesus is the experience of his "inner life," known through his moral teaching and example. It is the likeness of Jesus to the ideal of human personhood that makes him our Lord. In appropriating this value, Christians receive the primary benefit of religion, which is to provide meaning for humanity by affirming the world and attaining the fullness of personality.

In the figure of Herrmann, Machen encountered a sophisticated representative of the Protestant liberal tradition who anchored Christian belief in a principle of correspondence between divine nature and human nature. Machen was both attracted to Herrmann and disturbed by the implications of his theology. The struggle to understand Ritschlian liberalism eventually led him, after years of struggle, to reaffirm his "Old School" commitment to the plenary inspiration of Scripture, traditional dogma, and, above all, the historic accent of Reformed theology on the otherness of God. In Machen's view, the type of reconstruction of Christian faith that Herrmann represented meant the destruction of Christianity.

After his year abroad, Machen returned to Princeton, where he became Instructor in New Testament from 1906 to 1914. The agony of his quest for faith continued, and it was only in November 1913, at the age of thirty-two, that he sought ordination through the New Brunswick Presbytery. From 1914 to 1929 he served as assistant professor, interrupted by a year of service on the front lines in France during the First World War with the YMCA.

After the war, the controversy with modernism continued to plague the Presbyterian Church. As undisputed intellectual leader of the fundamentalist forces in Presbyterianism, Machen was in the thick of battle. He came under personal attack and engaged himself in acrimonious debate. After years of confusion and bitter rivalry among the faculty, Princeton Seminary reorganized under more liberal leadership in 1929. Machen resigned his post and was instrumental in founding Westminster Theological Seminary, where he served as full professor from 1929 to 1937. In March 1935 he was suspended from the ministry as a schismatic by the New Brunswick Presbytery for his efforts in 1933 as chief organizer of the Independent Board for Presbyterian Foreign Missions, the purpose of which was to counter liberal influence in worldwide evangelism activities of the Presbyterian Church. After appeal, the suspension was sustained by the General Assembly in 1936. On June 11 of that year, Machen led a small number of fellow dissidents in the founding of the Presbyterian Church of America (the Orthodox Presbyterian Church).

Machen died on New Year's Day in 1937 of pneumonia in Bismarck, North Dakota, while on a speaking tour undertaken to explain the stand of his infant denomination. A lifelong bachelor, he had spent his intellectual career in total absorption in the Presbyterian tradition. He loved his church deeply and died unreconciled to what it had become.

The Origin of Paul's Religion, in which Machen argues for the continuity between Jesus and Paul, appeared in 1921. *New Testament Greek for Beginners*, which is popular to the present day, was first published in 1923. Machen's *magnum opus* in New Testament scholarship is *The Virgin Birth of Christ*, first edition 1930. He was also the author of occasional essays and collections both scholarly and popular. But the work for which he is chiefly remembered is *Christianity and Liberalism* (1923), which Sydney Ahlstrom (1919-1984) has called "the chief ornament of American Fundamentalism."[35] It is to this work that we turn because it is the clearest theoretical statement of Machen's principles of biblical interpretation.

III. *Christianity and Liberalism*

Machen's credentials as a commonsense realist are evident on every page of this pivotal essay. He announces his aim "to present the issue as sharply and clearly as possible" (1).[36] He seeks "the attention of the plain man" (3) or the "simple Christian" (5), and is confident that the content of the Bible and Christian doctrine are "perfectly plain" (19) or "perfectly clear" (27). He

---

35. *A Religious History of the American People* (New Haven: Yale University Press, 1972), 912.

36. All page references are to J. Gresham Machen, *Christianity and Liberalism* (Grand Rapids: Eerdmans, 1946).

praises the human mind as having "a wonderful faculty for the condensation of perfectly valid arguments" (57). Accordingly, Machen refuses to indulge in any form of idealistic perspectivalism that drives a wedge between an "idea" and its "representation"; for him there are no "faded metaphors" (to use the phrase of Bushnell) in Christian speech. Machen's overriding interest is the "facts" of Christianity. The theologian's office is one of steward, guardian, faithful transmitter of received truth. In continuity with the American evangelical tradition, Machen takes the Bible for what it says and offers it to the "natural man," whom he trusts will be able to make proper distinctions and, under the guidance of the Holy Spirit, see the truth for himself.

This conviction about the clarity of the Bible leads Machen to affirm the plenary inspiration of the Scriptures: "[Plenary inspiration] supposes that the Holy Spirit so informed the minds of the Biblical writers that they were kept from falling into errors that mar all other books. . . . [A]ccording to the doctrine of inspiration, the account is a matter of fact, a true account . . ." (74). But Machen does not state this principle of his argument until the fourth chapter; and after he announces it, he leaves it quickly. Those who portray Machen as a wooden inerrantist do him disservice. Inerrancy is not for Machen the doctrine by which the church stands or falls. "There are many," Machen confesses, "who believe that the Bible is right at the central point, in its account of the redeeming work of Christ, and yet believe that it contains many errors." Such people are Christians, and to them Machen extends the hand of fellowship (75). Indeed, Machen's tolerance and flexibility, following a long and honored tradition of American evangelicalism, goes further. While insisting on a doctrinal basis for Christianity, he states unequivocally that not all points of doctrine are of equal importance. For example, Machen believes that premillennialists are in error in seeking to map out the specifics of Christ's return; but they are Christian. He is convinced that Luther was wrong at Marburg concerning the Real Presence; but "it would have been a far greater calamity if being wrong about the Supper he had represented the whole question as a trifling affair" (50). He rejects the Anglican doctrine of bishops as a mark of the church; he repudiates the Arminianism of Methodism; he acknowledges the gulf between the Church of Rome and Protestantism, and makes it clear on which side he stands. Yet in each case he affirms that there is a oneness to the Christian family that transcends even these profound divisions (48-52). On the matter of doctrine, Machen is, if anything, a radical ecumenist.

There is one doctrine, however, that he will not let go. It is the driving force of American evangelicalism from the beginning. Although he never states it outright in *Christianity and Liberalism*, Machen holds unshakably to the Reformed teaching of the perspicuity of Scripture. He trusts that the Bible may be placed in the hands of the common reader. The average Christian can study the Bible and comprehend its saving content. On the basis of this teaching, the Reformation gave the Scriptures to the people of the church. In the midst of crisis, Machen wants to insure that it remains among them.

This conviction does not make his theological argument simplistic. Machen drank at the well of German scholarship and spent a decade in intellectual and spiritual struggle trying to come to grips with its results. What it does mean, however, is that he sees the conflict between Christianity and liberalism to be nothing less than an epochal battle for the soul of the church.

Machen's objection against liberalism is that it is "a religion which is so entirely different from Christianity as to belong in a distinct category" (6-7). He describes liberalism as a form of "naturalism" or "paganism" insofar as it denies that God's transforming, creative power is able to break into the natural course of events described by modern science. According to liberalism, "this world is really all in all" (148). The defenders of liberalism do not find this situation disheartening; on the contrary, they are unfailingly optimistic. Having deep faith in the progress of Western civilization and the achievements of science, liberal theologians and preachers locate "the highest good of human existence in the healthy and harmonious and joyous development of existing human faculties" (65). At its root, liberalism means the loss of any consciousness of sin (64).

In the religion of liberalism there is no room for the Christian affirmation of the transcendence of God. Divinity has been reduced to a vague feeling of an affirming "presence" that symbolizes "the mighty world process itself" (68) or "the highest thing that men know" (110). The incarnation is interpreted with corresponding nebulousness. Its primary purpose is to endorse the idea that "man at his best is one with God" (68). This makes Jesus not the object of faith, but merely an example of faith, "the fairest flower of humanity" (96). Doctrines such as the virgin birth or the resurrection exemplify a superseded supernaturalism; the atonement is the leftover of a barbarous age that believed in a vengeful God demanding satisfaction for disobedience. At best, the death of Jesus on the cross provides an inspiring example of self-sacrifice.

Liberalism, of course, has some "doctrines" of its own. It teaches the sentimental principle of "the universal Fatherhood of God and the universal brotherhood of man" (18); it stands by the Golden Rule; it believes "that the world's evil may be overcome by the world's good" (136). In a world of sin, agony, and need, such teachings are shallow moralisms. "The truth is, the God of modern preaching, though He may perhaps be very good, is rather uninteresting" (133).

The effect of liberal preaching, intended or not, is to ratify the reigning culture. Machen sees plenty of evidence in the society of his day that "religion has become a mere function of the community or of the state." He laments the fact that the church has been co-opted in the effort to "Americanize" the great waves of immigrants landing on its shores by turning them from their customs and mother tongues "with a Bible in one hand and a club in the other" (149). The fear of "Bolshevism" and the concern for international peace after the Great War have been taken up by the church and made part of its missionary "program":

> "We are missionaries to India," they say. "Now India is in ferment; Bolshevism is creeping in; send us out to India that the menace may be checked." Or else they say: "We are missionaries to Japan; Japan will be dominated by militarism unless the principles of Jesus have sway; send us out therefore to prevent the calamity of war." (151)

In these developments, Christianity is being used as "a mere means to a higher end." When this world is made the beginning and ending of faith, when Christians do not seek the kingdom first, then the crass politicization of the gospel is the dire result.

Just as bad is liberalism's essential dishonesty in relation to average members of the church. It may use the traditional concepts of Christian faith. It speaks of "God," "Jesus," "Spirit," and the like. But in doing so it "offends . . . the fundamental principle of truthfulness in language." Honesty in language comes, "not when the meaning attached to the words by the speaker, but when the meaning intended to be produced in the mind of the particular person addressed, is in accordance with the facts" (112). By investing traditional Christian concepts with a meaning that is different from their meaning among ordinary folk, liberalism abrogates the trustworthiness and integrity of the common language shared by all. It turns theology into gnostic double talk. In this regard, "it is inferior to Unitarianism in the matter of honesty" (111).

Against the religion of liberalism, Christianity is "not a mere comprehension of eternal principles" but "an historical message" (29), a "telling of a story," "the narration of an event" (48). Positively, this means that Christianity is wed inextricably to the particularities of a history that are open to investigation and have the specificity and integrity to risk falsification. Negatively, it means that the identity of Christianity can never be abstracted in such a way as to satisfy the demands of universal human experience. It is a faith that requires letting go of what one finds secure and familiar.

For the scholar as well as the common reader, an investigation of the story of Christianity reveals that the early disciples grounded their proclamation less in what Jesus had said than in what he had done. "He is risen," they declared; he has "died for your sins." The passion of Jesus and his resurrection from the dead are not part of the excrescence of the New Testament, but its very center. The identity of Christianity is concentrated in the cross of Christ, who died that we might live (119).

Behind these central claims lie a host of others: that God is personal and that he acts in history to accomplish his will; that we have sinned against him; that we cannot change our predicament before God by our own merit; that God so values the moral order of his universe that he himself makes the sacrifice to uphold its rectitude. These claims are impossible to extrapolate from an analysis of general religious experience. This is because "The Christian gospel means, not a presentation of what always has been true, but a report of something new — something that imparts a totally different aspect to the situation of mankind" (121).

That God acts directly in human affairs is what the Bible plainly reports. In this sense, it is not at all hard to comprehend. Machen's confidence in the "common man" will not be shaken. But what is hard to accept is the clear implication of the gospel that we must give up control of our lives and place our trust in the power of Another greater than ourselves. The problem of the Christian message is less the difficulty of "facts" than its existential difficulty for the hearer trapped in sinful egoism. What the teaching of the Scriptures points to, above all, is "the real existence of a personal God" (58) who can neither be reduced to a philosophical principle nor made into the image of humanity.

The God of the Bible draws the hearer into his sacred orbit by the proclamation that "He is alive, He is sovereign, He is not bound by His creation or by His creatures, He can perform wonders" (134). Against the deist, who separates God from the world, and the pantheist, who identifies God with the world, Christianity teaches theism, which proclaims both the otherness of God and his dramatic activity in the course of history. "A gospel independent of history is a contradiction in terms" (121).

Christianity's essential point of contact with ordinary human experience may be found in the knowledge, common to all, that "the more serious wrongs are those that are done, not to the bodies, but to the souls of men" (129). When we set bad examples to the young, when we speak a harsh word to a loved one that leaves a scar for life, we know that expressing sorrow or pleading "to let by-gones be by-gones" is not enough. The agony of the world exceeds the human desire or capacity to make things right. "The truly penitent man longs to wipe out the effects of sin, not merely to forget sin. But who can wipe out the effects of sin?" (130). The gospel provides an answer to this agony in the death of Christ. It is Christ alone who takes on God's righteous wrath. "God has clothed us with Christ's righteousness as with a garment; in Christ we stand spotless before the judgment throne" (130-31).

The one who brought this proclamation is Jesus of Nazareth. Jesus can hardly be called "the fairest flower of humanity." The New Testament witnesses to his deity in every book. He himself claimed to speak for God with unique authority. The Gospels witness to him as being without sin. He taught "the outer darkness and the everlasting fire, [and] the sin that shall not be forgiven" (84). He calls on all humanity to "repent." He announces the kingdom of God both as present among people and as a future event. The kingdom of God upsets life as we live it. It calls on us to take ourselves out of the center. It is opposed to culture and custom. The message of Jesus is one of exclusiveness — all the more striking in that it arose in the syncretism of the Hellenistic age: "What struck the early observers of Christianity most forcibly was not merely that salvation was offered by means of the Christian gospel, but that all other means were resolutely rejected" (123). In short, as the comfortable exemplar of humanity Jesus of Nazareth fails completely. Either his claims are true or he is a madman.

The miracles of the Bible, above all the resurrection, attest to the authenticity of Jesus' claims. Miracles belong "to the very warp and woof" of the New Testament account (107). They are found at the deepest level of biblical traditions. They are an essential part of the historical identity of primitive Christianity. The most important fact of miracles is that they are "wrought by the immediate power of *God*" (102). To accept miracles is to accept the possibility of divine intervention in the course of human life, which is a fundamental assumption of biblical faith. To understand miracles, one must take to heart the biblical claim that God is not an arbitrary despot. His purpose, as the New Testament makes clear, is "the conquest of sin." For this to make sense one must know that one is lost in sin. Thus, "the acceptance of the supernatural depends upon a conviction of the reality of sin" (105). No doubt, without miracle the Bible would be far easier to believe. "But the trouble is, it would not be worth believing" (108).

Machen's remedy for the battle between the religion of liberalism and the religion of Christianity is a simple one whose roots go deep in the identity of American evangelicalism. The church must be a "brotherhood of twice-born sinners" (158). Its standards of membership, especially for the clergy, must be held high. When pastors take an oath to obey the Scriptures as "the only infallible rule of faith and practice" (163), they should be held accountable if they fail that oath. The language is plain; the duties are clear. The same is true with regard to confessional subscription. "A man may disagree with the Westminster Confession . . . but he can hardly fail to see what it means" (170). A denomination, to be faithful to the church, must discipline itself; otherwise its duties will be taken over by others.

IV. Assessment

Fundamentalism has been an emotional flashpoint in American church history. The common image is of a rearguard movement that considers verbal inerrancy to be the most crucial Christian doctrine, is hostile to all aspects of the modern temper, and rejects all who disagree as "unchristian."[37] The Scopes "monkey" trial of 1925 made the movement the object of ridicule in the national press. After the Second World War, fundamentalism became the whipping boy of cultural analysts, who used it to illustrate the dark strain of intolerance in American life. For example, *Inherit the Wind* (1955) by Jerome Lawrence and Robert E. Lee interpreted the Scopes trial as a prelude to the paranoia of the McCarthy era. As both a Broadway play and a popular film, it stereotyped fundamentalists in the minds of many secularists and mainline denominationalists. Richard Hofstadter (1916-70) saw in fundamentalism the intellectual roots of a defensive patriotism in anguish for a lost America that he called "the one hundred per cent mentality."[38] More recently, Robert Wuthnow has noted the "cultural residue" of the old battle from the 1920s. In the increasingly polarized denominational environment since the 1960s, which has been marked by opposing special interest groups fighting over a variety of issues, fundamentalism has emerged as the popular pejorative tag to demonize conservatives.[39] In the vast majority of mainline seminaries and divinity schools, the fundamentalist is the object of hostile suspicion and the butt of jokes.

Books decrying fundamentalism continue to crowd the shelves. The criticisms they make are familiar and often valid. Fundamentalism has been more of a protest movement than a theological school with a constructive program. When it has captured the attention of a denomination, its usual effect has been to divide and tear down. The stubborn defense on the part of

---

37. James Barr, *Fundamentalism* (Philadelphia: Westminster, 1978), 1.

38. *Anti-Intellectualism in American Life* (New York: Alfred A. Knopf, 1966), 121.

39. Robert Wuthnow, *The Restructuring of American Religion* (Princeton: Princeton University Press, 1988), 138.

many of its followers of a theory of verbal inerrancy inevitably leads to a sacrifice of the intellect. The theory itself is largely the product of seventeenth-century Protestant scholasticism and lacks deeper roots in the Christian tradition. In the hands of its most aggressive proponents, the theory is characterized by a level of insecurity that borders on unbelief. It refuses to accept the power of God's word to be its own interpreter and make its own disciples. It threatens to substitute an historical faith *(fides historica)* or reliance on the naked facts of the biblical narrative for a saving faith *(fides salvifica)* that clings to the promise of God's word.

But these weaknesses, serious though they are, are not the whole of the story, especially when one turns from a systematic appraisal of its teachings to an historical appreciation of its social impact. There are signs that a sympathetic historical assessment of fundamentalism is gaining ground. Scholars such as Ernest Sandeen and George Marsden have patiently examined the internal development of the movement and related it to the continuities of American Protestant history.[40] Garry Wills has even resurrected the Scopes trial, arguing that while Clarence Darrow (1857-1938) may have won the battle, fundamentalists won the war by successfully expunging Darwinism from American grade-school textbooks.[41] The fact of the matter is that, for good or for ill, fundamentalism is a continuing player in American Christianity; it demands serious attention, not dismissal.

What is true of fundamentalism is true of its finest intellect: J. Gresham Machen. Machen's arguments have frequently been maligned. For example, Lefferts Loetscher (1904-81), expressing the mainline Presbyterian viewpoint of the generation that followed the debacle at Princeton in 1929, accused Machen of "the fallacy of the 'undistributed middle.'" According to Loetscher, Machen distorts the idea of liberalism by defining it as radically as possible and then using it as a catchall classification to include "those who differed by implication from traditional orthodoxy even on subordinate points."[42] This is clearly not true. As we have seen, for Machen "traditional orthodoxy" is a radically inclusive phenomenon that he defines simply as faith in the atoning, resurrected Christ; within this orthodoxy, "subordinate points" from Baptist doctrine to Roman Catholic canon law are not rejected but embraced in the unity of the Christian cause. As for his characterization of liberalism, Machen no doubt paints his description with a broad brush;

40. Ernest R. Sandeen, *The Roots of Fundamentalism* (Grand Rapids: Baker, 1978); Marsden, *Fundamentalism and American Culture.*

41. *Under God* (Simon and Schuster, 1990), 108-37.

42. *The Broadening Church* (Philadelphia: University of Pennsylvania Press, 1957), 116.

but he was hardly alone at the time. Douglas Horton (1891-1968) reports that as a young pastor he came across Karl Barth's *Das Wort Gottes und die Theologie* (*The Word of God and the Word of Man* — 1925) on the new book shelf of the Andover-Harvard Library, losing himself totally in the book's sweeping argument:

> Only those who are old enough to remember the particular kind of desic-cated humanism, almost empty of other-worldly content, which prevailed in many Protestant areas in the early decades of this century, can under-stand the surprise, the joy, the refreshment which would have been brought by the book to the ordinary and, like myself, somewhat desultory reader of the religious literature of that time.[43]

Barth's attack, like Machen's, was a frontal assault on an entire movement. The years following the First World War were a time for dramatic generaliza-tions; and the generalizations stuck. "We live . . . in a time of hostility," wrote H. Richard Niebuhr (1894-1962) in 1935, "when the church is imperiled not only by an external worldliness but by one that has established itself within the Christian camp."[44] Niebuhr's argument against liberal theology differed not one wit from Machen's. And the most famous line Niebuhr ever wrote — "A God without wrath brought men without sin into a kingdom without judgment through the ministrations of a Christ without a cross"[45] — is an apt summary of the argument Machen made fourteen years before.

A much more sympathetic reading of Machen was made by a secular outsider to the faith, Walter Lippmann (1889-1974), in his classic essay of 1929, *A Preface to Morals*. Machen is right, says Lippmann, about the funda-mental nature of Christianity: it is grounded in an historical narrative; it de-pends upon the claims of external events. To separate the ideas and values of the faith from their history is to cut the nerve of Christianity: "There is gone that deep, compulsive, organic faith in an external fact which is the essence of religion for all but that very small minority who can live with themselves in mystical communion or by the power of their understanding."[46] The great mass of humanity cling to faith because they believe that it has been enacted upon the public stage of history; its creedal continuity embraces continents,

---

43. Karl Barth, *The Word of God and the Word of Man*, tr. Douglas Horton (New York: Harper & Row, 1957), 1-2.

44. H. Richard Niebuhr, Wilhelm Pauck, and Francis P. Miller, *The Church against the World* (Chicago: Willett, Clark & Co., 1935), 1.

45. *The Kingdom of God in America* (New York: Harper & Row, 1937), 193.

46. *A Preface to Morals* (New York: Macmillan, 1929), 32-33.

empires, and institutions. In knowing this, "the fundamentalist goes to the very heart of the matter."[47]

The debate over the external grounding of the Christian proclamation is the core of Machen's argument and is central to the whole fundamentalist-modernist controversy. Machen understood the integrity of Christianity to be a broad, generous thing whose tradition encompasses the Lutheran and the Calvinist, the predestinarian and Arminian, and even the historical critic who denies inerrancy. What finally matters is that this cloud of witnesses proclaims the Lordship of Christ in unambiguous constancy with the biblical narrative. The integrity of Christianity cannot abide the historical critic who, in the lineage of Spinoza and his children, denies a God outside the self and interprets God's word as man speaking to a mirror. To translate Christianity into the private world of the human psyche or the enclosed culture of Western intellectual development is to destroy the faith as a mass religion. It is to confine the followers of Jesus to a gnostic elite of intellectual religionists who rely on an invented language, unconstrained by tradition and common discourse, that has as its goal the wholesale redefinition of Christian symbols. It is, in short, untrue to the Bible.

The liberal tradition of biblical criticism, despite its achievements, had, by the beginning of the twentieth century, dispensed with the historical element of the faith, or at least treated it with cavalier independence, opened inherited dogma to radical reinterpretation, and turned the nodal points of the biblical narrative — creation, fall, incarnation, cross, and resurrection — into flexible images, subject to drastic reshaping. The immortal soul, once the seed of divine destiny, was replaced by the temporal self whose future was charted in the mundane regions of social science.[48] This led Christian thought to bind itself to extra-theological commitments in the reigning secular culture that made it vulnerable to an unending parade of therapies and programs of political engagement. Above all, it became inextricably wedded to the creed of the Enlightenment in its rejection of human corruptibility, its acceptance of this world as an end in itself, its assumption of unending progress, and its definition of the external grounding of faith as extraneous superstition.

If fundamentalism arose essentially as a protest movement, then J. Gresham Machen was its best theologian who walked the picket line. His witness to a Christianity of specific shape and public accountability, spoken in the plain language of American evangelical speech, reaches out from his

47. *Ibid.*, 33.
48. See Irving Kristol, "The Future of American Jewry," *Commentary* 92 (August 1991), 23.

time to ours. Machen entered the war of the worldviews on the side of Augustinian faith. And he did so at a time when such a choice was beginning to get a serious hearing, even among European theologians who approached the Scriptures in much different ways.

RUDOLF BULTMANN

Biblical Scholarship in Crisis and Renewal

I. At War with the Worldview

A. Contrary Tendencies

Nineteenth-century German historicism was a curious combination of contrary tendencies. On the one hand, it willingly embraced a radical relativism that viewed humanity as a constantly evolving creation whose character is not subject to a fixed standard of truth but is formed and reformed under the pressure of conditions and events. On the other hand, historicism adopted an increasingly conservative nationalism as its chief article of faith. The outcome of history, it firmly believed, would be the triumph of a German culture conceived as the pinnacle of European civilization.

Late nineteenth-century Protestant liberalism — in many ways an intellectual appendage to German historicism — displayed similar contrary tendencies. It was, first of all, a radicalizing intellectual force that rejected the dogmatic tradition as a guide to the identity of Christianity. Protestant liberals believed that only the results of unfettered historical scholarship could place Christian belief on a sure foundation. They accepted the challenge of critics from Spinoza to Strauss to uncover Jesus of Nazareth as an historical figure free from the distortions of ecclesiastical apologists. "They were eager to picture Him," writes Albert Schweitzer, "as truly and purely human, to strip from Him the robes of splendour with which he had been apparelled, and clothe Him once more with the coarse garments in which He had walked in Galilee."[1]

But this same liberalism was also bound to the Germanic culture that gave it birth. Its radical method was tempered by a conservative social allegiance. This allegiance deeply affected its portrayal of Jesus. For a generation of academics, Jesus came to embody the ideals of the *Bildungsbürgertum*, or educated elite. "The kingdom of God comes by coming to the individual, by entering his soul and laying hold of it," writes Adolf von Harnack in his famous lectures from the turn of the century. "It is not a question of angels and devils, thrones and principalities, but of God and the soul, the soul and its God."[2] In Protestant liberalism, Jesus and the Enlightenment worldview made peace.

This peace did not last. The irony of Protestant liberalism's contradictory dispositions was so transparent that it did not take long before the irony itself became the subject of attention. In his celebrated essay *The Quest of the Historical Jesus* (1906), Schweitzer shows in merciless fashion that the Jesus discovered by liberal theology was the mirror image of the scholars who made the quest. Whereas liberalism had set out to free Jesus from capitivity to ecclesiastical dogmatists, its effect was to bind him to the desires of the European intellectual elite.

By itself Schweitzer's book was not a fatal blow. What ultimately undermined the Protestant liberal enterprise of the nineteenth century and brought it to crisis was the unrelenting advance of historical-critical scholarship itself.

B. The Advance of Historical-Critical Scholarship

During the nineteenth century, the apologetic effort of liberal theology had been directed toward the identification of Jesus with modern culture as the prototype of universal religious experience. As God entered the heart of Jesus, so he enters our hearts, directing us to the just life. The kingdom of God was understood to be the key biblical symbol for this experience. In the latter decades of the century, historical scholarship began to cut the nerve of this apologetic by locating Jesus firmly in the historical context of apocalyptic ex-

---

1. *The Quest of the Historical Jesus,* 2nd ed., tr. W. Montgomery (London: A. & C. Black, 1922), 4-5.

2. *What Is Christianity?* tr. Thomas Baily Saunders (New York: Harper & Row, 1957), 56.

pectation. As early as 1873, Franz Overbeck, professor of New Testament and early Christianity at the University of Basel, argued that a strict reading of the earliest Christian sources reveals that the expectation of the world's imminent end and a world-denying ethic are the most prominent characteristics of the teaching of Jesus and the early Christian community. In its origin, Christianity was a radically apocalyptic religion. Apologetic efforts to make it otherwise, whether pursued by liberal or conservative theologians, are delusory.[3]

Overbeck's thesis was too uncompromising to secure a wide reading among liberal Protestants, but it was given at least indirect support by such scholars investigating the Jewish milieu of Jesus' age as Emil Schürer (1844-1910), Gustaf Hermann Dalman (1855-1941),[4] and, above all, Johannes Weiss and William Wrede (1859-1906).

In 1892, Weiss challenged the liberal establishment directly in his essay *Jesus' Proclamation of the Kingdom of God.* Theology must acknowledge, he argues, "whether and how far we today are removed from the original meaning of the concepts" of the New Testament. This is especially true with regard to the image of the kingdom. "The Kingdom of God as Jesus thought of it is never something subjective, inward, or spiritual, but is always the objective messianic Kingdom. . . ."[5] It is an eschatological event that breaks into human reality, and it cannot be equated with a value system meant to build Western civilization. As if Weiss's attack were not enough, Wrede raised the ultimate question concerning what could be known about Jesus. In *The Messianic Secret* (1901), he asserts that the portrait of Jesus in the Gospel of Mark — long considered a reliable source for the knowledge of the life of Jesus — is decisively colored by the author of the Gospel. This is especially true regarding Jesus' claim to be Messiah. This assertion is not authentic to Jesus, but reflects the imposition of the beliefs of the early church on the historical record. "The historical Jesus," says Albert Schweitzer, summing up the impact of this scholarly assault, "will be in our time a stranger and an enigma."[6]

---

3. Franz Overbeck, *Über die Christlichkeit unserer heutigen Theologie,* 2nd ed. (Darmstadt: Wissenschaftliche Buchgesellschaft, 1974); see also *Christentum und Kultur* (Darmstadt: Wissenschaftliche Buchgesellschaft, 1973).

4. Emil Schürer, *The History of the Jewish People in the Age of Jesus Christ,* tr. J. Macpherson, S. Taylor, and P. Christie, 5 vols. (Edinburgh: T&T Clark, 1885-90); Gustaf Hermann Dalman, *Christianity and Judaism,* tr. G. H. Box (London: William Norgate, 1901).

5. *Jesus' Proclamation of the Kingdom of God,* tr. Richard Hyde Hiers and David Larrimore Holland (Philadelphia: Fortress, 1971), 59-60, 133.

6. *The Quest for the Historical Jesus,* 397.

C. The Coming of War

This crisis in liberal scholarship was intensified by the crisis of liberal European culture. "We have left the land and have embarked," wrote Friedrich Nietzsche in 1882. "We have burned our bridges behind us — indeed, we have gone farther and destroyed the land behind us."[7] Nietzsche uses the metaphor of a ship adrift to describe late nineteenth-century Europe. It is surrounded by an ocean of cultural relativism and infinite space upon which it sails without a reference point in a firm tradition or a clear destination to guide its course. Modernity, says Nietzsche, is a frightening experience. It is so open, so pervaded with both choice and danger, that it can easily fill those who contemplate it with anxiety and dread.

There was good reason to fear. When societies are adrift, without clear focus, they are menacing. At such times, argued the Swiss historian Jacob Burckhardt (1818-97) in his posthumously published *Reflections on History* (1905), nations are prone to war even if they have been at peace with each other for decades. "Wars clear the air like thunderstorms," he writes despairingly. They force those who engage in them to chart a course, to choose a destination: "War alone grants to mankind the magnificent spectacle of a general submission to a general aim." Burckhardt agrees with the ancient Greek philosopher Heraclitus that "war is the father of all things."[8]

The First World War was, however, a father whom no one expected. The youth of Europe willingly went off to trenches in the late summer of 1914, only to find themselves mired in mud and death for four years. It was a war of attrition with each side taking enormous casualties while winning very little ground. In the battle of the Somme, for example, which raged from July to the middle of November 1916, the total carnage amounted to 1.2 million dead and wounded. By war's end, nearly 8.5 million died on both sides of "no-man's-land."

If ever the Enlightenment worldview has been called into question in the last two hundred years, it was during this epic conflict, this terrible epiphany for European culture. During the war, there began to emerge an altered religious sensibility, nothing less than the reassertion of Augustinian faith with its harsh view of the human condition, its austere spirituality, and its exultation in the strangeness and otherness of God.

For example, Rudolf Otto (1869-1971), newly appointed professor of theology at Marburg, took up the question of theological method in 1917.

---

7. *The Gay Science,* tr. Walter Kaufmann (New York: Vintage, 1974), 180.
8. *Reflections on History,* tr. M. D. Hottinger (Indianapolis: Liberty, 1979), 217-18.

The obligation of the modern theological enterprise, he writes, has customarily been to think of God "by analogy with our human nature and personality." Thus we naturally draw upon such notions as reason, purpose, goodwill, unity, selfhood, and the like. But this procedure is fraught with difficulties. "We have to be on our guard," says Otto, "against an error which would lead to a wrong and one-sided interpretation of religion. This is the view that the essence of deity can be expressed completely and exhaustively in such 'rational' attributes." The "idea of deity," in fact, implies a "non-rational or suprarational Subject" who stands behind and beyond all human analogy. To encounter this "Subject" and bow before it in adoration is the original motivation and driving force of the human religious quest. It fills the pages of sacred books with their strange narratives. It inspires the building of hallowed places and furnishes them with works of art that form a precious heritage of civilization. Before anything else, the idea of deity that undergirds religion is "the idea of the Holy."[9]

The Idea of the Holy (Das Heilige) was an immediate success upon its publication during the darkest days of the war. After the war, it was quickly translated into several languages, including Japanese. It reached its twenty-fifth edition in less than twenty years. By the 1960s it was hailed as "the most widely read theological work in German of the twentieth century."[10]

Otto concentrates his analysis on the ways in which humanity experiences the difference between the infinite power of God and its own weakness and mortality. These experiences, he argues, are not adequately described by Schleiermacher's concept of a "feeling of dependence." Schleiermacher's understanding is too vague; his description of fundamental religious apprehension too closely tied to mundane analogies. Authentic religious perception takes a more definite and dramatic shape. When Abraham, pleading for the men of Sodom, confesses: "Behold now, I have taken upon me to speak unto the Lord, which am but dust and ashes" (Gen. 18:27, KJV), he is not engaging in sentimental reflection meant to comfort a family on a cozy Christmas Eve. Rather, his is the unsettling experience of "creature-consciousness": "the emotion of a creature submerged and overwhelmed by its own nothingness in contrast to that which is supreme above all creatures." It entails both the realization of the self as unworthy and a vital concern for the Object whom one

9. *The Idea of the Holy,* tr. John W. Harvey, 2nd ed. (London: Oxford University Press, 1950), 1-2.

10. Heinz Zahrnt, *The Question of God,* tr. R. A. Wilson (New York: Harcourt, Brace & World, 1969), 48.

faces, the *numen praesens* who determines the course of one's fate. "The numinous is thus felt as objective and outside the self."[11]

Otto divides the awareness of the numinous into two separate but related "determined states." First there is the *mysterium tremendum*. To this belongs all that thrills and frightens, all the weird and the fearful, the majesty, anger, and unpredictable energy of God. In the words of the ancient Israelite confession:

> See now that I, even I, am he;
> there is no god beside me.
> I kill and I make alive; . . .
> and no one can deliver from my hand. (Deut. 32:39)

The holiness of God brings death not only to Pharaoh's son but also to the child of David and Bathsheba's adultery. It destroys the sanctuary at Shiloh, divides the kingdom, lays Jerusalem waste, and drives the people into exile. Before this same mystery, Jesus himself cries from the cross, "My God, my God, why hast thou forsaken me?"

The numinous is also experienced in another way. This is "the element of fascination," that which makes the numinous uniquely attractive and compelling. God speaks in Exodus, drawing the people to himself: "I bore you on eagles' wings and brought you to myself . . . you shall be my treasured possession out of all peoples" (Exod. 19:4-5). The mystic is filled with joy and an uncanny intuition of the unity of all things. The hope of the world is seen in the birth of a child. Death loses its sting; miracle reverses tragedy.

In seeking to understand the numinous as this twofold experience of the divine, Otto draws upon the Old and New Testaments, the theology of Luther (whose *Bondage of the Will* he acknowledges as his initial guide in these reflections), and a host of cross-cultural references in art, music, and poetry. Sin, atonement, and predestination — the pillars of Augustinian theology and the bane of nineteenth-century liberal apologists — are essential topics that help to shape Otto's argument. The book is an unrelenting assault on the Enlightenment worldview and, at the same time, a model of thorough German scholarship. Drawing upon the same historicist tradition that guided liberal Protestantism, Otto seeks to let the voice of religion as manifest in different epochs and cultures speak on its own terms.

The Idea of the Holy made sense of the European crisis. The First World War had, in fact, placed Europe before the awesome power of *mysterium tremendum*. The English war poet Wilfred Owen (1893-1918), who died on

11. Otto, *The Idea of the Holy*, 11.

the battlefield one week before the war's end, gave expression to this experience in poetry that breathes deeply an Augustinian awareness of human corruption and the judgment of God. This awareness is reflected in his sonnet "On Seeing a Piece of Our Artillery Brought into Action":

> Be slowly lifted up, thou long black arm,
> Great gun towering towards Heaven, about to curse . . .
> Reach at that Arrogance which needs thy harm,
> And beat it down before its sins grow worse;
> Spend our resentment, cannon, — yea, disburse
> Our gold in shapes of flame, our breaths in storm.[12]

Owen's poetic vision, describing the engines of war in the cadence of biblical speech, typifies the consciousness of the period. In the face of war, many intellectuals, interested in the matter of religion and its relation to culture, boldly rejected the values inherited from liberalism. For example, Thomas Ernest Hulme (1883-1917), another Englishman who died on the battlefield, inspired many in the "lost generation" after the war with his harsh reflections on the contrast of humanism and religion:

> It is necessary to realize that there is an absolute, and not a relative, difference between humanism (which we can take to be the highest expression of the vital) and the religious spirit. The *divine* is not *life* at its intensest. It contains in a way an almost *anti-vital* element; quite different of course from the non-vital character of the outside physical region. The questions of Original Sin, of chastity, of the motives behind Buddhism, etc., all part of the very essence of the religious spirits, are quite incomprehensible for humanism.[13]

Like Otto and Owen, Hulme is searching for that which is objective and authoritative. To be enduring, especially in a time when so much was violently reduced to rubble, religion had to rediscover its unapologetic core.

Of all the young men who began the war with the inherited worldview of the Enlightenment, only to change drastically as events unfolded, none is more famous than Karl Barth. It has often been stated that Barth's commentary on Paul's Epistle to the Romans inaugurated a new era of theology. The first edition appeared in 1919, in a tiny Swiss publication. Two years later a

---

12. C. Day Lewis, ed., *The Collected Poems of Wilfred Owen* (New York: New Directions, 1963), 85.

13. *Speculations: Essays on Humanism and the Philosophy of Art*, ed. Herbert Read (London: Routledge & Kegan Paul, 1924), 8-9.

new, drastically revised edition emerged from a publishing house in Munich. In his prefaces to these and still further editions, Barth leveled biting criticism against the humanism of current biblical interpretation, and demanded an approach to the text bent to its subject matter. Instead of beginning with the human, with human speech or human thought about God, one had to begin with God, with God's speech and God's thought about human existence. The *Römerbrief* bubbled and boiled like a volcano:

> God, the pure and absolute boundary and beginning of all that we are and have and do; God, who is distinguished qualitatively from men and from everything human, and must never be identified with anything which we name, or experience, or conceive, or worship, as God; God, who confronts all human disturbance with an unconditional command "Halt," and all human rest with an equally unconditional command "Advance"; God, the "Yes" in our "No" and the "No" in our "Yes," the First and the Last, and consequently, the Unknown, who is never a known thing in the midst of other known things; God, the Lord, the Creator, the Redeemer: — this is the Living God.[14]

The young Swiss pastor had had no revelation, no "tower experience," no experience of a heart "strangely warmed." The simple fact was that his theological preparation bore no relation to his task as a parish pastor. The entry of his theological professors into the propaganda front of the First World War gave proof that "the theology of the nineteenth century no longer had any future." Either one continued to establish God from the perspective of the human and thus distance oneself more and more from what was specifically Christian, and in the last analysis — as the war made clear — lose both Christianity and what was human, or take seriously the revelation witnessed to in the Bible and acknowledge it as the measure of all things. At issue was Christian thinking that did not simply develop axioms into some sort of system, but that was impelled, moved from outside itself, a thinking that had a partner, Another — Scripture, the fundamental, canonical witness to the revelation.

This new Augustinian sensibility outlasted the First World War. The crisis did not end with the Armistice in November 1918 but passed on to other cataclysmic events: revolution in Germany and Russia that ended monarchical rule, the failure of the Weimar experiment in liberal democracy, economic depression, the solidification of fascist and communist rule, the Second World War and the second defeat of Germany, the Holocaust, the birth of the

---

14. *The Epistle to the Romans*, tr. Edwyn C. Hoskyns (London: Oxford University Press, 1950), 330-31.

atomic age, and the Cold War. The generation that entered adulthood in 1914 experienced all these events. Social upheaval was their way of life; a "theology of crisis" their response. Their war with the Enlightenment worldview was an experience not of years, but of decades. It did not mean a turning away from modernity and its demands, but a new and more critical encounter with its significance for the life of faith.

Among biblical scholars deeply influenced by these new trends of thought and acutely aware of the war of the worldviews, none is more important than Rudolf Bultmann, the subject of this chapter, and Ernst Käsemann, the focus of the next.

II. Biography

Rudolf Karl Bultmann was born 20 August 1884, oldest son of the Evangelical Lutheran pastor Arthur Bultmann, in Wiefelstede near Oldenburg, on the North Sea. After passing his preparatory examination at Oldenburg, Bultmann began university studies at Tübingen, Berlin, and Marburg. Following his first theological examinations in 1907, he served for a year as instructor in the Oldenburg Gymnasium, then spent three years in the Marburg Seminarium. In 1910, on the basis of his research on Paul and the Cynic-Stoic diatribe,[15] Bultmann received the Licentiate of Theology degree (usually restricted to theological faculties), and two years later he was granted the right to serve as instructor in New Testament at Marburg, where he taught until 1916.[16] In 1916 Bultmann was called as associate professor to Breslau. In 1920 he was invited to follow Wilhelm Bousset (1865-1920), co-founder of the History of Religions School, as full professor at Giessen, and from there in 1921 he returned to Marburg as the successor of Wilhelm Heitmüller (1869-1926). Early in his Marburg years, from 1923 to 1928, Bultmann carried on an exchange with Martin Heidegger (1889-1976), who had been called to succeed Paul Natorp (1854-1924) in the chair of philosophy. In the 1930s Bultmann's encounter with fascism began.

In American studies of the German churches under Hitler, little or nothing is said of Bultmann's resistance to the policies of Germany's Third Reich, which came to power in 1933. Usually, others are singled out for laurels

---

15. Bultmann, *Der Stil der paulinischen Predigt und die kynisch-stoische Diatribe* (Göttingen: Vandenhoeck & Ruprecht, 1910).

16. Bultmann's *Habilitationsschrift* or qualifications thesis, a second dissertation required for entry upon teaching duties, was entitled *Die Exegese des Theodor von Mopsuestia* (Stuttgart: W. Kohlhammer, 1984).

by virtue of their greater visibility and heroic appeal.[17] A member of the Confessing Church since its founding in 1934, Bultmann bitterly opposed the exclusion of persons of non-Aryan origin from official service in the church. On 7 April 1933 a law was passed in Germany entitled "Ordinance for the Restoration of Career in Government," the third paragraph of which read that persons of non-Aryan origin were to be excluded from state positions. On May 6 this law was interpreted as inapplicable to non-Aryans employed by the legally recognized churches of Germany. Nonetheless, voluntarily, without pressure from the state, at least nine of Germany's established state churches adopted the so-called "Aryan paragraph," relieving Jewish pastors and laity from positions of responsibility in Christian congregations. The following September, representatives of three church districts of the Evangelical Land Church of Hesse-Kassel gathered at Marburg and issued a plea to the theological faculties of Marburg and Erlangen for "solemn and responsible instruction" concerning whether or not the Aryan paragraph obeyed or contradicted Holy Scripture, the gospel, the nature of the sacraments, the ecumenical creeds, Reformation teaching, as well as the preamble to the Constitution of the German Evangelical Church.

In contrast to the equivocal statement of the Erlangen faculty, Bultmann and his Marburg colleagues authored an opinion opposing the adoption of the paragraph. The opinion in part read that the church's task is not political, but, in the given instance, it may require a critical stance toward national events. The opinion further states that no church or national law recognizes Jewishness in terms of race, concluding with the statement that whoever does not acknowledge total unity between Jewish and non-Jewish Christians in the church deceives himself when confessing that Scripture is God's word and Jesus God's Son and Lord of all.[18] A further opinion, released by New Testament scholars throughout Germany sometime before October 5 and to which Bultmann was signatory, stated that New Testament teaching concerning the equality of all persons before God is not calculated to result in an economic or political program, but nonetheless has its consequence in the total equality of believers within the community.[19] In reaction to the opinion and individual essays submitted by members of the Erlangen faculty, in which

17. See, however, Walter Schmithals's account of Bultmann's anti-Nazi activity in his *An Introduction to the Theology of Rudolf Bultmann*, tr. John Bowden (Minneapolis: Augsburg, 1968), 295-99.

18. Heinz Liebing, ed., *Die Marburger Theologen und der Arierparagraph in der Kirche: Eine Sammlung von Texten aus den Jahren 1933 und 1934* (Marburg: N. G. Elwert, 1977), 9-15.

19. *Ibid.*, 16-19.

Scripture, tradition, confession, and *praxis* were all warped to the notion of *Volkstum* or nationality, Bultmann made separate reply:

> If I were a non-Aryan or not a pure Aryan Christian, I would be ashamed to belong to a church in which I of course may listen, but must keep silent. . . . In 1 Corinthians 7:17-24 [Paul] turns on such fools who would make the principles of the church's fellowship laws for the world. . . . And now we should commit the reverse folly, and make the laws of the world the laws of the church? . . . Has [the church] then forgotten that the word of the cross is scandal and folly to the natural man? May it presume to lop off something of this scandal and folly and obtain by stealth the applause of the nation at the expense of a falsification of the word? . . . A church which does not look to the left or to the right performs for nation and state the sole genuine and true service which it alone can perform.[20]

Later, members of Erlangen's "orthodox" faculty, who had disavowed the church's history respecting Judaism, would join the chorus of Bultmann's critics, anxious for the historical basis of the church,[21] and withal would shun any of their kind who had condemned adoption of the Aryan paragraph.[22]

By modern standards, perhaps by any standards, Bultmann's literary output could only be described as massive. From the first brief articles and reviews in 1908 and 1909 until the publication of the second fascicle of his *Theology of the New Testament* in 1951, the books, monographs, articles, and reviews carrying Bultmann's name numbered over three hundred. In the midst of this flurry of production, Bultmann took time to travel to Scandinavia, England, Holland, and Switzerland prior to World War II, and after it to Sweden, England, and twice to the United States. Bultmann remained at Marburg until his retirement in 1951, and died at the age of ninety-two on 31 July 1976.[23]

20. *Ibid.*, 32-45.

21. See Paul Althaus, *Das sogenannte Kerygma und der historische Jesus* (Gütersloh: Carl Bertelsmann, 1958).

22. See Gordon J. Gerhardy, "Hermann Sasse on Confession and Culture for a Younger Church" (diss., St. Paul: Luther-Northwestern Seminaries, 1981), 39-69.

23. See Bultmann, "Autobiographical Reflections," in *Existence and Faith*, tr. Schubert M. Ogden (New York: Meridian, 1960), 283-88; Charles W. Kegley, ed., *The Theology of Rudolf Bultmann* (New York: Harper & Row, 1966), xix-xxv; *Karl Barth–Rudolf Bultmann: Letters, 1922-1966*, tr. Geoffrey W. Bromiley (Grand Rapids: Wm. B. Eerdmans, 1981), 158-62.

III. New Testament and Theology

A. What Is Myth?

Before 1941 Rudolf Bultmann excited no greater interest than did any other scholar of his time. Neither his volume on the Synoptic tradition, earning him a place as pioneer in form-critical investigation of the Gospels, nor his book on Jesus, reducing to a bare minimum what was genuine in the New Testament, caused great furor.[24] But when his brief essay, first delivered to pastors of the Confessing Church at a pastoral conference, and later published under extreme handicap in Nazi Germany, found its way to the bookstalls, the Marburg scholar was catapulted to an eminence that only Barth could rival. For some Bultmann was a champion, for others the very devil. Lines were drawn, factions emerged, "schools" arose, bishops warned their congregations, professors debated, and a welter of literature resulted.

The name of the essay was "New Testament and Mythology."[25] Bultmann begins bluntly and without flourish. The thought-forms of the New Testament, he says, are "mythical." They depict the universe as divided into three parts — the center occupied by earth, sandwiched between heaven and hell representing the supernatural world (1). To this mythical worldview corresponds the biblical description of the events of salvation (2). And to this worldview the "aggravatedly modern man" is irreconcilably opposed (3). The reason is not that he holds another worldview but that he conceives of himself as a self-contained being who is not open to the seizure of supernatural powers (7). To retain the "myth," to repristinate it, is tantamount to returning to a primitive era and making of faith a sacrifice of the intellect (4-5). Faith requires responsibility in thought and judgment. Moreover, Bultmann adds, the basic intention of the New Testament is not to tell tales, but to provide its reader-hearer with self-understanding (10-11). And since the mythological screens the true intention of the New Testament — that is, since it adds to the "scandal" of the cross the "offense" of the mythological — that intention has to be exposed.

Bultmann goes on to argue that biblical exposition can no longer occur

24. Rudolf Bultmann, *The History of the Synoptic Tradition,* tr. John Marsh (New York: Harper & Row, 1963); *Jesus and the Word,* tr. Louise Pettibone Smith and Erminie Huntress Lantero (New York: Charles Scribner's Sons, 1958).

25. Bultmann, "New Testament and Mythology," in *Kerygma and Myth,* ed. Hans Werner Bartsch, tr. Reginald H. Fuller (London: S.P.C.K., 1953), 1-44. The text first appeared under the title "Offenbarung und Heilsgeschehen" in *Beiträge zur evangelischen Theologie* (München: Christian Kaiser, 1941). Citations in the text refer to the English translation.

after the fashion of the old liberal by peeling the historical "hull" from its "kernel." The gospel leaves nothing after peeling, since it resembles more an onion than a walnut (12-14). Authentic exposition occurs through a method that takes the mythology seriously but that "demythologizes," or, better, "reinterprets" it (Bultmann eventually preferred the latter word) in terms of a self-understanding for which the mythology furnishes the vehicle (16). And, indeed, the New Testament itself, particularly Paul and John, already pave the way for such a "reinterpretaion" (20-21).

Bultmann insists that the term "myth" as he uses it does not merely spell ideology. Rather, it denotes a mode of conception in which what is unworldly and divine appears as worldly and human; in which what is beyond appears as though it is here and now; in which God's distance from the world is construed as spatial, and as a result of which the cultus is conceived as an activity in which nonmaterial powers are mediated through material means (10). It is this "objectifying" mode of conception that obscures the myth's true intent. Since, however, the myth does not intend to communicate such a mode but rather an understanding of existence, the New Testament mythology is not to be inquired into for whatever mode of conception it may reflect, but solely for the existence that underlies it. This distinction between what Bultmann calls the "content of ideas" *(Vorstellungsgehalt)* attaching to the mythological worldview and the actual intent of the mythology will not always be clear to his readers, who often reproach him for his program of "elimination." For Bultmann, the distinction is crucial, since he will not eliminate but "reinterpret." For Bultmann, ultimately, the distinction concerns the truth of an understanding of existence free of obligation to a particular content of ideas.

Readers of Bultmann's essay were alarmed when he proceeded to indicate how his "existential reinterpretation" functions, particularly with reference to the cross and resurrection of Jesus Christ. To the question whether or not the meaning of the cross derives from the cross as an actual, historical event, Bultmann replies that such was true for the first preachers of the gospel who were linked to the historical Jesus, but it could not be true for us since that link is not reproducible. In fact, Bultmann adds, the New Testament does not proclaim the meaning of the cross in this sense. It rather proclaims Jesus Christ as the crucified *and* risen one. In other words, the cross and resurrection comprise a unity (37-38). But if the cross and resurrection are together the one "cosmic" event by which the world is judged and the possibility of genuine life created, then the resurrection alone as an actual historical event cannot be a faith-creating miracle. Bultmann agrees that the New Testament often regards it as such, for example, in the "legends" of the empty tomb and in the narratives treating of Jesus' corporeality. But the resurrection as witness to the eschatological fact of the conquest of death, as proclamation of the meaning of the cross, as object of faith, cannot be supported by yet another faith — that is, belief in its having actually occurred (39-40). It would be an error, Bultmann declares, to inquire into the historical origin of gospel proclamation. The proclamation encounters us as God's word, to which we cannot put the question of legitimacy. Summoning us to believe in the death and resurrection of Christ as an eschatological event, that word opens to us the possibility of understanding ourselves (41-42). Precisely this quality of nondemonstrability attaching to the gospel, Bultmann concludes, preserves Christian proclamation from the reproach of the mythological (44).

The reaction was continental, if not global. On one side there was bitter opposition, even biting irony. In Erlangen, Hermann Sasse (1895-1976) recited the Apostles' Creed à la Bultmann:

> . . . not conceived by the Holy Ghost,
> Not born of the Virgin Mary:
> Suffered, indeed, under Pontius Pilate,
> Was crucified, dead, and buried;
> He did *not* descend into hell;
> The third day he did *not* rise from the dead;
> He did *not* ascend into heaven,
> And thus does *not* sit at the right hand of God the Father Almighty;
> From whence therefore he shall *not* come to judge
> the quick and the dead.[26]

The New York Times' report of Bultmann's death in 1976 stated that the logical conclusion of his concentration on Christianity was to deny the physical resurrection of Jesus.[27]

On the other side there was caution. The Tübingen faculty hazarded the opinion that Bultmann's theology was admittedly *one* voice in the theological choir, that discussion of its propriety should be unrestricted, and the correction of its errors left to the continuance of theological work.[28] To the present day, the debate has not ceased. Paul Tillich's (1886-1965) prediction that the discussion concerning demythologization would continue for a long

---

26. "Flucht vor dem Dogma," in *Luthertum* (Leipzig: A. Deichert, 1942), 161ff.

27. *The New York Times*, 1 August 1976.

28. *Für und Wider die Theologie Bultmanns: Denkschrift der Evangelischen theologischen Fakultät der Universität Tübingen*, 3d ed. (Tübingen: J. C. B. Mohr, 1952), 42.

time to come, both in Europe and America, achieved an accuracy bordering on the trite.[29]

Two factors furnished Bultmann the motivation for his program. First, people were asking, "What have Copernicus or Einstein to do with 'descended into hell,' and 'ascended into heaven'?" And the people who were asking were not just any at all but, as a friend of Bultmann put it, people whose imminent death was their truest possibility — men at arms. The questions were not academic. Second, Bultmann's companion in the church struggle, Karl Barth — who had played St. George to the old dragon of liberalism, and whose *Church Dogmatics* since 1948 were written with one eye on Bultmann — had insisted that the gospel creates such complete discontinuity between life apart from and life within faith that the believer is in reality annihilated and created *ex nihilo* by its message. For Bultmann, Karl Barth's "revelation purism" had been too violent a reaction to liberal Protestantism. There *had* to be continuity between unbelief and faith; unbelief *had* to have an inkling of that "authentic life" of faith, though without the power to appropriate it. After all, it was Augustine who had written, "Thou hast formed us for Thyself, and our hearts are restless till they find their rest in Thee." The gospel has to confront its addressee as a valid alternative in the midst of all the others encountering human existence.

This was Bultmann's axiom, his given. It furnished him justification for his existential reinterpretation of the mythological utterances of the New Testament. Underlying the whole of his effort was this evangelistic motif, the passion that the accosting, demanding, and proclaiming word of the gospel be heard and understood in all its clarity.

B. Bultmann and Heidegger

In contrast to Barth, who insisted that the biblical revelation is without any contact point in human existence, Bultmann contended that just such a contact point exists and is to be exploited in the intelligible proclamation of the Christian message. Bultmann's view of the interpretative task is of a piece with his insistence upon a "natural theology," not in the classical sense of the great theological systems, but in the simplest sense of a continuity between life apart from faith and life within faith. If theology is not to fall prey to ob-

29. "The European Discussion of the Problem of the Demythologization of the New Testament," delivered as one of the Auburn Lecture Series at Union Theological Seminary, 10 November 1952.

scurantism, broken off from human reason and judgment, then such continuity must exist, and the biblical message must thus be a clear and lucid appeal to that true and genuine life of which the person even apart from faith has an "inkling."

Barth would have none of this. Ten years before "New Testament and Mythology," in a letter to Bultmann dated 27 May 1931, he wrote:

> With your definition of the relation between anthropology and theology you have won so little freedom from the eighteenth and nineteenth centuries, that you have scarcely realized or rejected the old impudent dictatorship of modern philosophy. . . . In the end I feel you have simply returned me to the same Egyptian house of bondage which I thought we were supposed to have abandoned with the rejection of Schleiermacher and with the new links to the theology of the reformers.[30]

In response to criticism that his idea of a proclamation intelligible to modernity denies humanity's radical fallenness and that it furnishes a substitute for the power of God who alone can bring about new life, Bultmann acknowledged that the interpreter or preacher cannot raise the dead to life — from that perspective God has no contact point in humanity! On the other hand, however, Bultmann asserted in no uncertain terms that the preacher-interpreter is responsible for setting the scene, for creating the possibility of God's word becoming radical judgment and grace in a speech, a language that does not strike the hearer as meaningless and absurd. Thus, in addition to historical-critical examination of the biblical text, Bultmann insisted that to an intelligible proclamation and thus to a proper interpretation of the Bible belongs a specific, concrete "pre-understanding" (Vorverständnis), a pre-understanding rooted in the interpreter's life-relation to the subject matter of the Bible, and which in turn gives rise to a specific, concrete inquiry into the biblical text.

Throughout his work, Bultmann assumes that the average person has a "hint," a "clue" as to what the Bible is saying because, consciously or unconsciously, willingly or no, all share with the biblical authors the question about the meaning of God in relation to human life. The questions put to the Bible grow out of this sharing of the question, and out of the "inkling" this sharing gives into the meaning of the Bible's content.

When Bultmann came to describe what that "inkling" is, what "hint" or "clue" one might have of the biblical message, he turned to Martin Heidegger's analysis of human existence. To those who protested that he forced the

---

30. *Barth-Bultmann: Letters,* 58.

biblical interpreter to arm himself with presuppositions alien to the Bible, Bultmann retorted that if there is such a thing as a natural theology, that is, an "inkling" of the meaning of Christian existence; if Heidegger's analysis is merely a secular descendant of the theology of Paul, Luther, and Kierkegaard; and if that analysis is not concerned with the specific act of faith but merely with the broad structures of human life within which such an act must fall, then the Heideggerian analysis, far from being an alien presupposition, is actually required for a true exposition of the gospel in this era.

Heidegger's scheme, as Bultmann employs it, is roughly as follows:[31] human existence is a possibility, never an achievement or a "having arrived." It is always a becoming, a deciding to be one thing or the other. Human being, thus, never "is"; it is rather "about to be." Further, the essential state of human existence is being-in-the-world. That is, to be human means to be of a piece with the world, things, and other persons, a creature of time and change, of history. No one starts from scratch, but everyone is "thrown" out over a field of being that already exists and includes the world, things, and other persons. Next, to be human means to be "fallen," that is, absorbed in concern for the world of things. This sketch of existence according to its "broad, empty structures" of possibility, thrownness, and fallenness, Heidegger sums up in the word "care" *(Sorge),* then cites the old Latin myth according to which the gods dispute over the name of the human creature but finally concede that its name should be "man" *(homo)* since "care" had first shaped it from the earth *(humus).*[32]

For Heidegger, again as Bultmann employs him, the *type* or *kind* of one's existence depends upon whether the shock of one's finitude, of one's being as possibility, thrownness, and fallenness — a shock produced by some "boundary situation" such as the imminent possibility of one's own death — produces an anxiety sufficient to make one hear the call of the self, or the call of "care" to be truly oneself, to live authentically, or whether that shock results in recoiling from one's finitude to live spuriously or inauthentically. Inauthentic existence can take the shape of losing oneself in the crowd, becoming anonymous, a speck in that generalization called "they," as in "they say." But it can also express itself in developing an appetite for the world, things, and others as tools to be exploited and possessed. Authentic existence, however, means to let that gnawing suspicion that life is slipping from one's grasp call one back to oneself; it means to let that "anxiety" bring one face-to-

---

31. For the review appearing in this paragraph, see Martin Heidegger, *Being and Time,* tr. John Macquarrie and Edward Robinson (Oxford: Basil Blackwell, 1967), 41-49, 78-90, 219-24, 235-41.

32. *Ibid.,* 242.

face with the cold, hard fact of one's own finitude, temporality, and, in the encounter, resolve to understand oneself as finite, resolve to be destined for nothingness, to give death a home in one's existence and thus transcend it, to become a true self, a being-unto-death, a being open to the future.[33]

Whatever else this phenomenological analysis may be — some called it a heroic defiance of every particular of human thought from Thales to Husserl; others called it nihilism, atheism — it is a summons to a specific understanding, a specific view of oneself as the condition for true and authentic existence. And though Bultmann denies Heidegger's assumption that the mere awareness of our finitude, our being-unto-death, can catapult us into true existence, he believes that Heidegger's description corresponds to the biblical analysis of existence, and furnishes that "inkling" or "pre-understanding" with which the interpreter can legitimately approach the text.

The lucid and ingenious fashion in which Bultmann interprets the movement from unbelief to faith within the context of Heidegger's formal analysis is reflected in his discussion of the Pauline anthropology in the first volume of his *New Testament Theology*. Bultmann writes that the term *sōma* ("body") as used by Paul denotes man in relation to himself, thus either at one with or estranged from himself. A duality thus inheres in the term. By contrast, the terms *sarx* ("flesh") and *pneuma* ("spirit") are used unambiguously to denote the one or the other relation, never both. Thus *sarx*, in addition to denoting the concrete, fleshly body, refers to man as estranged from himself, as "fleshly," lost to the world, existing in inauthenticity. And *pneuma*, often used synonymously with *psychē*, is descriptive of that way of being in which man is oriented to God, thus living authentically. The terms *nous* ("mind"), *syneidēsis* ("conscience"), *kardia* ("heart"), *psychē* ("soul"), and *zōē* ("life") as employed by the apostle oscillate between *sarx* and *pneuma* to describe now this or the other aspect of somatic existence in its authenticity or inauthenticity. *Nous* denotes practical understanding issuing in a conscious or unconscious willing; *syneidēsis* denotes such understanding in light of a requirement. *Kardia*, often used in the sense of *nous* as willing, planning, and intending subject, nevertheless accents resolve as dominated by feeling. *Psychē*, like *zōē*, denotes the specifically human quality of being alive, of being directed toward something, though the latter term comes more and more to be used of true and authentic existence. The anthropological terms *nous*, *syneidēsis, kardia, psychē*, and *zōē* thus reflect an ontological rather than an ontic structure. That is, they describe what belongs to human nature and which in itself is neither good nor evil, but which offers the possibility of de-

33. *Ibid.*, 165-66, 309-11, 319-25.

ciding for good or evil. The terms may thus be predicated of man in his true and genuine existence or in his inauthentic existence. Finally, the broad, empty structures of human existence as outlined in Heidegger's analysis — possibility, thrownness, and fallenness — are signaled in Paul's use of the term *kosmos,* or "world," for it is into the world that one is "thrown," into the world that one falls or to which one surrenders, or it is against the world that one decides to be open to the future and live for God.[34]

C. The Quest for the Historical Jesus

For Bultmann, everything must be removed that can conceivably serve as a prop or support for faith, faith thus construed as self-understanding, as the resolve to be temporal, finite, to be a being unto death, open to the future, to God. In this assertion, Bultmann turns away decisively from the Enlightenment worldview with its commitment to life as an end in itself to which the traditional Christian notion of God must be reconciled. The task of the historian is thus not to prove that God can be proved to the satisfaction of modernity, *but rather to prove that God cannot be proved!* In other words, historical criticism is nothing but the obverse side of justification by which the sinner holds exclusively to a word, decides for the *kerygma* as heard and preached now, in this moment. Any attempt to buttress this decision through external means, whether by idea, dogma, or historical science, is illegitimate since it is motivated by unbelief. The "quest for the historical Jesus" had been nothing but a century-old attempt to give the believer a reason for believing. On this fundamental point Bultmann remained adamant.

To the question, "Of what significance, then, is the Jesus of history?" Bultmann replies, "only *that* he lived and died." As early as in 1921, Bultmann had attempted to demonstrate that the material in the Synoptic Gospels had undergone powerful changes until it achieved its present form. He writes that scarcely a piece of the Synoptic tradition had not been altered in form or content before arriving at its present status. This process of renovation, along with the interpolation of Jewish materials, had already begun in the Palestinian community, prior to the gospel's transplantation to Hellenistic soil. Then, with the influx of Hellenism in the Christian community, came an era of even

---

34. Bultmann, *Theology of the New Testament,* tr. Kendrick Grobel (London: SCM, 1952), 1:192-239, 254-59; see also the discussion of Bultmann's interpretation of New Testament anthropology against the background of Heidegger's analysis in James Macquarrie, *An Existentialist Theology* (New York: Macmillan, 1955), 43, 45, 51, 65, 78, 105, 137, 138, 151.

greater change. In sum, the Gospels were expanded cultic legends, their kerygmatic unity supplied by means of the myth, not by history or biography.[35] In this fashion, material continuity between the Jesus of history and the Christ of the *kerygma* must be recognized as impossible to achieve.

Bultmann does not, however, deny *historical* continuity between the Jesus of history and the primitive Christian proclamation. Indeed, he writes, there would be no *kerygma* apart from the historical Jesus. The *kerygma* announces that God made Jesus *Kyrios* and thus presupposes the historical Jesus. But, he contends, the *Christ* of the *kerygma* is not an historical figure who may enjoy continuity with the historical Jesus.[36]

To the question, "Can anything at all be known of the historical Jesus?" Bultmann ventured the following response:

> With a bit of caution we can say the following. . . . Characteristic of him are exorcisms, the breach of the Sabbath commandment, the abandonment of ritual purifications, polemic against Jewish legalism, fellowship with outcasts such as publicans and harlots, sympathy for women and children; it can also be seen that Jesus was not an ascetic such as John . . . but gladly ate and drank a glass of wine. Perhaps we may add that he called disciples and assembled about himself a small company of followers. . . . We can only say of his preaching that he doubtless appeared in the consciousness of being commissioned by God to preach the eschatological message of the breaking-in of the Kingdom of God. . . . We may thus ascribe to him a prophetic consciousness. . . . The greatest embarrassment to the attempt to reconstruct a portrait of Jesus is the fact that we cannot know how Jesus understood his . . . death. . . . What is certain is merely that he was crucified by the Romans, and thus suffered the death of a political criminal. . . . It took place because his activity was misconstrued as a political activity. In that case it would have been — historically speaking — a meaningless fate. We cannot tell whether or how Jesus found meaning in it. We may not veil from ourselves the possibility that he suffered a collapse.[37]

The conclusions to be drawn are threefold: first, in place of the historical Jesus, the Gospels present the figure of the Son of God. Second, whereas the

---

35. See Bultmann's discussion of the form and history of the apophthegms, dominical sayings, miracle stories, historical stories, and legends in *The History of the Synoptic Tradition*, 39ff., 81ff., 125ff., 145ff., 179ff., 218ff., and 302ff.

36. Bultmann, "The Primitive Christian Kerygma and the Historical Jesus," in *The Historical Jesus and the Kerygmatic Christ*, ed. Carl E. Braaten and Roy A. Harrisville (Nashville: Abingdon, 1964), 18, 30, and *passim*.

37. *Ibid.*, 22-24.

historical Jesus preached the coming rule of God, in the *kerygma* he is proclaimed as dying vicariously for our sins and rising for our salvation. Third, for the historical Jesus, the proclamation of God's will went hand in hand with the announcement of the end, but in the *kerygma* the ethical command takes second seat.[38]

To these assertions there have been many and loud objections. Joachim Jeremias of Göttingen wrote that if Christianity actually began with the proclamation of the risen Christ, then it logically follows that Jesus does not belong to Christianity. Modern scholarship is about to surrender the phrase "the Word become flesh"; about to dissolve the holy history, the activity of God in Jesus and his preaching; about to become docetic, to embrace the Christ-idea; and about to substitute the preaching of the apostle Paul for the message of Jesus.[39] Ethelbert Stauffer of Erlangen agreed that a biography of Jesus is unattainable, but that a history of Jesus in terms of a "strict clarification of those facts which can be ascertained" is within reach. Stauffer remonstrates: "I shall proceed along pragmatic lines, refraining from any psychologizing. Chronology will be my guide. I shall synchronize but not invent or speculate."[40] The Erlangen systematician Paul Althaus protested that faith's ground is not a *kerygma* without historical links, that while a *fides humana* or mere acknowledgment of the historicity of an event can never create *fides divina*, or saving faith, the latter is nevertheless not without the former.[41]

Bultmann's pupils have taken another tack. In contrast to a Jeremias or Stauffer who insisted that Jesus' life and work are actually contained in or at least presupposed by the *kerygma*, they argued that the faith of the community in its substance, in its conception of the person of Jesus, harks back to Jesus himself.

At a meeting of old Marburgers in 1953, Ernst Käsemann, then of Göttingen, opened the debate. In his famous speech "The Problem of the Historical Jesus," Käsemann states that he cannot agree that resignation or skepticism has the last word in historical study. Disinterest in the earthly Jesus not only ignores the primitive Christian concern for the identity of the exalted with the earthly Lord, but overlooks the fact that there are portions of the Synoptic tradition that the historian must recognize as authentic. True, says

38. *Ibid.*, 16-17.

39. Joachim Jeremias, *The Problem of the Historical Jesus*, tr. Norman Perrin (Philadelphia: Fortress, 1964), 9, 11, 22.

40. *Jesus and His Story*, tr. Richard and Clara Winston (New York: Alfred A. Knopf, 1960), xiii.

41. Paul Althaus, *Das sogennante Kerygma und der historische Jesus* (Gütersloh: Carl Bertelsmann, 1958), 37.

Käsemann, in the Gospels the exalted Lord has all but swallowed up the earthly Jesus, but the church has nevertheless maintained their continuity and identity. Herein lies justification for resuming the quest, though without sharing the liberal, nineteenth-century point of view. For Käsemann, those portions of Synoptic tradition that the historian is required to recognize as authentic are concentrated in the first, second, and fourth antitheses of the Sermon on the Mount (Matt. 5:21-22, 27-28, 33ff.). These antitheses, Käsemann states, reflect Jesus' consciousness of his mission. This, then, is the point at which to fix continuity between the Jesus of history and the Christ of the *kerygma*.[42]

In *Jesus of Nazareth,* Günther Bornkamm (1905-90) of Heidelberg wrote that if we were to accept uncritically everything transmitted in the Gospels as historical report, we would be doing violence to the Gospels. On the other hand, if we critically reduce the gospel tradition merely to what could not be contested on historical grounds, only a torso would remain. The Gospels attest to the fact that faith does not begin with itself, but lives out of a history. The task is thus to seek the history of Jesus in the *kerygma* of the Gospels, but also to seek the *kerygma* in this history. The Gospels afford no occasion for skepticism, but rather allow the historical figure of Jesus to appear before us in all its immediacy. What the Gospels report concerning Jesus' message, his deeds, and his story is marked by a genuineness, freshness, and uniqueness that the Easter faith did not materially alter.[43]

Ernst Fuchs, later to occupy Bultmann's chair at Marburg upon the latter's retirement, wrote in *Studies of the Historical Jesus* that inquiry into the New Testament concept of faith would establish what Jesus himself said. He then turned to the parable of the two sons in Luke 15 as fixing continuity between the Jesus of history and the Christ of faith. In this parable, asserts Fuchs, the historical Jesus dares to validate God's will as though he himself stands in God's place. But this means that the historical Jesus requires a decision from his hearers, a requirement simply echoing his own decision to range himself on God's side. In the church's present proclamation, Fuchs concludes, the relationship to God as disclosed in Jesus requires our decision. In the proclamation, therefore, the historical Jesus has come to us.[44]

To these voices and myriad others, the Zürich systematician Gerhard

42. Ernst Käsemann, "The Problem of the Historical Jesus," in *Essays on New Testament Themes,* tr. W. J. Montague (London: SCM, 1964), 15-47.

43. Günther Bornkamm, *Jesus of Nazareth,* tr. Irene and Fraser McLuskey with James M. Robinson (New York: Harper and Row, 1960).

44. Ernst Fuchs, *Studies of the Historical Jesus,* tr. Andrew Scobie (London: SCM, 1964), 11-31.

Ebeling added his own: as scanty as our knowledge of the historical Jesus may be, the point at which everything comes together in astonishing agreement can be summed up in one word — "faith." This concentration of all lines of the tradition, Ebeling contends, is not the product of fantasy, but occurred in existence. In Jesus faith had found its speech; encounter with the historical Jesus culminates in an encounter with the witness to faith. At Easter this witness to faith became the basis of faith. It is thus Jesus' solidarity with faith that establishes continuity between the Jesus of history and the Christ of the *kerygma*.[45]

IV. Assessment

A. Myth and Bultmann

To Bultmann's definition of myth, Julius Schniewind (1883-1948) of Halle, described by Bultmann as his ablest opponent in the demythologizing debate, proposed an alternative: "By 'mythological' we mean the presentation of unobservable realities in terms of observable phenomena." Schniewind preferred this definition because, as he says, "the most striking feature of the myths about the pagan gods is the way they speak of persons and events in an invisible world as if they were like those with which we are familiar on earth."[46]

Schniewind's definition is broad enough to escape reinterpretation solely in terms of self-understanding. Further, his definition is suggestive of the anthropomorphic, of the attribution of human form or personality to God, frequently characteristic of the language and thought-world of the Bible. More to the point, Schniewind doubts the possibility of avoiding the myth, of escaping that "ever-refined mythologizing of human thought." His answer is that the necessity of thinking in pictures and figures taken from the world of space and time reflects the search for the invisible. All human thought constitutes a single inquiry after the invisible, its answer given in the confession that the invisible God has surrendered himself to our world of visibility.[47] Schniewind's company of assenters grew and grew.

Karl Jaspers (1883-1969), across the hall from Barth at Basel, was the

45. Gerhard Ebeling, "Die Frage nach dem historischen Jesus und das Problem der Christologie," *Zeitschrift für Theologie und Kirche* 56 (1959), Beiheft 1:14-30; *The Nature of Faith,* tr. Ronald Gregor Smith (Philadelphia: Muhlenberg, 1961), 44-71.

46. "A Reply to Bultmann," in *Kerygma and Myth,* 46.

47. *Ibid.,* 47-52.

239

first among the philosophers to engage Bultmann in sustained debate. He asks:

> Does the splendour of the sunrise cease to be a tangible, ever new and in-spiring reality, a mythical presence, just because we know that the earth is revolving around the sun . . . ? Does the appearance of the deity on Mount Sinai or in the burning bush cease to be a poignant reality even when we know that in terms of space and time the phenomena in question were human experiences? To demythologize would be to do away with an essential faculty of our reason.[48]

Appeal was made to Plato, who employed the myth or the analogy of human agency to describe whatever in the realm of values could not be described in terms of the mechanical processes. Appeal was made against Plato, whose use of myth was often cosmological, whereas the purpose of myth in the New Testament was soteriological, intent on mediating a specific concept of human existence and a specific picture of God.[49]

It is necessary neither to defend Bultmann's definition of myth, his de-scription of the biblical universe as alien to the "aggravatedly modern man," nor to plead his evangelistic purpose in its existential reinterpretation. Be-hind his irritation with the mythological lies the conviction that allegiance to it spells bondage to a view of the world that everlastingly seeks to hold the hu-mane sciences, thus theology, in thrall. One of his star pupils spends over five hundred pages attempting to wrest the humane sciences from the grip of the natural sciences.[50] The link between fundamentalist insistence upon the ob-jective reality of the mythical and modern man's captivity to a worldview de-termined by natural science is not accidental and occasional but intimate and causal. Eleven years after he addressed the issue of the New Testament and mythology, Bultmann wrote to Barth:

> At issue first of all is liberation from the Bible's mythological worldview, because it has become totally alien to the man of today, and because adher-ence to it causes him offence — in fact, spurious offence — and bars his understanding. . . . Now, the present situation appears to me to be as fol-lows: Man lives totally within the worldview as sketched by objectifying sci-

48. "Myth and Religion," in *Kerygma and Myth*, vol. 2, ed. Hans-Werner Bartsch, tr. Reginald H. Fuller (London: SPCK, 1962), 144.

49. See Regin Prenter, "Mythos und Evangelium," in *Kerygma und Mythos*, ed. Hans-Werner Bartsch (Hamburg-Volksdorf: Herbert Reich, 1952), 2:81.

50. Hans-Georg Gadamer, *Truth and Method*, 2nd rev. ed. Joel Weinsheimer and Don-ald G. Marshall (New York: Crossroad, 1988), 218-42, 282-85, 450-56.

ence; but he has come more and more to realize (or is beginning to realize) that he cannot understand his own existence from out of that view of the world.[51]

The second sentence makes clear that the term "offence" in the first does not spell mere pique or irritation, but a stumbling block. The problem of the "man of today" is that his subservience to the natural scientific worldview has led him to a misapprehension of existence, thus rendered him lame respecting choice, faith, and genuine life. Bultmann contends that modern man is aware of the condition — this is the "offence" — but ignorant of the means for deliverance. Four hundred years earlier, the one whose thought Bultmann always complained he had merely struggled to bring to its logical conclusion wrote:

> You know that natural philosophy has always brought and still brings something evil and disagreeable to theology. The reason is that each and every art has its own terms and vocabulary. . . . Judges have theirs, doctors theirs, natural philosophers theirs. If you ever wished to transfer them from their locale or place to another, the confusion will be unbearable. It will obscure everything. So, if you wish to use these words, I ask that you first give them a good scrubbing. Take them off to the tub.[52]

For Luther's term *physica,* or "natural philosophy," substitute Bultmann's "objectification via the mythological," and one finds virtually the same argument.

B. Bultmann and Heidegger

Criticism of the work of Bultmann has often assumed that the old master's theology had its stimulus and final court of appeal in Martin Heidegger's phenomenology. Bultmann has been charged with captivity to a notion of reality that drives a wedge between existence conceived as possibility and whatever is objectifiable. This dichotomy, the argument continues, results in an epistemological division between histor*ic* self-understanding and historic*al,* factual knowledge. It creates a gulf between kerygmatic address and language "about" God. Or again, this separation of existence as possibility from what is objectifiable opens a chasm between a conceptuality that accosts or encounters and a conceptuality that merely refers.

51. *Barth-Bultmann: Letters,* 88.
52. *WA,* 39, 1:229.

It is alleged that allegiance to this division, to this "fact-value" split, induced Bultmann to reject by reinterpretation or demythologization all "worldly" talk of God, of human existence, of faith, and of Christian behavior that might endanger existence as a possibility, and thus forced him to squeeze the content of the biblical revelation into the single mode of "self-understanding."

The results of this "empire" of division between existence and the objectifiable world, so stated the critics, are as follows: faith is reduced to the punctiliar; its object rendered a cipher (in favor of the "here-and-now" character of the *kerygma*); the obedience of faith is voided of specificity (due to its definition as mere repetition of the resolve "to be"); the future is mulcted of content; the self deprived of any identity. Bultmann's self-contradictions, his offenses against this architectonic, are said to include an objectifying, "worldly" description of authentic existence — the refusal to demythologize such terms as "God," "grace," "forgiveness," and "salvation," and the occasional, "puzzling" accent upon the factual account of Jesus of Nazareth as possessing saving efficacy.

The topic for discussion is whether or not Bultmann's work looks as it does because of philosophical or because of theological commitments; whether or not appraisal begins with assuming Bultmann's membership in the circle of Adolf Schlatter and Karl Barth, devoted to the principle that the interpreter of the New Testament must hear its promise and claim, *or* with his affection for phenomenology — which, chronologically at least, did not surface till after his characteristic patterns of thought were formed.

In face of indecision respecting the reading of Bultmann — whether to give the nod to an interpretation of Bultmann from the side of his philosophy or of his theology — it may be asked: Why did Bultmann persist in his exclusivistic claim on behalf of Jesus when the philosopher and the theologian invited him to give Jesus the status of a mere paradigm or model of authentic existence available to humanity as such? Why the criticism to the effect that Bultmann did not proceed far enough with his demythologizing, but built a citadel for God and sin and grace? Are these not a signal that after all the man could not live without the "mythological," that the inconsistencies and self-contradictions were clues to his real intention, that what he said of existence as possibility, thrownness, and fallenness was already prejudiced by a theological commitment? More than one critic argues that it was not Bultmann's appropriation of the Heideggerian analytic, but rather certain alien commitments to historical criticism that effected the "damaging" results in his interpretation. For example, Bultmann left uninterpreted such New Testament utterances concerning the future as appear in Revelation or in

Paul. The "cosmic" christology of Ephesians and Colossians was expunged, not on hermeneutical grounds, but because Bultmann regarded them as pseudo-Pauline.[53] Hans Conzelmann (1915-89) charges his old teacher with confusing systematic and methodological questions, with drawing systematic conclusions from historical-critical premises.[54]

At any rate, if the answer to the question whether or not Bultmann "loads the dice" theologically is in the affirmative, it was not an answer Barth could give. He fully expected that the attraction to phenomenology would lead Bultmann to Nazism. Anyone who worked in a positive sense with a natural theology, he said, could and ultimately would join the "German Christians," that ecclesiastical monstrosity concocted by Hitler and shaped after his pattern of *Führertum*. Bultmann was shocked, affronted, and Barth relented.[55]

The argument is an old one. Bultmann's remarkable wedding of scientific concerns with those of the community's faith and confession, and its attendant reduction of the biblical witness to a single mode — self-understanding — can no longer serve. But the argument that its stimulus and last resort lay with Heidegger is premature.

C. The Question of Continuity

Nowhere else than in his Life-of-Jesus Research is Bultmann's theological orientation more clearly reflected.

In his exposition of the Gospels, Martin Luther never tires of emphasizing the insufficiency of a mere "historical faith." Preaching has to occur in such fashion that the gospel "should not remain in the history . . . but be preached so as to be useful to me and to you."[56] In agreement with Luther, Philip Melanchthon (1497-1560) writes:

> This sophistic faith . . . by which the impious give assent to the evangelical histories much as we are accustomed to do in the case of the history of Livy or Sallust, is no faith at all. . . . Faith is nothing other than reliance upon the

53. Günther Backhaus, *Kerygma and Mythos bei David Friedrich Strauss und Rudolf Bultmann* (Hamburg: Herbert Reich, 1956), 72-76.
54. "Zur Methode der Leben-Jesu-Forschung," *Zeitschrift für Theologie und Kirche* 56, Beiheft 1 (1959): 1.
55. *Barth-Bultmann: Letters*, 75-76.
56. Walter von Loewenich, *Luther als Ausleger der Synoptiker* (Munich: Chr. Kaiser, 1954), 83-84.

divine mercy promised in Christ, and therefore without any sign whatso-ever.[57]

For Melanchthon, *fides historica,* or "historical faith," bears no relation to the faith that justifies.

Obviously, the problem of the historical Jesus did not exist for Luther or Melanchthon. All gave assent to the evangelical histories. What concerned the Reformers was that the *vobis,* the "to you," get the priority. As Luther argues: "All the actions that Christ performed visibly should be interpreted to signify the actions Christ performs spiritually."[58] And, in response to a Jeremias or a Stauffer, Ernst Käsemann asserts that our relation to past history is not medi-ated exclusively through research on the sources. Past history is ambiguous; only the word that accompanies it can give it contemporaneity. The message of Paul or of John make clear that they are not mere brute, naked facts that are to be proclaimed.[59]

Of course, Bultmann's theological orientation is not his own invention. In the series of theological studies Karl Barth edited, he included his own fifty-page essay on demythologizing, titling it *Rudolf Bultmann: Ein Versuch, ihn zu verstehen (Rudolf Bultmann: An Attempt to Understand Him).* The title is replete with irony: "I must confess I know of no contemporary theologian," writes Barth, "who has so much to say about understanding, or one who has so much cause to complain of being misunderstood."[60] Then, toward the con-clusion of the essay, Barth argues that Bultmann, unlike Strauss, does not cling to the modern worldview as an article of faith but rather relativizes it, adding that Bultmann is an apologete, historian, or philosopher only second-arily, and fixes the dominant elements of Bultmann's theology in the "young Luther," whose portrait his old teacher Wilhelm Herrmann had drawn. Barth concludes: "Bultmann's work is inconceivable apart from his Lutheran back-ground. Of course, this is not the whole story. But those who throw stones at Bultmann should be careful lest they accidentally hit Luther, who is also hov-ering somewhere in the background."[61] Barth's statement takes on greater rel-evance when attention is given to Bultmann's proximity to the Reformer — a feature missing from the great bulk of the literature. To enlarge on one in-

57. *Loci Communes,* tr. Charles Leander Hill (Boston: Meador, 1944), 175, 177, see 184.

58. *WA,* 17, I, 421, 35.

59. Ernst Käsemann, *New Testament Questions of Today,* tr. W. J. Montague (Philadel-phia: Fortress, 1969), 13.

60. "Rudolf Bultmann: Ein Versuch, Ihn zu Verstehen," *Theologische Studien* 84 (1953): 3.

61. *Ibid.,* 47-48.

stance closest to Bultmann's concern, the Marburger joins hands with Barth in asserting that the freedom to act and the reception of grace or forgiveness are indissolubly linked. He agrees with Barth that it makes all the difference in the world which of these two establishes the other. Together with Barth, he denies the Pelagian notion that the freedom to act is given with existence, and maintains that only the gift of grace makes possible this freedom. All this attack upon the liberalism of his teachers Bultmann shares with Barth. And for this reason, no doubt, he applauded the appearance of Barth's *Romans*.[62]

On the other hand, Bultmann parts company with Barth when the latter denies to existence apart from faith a knowledge about the freedom to act or to receive grace. According to Bultmann, the difference between philosophy and faith, for example, is not that the one is aware of the command to love while the other is not. The difference consists in the fact that the one regards love as one more inherent, native, human possibility among others, and not as gift, a gift from Another. With Barth, knowledge of love is reserved for faith; for Bultmann the fulfillment of love's requirement is reserved for faith.

At bottom, these are not two points, at one of which Bultmann joins hands with Barth while at the other parting company with him, but only one, the point of an Augustinianism nuanced by Luther. In Luther's *On the Bondage of the Will*, the Reformer concedes to existence apart from faith the capacity for being "caught up by the Spirit and touched by God's grace" — an affirmation for which Emil Brunner (1889-1966) hundreds of years later would hear a thunderous "No!" from Barth[63] — then added, "as the proverb says, God did not make heaven for geese!"[64] But Luther roundly denies to existence apart from faith the realization of that capacity: "Grace is given freely to the undeserving and utterly unworthy, and is not attained by any of the efforts, endeavours, or works, small or great, of even the best and most upright men who seek and follow after righteousness with flaming zeal."[65]

In the 1920s Bultmann held lectures on the introduction or propaedeutic to the study of theology. In those lectures themes that later would be accented or hammered home were already being struck. What characterizes those efforts at "theological encyclopedia," as they then were called, is not so much Bultmann's appetite for existence-philosophy and the like, but his allegiance to a particular Reformation heritage in face of the liberalism of the

---

62. Barth, *The Epistle to the Romans*, 16.

63. *Natural Theology*, comprising "Nature and Grace" by Emil Brunner, and the Reply "No!" by Karl Barth, tr. Peter Fraenkel (London: Bles, 1946).

64. Martin Luther, *On The Bondage Of The Will*, tr. Packer and Johnston (London: James Clarke, 1957), 105.

65. *Ibid.*, 302.

nineteenth century, and thus his proximity to, but also his distance from, other "neo-orthodox," "crisis," or "dialectical" theologians. In 1926 Bultmann wrote: "Both philosophy and faith know of human limitations, of the quest for authenticity. . . . The difference is that faith contests that authenticity can be achieved through courageous resolve. . . ."[66] It is all there in Luther — the concession that existence apart from faith possesses a "hint" or "clue" regarding authentic existence (Luther's term: "passive aptitude"), thus the refusal to give the cognitive preeminence over trust in the definition of faith; the denial that knowledge of genuine existence assumes the capacity to achieve it (in Luther the denial of the freedom of the will); the reserving of its achieving to the hearing of a word of forgiveness calling away from self to the other, thus to trust that self will not be lost in its being lost to or for the other (in Luther, the summons from being "turned in upon the self to a going out of self to the other") — it is all there, but now nuanced, retranslated, given speech in a new vehicle. That vehicle would tempt the translator to betray the original, but, as Bultmann argued, against his will: "Why won't they understand that I am merely trying to carry the Pauline, Lutheran understanding of faith to its logical conclusion?"

Bultmann's students, particularly those responsible for the "post-Bultmannian" quest, all acknowledged their indebtedness to Bultmann. Käsemann writes:

> As it is not uncommon today to speak of the "school of Bultmann," it may be allowable to emphasize that there is probably none of Bultmann's older and better-known pupils who do not adopt a thoroughly critical attitude towards the master. But this tells in favour of the master and not against him. For this state of affairs which is really very rare today only proves that the master has succeeded in supplying that Socratic midwifery which leads to truth and freedom.[67]

Yet all deviated from Bultmann, and for the reason that the *extra nos* (that term for what is outside me and occurs toward me), the fact that faith does not begin with itself; that Jesus first brings faith to speech and thus is its ground; that the *kerygma* retains its character from the fact that it lays bare a relationship to God that Jesus disclosed — this was in danger of being swallowed up by the *vobis* or *pro me* (that theological term for what concerns me).

But if in Bultmann the danger is that the *pro me* may swallow up the *ex-*

66. *Theologische Enzyklopädie,* ed. Eberhard Jüngel and Klaus W. Müller (Tübingen: J. C. B. Mohr, 1984), 89.

67. *New Testament Questions of Today,* 10-11.

tra nos, there is another danger to which Bultmann did not fall prey — the danger of objectification, of abstracting the *extra nos* from the *pro me* and regarding it as separate from the movement of faith.[68]

The topic for discussion is whether or not Bultmann's programmatic christology paid the price for nondemonstrability or nonverifiability, and whether or not the burden of nondemonstrability should be borne by faith, that is, that in the movement of faith what is nonverifiable is affirmed, namely, that God is there before I believe. Bornkamm believes that with Bultmann christology has indeed paid such a price. He writes: "Jesus Christ has become a mere saving fact and ceases to be a person"; the speech of the New Testament "is transformed into a system of significances, it is dissolved into a mere *significat* and has lost the force of the *est.*"[69]

Hans Conzelmann turns up the other side of the coin, writing that only when "the event of the proclamation is taken up into the problematic" can we escape the dangers inherent in the old as well as in the new quest of the historical Jesus. This means that when it is recognized that Jesus does indeed rise in the *kerygma,* not merely because it is his word that involves the hearer in the *kerygma* — as though that word could be abstracted from the person, hypostasized, and called by the name "Jesus" — but because he himself is the word that speaks of him, or when the self-authenticating character of the *kerygma* is acknowledged, then we shall be spared either the objectification of the revelation or its reduction to a mere psychic phenomenon.

Where historical-critical research can only demonstrate *that* Jesus lived and died, and in face of the event of the resurrection can only maintain a discontinuity, the *how* and the *what,* the continuity in christology is the burden that faith must bear. "There are cases," writes William James, "where a fact cannot come at all unless a preliminary faith exists in its coming." The recognition of the contingency of the eschatological event in this one person, and hence of the *extra nos,* the conviction that "faith does not begin with itself" but has its "ground" in Jesus of Nazareth, is part and parcel of the movement of faith. And though it is an error to assume that because of

68. The distinction in "process thought" between God's "primordial" and "contingent" natures, the latter only an "illustration" of the former, is a distinction to which neither Bultmann nor Barth would consent. See Eberhard Jüngel, *Gottes Sein Ist im Werden* (Tübingen: J. C. B. Mohr, 1976), 113-14 n. 148.

69. In G. Bornkamm and W. Klaas, "Mythos und Evangelium: Zum Programm R. Bultmanns," *Theologische Existenz Heute,* Neue Folge 26 (1953): 18-19; see also Bornkamm's remarks in the discussion between himself, Rudolf Bultmann, and Friedrich Karl Schumann in *Die christliche Hoffnung und das Problem der Entmythologisierung* (Stuttgart: Evangelisches, 1954), 55.

its nondemonstrability the contingency of this event is irrelevant to faith, not because faith "needs" this contingency, but because it is of the nature of faith to affirm the divine initiative, it must be asserted that the "ground" of faith is disclosed to faith *alone,* and that any attempt at legitimizing it is a domestication, a robbing faith of its establishment *sola gratia,* by grace alone.

But to return to our question: Did Bultmann suppress the *est* for the sake of the *significat?* One American author has interpreted Bultmann thusly:

> Objects of faith cannot be objects of historiography (major premise). A Jesus with an identity is an object of historiography (minor premise). Therefore, a Jesus with an identity cannot be the object of faith (conclusion).[70]

The syllogism appears unimpeachable, but it rests upon a prior argument that gives advantage to the term "identity." What if that prior argument were to give the advantage to "faith"? Then the syllogism might read:

> Objects of historiography cannot be objects of faith (major premise). The Christ of the *kerygma* is an object of faith (minor premise). Therefore, the Christ of the *kerygma* cannot be an object of historiography (conclusion).

The use of the name "Jesus" in the first and of "Christ" in the second syllogism renders the two highly dissimilar. But suppose the *that,* the mere fact *that* Jesus lived and died, could span the two — historically if not materially? In other words, suppose that faith is not assent to an object of historiography, to the mere historical fact of Jesus of Nazareth, but nevertheless the belief that history has been qualified as a history of salvation through that very object? In that case, what for Bultmann's crtics is the most difficult sentence in all his writing to interpret would be rendered less difficult. The sentence reads: "The word of God is not some mysterious oracle, but a sober, factual account of a human life, of Jesus of Nazareth, possessing saving efficacy for man" (44).

Bultmann's grave is not easy to find in the old Marburg cemetery. That fact is in inverse proportion to the weight of his influence and the comprehension of his thought to the present moment.

70. Robert C. Roberts, *Rudolf Bultmann's Theology* (Grand Rapids: Wm. B. Eerdmans, 1976), 108.

12

ERNST KÄSEMANN

Biblical Theology under the Cross

Rudolf Bultmann dominated New Testament scholarship for nearly three decades with his method of "demythologizing" or "existential interpretation." His reign was anything but serene. Not only did he face formidable opposition from biblical conservatives and neoorthodox dogmaticians, but he also had to deal with rebellion within the ranks of his own students. Barth had his Barthians and Bonhoeffer his devotees, but Bultmann's regular reunion of "old Marburgers" was not anything like the gathering of disciples or the founding of a school. Instead, his best students chose to honor their teacher by calling even the most fundamental elements of his work into question. Among the first of the truants was Ernst Käsemann.

I. Biography

Born in Bochum-Dahlhausen, 12 July 1906, Käsemann entered upon his theological studies in 1925. "We found ourselves," he writes, "in the mighty train of German Idealism which for one hundred years unchallenged linked the middle class with the cultural program of its classical poets and thinkers."[1] In 1931 Käsemann received his licentiate in theology, and two years later he took up his duties as pastor of the Lutheran congregation in Gelsen-

---

1. *Kirchliche Konflikte* (Göttingen: Vandenhoeck und Ruprecht, 1982), 1:226.

kirchen-Rotthausen. While in Gelsenkirchen, he was seized by the Gestapo for his exposition of Isaiah 26:13 ("O Lord our God, other lords besides thee have ruled over us, but thy name alone we acknowledge").[2] During his four-week incarceration, Käsemann drafted the outline for his monograph on Hebrews, *The Wandering People of God*, with the Confessing Church in mind, "which in Germany opposed tyranny and had to be called to patience."[3] In 1942 Pastor Käsemann was drafted into the *Wehrmacht*. Following a tour of duty in Paris, he was released, then drafted a second time for duty in Greece. At war's end, Käsemann surrendered to the Americans on 5 May 1945. Until his release, he was interned with 80,000 other prisoners in a prison camp at Kreuznach.[4] In 1946, Käsemann was invited to the University of Mainz as associate professor, and in the year following he received his doctorate from the University of Marburg. In 1951 he was called as full professor to Göttingen, then in 1959 to Tübingen, where he taught until retirement in 1971. He died in 1997.

II. Biblical Theology under the Cross

A. Bultmann

From Rudolf Bultmann, Käsemann learned the necessity and the art of radical historical criticism. Writing that biblical criticism should no longer be treated as a horror to children or as an excuse for cowardice in a Christianity turned bourgeois, he insists that Protestant theology has always been critical, and for this reason can be linked to the historical-critical method. Käsemann asserts that the gospel actually begets the critical faculty, whereas its absence tokens spiritual impoverishment and deprivation, adding that the only possible alternative to the scientific method is the violence done by the devout.[5] As to the method's function, Käsemann is in agreement with Bultmann: the method serves the doctrine of justification by faith. He writes: "We learned . . . to read our texts no longer primarily as historical sources, because . . . their

2. Käsemann, *Widerstand im Zeichen des Nazareners* (Lucerne: Romero-Haus, 1987), 17-18.
3. *The Wandering People of God*, tr. Roy A. Harrisville and Irving L. Sandberg (Minneapolis: Augsburg, 1984), 13; *Kirchliche Konflikte*, 17.
4. Käsemann, *Widerstand im Zeichen des Nazareners*, 18, 28, 41.
5. Käsemann, *Kirchliche Konflikte*, 171; "Theologie des Neuen Testaments: Vorlesungsnachschrift für den internen Studiengebrauch" (unpublished manuscript, n.d.), 4; *New Testament Questions of Today*, tr. W. J. Montague (Philadelphia: Fortress, 1969), 264, 269.

kerygmatic character and their theological intention became more clearly recognizable."[6]

In other words, historical criticism makes clear that the right and promise of faith are not immediately derived from history. Only that illumination of existence is Christian which acknowledges this truth. But this means acknowledging that the understanding of existence and the world is determined by the doctrine of justification.[7] "No old Marburger," says Käsemann, "will forget how passionately Luther was studied in the early days."[8]

For this reason Käsemann perennially took Bultmann's part in the debate over demythologizing. The 1962 Ecumenical Conference in Montreal tested whether or not the voice of radical historical criticism from the Bultmann school was fit for "membership in the great choir."[9] Following Käsemann's address on the Bible as evidencing a plurality of confessions rather than the unity of the church, the General Secretary, Willem Visser 't Hooft (1900-85) concluded that such a voice was not fit, and forever after refused to shake Käsemann's hand.[10] Together with Bultmann, Käsemann believed that historical criticism furnished the best access to past reality, and together with Bultmann he acknowledged that radical criticism removed from the canon any binding character and destroyed the "gold background" of the life of Jesus. But he did not believe that historical criticism furnished the only access to past reality — history could be more or less "naively discovered."[11]

Beneath what he had learned from Bultmann, Käsemann detected a reduction of the biblical message. Bultmann's existential interpretation had obscured the historian's concern. Bultmann had read the variations on eschatology in the New Testament as expressions of a changing Christian self-consciousness. He had interpreted justification as the vehicle for believing self-understanding. He had fixed continuity between unbelief and faith in the creature's indirect knowledge of God — in spite of the Pauline assertion that continuity lay solely in God's refusal to abandon his creation. He had defined the biblical notion of freedom in terms of the search for identity. Not even the "historicality" of human existence by which Bultmann had set such great store was given its due, for he spoke only of the acting and suffering person,

---

6. "Vom theologischen Recht historisch-kritischer Exegese," *Zeitschrift für Theologie und Kirche* 64 (1967): 272.

7. *Ibid.*, 270, 273.

8. *Ibid.*, 273.

9. Käsemann, *Kirchliche Konflikte,* 23, 29; see also *Perspectives on Paul,* tr. Margaret Kohl (Philadelphia: Fortress, 1971), 24.

10. Käsemann, *Widerstand im Zeichen des Nazareners,* 22.

11. Käsemann, "Theologie," 16, 38; "Vom theologischen Recht," 261, 262.

whereas *hearing* as a mark of historicality was totally ignored.[12] Quoting from Bultmann's 1957 Gifford Lectures, in which his teacher states that with Paul the idea of salvation is oriented to the individual, Käsemann replies: "This sentence clearly shows the stimulus and basis of all Bultmann's thought. Nowhere is stronger objection to be raised than here."[13]

In Käsemann's view, Bultmann's preoccupation had led him to ignore the New Testament's concern for world history, for the cosmos. "Authentic existence" was abstracted from nature, from society, and from creation as a whole. But this means snapping the link between the Testaments, and reducing the world to a theater of individual decisions. In the New Testament, Käsemann contends, God does not surrender his creature to other powers; in the Nazarene he claims every spot on earth. Removed from the sphere of apocalyptic — thus, from any concept of judgment — Bultmann's view of justification is unable to speak of the dominion of Christ in its worldwide dimension.[14]

The debate with Bultmann, begun principally over Pauline and Johannine texts, now led to conflict over the historical Jesus — that is, over the question of material-theological continuity between the Jesus of history and the Christ of faith, and in the teeth of Bultmann's assertion that the *kerygma* allowed only for the "that" of Jesus' life. At a meeting of "old Marburgers" at Jugenheim on 21 October 1953, Käsemann reopened the quest with a twenty-eight-page, seven-point address entitled "The Problem of the Historical Jesus."[15]

The essay begins with an analysis of contemporary scholarship that, by now, assigns greater credibility to the Synoptic tradition and has attained to a systematic conception of a history of salvation, lodged in world history, yet with its own laws and its own continuity. Käsemann then proceeds to the problem of the historical element in the Gospels, writing that the earliest Christian *kerygma* did indeed conceal the picture of the historical Jesus, in-

12. Käsemann, "Theologie," 12, 40, 61-62, 64; *Perspectives on Paul*, 76, 27n.; *Commentary on Romans*, tr. Geoffrey W. Bromiley (Grand Rapids: Wm. B. Eerdmans, 1980), 172; unpublished "Lectures on Romans" (Tübingen, 1962), 130-31, 140; *Kirchliche Konflikte*, 66-67, 238-39.

13. Käsemann, "Theologie," 63; see Bultmann, *Geschichte und Eschatologie* (Tübingen: J. C. B. Mohr, 1958), 48.

14. Ernst Käsemann, *Jesus Means Freedom*, tr. Frank Clarke (Philadelphia: Fortress, 1969), 132-33; *Perspectives on Paul*, 23; *Commentary on Romans*, 56, 93, 236, 255; "Die göttliche und die bürgerliche Gerechtigkeit," *Sexauer Gemeindepreis für Theologie* 5 (1986): 10; *Widerstand im Zeichen des Nazareners*, 11.

15. *Essays on New Testament Themes*, tr. W. J. Montague (London: SCM, 1964), 15-47.

tent on the decision between faith and unbelief. Because primitive Christianity held fast to the identity of the earthly with the exalted Lord, it could only have regarded the historical question as an abstraction.

Acknowledging the mingling of myth and history in early Christianity's portrait of Jesus, Käsemann asserts that the Gospels clearly point to the contingency with which the saving event is tied to a particular person, place, and time. Such contingency reflects the freedom of the acting God who sets the time and place in which faith becomes a possibility. Because primitive Christianity experienced Jesus' earthly history as a *"kairos,"* it wrote Gospels.

Next, conceding that no formal criteria exist for reconstructing authentic words of Jesus, Käsemann nevertheless asserts the genuineness of utterances in the Gospels, in which Jesus reflects a dialectical relationship to the Torah, displays the immediacy of a teacher of wisdom, and employs terms such as "Amen," denoting a direct relation to the divine as mediated through inspiration — all of it expressing the uniqueness of Jesus' mission, which the church later acknowledged in confessing him as Messiah and Son of God.

In the final portion of the essay, Käsemann states that the question concerning the historical Jesus is "the question concerning the continuity of the gospel within the discontinuity of the times and within the variation of the *kerygma.*" Or, as he repeated in the unpublished "Theologie des Neuen Testaments," prepared for students at Göttingen, at issue was the *eph' hapax,* the "once," from the perspective of which the "once-for-all" has to be seen.[16] The Jugenheim essay concludes with the word that the problem of the historical Jesus is a riddle Jesus himself had posed, a riddle the historian could establish but could not solve: "It is only solved by those who since the Cross and the Resurrection confess him as that which, in the days of his flesh, he never claimed to be and yet was — their Lord. . . ."[17]

Methodologically, Käsemann embarked on his "New Quest" from the perspective of the *kerygma,* that is, he attempted to lift out from the New Testament proclamation whatever reflection of the historical Jesus it might contain.[18] In doing so, he fixed the approach for a series of "questers" to follow. Günther Bornkamm, Hans Conzelmann, Ernst Fuchs, and James M. Robin-

16. Käsemann, "Theologie," 75, 85.

17. *Essays,* 47. These same points are made in "Theologie," 47, 72-74, 78-79.

18. "Theologie," 102: "There is only discontinuity between the historical Jesus and the *kerygma.* Bultmann is correct on this point. The continuity between the historical Jesus and the post-Easter community can only be seen in retrospect. . . . The exalted Lord creates continuity with the historical Jesus"; 107: "We have known Jesus in the exalted Lord." See also *Essays,* 59: "There is no access to the historical Jesus other than by way of the community's faith in the Risen Lord."

son, to name only a few, would commence their quest from the perspective of the *kerygma,* not conversely, as did, for example, Joachim Jeremias of Göttingen or Ethelbert Stauffer (1902-79) of Erlangen. For this approach Käsemann acknowledged indebtedness not only to Bultmann but also to the one-time Tübingen scholar Adolf Schlatter, "spiritual father" of the new quest and the first to inquire into the theological significance of the historical Jesus.[19]

Käsemann's criterion for determining authentic Jesus tradition consists of assigning to Jesus only what cannot be explained from Judaism or earliest Christianity. But this criterion, he adds, comprises a merely heuristic principle, since Jesus advocated much that belonged to the Judaism of his time.[20] Again, the culprit is the same — Bultmann's reduction of the kerygmatic to the "existential," thus his substitution of the kerygmatic for the historical. Käsemann attacks:

> When the kerygma takes the place of the historical Jesus, the inference to be drawn is that there is no faith in Christ which is not also faith in the church. . . . Nowhere does the New Testament allow us to conclude that the Easter faith is also faith in the church as bearer of the *kerygma.* . . . Bultmann's resistance to the historical knows no bounds.[21]

According to Käsemann, the Jesus of history is no apocalypticist. Nowhere, he writes, does the genuine material reflect Jesus' urge to usher in the kingdom. Scarcely one scholar agrees with Schweitzer that Jesus, inspired by expectations of the End, sent his disciples on a hasty mission to Palestine, proclaimed an "interim ethic," and when his hopes proved false, sought to force God's hand at Jerusalem. Apocalyptic is nevertheless the oldest *interpretation* of the *kerygma.* Here the concept of "interim ethic" applies. And here again Käsemann differs with Bultmann, who viewed anthropology as the *kerygma's* oldest variation. From their Easter experience, writes Käsemann, the earliest disciples derived their hope in the return of Jesus as heavenly Son of Man. The exalted and returning Lord thus became the midpoint of Christian proclamation, and primitive Christian enthusiasm the community's response to it. It was at this point that Jesus' earthly life began its retreat.

As for Paul — Jesus' greatest interpreter — the sign under which he understood himself and his mission and carried on his battle with his opponents was that of apocalyptic. Käsemann insists that the meaning of the Pauline doctrine of justification, that is, that in Christ God is becoming *cosmo-*

---

19. Käsemann, "Theologie," 3, 10, 11.
20. *Ibid.,* 73.
21. *Ibid.,* 79.

crator, and not merely the Lord of believers or a cultic deity, had its roots in apocalyptic.[22] Due to his discomfort over mythology, Bultmann could not see that Paul's dialectic of the "now already" and the "not yet" does not mirror a dialectic of existence, but an apocalyptic posture; more, that Paul's anthropological reflection is an important function of his theology, but not its center. With Bultmann, however, the consequence of Paul's theology had been made its basis. This, writes Käsemann, is the result of reduction and soteriological actualization of Christianity. The way from the preaching of Jesus to the earliest community's apocalyptic posture, however, is not the way of organic development — the community had been strongly influenced by mythology.[23]

It was inevitable, says Käsemann, that the apocalyptic of the oldest community should be surrendered, and in a confession of Christ no longer as coming but as seizing the world here and now. The result of this fading of imminent expectation was concentration on things of this earth. Now the matter at issue was the means or structure by which Christ was to seize the world here and now. The legitimizing of community leadership thus became the church's most urgent task. As a result prophets, charismatics with their message of the priesthood of all believers, came to be regarded as carriers of infection, to whom one could not entrust leadership. In their place appeared presbyters, eventually monarchical bishops, tracing their succession to disciples of the apostles, and in it all Jewish Christianity functioning as godfather. "Early catholicism" was the term given this revolutionary change, this preoccupation with legitimizing leadership. The New Testament itself reinforced such preoccupation in the Pastoral Epistles.[24] And to it the Gospel of John furnished resistance.

In his study of John 17, Käsemann writes that the Johannine writings have to be interpreted as antithetical to early catholicism, while at the same time influenced by gnosticism. In fact, the author of the Johannine Gospel and letters belonged to a conventicle that, although later hereticized by the Great Church, was by "human error and the providence of God" allowed into the canon. This author, a presbyter of docetic persuasion, nonetheless waged war on behalf of the "Word become flesh."

22. Käsemann, "Lectures on Romans," 124, 145, 147, 151; *New Testament Questions of Today,* 127-28, 132-33, 135, 136-37, 181; *Perspectives on Paul,* 44, 75; "Theologie," 49, 50-52, 55, 64, 92, 94, 105; *Commentary on Romans,* 217.

23. Käsemann, "Theologie," 49, 50-52, 64, 92, 94, 105; "Lectures on Romans," 145, 147, 151; *New Testament Questions of Today,* 127-28, 135.

24. Käsemann, "Theologie," 53-54, 57; *Kirchliche Konflikte,* 16, 43; "Evangelischer Wahrheit in den Umbrüchen christlicher Theologie," in *Theologen und Theologien in Verschiedenen Kulturkreisen* (Düsseldorf: Patmos, 1986), 267.

Throughout his discussion of the displacement of apocalyptic in the later history of the church, Käsemann echoed his teacher's hypothesis respecting the pre-Christian, gnostic "redeemed Redeemer," a title invented by the great historian of religions Richard Reitzenstein (1861-1931), for the idea of a Savior who descends to free all "souls" that sit in darkness through revealing to them knowledge of their true, "light" essence and, in thus liberating them, also redeems himself. It was this "redeemed Redeemer," a construct or conclusion drawn from research into Manichaeism, and long advocated by Bultmann and the Marburg school, that was alleged to have sat for the portrait of the Christ at various points in the New Testament literature. Later, Käsemann would express embarrassment at having accepted that construct, but would retain his opinion of the Fourth Evangelist as the first to reject the tenet that it was enough to believe with the church.[25]

B. Cullmann

Käsemann reserves his bitterest criticism for what he terms an "enthusiastic theology of history" attaching to the perspective known as *Heilsgeschichte* or "salvation history," and principally as advocated in the twentieth century by Oscar Cullmann of Basel. Though Cullmann is often mentioned in the same breath with the great nineteenth-century *Heilsgeschichtler* von Hofmann, there is less similarity between the two than first appears. Cullmann does not commence his work by reflecting on Christian experience, then move toward demonstrating its recapitulation in the events of salvation history.[26] He rather concentrates on those events themselves as yielding a measurable, demonstrable continuity within the historical process, a process, moreover, with Christ at its center.

This reference to Christ as the "midpoint of time" furnishes the occasion for Käsemann's attack on Cullmann and his *heilsgeschichtlich* sketch. According to Käsemann, *Heilsgeschichte* refuses to recognize apocalyptic as the oldest and supporting layer of post-Easter Christianity. It is an impersonal thing, an empty *mysterium tremendum,* without any idea of the horror in history. Its effect is to relegate faith to a *gnosis,* a retrospection on saving "facts,"

25. Käsemann, "Theologie," 60; *The Testament of Jesus,* tr. Gerhard Krodel (Philadelphia: Fortress, 1968), 15, 26-27, 40, 66-67, 70, 73, 75; *Exegetische Versuche und Besinnungen* (Göttingen: Vandenhoeck und Ruprecht, 1960), 1:174, 178, 182; *Essays on New Testament Themes,* 154-55; *Kirchliche Konflikte,* 17.
26. See the discussion of "The Task and Method of Theology" according to von Hofmann, 238-45.

of which none — preexistence, incarnation, crucifixion, resurrection, exalta-tion, return — takes precedence over the other. Käsemann charges that Cullmann had joined forces with Luke, for whom God's activity had to be rendered historically tangible, first in a progressive reduction beginning with Abraham and ending with Israel as representative of humanity, then in a pro-gressive expansion, beginning with Christ and ending with the church. Such, Käsemann contended, paralyzed Paul's doctrine of justification by incorpo-rating it in a salvation-historical scheme. In Wolfhart Pannenberg, Käsemann believes that Cullmann found a comrade-in-arms who is also willing to de-scribe history as the revelation or self-disclosure of God. Had not Germany enough of this type of thinking with Hitler? Was not *Heilsgeschichte,* in a sec-ularized and political form, the driving force of the Third Reich?[27] To all of this "boasting in isolatable saving facts," Bultmann's program, despite its faults, is far superior.

History, Käsemann contends, cannot define and interpret the gospel, for the simple reason that history is ambiguous. The eschatological contin-gency of the revelation makes clear that the true God as well as true human existence is totally hidden in the fallen world. Consequently, it is the gospel that defines and interprets history. On the other hand, Käsemann cannot deny a *Heilsgeschichte* of sorts, that is, a history of salvation that consists in a continuity of the divine will; thus a paradoxical history, a history in which the divine will cannot be read off from events but only heard in the word of promise. It is just such a *Heilsgeschichte* that is linked to the Pauline doctrine of justification, serving that doctrine as its horizon, its historical depth, not as its superstructure or completion. "The worldly," writes Käsemann, "even in the shape of a *Heilsgeschichte,* cannot be the content and ground of our faith. Yet it remains its battlefield, and the horizon of divine grace."[28]

Whether it is believing "self-understanding," which reduces justifica-tion to its mere vehicle, or salvation history, which subordinates justification to a polemical, thus provisional, thus disposable motif within the superstruc-ture of a theology of saving facts, it is clear to Käsemann that both spring from the same parent root: German Idealism — an ideological philosophy linked to the middle class, unchallenged for a century, fed by its classical thinkers and poets. In face of Bultmann's passionate defense against identify-

27. Käsemann, *Kirchliche Konflikte,* 49; "Theologie," 59, 66-69; *Perspectives on Paul,* 48-49, 52-53, 64; *Commentary on Romans,* 254; "Vom theologischen Recht historisch-kritischer Exegese," 276; "Justification and Salvation History," 64.

28. Käsemann, ed., *Das Neue Testament als Kanon* (Göttingen: Vandenhoeck und Ruprecht, 1970), 407; *Perspectives on Paul,* 41-42, 68, 76, 89; *Commentary on Romans,* 116-17, 317.

ing self-understanding with "self-consciousness" in the idealistic tradition, Käsemann denies that the distinction can be drawn, much less retained.[29]

C. Crux sola nostra theologia

The event that required Paul's radicalization of the tradition within the context of apocalyptic was the cross. Both Testaments have to be understood from the perspective of the Crucified One. This does not spell the elimination or abbreviation of parts of the canon, but involves its proper interpretation. From the perspective of the cross, demythologizing as well as existential interpretation is necessary, and in more radical fashion than from the standpoint of a worldview or self-understanding. Käsemann's critical work had forced him to this conclusion. For this reason he regarded his critical work as serving that event together with its christological exposition in the doctrine of justification: "Theologically, the right of historical criticism lies in its breaking through the docetism dominating the community. That is not its concrete task or intention, which consists in uncovering historical reality. But that is its effect . . . it frees for a sight of the cross. . . ."[30] If material continuity between the Jesus of history and the Christ of the kerygma is to be fixed in the uniqueness of Jesus' mission, then it is the event of the cross that fixes such continuity, since Jesus' mission culminated in the cross. Käsemann writes that the Risen One would have no face at all if it were not the face of the crucified; that the resurrected Lord is identifiable with Jesus of Nazareth only as the man of the cross. If the "iron ration" of the Christian and of the church consists solely in obedience to the first commandment, then it is to the God whose earthly place was the cross of Golgotha. Of course, Käsemann adds, cross and resurrection belong together; but before all it is the crucified who was raised. In short, theological discussion commences neither with the creation nor the hope of resurrection, nor with an enumeration of the mighty acts of God. Such could occur either side of Golgotha.[31]

If then it is the sign of the cross under which God is winning back the world, then justification has to be nothing less than justification of the godless. This, Käsemann asserts, is the unmistakable feature and unifying center of Paul's theology. The apostle developed no fixed exegetical method or dogmatic system, but the theme that dominates his theology, and determines

---

29. *Perspectives on Paul*, 13; *Kirchliche Konflikte*, 37-38, 144; *Widerstand im Zeichen des Nazareners*, 6.

30. "Vom theologischen Recht historisch-kritischer Exegese," 281.

31. Käsemann, "Die göttliche und die bürgerliche Gerechtigkeit," 11, 29-31; *Jesus Means Freedom*, 68-69; *Kirchliche Konflikte*, 77.

throughout his exposition of Scripture under the aspects of law and gospel, is the justification of the sinner. For Paul, this solidarity of God with the godless unites Israel with those who previously were not the people of God. At this point, writes Käsemann, Paul and the synoptists join hands, since the Jesus of the Gospels had promised salvation to those who "sat in darkness and the shadow of death." This then, is the consequence of that event in which the uniqueness of Jesus' mission culminates, and which thus fixes material continuity between Jesus of Nazareth and the Christ of faith. The justification of the godless spells an end to the distinction between sacred and profane. For if the eschatological event consists in the fact that God is reclaiming the world he has made, nothing is sacred in the cultic sense but the community of the saints and their self-sacrifice in the worship of the Lord. In fact, with religiosity begins the guilt that led to all other blasphemies.[32]

Käsemann is adamant: the rule of Christ who before and after his exaltation traffics with the godless is the nonnegotiable midpoint of all Christian proclamation and thus of Scripture. In a score of ways, through a score of years, the Tübingen scholar swore allegiance to this single theme. At the end of his teaching career:

> What for me may under no circumstance go overboard is this one single thing: The message of the justification of the godless. . . . Our God is not chiefly concerned with the strengthening, bettering or preserving of the pious and the victory of religiosity in the world, but with freeing people and the earth from the demonic power of godlessness;[33]

at its midpoint:

> If the Bible has anything to say to the realities of our own time, if the interpretation of Scripture must by critical necessity be orientated around one central point . . . it is this: Jesus did not come primarily and solely to the religious;[34]

and at its beginning:

> The field of the Church's operation must be the world in its totality, for nothing less can be the field of Christ the *Cosmocrator*. The secular is no

---

32. Käsemann, *New Testament Questions of Today*, 184, 187; "Theologie," 76, 109; *Perspectives on Paul*, 164, 166, 190-191; "Lectures on Romans," 148; *Das Neue Testament als Kanon*, 404-5.

33. *Widerstand im Zeichen des Nazareners*, 29-30.

34. *New Testament Questions Of Today*, 282.

longer abandoned to demons and demonic energies. Grace pushes home its attack to the very heart of the world. . . .[35]

Since the justification of the godless gives definition to what is specifically Christian, it constitutes the "canon within the canon." More accurately, as the criterion for Bible exposition it gives the Bible its theological authority.[36]

But if justification of the ungodly is the premise, then the law with its requirement of performance has to be proclaimed as set aside. Freedom from the law is thus identical to the annulment of the law. The law is not a bridge to grace.[37] In Käsemann's opinion, the stress he gives this point in his Romans commentary renders him liable to the charge of anti-Semitism. It resulted in the commentary's eventual rejection by the editors of a series who for several years had retained the right to its translation and publication. As he himself wrote, "I've obviously put my foot in it *(ins Fettnäpfchen getreten),* and again made new enemies of old friends."[38]

Käsemann readily acknowledges that this "apocalyptic" interpretation of the gospel is not alone in bidding for first place. It is as clear to him as to Ferdinand Christian Baur before him that variety rather than unity lay at the beginning of the church's history. The biblical canon thus does not establish the unity of the church; it establishes a variety of confessions. And because the historical-critical method reveals this truth, Käsemann can speak of it as "splintering" the canon. The view of the original unity of the Christian community, he writes, is merely the transference to the church of the myth of the "golden age." Historically, the truth is that the admixture of the earthly people of God is reflected in a variegated Bible.

At this point Käsemann advances to the question of the relation between canon and gospel. The two cannot be separated, he contends, since the canon is the vessel that holds the gospel. There is, writes Käsemann, no *viva vox evangelii* apart from the canon. Hearing the gospel cannot occur apart from the scriptural word. For this reason, the place at which the gospel is heard has to be defined in exemplary fashion, hence the emergence of a canon. From this perspective, the historical criticism of this discrete, singular

35. *Essays on New Testament Themes,* 72. The address was delivered in October of 1949 before a gathering of "old Marburgers."

36. Käsemann, *Das Neue Testament als Kanon,* 368-69, 376.

37. This in contrast to the Reformed tradition, particularly as articulated by Karl Barth. See Käsemann, "Lectures on Romans," 118, 120, 123; *Perspectives on Paul,* 146-47, 159; *Essays on New Testament Themes,* 56-57; *Das Neue Testament als Kanon,* 132.

38. Letter to Roy A. Harrisville, 27 September 1974; see also Harrisville's review of the commentary in *Word and World* 2 (1981): 313-16.

collection of writings called Old and New Testaments is justified. At the same time, Scripture and canon cannot be identified, lest Christianity be surrendered to syncretism or to hopeless strife among the confessions — a danger to which Protestant scholasticism was continually prey. The place at which the gospel is to be heard requires defining, but its "surface" is not on that account sacrosanct. From this perspective, the task of historical-criticism is to indicate where encounter with the gospel can occur in "sufficiency, clarity, and perspicuity, where and when it pleased God." In accomplishing this task, historical criticism is justified as a scholarly, theological discipline.[39]

If the "apocalyptic" interpretation had its rivals in the early church, it was ultimately fated for oblivion. According to Käsemann, the view of the individual and world history from the aspect of justification is the most vulnerable component in Paul's theology. The one partner soon tore loose from the other — justification gave way to anthropology. Salvation history came to mean development, free of paradox. The "institutional" corollary of the aspect of justification — that is, church leadership by charismatic means, by which each fellowship in more or less spontaneous fashion ruled over its own occasions, the sole criterion of authenticity comprising usefulness to the "neighbor" — had to give way to a fixed, established order by which the church could survive heresy and the *parousia*'s delay. Enter "early catholicism" — for Käsemann a term applied to the post-apostolic period in which the Christian community harked back to old means, to churchly offices protected through ordination, to confessions of faith made normative, and to a specific theology of history. The retrogression originated with the disciples of Paul, the Pastoral Epistles, and Luke. The righteousness of God was now construed as requiring performance and operating in a punitive fashion, resulting in a satisfaction theory of Christ's death. The concept of the *charismata* was still retained, but bereft of its Pauline interpretation. It served to mark those members of the community who were separate from the rest. The regression was due not merely to Jewish-Christian habit but also to Hellenistic dualism. In 2 Peter, for example, the cross disappears from proclamation; christology and eschatology suffer divorce; the Spirit is bound to the office; and the delay of the parousia is relativized.[40] Could Paul himself have been responsible for this declension, for the regress? Battling enthusiasm throughout his life, but unable to establish churchly tradi-

39. Käsemann, "Theologie," 2, 6, 19, 25, 27; *New Testament Questions of Today*, 275; *Das Neue Testament als Kanon*, 130, 362, 369; *Essays on New Testament Themes*, 55-58.

40. Käsemann, *Commentary on Romans*, 296, 392; "Theologie," 56; *Exegetische Versuche und Besinnungen*, 2:3; *Essays on New Testament Themes*, 92-93, 179-80, 183, 187-88, 190-91, 193.

tion, was he able to destroy it only because he overexerted Christians and their fellowship, and thus in his turn led to enthusiasm, to those "native" counterparts to gnosticism?[41] Or perhaps the reason lay deeper. On occasion Käsemann can describe the Pauline gospel as an alien, and its emphasis as evoking reaction: "This message with its focus on faith alone apart from law was and remained in primitive Christianity in the position of a theological outsider and . . . represents a provocation which has not found total acceptance even to this day."[42]

D. Christian Existence as the Body of Christ

Early on, and in contrast to Bultmann's conception, Käsemann had described Christian existence from the perspective of apocalyptic christology as communal. In *Leib und Leib Christi (Body and the Body of Christ)* he argues that, viewed in their individuality, members of the church mean nothing to Paul: "We can no more speak of Paul's reshaping the mysticism of the cult or fellowship into an individual mysticism . . . than we can speak of the apostle's ecstatic piety."[43] This theme is broadened in *The Wandering People of God* to read that Christian existence is the journey of the "people of God" through the zone of battle and death, borne along by promise and hope, the fulfillment of which is hidden or still lies ahead.

Käsemann later concludes that the concept of the "Body of Christ" denotes more than can be expressed under the category of a people. This concept as developed and finally given preference in Paul is "realistic": it conceives the exalted Christ as possessing an earthly body into which believers are incorporated. Obviously, the incorporation is not into that body on the cross, but into the Body of the Risen One, into the sphere of his rule, the sphere of the *pneuma*.

This conclusion is not reached without compunction in Käsemann's work. Although the motif of the Body is far more comprehensive, denoting a new creation in a world dimension, it is possible — in fact, evidence for the possibility lies strewn about in contemporary ecclesiology — to use the motif to give definition to christology, rather than to construe the motif with its ecclesiological and anthropological implications *from the perspective* of chris-

41. Käsemann, *Essays on New Testament Themes*, 93.

42. *Commentary on Romans*, 392.

43. *Leib und Leib Christi* (Tübingen: J. C. B. Mohr, 1933), 183; see *New Testament Questions of Today*, 176; *Perspectives on Paul*, 114.

tology.[44] The one approach detracts from the Lordship of Christ, while the other gives accent to it.[45] Ironically, it is precisely such detraction from Christ's Lordship that Käsemann finds lurking in his old teacher's aversion to the historical:

> I cannot conceive of the position Bultmann is actually taking. . . . To combine Easter faith and church actually contradicts the New Testament. In the New Testament, Easter faith is not faith in the church, but faith in the risen Christ. . . . He takes absolutely no position on the real problem of historical Jesus research as it is presented today. In Bultmann, the concepts of proclamation, Spirit, church, and the present Christ are all impossibly mixed together.[46]

These sentences from the early Göttingen lectures on New Testament theology are an omen of struggles to come with those who conceive the church as in some fashion an "extension" of the incarnation, thus robbing the future of content for the sake of a present realization.

The question is legitimate, whether Käsemann's refusal to identify the *kerygma* or Easter faith with the church, either as institution or as "eschatological event" (Bultmann's term), thus his intention to preserve the apocalyptic scheme, and not mere personal pique, furnishes the occasion for his attacks on the church of Baden-Württemberg. At the celebration of the 450th anniversary of the founding of the Tübinger *Stift*, Käsemann, now professor emeritus, broke in on a three-hour academic dialogue on faith, science, and responsibility, held between the Protestant faculty of the University and members of the *Stift*. He reproached his church for its preoccupation with balance and its assemblage of the pious. The hour of the dialogue to follow proceeded as before. Käsemann then burst in, indicting science for its preoccupation with arms, for its exploitation and oppression, and charging the church with rejection of the gospel of the justification of the godless and for its worship of mammon. Two sentences served as the *inclusio* or frame for Käsemann's remarks: the first, "within the Württemberg Church I can nei-

---

44. For example, in an essay on the body of Christ, the Swedish scholar and bishop Anders Nygren (1890-1978) writes: "The issue of the church as the body of Christ lies at the very center of Christianity. Christology itself is here involved, inasmuch as Christ is what he is only in relation to the church." Anders Nygren, "Corpus Christi," in *This is the Church*, tr. Carl C. Rasmussen (Philadelphia: Muhlenberg, 1952), 5. See also the literature referred to in Käsemann, *Commentary on Romans*, 189, 336-38.

45. Käsemann, "Lectures on Romans," 117; *Perspectives on Paul*, 104, 108; *Commentary on Romans*, 143.

46. "Theologie," 79.

ther think nor believe," and the second, "there is nothing more provincial than the Württemberg Church."[47]

E. Christian Existence as the Cruciform

For Käsemann, the element of hiddenness attaching to Christian existence is epitomized in the Pauline concept of weakness, *astheneia*. He writes repeatedly that, as defined by Paul, "weakness" denotes Christian existence, not simply human existence. Citing 2 Corinthians 5:16 ("Even though we once regarded Christ from a human point of view, we regard him thus no longer") — a passage that in Bultmann's interpretation expressed disinterest in Christ "as an empirical phenomenon in the world"[48] — Käsemann states that Paul may not have wanted to know the Christ "from a human point of view," but nevertheless lived in the continuation of such a Christ. Paul was himself the mode of such a Christ after his ascension. And when rapture lifted him from his apostolic existence, God tore him back into the historical context of the members of Christ's body through the "thorn" that was never removed. Paul submitted and resolved that none should credit to his account more than could be seen or heard (2 Cor. 6:1-10). With the concept of "weakness" Käsemann associates even such manifestations of the Spirit as majority opinion would link to power. He writes that it was in ecstasy, and especially in glossolalia, that Paul heard the groaning of those who, called to freedom, still lay suffering and dying, waiting to be reborn with the new creation.[49]

F. Christian Existence as Obedience

If the shape of Christian existence is cruciform — thus hidden and capable of misinterpretation — Käsemann roundly denies that its corollary is inactivity: "My life should not run out into the sand without a trace, and God does not speak or act without making known his claim to lordship, leaving behind witnesses to his victory."[50]

47. *Tübinger Chronik,* 2 June 1986.

48. Rudolf Bultmann, *Theology of the New Testament,* tr. Kendrick Grobel (London: SCM, 1952), 1:238.

49. Käsemann, "Lectures on Romans," 114; *Die Legitimität des Apostels* (Darmstadt: Wissenschaftliche Buchgesellschaft, 1964), 38-39, 41, 45, 64-65; *Perspectives on Paul,* 113-14, 127, 134.

50. *Kirchliche Konflikte,* 75.

In his struggle with the enthusiasts, Käsemann states, Paul was forced to a resolutely christological orientation of the doctrine of the Spirit. *Charisma* was no longer limited to the sphere of ecstasy or miracle, but viewed as an individuation of the grace given every Christian at baptism. But that means that the gift is also task, since the Spirit aims at the visible, the corporeal. And this can only mean that no fundamental distinction is to be drawn between justification and sanctification, since faith spells a new obedience. If, writes Käsemann, the righteousness of God is seen solely or primarily in terms of gift, justice cannot be done to Paul's ethics. The salvation event established by Christ, though not to be repeated, nevertheless has to be "verified" in discipleship. In "Justification and Salvation History in the Epistle to the Romans," Käsemann takes issue with fellow Marburger Hans Conzelmann's disparagement of Schlatter's judgment respecting the formula "the righteousness of God." According to Schlatter, the formula at times has the same sense and is always related to the same state of affairs as the genitival constructions "gospel of God," "power of God," "wrath of God," and so forth. This is not a "philological error," writes Käsemann, but a "philological achievement" that can also be exegetically justified.[51] Wherever "the righteousness of God" does not simply denote gift, it is to be construed as a salvation-creating power. For this reason, the distinction between a forensic-imputed righteousness and an "effective" righteousness are false alternatives. Similarly, the sacraments are not to be construed as guaranteeing salvation, but as laying claim to corporeality. Here, writes Käsemann, lay the difference between Paul, who understood the sacraments as the possibility of the new obedience, and the enthusiasts, who understood them as guarantees of security. Christian freedom is by way of obedience. Finally, by submitting to Christ in bodily obedience that piece of the world which they are, Christians witness to his Lordship as *Cosmocrator* and anticipate the future of his uninhibited reign. The Christian is thus the means by which Christ's will, his word, his deed, his presence following his cross and exaltation, seize the earth.[52] With this statement, Käsemann projects the justification of the godless into the social dimension.

---

51. *Perspectives on Paul*, 77-78.

52. Käsemann, *Perspectives on Paul*, 21, 58, 77-78, 82; *Essays on New Testament Themes*, 72, 75; *Commentary on Romans*, 159, 171, 174, 226-27; "Geist und Geistesgaben im Neuen Testament," in *Die Religion in Geschichte und Gegenwart*, ed. Kurt Galling (Tübingen: J. C. B. Mohr, 1958), 2:1274-76; *Kirchliche Konflikte*, 96, 165, 184; "Lectures on Romans," 113, 118, 133, 136, 138, 141, 152; *New Testament Questions of Today*, 136, 181-82, 191; *Exegetische Versuche und Besinnungen*, 1:95.

G. Christian Existence and Politics

Käsemann writes that in that no-man's-land in which the Nazarene died we have to do with politics, like it or not. When in prison, officials visited Käsemann, asking what it was he really wanted. "Heaven?" they said; "you and the sparrows all have it, but the earth belongs to us!" With that, says Käsemann, it was made clear to him that from the outset, as early as from the Old Testament, the gospel had a political dimension. The sociologist Max Weber's (1864-1920) distinction between an ethics of intention and an ethics of responsibility, by which the politician controls impulses and effects policies while Christianity furnishes the basic morality, needs abandoning. "Church" is to be defined as the resistance of Christ on earth.[53] During the Third Reich, the resolute wing of churchly resistance had weakest support among the bourgeoisie. For one brief moment, however, in the "Darmstadt Declaration" of 1947, authored by his friend Hans-Joachim Iwand (1899-1960), systematician at Königsberg, Riga, Göttingen, and finally at Bonn, the church was true to its definition. Here, and almost here alone, Christianity in Germany reflected on its public responsibility and confessed its political guilt and the peril resulting from it. For the rest, national destiny was shaped by old men from the previous century, who spurned the heritage and organizational forms of the Confessing Church and engaged in restoration.[54] "Christianity," writes Käsemann, "can only side with the revolutionaries, because it sides with humanity. If it does not, then it must belong to the exploiters."[55] This conviction led Käsemann to support the Christian-Marxist dialogue among the students at Tübingen, and it was the refusal of continued support for the dialogue on the part of the provincial church of Baden-Württemberg that led him to consider departure from it. To that conviction his own daughter, Elisabeth, gave her life. On 16 June 1977, the friends of Margrit and Ernst Käsemann received this notice:

> Today we buried our daughter Elisabeth at the Lustnau cemetery. Born on May 11, 1947, and murdered on May 24, 1977, by functionaries of the military dictatorship in Buenos Aires, she gave her life for freedom and a better righteousness in a land she loved. Entirely of one will with her, we bear our pain in the power of Christ, and do not forget the goodness and joy we learned through her. . . .

53. Käsemann, *Kirchliche Konflikte*, 169, 205; *Widerstand im Zeichen des Nazareners*, 43-44; see also 12-13.

54. Käsemann, "Evangelischer Wahrheit in den Umbrüchen christlicher Theologie," 260, 263, 269; *Kirchliche Konflikte*, 34, 236.

55. *Kirchliche Konflikte*, 31.

Under that sign by which God seizes what he has made, the hieroglyph "humanity" requires reinterpretation. The idols of the age, camouflaged behind ideologies, require tearing down. Among those idols, according to Käsemann, stands the church. To begin with, the church does not so much represent the Body of Christ as a middle-class society, stamping Christ according to the model of its yearnings or fears, its view of the world and morality. The church, with its identification of unity with empirically establishable theological and organizational uniformity, its conception of itself as the body of deity and not the Body of the crucified and exalted Christ, its promise of freedom as inherited and secured by institutions — the church, more than all other things Christian, requires demythologizing. Time and again Käsemann repeats his contention that there never is a unified organization of Christianity, never a confession in which all important articles are formulated and recognized in agreement. "How could that be overlooked!?"

Contemporary notions of Christian unity are heirs of an idealistic tradition that promises humanity the right and power to realize itself. This is a repression of the christological. To the leading ecumenical notion of the church as the extension of the incarnation, Käsemann opposes the Pauline idea of the Body as made for service, as participating in the glory of the exalted Lord only insofar as it remains his tool in earthly humility. For this reason, writes Käsemann, Paul is intent on the community's remaining polyform. As for order, the Tübinger insists that the New Testament never postulates the order of the church. From the motif of Christ's Body, no ecclesiastical hierarchy can be deduced as constitutive. The concept of "office" can neither be maintained in general, since it assumes a separation of the public from the private sphere, nor in particular, since the *charisma* of the individual constitutes that office or service owed always and everywhere to the Lord of the world. To be sure, resistance to the domestication of the Spirit renders the Pauline concept vulnerable to the perils of neopentecostalism, a peril with which the later portions of the New Testament were already coming to grips.

In any event, Käsemann does not consider himself choleric on the subject of "early catholicism." As he put it, "I have not the least interest in a doctrinaire purism." What is intolerable to him is a theory of legitimacy in ecclesiastical order[56] — a position that no doubt makes many a professional ecumenist sputter.

---

56. Käsemann, "Die göttliche und die bürgerliche Gerechtigkeit," 12; *Kirchliche Konflikte,* 56, 58, 65, 101; *Perspectives on Paul,* 117-21, 124; "Urchristliche Konflikte um die Freiheit der Gemeinde," 56, 58, 65; "Theologie," 4-5; *Commentary on Romans,* 339; *New Testament Questions of Today,* 194; *Das Neue Testament als Kanon,* 374.

III. Assessment

On at least three separate occasions, Bultmann replied to Käsemann publicly. On one occasion he opposed Käsemann's interpretation of "the righteousness of God" as God's salvation-creating power, thus as reflecting Jewish apocalyptic. Bultmann insisted that the phrase never had such significance in Judaism, that though it could conceivably be eschatologically freighted, it certainly was not as applied to concrete events. Paul, Bultmann concluded, did not radicalize the Jewish concept of God's righteousness; the idea was Paul's invention.[57] Later, Bultmann devoted a paragraph to Käsemann in a response to his pupils who had taken up the "New Quest." Käsemann, writes Bultmann, clearly saw that history acquires relevance through interpretation, that is, through understanding events of the past as solidified in data, and not through the mere establishment of facts. "Unfortunately," Bultmann adds, Käsemann does not employ this "fundamental insight" to proceed toward an existential interpretation of the activity of Jesus or the *kerygma*, concluding that Käsemann's remarks on the "uniqueness of Jesus' mission" are not an existential interpretation but the description of an historical phenomenon.[58]

In the fourth volume of Bultmann's collected essays, the old master replied to Käsemann's reproach that he had set up an antithesis between historical and material continuity, that is, between objective investigation and existential interpretation. The charge is false, writes Bultmann. Subjectivity belongs to objective investigation. Bultmann claims that he had drawn a distinction between historical continuity and material *relation (sachliches Verhältnis)*, a distinction Käsemann fails to recognize, for which reason he construes the relation of continuity to discontinuity as dialectical. But discontinuity, even the most radical, writes Bultmann, is to be understood within the continuity of history. The relation between the historical Jesus and the primitive Christian *kerygma* is thus not to be construed as dialectical. The *kerygma* is not the preaching of Jesus, but it does assume or requires the very same self-understanding.[59]

Had Käsemann misunderstood? Bultmann insisted that he had, and repeatedly — a complaint often aimed at critics, and turned to irony in Barth's own attempt to "understand."[60] Had Käsemann, due to gaps in his education,

57. Rudolf Bultmann, *"Dikaiosynē Theou," Journal of Biblical Literature* 83 (1964): 12-16.

58. Rudolf Bultmann, *The Historical Jesus and the Kerygmatic Christ,* tr. and ed. Carl E. Braaten and Roy A. Harrisville (Nashville: Abingdon, 1964), 35.

59. Rudolf Bultmann, *Glauben und Verstehen* (Tübingen: J. C. B. Mohr, 1965), 4:190-98.

60. Karl Barth, *Rudolf Bultmann: Ein Versuch, ihn zu Verstehen,* Theologische Studien 34 (Zollikon-Zürich: Evangelischer, 1953).

failed to grasp the nuances of existence philosophy and thus botched his criticism of Bultmann? Or had Bultmann altered his position, had he tacked and filled, due to contrary winds blown by his students? If, in the opinion of some, search for the historical Jesus lay beneath Bultmann's perpetual demurral, the distinction between "historical continuity and material relation" was scarcely calculated to repress it. The evidence points to Käsemann's having laid bare Bultmann's weakness, which the old scholar later struggled to supply.

Käsemann's debt to Baur is almost as great as his debt to Bultmann. The refusal to embrace the notion of a "golden age" in primitive Christian history and the assignment of antithetical forces or views to the beginning of that history are the lessons learned from Ferdinand Christian Baur — in Käsemann's opinion, Bultmann's superior by far. And it was Baur who first coined the epithet "early catholicism" for those portions of the New Testament that marked the move toward reconciliation of the opposing views. If it is Bultmann who whetted Käsemann for the fight, it is Baur, in a measure at least, who provides the weapon, and the copy of whose portrait in the Tübinger Aula Käsemann requested as retirement gift.

But there is more to the explanation of Ernst Käsemann than a Bultmann or a Baur, and as a result of which the debt owed to Bultmann is greater. During his years under Bultmann, Käsemann read with others for whom the future was not simply linked to the past in a "material relation." That view lived from an idealistic conception that allowed no "real discontinuity" (the words are Bultmann's) in history. There were "dialogicians" who insisted that discontinuity *did in fact exist,* that the future was not simply exfoliated out of the past, for the reason that encounter with the new, strange, or "other" spelled displacement. These dialogicians were furnishing grist for the mill of a breed of scholars preoccupied with the Luther renaissance. For example, the similarities between Iwand the systematician and Käsemann the biblical scholar are striking. The reference to God as hidden to natural thought; the assignment of preeminence to a christological over an historical understanding; the description of the cross of Christ as the key to all of Scripture; the insistence upon justification as the decisive theological element in the deed of God at the crucifixion; the accent upon the doctrine of Christ as power and not merely theory — all these themes are shared by the two old friends.[61] And, with respect to the

---

61. See Hans-Joachim Iwand, *Glaubensgerechtigkeit nach Luthers Lehre* (München: Christian Kaiser, 1941); *Rechtfertigungslehre und Christusglaube: Eine Untersuchung zur Systematik der Rechtfertigungslehre Luthers in ihren Anfängen* (München: Christian Kaiser, 1961); *Predigt-Meditationen* (Göttingen: Vandenhoeck und Ruprecht, 1984).

concept of justification as denoting not merely gift but also power, Käsemann could as well have penned these lines:

> Faith must always be *"in actu."* . . . So also works. Faith can never turn into reflection. In my opinion, the altering of faith to reflection as occurs later in pietism was the greatest misfortune for an understanding of the Reformation. In faith I come under God's command, and his command leads to action, not to my own performance, but to the deed which God promises to me in his command. . . .

and these lines:

> Encounter with the reality of this world has set the believer the task of employing faith in Christ's victory to oppose [the world's] powers and shapes. But in that use there arises in turn the Christian's inner conflict *(Anfechtung)*. . . .

and finally, respecting the structure of the church, these lines:

> It is impossible that . . . a specific, visible church should represent the true church. Since there is no such thing, people cling to the churchly office. Their anxiety binds them to the only thing they have in hand. As a result, the visible church becomes the magnet to attract them. In this way they withdraw from the word of God and its power.[62]

There is no dependence of the one upon the other, but a dependence of both upon another — "No old Marburger will forget how passionately Luther was studied in the early days."[63]

Käsemann's identification with the political left may have proved to be his Achilles' heel. If justification is of the godless, how dare he so neatly distinguish oppressor and oppressed? Recently, the left and all its reflection in Marxist structure has collapsed, leaving the entire inhabited world a candidate for free enterprise. But with this change the demonic has not ceased to exist — neither in the world nor in the church. And who is to say whether or not that evil spirit will bring into this house swept clean seven others worse than himself?

---

62. Hans-Joachim Iwand, *Luthers Theologie: Nachgelassene Werke,* ed. Helmut Gollwitzer, Walter Kreck, Karl Gerhard Steck, und Ernst Wolf (München: Christian Kaiser, 1974), 164, 168, and 253.

63. Käsemann, "Vom theologischen Recht," 273.

13

PAUL RICOEUR

The Risk of Reading the Bible

I. The Secular Challenge

Writing to his friend Eberhard Bethge from his prison cell on 8 June 1944, Dietrich Bonhoeffer (1906-45) reflected on the predicament of Christian faith in a secular age. Since the thirteenth century, humanity has gradually gotten used to the experience of living without God. "[I]n our time," he states, this movement has "reached an undoubted completion. Man has learnt to deal with himself in all questions of importance without recourse to the 'working hypothesis' called 'God'. In questions of science, art, and ethics this has become an understood thing. . . ."[1] This is man's "coming of age,"[2] a theological theme that would make Bonhoeffer posthumously famous. In compelling correspondence, written under extreme circumstances, Bonhoeffer made his case. Bultmann, he said, "didn't go far enough." It is not just the concept of the miraculous that needs revision, but "religious concepts generally which are problematic." Likewise Barth must be reassessed. His "criticism of religion" is an important contribution, but not what he replaced it with: "a positivist doctrine of revelation which says in effect, 'Like it or lump it': virgin birth, Trinity, or anything else; each is an equally significant

---

1. *Letters and Papers from Prison,* enlarged edition ed. Eberhard Bethge, tr. Reginald Fuller, Frank Clarke, et al. (New York: Macmillan, 1972), 325. See Franklin L. Baumer, *Modern European Thought* (New York: Macmillan, 1977), 439-55.
    2. *Letters,* 360.

and necessary part of the whole, which must simply be swallowed as a whole or not at all."[3] We live in a world that has been shaped by the likes of Machiavelli and Spinoza. The traditional assertions of dogmatic Christianity are no longer convincing. We need to live as if God did not exist. The "working hypothesis" of God "should be dropped, or, as far as possible, eliminated."[4]

Bonhoeffer was not alone in recognizing the pervasiveness of a radical secular viewpoint. Theologians such as Helmut Thielicke (1908-81) and Hermann Diem (1874-1958) spoke of "genuine 'men of the world'" in wartime "barrack rooms and officers' messes" who were never bothered by questions such as "'How can God allow it?' or 'Yet God says nothing?'"[5] What made Bonhoeffer stand out was that he embraced secularism with singular courage and openheartedness not only as a fact of the age, but as the way to the future. He convinced a generation of scholars that the secular mind-set was inevitable. This gave new life to the cause of liberal Protestantism, whose key idea had always been that Christianity must accommodate itself to the triumph of modernity. Liberal theology had been shaken to its roots in the debacle of the First World War. It retreated before the attacks of fundamentalism and neoorthodoxy. Now ironically, in the darkest days of the Second World War, it was given a new lease on life by a thirty-nine-year-old Lutheran pastor and martyr.

Bonhoeffer's own method of accommodation to modernity was a version of the traditional Lutheran theme of "the theology of the cross." In one of the most famous and intriguing passages in his letters, he describes this way to God as both a knowing and an unknowing: "God would have us know that we must live as men who manage our lives without him. The God who is with us is the God who forsakes us (Mk. 15.34). Before God and with God we live without God. God lets himself be pushed out of the world on to the cross."[6] Because of his execution by the Nazis a month before the end of the war, Bonhoeffer left his ideas in unfinished form. This made them all the more influential as they served in protean fashion to inspire others.

For example, Harvey Cox, Bonhoeffer's most famous liberal disciple, used the theme of man's coming of age to construct his theology of "the secular city" in the mid-1960s. Secularity means "the defatalization of history."[7] Humanity is not subject to superstitious forces beyond its control, but shapes

3. *Ibid.*, 285-86.

4. *Ibid.*, 360.

5. Karl Heim, *Christian Faith and Natural Science,* tr. Neville Horton Smith (London: SCM, 1953), 16. See Baumer, *Modern European Thought*, 440.

6. *Letters*, 360.

7. *The Secular City,* rev. ed. (New York: Macmillan, 1966), 2.

the future by its own achievements. This is seen most clearly in urban civilization, the "technopolis" that signifies "the fusion of technological and political components into the base on which a new cultural style has appeared."[8] Not even the cold war and the shadow cast by the prospect of nuclear annihilation could dampen the enthusiasm for this new vision. Along with a host of theologians, Cox reaffirmed the liberal virtues of autonomy and freedom as central to the biblical task.

Confident in the power of their hard-won secular viewpoint, the new liberals sought not only to defend Christianity but to embrace its fiercest critics: Karl Marx (1818-83), who taught that religion is a disguise for class privilege; Friedrich Nietzsche, who derided Christian morality as the resentment of a conventional middle class against progressive ideas and heroic individuals; and Sigmund Freud (1856-1939), who warned against the destructive capability of religion as the battleground for Oedipal conflict, the excuse for false and immature security, and ultimately the basis for otherworldly illusion. These hostile thinkers were thought to discipline theology in the "hermeneutics of suspicion," which teaches that no theology can exercise authority unless it has been purged of its ideological underpinnings. Instead of defending the status quo, theology must serve social transformation and psychological liberation.

With regard to social transformation, Bonhoeffer had observed: "With us thought was often the luxury of the onlooker; with you it will be entirely subordinate to action."[9] This was interpreted as a call to political theology "in which politics is understood as the comprehensive and decisive sphere in which Christian truth should become praxis."[10] Purveyors of privatized religion too easily corrupt traditional dogmatic appeals to the "forgiveness of sins" and "sanctification." The church can be its authentic self in the world only when "it makes clear God's renewed authorization, commandment, and liberation to man to be human, to create his own history and culture, to love and to transform the world, to claim and exercise the glorious freedom of the children of God."[11]

Psychological liberation is also a crucial task. A religion that traffics in anxiety and repression through "obsessional authoritarian and legalistic structures of church practice" separates humanity from the emotional core of

8. *Ibid.*, 5.
9. *Letters*, 298.
10. Dorothee Soelle, *Political Theology*, tr. with intro. John Shelly (Philadelphia: Fortress, 1974), 59.
11. José Míguez Bonino, *Doing Theology in a Revolutionary Situation* (Philadelphia: Fortress, 1975), 169.

its being. What needs to be taught is that the God known in Jesus Christ frees "the oppressors and the oppressed from oppression . . . to open up to them the situation of free, sympathetic humanity." Faith means psychological freedom "a new spontaneity of the heart. But this only emerges when the emotions of anxiety and hate have been overcome and man emerges from his Oedipal situation."[12]

Liberal Protestant theologians of the Cold War period were especially attracted to a bold, new form of secularism because of its constructive possibilities. There was, however, what Franklin L. Baumer calls "another kind of secularism" at work in twentieth-century thought that reflected a different mood and tone. Instead of being confident in man's "coming of age," this view found no comfort in the much-vaunted autonomy and freedom of the modern condition. These apparent virtues bring neither peace nor rest. Beneath the "maturity" of modern humanity is a much more fundamental condition: dissatisfaction with the self. "Men become dissatisfied with themselves," writes the political philosopher Joseph Cropsey, "when, and only if, what they are does not possess them exhaustively and to the exclusion of a power to scrutinize what they are."[13] Dissatisfaction is a condition that humanity cannot escape. It is the curse of the human species, bedeviling man since the dawn of time. "Man," observes Albert Camus (1913-60), "is the only creature who refuses to be what he is."[14] No gleaming technopolis will bring permanent rest. No amount of social change or therapy will make dissatisfaction disappear.

Dissatisfaction teaches modern, secular selves that, despite autonomy and freedom, they are alone in the universe. There is no benevolent power that hears their cries. People as individuals are also under constant threat by the irrationality of human behavior and the randomness of events. Humanity may be able to accomplish all sorts of things without the need of the "working hypothesis" of God, but the divine absence causes deep anguish. This anguish is explored in twentieth-century literature by the likes of Franz Kafka (1883-1924), Jean-Paul Sartre (1903-80), Camus, and others. Antoine Roquentin, the protagonist in Sartre's *La Nausée* (1938), finds himself in the peculiar state of having revulsion for all things. His passion to live is dead. He is indolent, overtaken by "a voluminous, insipid idea" that existence has no meaning.[15] "I pro-

12. Jürgen Moltmann, *The Crucified God,* tr. R. A. Wilson and John Bowden (New York: Harper & Row, 1974), 306-7.

13. *Political Philosophy and the Issues of Politics* (Chicago: University of Chicago Press, 1977), 3.

14. *The Rebel,* tr. Anthony Bower (New York: Vintage, 1956), 11.

15. Jean-Paul Sartre, *Nausea,* tr. Lloyd Alexander (New York: New Directions, 1959), 13.

claim that I believe in nothing," states Camus, "and that everything is absurd."[16] What is left is an act of protest, a "metaphysical rebellion" against the suffering, both external and internal, that is the lot of human beings.

"Thou hast made us for Thyself," declares St. Augustine, "and our heart is restless until it rests in Thee."[17] Could it be that the dissatisfaction and despair of the modern self is not only a protest but a pointer to something beyond? Gabriel Marcel (1889-1973) in his Gifford Lectures (1949-50) asserts that the question, "Do you believe in God?" may not be able to be answered in the present age with a simple yes or no. There are many people "who imagine that they believe in God when in fact they are bowing down to an idol." There are also convinced atheists who "reveal by their acts, which far transcend their professed opinion, a totally inarticulate religious belief." Perhaps the foundational question for the age is, "What does believing in God mean?"[18] To ask about God may be the same as asking about the ultimate ideas behind contemporary civilization, a civilization imperiled by its ability to destroy itself and all life.

To engage in this type of foundational inquiry is to travel an intellectual path made familiar by René Descartes. At the birth of modernity, in a time of change and crisis not unlike the present, Descartes pitted the doubting, struggling self against a confusing, threatening world. Marcel emphasized this important aspect of the Cartesian tradition. He was not alone. Edmund Husserl (1859-1938) invested the Cartesian method with existential urgency during the interwar years. "Anyone who seriously wants to become a philosopher," said Husserl in an influential passage, "must 'once in his life' withdraw into himself and attempt, within himself, to overthrow and build anew all the sciences that, up to then, he has been accepting. Philosophy — wisdom (*sagesse*) — is the philosopher's quite personal affair."[19] For Husserl this meant taking up a "phenomenological" inquiry that examines the whole range of reality as it impinges upon the ego and is experienced. This examination involves not merely mundane objects of perception. Nor is it exhausted by the abstract mental activity of scientific abstraction and mathematics. It also includes moral imperatives, traditions, even the idea of God. That God exists may be impossible to know definitively. But there is no doubt that as a phenomenon from the outside world, it affects human beings individually and corporately. It is part of the concrete data of experience and as such is a legitimate subject for philosophical inquiry.

---

16. *The Rebel,* 10.
17. *Confessions* 1.1.
18. *Mystery of Being,* tr. G. S. Fraser (Chicago: Henry Regnery, 1960), 1:14-15.
19. *Cartesian Meditations,* tr. Dorion Cairns (The Hague: Martinus Nijhoff, 1973), 2.

It is in this intellectual milieu that Paul Ricoeur found his bearings as a thinker and exercised his considerable abilities to examine that part of the data of human experience which is made up of the biblical text and other religious phenomena associated with it. Through the religious community and cultural traditions, Scripture encounters the dissatisfied self of modernity as it struggles to understand without the certainty that it will find rest. As Ricoeur describes the contemporary religious quest in terms of preaching, that most traditional act of the church:

> To preach is not to capitulate before the believable and unbelievable of modern man, but to struggle with the presuppositions of his culture, in order *to restore the interval of interrogation* in which the question can have meaning. If we consider the problem of secularization no longer only as the end of mythology and the religious era . . . but as an estrangement from the kerygmatic situation itself, then the whole problem of myth will from this point of view become immediately changed.[20]

II. Biography

A. Achievements

Jean Paul Gustave Ricoeur was born on 27 February 1913, in Valence, France. In September of that year Ricoeur's mother died, and two years later his father, professor of English at the Valence secondary school, was killed in the battle of the Marne. Together with his older sister Alice, the three-year-old boy was taken in at Rennes by his paternal grandparents, descendants of two old Protestant families. Each year, as an "orphan of the state," he received a small stipend for texts and other school expenses. After earning his degree from the University of Rennes, he began his teaching career at a secondary school in Saint-Brieuc. In 1934 he received a scholarship from the Sorbonne. During his year at the Sorbonne Ricoeur met Gabriel Marcel. In his own words, he read "everything that Gabriel Marcel had written"[21] and visited him each week at his home.

In that same year, 1935, Ricoeur married Simone, a childhood friend

---

20. Charles E. Reagan and David Stewart, ed., *The Philosophy of Paul Ricoeur* (Boston; Beacon, 1978), 227, cited in the introduction to Paul Ricoeur, *Essays on Biblical Interpretation,* ed. with intro. Lewis S. Mudge (Philadelphia: Fortress, 1980), 9.

21. *Critique and Conviction: Conversations with Francois Azouvi and Marc de Launay,* tr. Kathleen Blamey (New York: Columbia University Press, 1998), 9.

from his Protestant community in Rennes, and left to teach at Colmar in the Alsace. In the year following he was sent to the military school at St. Cyr. After obligatory military service in the infantry he left for Lorient in Brittany, where he taught at the *lycee,* or secondary school, from 1937 to 1939. During these years Ricoeur began his career as author, concentrating on pacifist themes. He became involved in socialist youth movements and, under the influence of the French Barthian Andre Philip (1902-70), took part in the marches of the Popular Front, French political parties united against fascism in defense of the Republic. In August of 1939, Ricoeur received a small grant for study at Munich, but in September he was called to military service and assigned to a regiment of Bretons barracked at St. Malo.

After the Germans captured Paris, the Bretons continued fighting in the Marne valley near Rheims. For his bravery in this action Ricoeur received the *Croix de Guerre* with three palm leaves. He has never referred to this action in public nor worn the decoration. Captured at Dormans, a small village near Chateau Thierry, he began almost five years' imprisonment, first in Pomerania. While in camp, Ricoeur worked to establish a regulated cultural life with his fellow prisoners. Together with them he studied Russian, Chinese, Hebrew, and Arabic, and on his own he began translating the first volume of the *Ideen* of Edmund Husserl. Following his release, Ricoeur marched west, arriving in Paris in May of 1945. There he again met Andre Philip, who persuaded him and his wife to move to Le Chambon-sur-Lignon, a village in the south of France celebrated for giving Jews shelter from the Nazi terror. During his first winter at Chambon, Ricoeur met American Quakers, at whose invitation he visited Haverford College in 1955. Ricoeur's first published work after the war was a study of Karl Jaspers, coauthored with his friend and fellow prisoner, Mikel Dufrenne.[22]

After three years in Chambon-sur-Lignon, in 1949 Ricoeur received an appointment to the University of Strasbourg, where he remained for eight years. In 1950 he received the *Doctorat d'Etat I,* the highest academic degree obtainable in France. Both of his doctoral theses were published, the minor dissertation consisting of his translation of Husserl's *Idees,* and the major *Le Volontaire et l'involontaire.*[23]

In 1956 Ricoeur was appointed to the Sorbonne, and in the following year he moved with his family to a new residence at Chatenay-Malabry, the

22. *Karl Jaspers et la philosophie de l'existence* (Paris: Editions du Seuil, 1947).

23. *Idées directrices pour une phénomenologie,* tr. Paul Ricoeur (Paris: Editions Gallimard, 1950); *Le Volontaire et l'involontaire* (Paris: Aubier, 1950) is translated into English as *Freedom and Nature: The Voluntary and the Involuntary,* tr. E. V. Kohak (Evanston: Northwestern University Press, 1966).

birthplace of Voltaire. Ricoeur was immensely popular at the Sorbonne. More than a thousand students crowded the amphitheater to hear him, and loud-speakers had to be set up in the courtyard for the overflow. His books *Fallible Man* and *The Symbolism of Evil*, the first two parts of a project entitled *Fini-tude and Guilt*,[24] were widely read. The first volume led to including psycho-analytic interpretation in his hermeneutics, and the second to reading the principal Protestant theologians of the century. During this same period, Ricoeur increased his political profile by opposing French involvement in the Algerian civil war, a conflict that had been ranging since 1954. Ricoeur often participated in demonstrations against the war. Accused of hiding arms for the FLN (*Front de Liberatione Nationale* = Algerian National Liberation Front), he was arrested and after his release placed under house arrest.

In 1967 a new campus of the University of Paris was being built in the western suburb of Nanterre. Invited to Nanterre, Ricoeur resigned from the Sorbonne. He served as a member of the Nanterre faculty beginning in 1966, and three years later was elected dean of the Faculty of Letters by the univer-sity council. During the 1968 academic year, political demonstrations oc-curred on campus, and in the year following, remnants of leftist groups from Paris gravitated to Nanterre, where they left the campus in shambles. Ricoeur resigned his post in 1970, and requested a three-year leave from the French university system.

While disappointed over events at home, Ricoeur began to achieve world-wide fame. Due largely to his friendship with the philosopher-theologian Paul Tillich and the political philosopher Hannah Arendt (1906-75), the University of Chicago invited him regularly to give courses there. He thus came to occupy Tilllich's chair, and in 1991 at the age of sixty-seven he received the title of John Nuveen Professor Emeritus, with teaching responsibilities for one quarter per year. In the summers of 1983, 1985, and 1994, Ricoeur was invited by Pope John Paul II along with a small party to join him at the papal retreat at Castel Gondolfo.

Throughout the years Ricoeur was an extraordinarily active scholar. In 1965 he published his fourth major work, *De l'interpretation: Essai sur Freud* and in 1975 *La metaphore vive*. Both works have been translated.[25] In the '80s he published the three volumes of *Temps et Recit* (1983-85)[26] and *Du Texte a*

---

24. *Finitude et Culpabilité*, 1: *L'homme faillible* (Paris: Aubier, 1960); *Finitude et Culpabilité*, 2: *La Symbolique du mal* (Paris: Aubier, 1960).

25. *Freud and Philosophy*, tr. Denis Savage (New Haven: Yale University Press, 1979); *The Rule of Metaphor*, tr. Robert Czerny et al. (Toronto: University of Toronto Press, 1977).

26. *Time and Narrative*, tr. Kathleen McLaughlin and David Pellauer (Chicago: Uni-versity of Chicago Press, 1984).

l'action,[27] consisting of articles published in English during the late '70s and '80s. In 1990 he published *Soi-Meme Comme Un Autrer*.[28] With the publication of *Temps et Recit,* Ricoeur burst back on the French intellectual scene, which had paid him little attention since his retirement from Nanterre. In 1995 he published two slight volumes, one containing his intellectual autobiography, and the other a collection of articles on justice and its application.

Ricoeur's interviewer and friend, Charles Reagan, reports his subject's reluctance to furnish biographical details, and quotes him as stating that "no one is interested in my life; and, besides, my life is my work. If you want to write about me, just write about my philosophical books and articles." With his wife Simone, constant companion and mother of his five children, Ricoeur makes his home today at Prefailles, on the Brittany coast.[29]

B. Influences

At the outset of his intellectual journey, Ricoeur was influenced by Roland Dalbiez. Dalbiez, who was instructor at the Rennes *lycee,* introduced the young boy to the powers of philosophy. As he attests, Dalbiez's influence has remained with him throughout his career. Ricoeur writes that it is to Dalbiez that he owes his didactic model, or that his chapter on the unconscious in the *Philosophie de la Volonte* consists of an extended discussion with his old teacher. Dalbiez's avowed enemy was Idealism in all its forms: Descartes, Berkeley, Hume, and Kant were the objects of sustained refutation. Ricoeur often cites Dalbiez's metaphor of the Idealist's notion of consciousness: a giant pincers thrust out into space and, without anything to seize on to, doomed to grab hold of itself in a useless doubling back. According to Dalbiez, Idealism was a species of mental illness. And it was Dalbiez who linked this "clinical" treatment of Idealism with his researches in Freudian psychoanalysis, however poorly his students perceived the connection. Ricoeur writes of the severest lesson his first teacher taught him: noting Ricoeur's hesitation over committing himself to a career in philosophy for fear of losing certainties, Dalbiez said, "do not turn away from what you are

---

27. *From Text to Action,* tr. Kathleen Blarney and John B. Thompson (Evanston: Northwestern University Press, 1991).

28. *Oneself as Another,* tr. Kathleen Blarney (Chicago: University of Chicago Press, 1992).

29. For more complete biographical data, cf. Charles E. Reagan, *Paul Ricoeur: His Life and His Work* (Chicago: University of Chicago Press, 1996) and *Critique and Conviction,* 1-49.

afraid to encounter; never go around the obstacle, but meet it head on." The teacher's evocation of a "concession to necessity," his appeal to patience with oneself, his opposition to the arrogance of supposing one has mastered understanding — of it all Ricoeur asks, "do they not harmonize with the critique of the 'idealism' of the Cartesian *cogito,* with which the walls of the Rennes lyceum still resound?"[30]

As mentioned, Ricoeur maintained a deep relationship with Gabriel Marcel, a friendship that began the year of Ricoeur's qualifying examination. When he was released from internment and reached Paris in May 1945, it was Marcel whom Ricoeur first came to see. After coauthoring the book on Jaspers, Ricoeur published a second in which he compared the German psychiatrist turned philosopher and Gabriel Marcel.[31] Following the publication of Ricoeur's volume on Freud, Marcel "disavowed" him. While at Chambon-sur-Lignon, Ricoeur met Maurice Merleau-Ponty (1908-1961), phenomenologist on the faculty of the College de France. A lecture of Merleau-Ponty on the phenomenology of language made a profound impression on him. Ricoeur speaks of his "deep and faithful" friendship for Mircea Eliade (1907-86), member of the "Romanian trio" at Paris together with the playwright Eugene Ionesco (1809-1994) and the "hagiographer" Emile M. Cioran (1911-95). Eliade had begun his career at Budapest, then moved to France, where he joined the Sorbonne faculty, and finally immigrated to the United States, where he held the chair in the history of religions at the University of Chicago.

Among the Germans, Ricoeur acknowledges the influence of Edmund Husserl, Martin Heidegger, and Hans-Georg Gadamer. Of the theologians Rudolf Bultmann seems to have had the greatest influence. Husserl had refuted Wilhelm Dilthey's attempt to furnish the humane sciences with a method as objective as the natural sciences, and, more importantly, accented the "life-world" or level of experience prior to any "subject-object relation." From Heidegger Ricoeur gleaned his accent on language or speech as constitutive and not merely expressive of human existence, in Heideggerian terms, as belonging to that "field of being" over which human being *(Da-sein)* had been "thrown." From Gadamer he gained support for his understanding of the hermeneutical enterprise as "merging the horizons," as diminishing the space and time between text and interpreter, and from Bultmann the restoration of the myth's intention. Nor would Ricoeur deny the influence of the six-

---

30. "Mon Premier Maître en Philosophie," in *Honneur aux Maîtres: Presente par Marguerite Lena* (Paris: Criterion, 1991), 221-22; *Critique and Conviction,* 7.

31. *Gabriel Marcel et Karl Jaspers: Philosophie du mystère et philosophie du paradoxe* (Paris: Temps Present, 1948).

teenth-century Reformers. He had long admired Luther's treatise on Christian freedom and "the servile will," and acknowledged the influence of his formative training in Calvin's theology of predestination. Ricoeur's taste for Greek tragedy with its accent on fate or destiny may have derived from that earlier encounter with Luther or Calvin.

Finally, the more Ricoeur came to concentrate on language as central to thought and discourse, the more he came to appreciate the British and American schools of ordinary language philosophy, according to which the proper activity of philosophy was to clarify language since philosophical problems originated in linguistic confusion. As he put it, this school was "at least a necessary first stage in philosophical inquiry," since the "polysemic" feature of our words in ordinary language, that is, their openness to many or several meanings, was the basic condition for symbolic discourse.[32]

III. The Hermeneutical Interest

Ricoeur is convinced that philosophy should not be concerned with the structure of language, but with its use, for it is in its use that existence is reflected. In fact, language would be "empty" if it were not rooted in existence. The philosopher's task, therefore, is to attend to the way in which existence manifests itself in language. And since the relation between existence and language exists only in signs or symbols, the philosopher must deal with semantics or the system of signs *(langue)*. Of course, these signs or symbols are open to several meanings and give rise to a variety of interpretations, for which reason the philosoper must arbitrate among absolutist claims. This polysemy, however, is not a malady of language. The ability of the word to take on a new sense without losing its old meaning is the basis or condition for metaphor, the "transfer" of sense. Further, each of these interpretations has its home in a particular existential situation.

Philosophy, however, cannot remain with signs. It must move on to the event of discourse *(parole)*, toward which the signs are a first step. It is there, at the point of discourse, that "something comes to us." Most important, since the universe of signs or symbols is the milieu of self-understanding, in other words, since there is no direct apprehension of the self by the self but only by way of the interpretation of signs, the ultimate goal of "linguistic philosophy" is self-understanding.

As he readily acknowledges, Ricoeur is indebted to phenomenology,

32. Reagan and Stewart, *The Philosophy of Paul Ricoeur*, 92.

which assigns priority to meaning or sense over communication or expression, as well as to the philosophy of Martin Heidegger with his call to leave the enchanted circle of signs and in the act of speaking recover the modality of "Being," that is, to appreciate the way in which existence, prior to language, is nevertheless manifest in language.[33]

Ricoeur's fascination with biblical hermeneutics derives from its similar claim that existence is unveiled in the word or discourse. It also is concerned with a phenomenology of discourse rather than with the analysis of signs. To this extent it is a particular instance of general hermeneutics. But it is also unique insofar as all the symbols within the variety of biblical discourse have a single sign as their center of gravity, the word "God" or "Christ." This word says more than the word "to be" since it adds the dimension of God's relation to us and the dimension of our relation to God. Biblical hermeneutics is also unique insofar as the existence opened up by its discourse cannot be sought anywhere else. By virtue of this originality, biblical or theological hermeneutics enjoys preeminence over philosophical hermeneutics. For these reasons the theologian is "sentenced" to deal with all the problems posed by the linguist, the semiologist, the logician, the philosopher, the psychoanalyst, and so on.[34]

Due to the polysemic character of signs resulting in a variety of interpretations, each reflective of a particular problem or situation, Ricoeur insists that there is no "innocent" or objective interpretation. The philosopher or theologian always interprets his texts in relation to a theory with its own axioms. In this connection he cites Paul Beauchamp, who writes that "to explicate a text is and always has been to say what it did not say and which one largely gets on one's own."[35] But despite this lack of "innocence," Ricoeur insists that the interpreter must take a stand — it is not possible to live and work according to many theories at once.

As for his own theory and axioms, Ricoeur writes that by virtue of being born in a certain family — a condition "transformed into a destiny through a

33. Paul Ricoeur, "Contribution d'une Reflexion sur le Langage à une Théologie de la Parole," *Revue de Théologie et de Philosophie* 18 (1968): 341, 343, 344-45, 346; Paul Ricoeur, *The Conflict of Interpretations,* ed. Don Ihde (Evanston: Northwestern University Press, 1974), 11, 15, 169, 170.

34. Ricoeur, "Contribution d'une Reflexion," 334, 343, 347; "Philosophical Hermeneutics and Theological Hermeneutics," in *The Center for Hermeneutical Studies in Hellenistic and Modern Culture* (Chicago: University of Chicago Press, 1976), 4, 15-16; *From Text to Action,* 90, 91, 92, 95.

35. Quoted in Paul Ricoeur, *Exégèse et Herméneutique, Parole de Dieu* (Paris: Editions du Seuil, 1971), 80.

continual choice of preferences" — he has gained more understanding of himself, others, and of existence from an interpretation rooted in "a scriptural foundation tied to the Jewish and Christian experience." Ricoeur is aware of the duality resulting from this stand. He writes that he is prepared to live with the difficulties arising from his concern for both, but he states that since existence is manifest in discourse outside the Christian gospel as well as within it, the "two affiliations" enjoy a circular relation that justifies giving attention to both. To this attention Ricoeur assigns the formulation "conviction and critique."[36]

This moving back and forth between the biblical and rational poles Ricoeur has termed a "controlled schizophrenia." He is at pains to separate the two. For one thing, he does not do philosophy or theology on the basis of the same texts. For another, he acknowledges that it is at the point of a *kerygmatic* reading of the biblical texts that "the opposition between Jerusalem and Athens" is sharpest. But whereas once, under the influence of Karl Barth, he contrasted them to the point of excluding any encounter with God in philosophy and therefore of treating philosophy as anthropology, now, in his maturer years, though assigning more sense to the word "God" than to the word "Being," he gives larger space to "indications of the manifestation of Being" outside the gospel.[37]

IV. Critique

A. Idealism

Like his teachers before him, Ricoeur resists idealism's separation of knowledge into two different worlds. This is a form of Enlightenment tyranny over Protestant thought. Dialectical theology, far from ridding the world of the Enlightenment, merely radicalized nineteenth-century historical criticism, so that Barth, for example, could be understood as a radical representative of the Enlightenment.[38] At any rate, one result of this "Kantian" separation of the

---

36. *Ibid.*, 80, 285-86; Ricoeur, "Contribution d'une Reflexion," 347; Reagan and Stewart, *The Philosophy of Paul Ricoeur*, 126; Reagan, *Paul Ricoeur: His Life and His Work*, 18; Ricoeur, *Critique and Conviction*, 139, 169.

37. Ricoeur, "Contribution d'une Reflexion," 347; *Critique and Conviction*, 2, 6, 142, 144, 150.

38. Paul Ricoeur, "Religion, Atheism and Faith," in *The Religious Significance of Atheism*, ed. A. MacIntyre and P. Ricoeur (New York-London: Columbia University Press, 1969), 66; Paul Ricoeur and Eberhard Jüngel, *Metapher: Zur Hermeneutic religiöser Sprache*, intro. Pierre Gisel (Munich: Chr. Kaiser Verlag, 1974), 18-19, 22.

intelligible from the sensible world was the positivistic attempt to give the humane sciences equal validity with the natural sciences. Another was the romantic attempt to reduce theology to "inwardness" or feeling — both attempts linked to the names of Schleiermacher and Wilhelm Dilthey. Schleiermacher construed understanding as the transference of the hearer or reader into the spiritual life of another. Dilthey opposed "explanation," borrowed from the natural sciences, to "understanding," Both paths are now closed off. This is because the notion of hermeneutics as a method competitive with that of the natural sciences needs jettisoning, since "explanation" does not derive from the natural sciences. It is furnished by semiotics, the science of language. Moreover, that "intolerable state of opposition between a mentalistic order of understanding and a physicalist order of explanation" requires abandoning. Understanding and explanation are not two methods; the former precedes and envelops the latter, while the latter in turn develops the former. The task, therefore, is to articulate understanding and explanation dialectically rather than seeing them as polar opposites.[39]

Further, the consideration of texts as autonomous, thus the application of structural analysis, renders obsolete the notion of reactualizing some inspired subjectivity behind a text through becoming contemporary with it.[40] What is accessible in the text is the sense of the text and its readers, not the intersubjectivity of author and reader. The understanding of a text is thus an understanding at a distance, and whatever recognition of its author there may be is indirect. Ricoeur calls this the recognition of an "implied author."[41] The notion of the intersubjectivity of author and reader, and the consequent ambition "to understand an author better than he understood himself," rests on the illusion of a sovereign consciousness.[42] Ricoeur thoroughly rejects the romantic notion of a self absolutely settled or sovereign, which he identifies by the term *moi*, in favor of a "called self" *(le sujet convoque)*, a self-in-relation, a self "received" by the text, and which he identifies by the term *soi*.[43]

39. Ricoeur, *The Conflict of Interpretations*, 5, 7; "Philosophical Hermeneutics and Theological Hermeneutics," 8-9; Reagan and Stewart, *The Philosophy of Paul Ricoeur*, 149-66.

40. Ricoeur, *The Conflict of Interpretations*, 7; "Philosophical Hermeneutics and Theological Hermeneutics," 8-9; "Rhetoric-Poetics-Hermeneutics," in *Rhetoric and Hermeneutics in Our Time: A Reader*, ed. Walter Jost and Michael J. Hyde (New Haven: Yale University Press, 1997), 69-70.

41. Ricoeur, *Exégèse et Herméneutique*, 53; *From Text to Action*, 16.

42. *Ibid.*, 11-12.

43. Ricoeur, *Exégèse et Herméneutique*, 53; *The Conflict of Interpretations*, 20; "Philosophical Hermeneutics and Theological Hermeneutics," 17; "Hermeneutic of the Idea of Revelation," in *The Center for Hermeneutical Studies: Protocol of the Twenty-Seventh Colloquy*

B. Structuralism

Ricoeur is equally critical of structuralism, though he believes structural analysis yields considerable gain. It involves distancing oneself from the text, thus allowing its singularity to appear, free of psychologism. To illustrate its benefit, Ricoeur refers to the celebrated Old Testament scholar Gerhard von Rad (1901-71), who made "implicit use" of structural analysis. With von Rad, the "kerygmatic" element or confession of Israel's faith furnished the centrifugal force drawing in texts of vastly different origins.

On the other hand, with structuralism language refers to nothing outside itself. All reference of the text to an external world, to an author or reader is excluded. At the same time history is excluded, since stories or narratives consist merely of the functioning of codes. The structuralist model is also anti-sociological; it ignores any causal relation between a text and its economic or political context. With such "immanence" at its heart, structuralism leaves us with a truncated linguistic model, and against it the exegete needs to be warned.

Above all, writes Ricoeur, structuralism excludes the primary intention of language, that is, "to say something about something." For it is in saying something about something, in discourse that language has a reference, first in the relation of predicate to subject, then in its relation to an outer reality, that implies a claim to truth. As system, language has no subject; discourse "puts language to work" through a speaker. As system, language consists solely of an internal dependence among the elements making it up; discourse is related to a world about which something is said. As system, language is merely the instrument of communication; discourse is addressed to someone; it has an addressee. As system, language renders the narrative "virtual," or strips it of its character as event; discourse gives the narrative its actuality. Upon this irreducible nature of discourse, writes Ricoeur, hermeneutics is built, whereas structuralism "has a secret affinity with a certain aesthetics of the dead text."[44]

(Chicago: n.p., 1977), 11-12; "Le sujet convoque à l'Ecole des Récits de Vocation Prophétique," *Revue de l'Institut catholique de Paris* (1988): 83; Reagan and Stewart, *The Philosophy of Paul Ricoeur*, 144.

44. *The Symbolism of Evil*, tr. Emerson Buchanan (Boston: Beacon, 1967), 306; "Contribution d'une Reflexion," 335, 337-40; *Exégèse et Herméneutique*, 37-39, 44, 48, 287, 289; *Paul Ricoeur on Biblical Hermeneutics, Semeia* 4, ed. John Dominic Crossan (Missoula, Mont.: Scholars, 1975), 29; "Philosophical Hermeneutics and Theological Hermeneutics," 5; Reagan and Stewart, *The Philosophy of Paul Ricoeur*, 90, 111-12, 114-15, 153-54.

C. Historicism

Ricoeur notes the affinity of historical-critical method with philosophical historicism. Historicism, he writes, oscillates between two extremes: the idea of the human spirit as evolving toward an ever purer spirituality, and the recognition of the irrational emergence of forms of life as expressed in literary styles. Nevertheless, writes Ricoeur, the method cannot be replaced since the texts we read are not "texts about texts" but about witnesses dealing with events. The fundamental motif of the historical-critical method is that exegesis is not, as per the structuralist's view, a reflection on "codes" governing the text but a way of returning to those witnesses at the origin of the text.

Ricoeur is quick to add that the historical-critical method requires correcting since it suffers from three illusions — the illusion of the source, the author, and the addressee. Ricoeur's prescription for the first is the recognition that the source does not facilitate understanding of the text but rather *the text* chooses and articulates its source. His prescription for the second is the awareness that the author is author of a *text,* and for the third the understanding that interpretation is an activity or operation of *the text* prior to any activity on the part of the reader.[45]

In an essay delivered at Marquette University in Milwaukee, Wisconsin, in 1984, Ricoeur dealt with three ways by which to speak of the past, as the Same, the Other, or the Similar. Citing R. G. Collingwood (1889-1943) as representing the first, thus of history solely as "reenactment" of the past, Ricouer asks whether or not it was necessary for the past itself to survive in order to be reenacted. Citing linguists and semiologists for whom the past is the Other in its extremest form, as "deviation," Ricoeur asks how the Other, how a difference relative to an abstract system and without any link to time, can take the place of what was once real and living. Ricoeur then suggests that the way by which to save whatever benefits accrue from the Same or the Other is to link them under the category of the Similar. Such would involve recourse to tropes, to figures of speech, in which metaphor occupies an eminent place. This type of analysis implies only one thing: events must have occurred *as* narrated. In other words, against the notion that the facts speak for themselves, and against the notion that historical imagination has no hold on reality, analysis by way of the Similar regards what is "real" or what "really" happened in terms of "such as" or "like this."[46]

---

45. Ricoeur, *Exégèse et Herméneutique,* 36, 291-93.
46. Paul Ricoeur, *The Reality of the Historical Past: The Aquinas Lecture, 1984* (Milwaukee: Marquette University Press, 1984), 5-35 *passim.*

D. Existentialism

In an extended essay titled "Preface to Bultmann," Ricoeur is at considerable pains to evaluate the work of the great Marburger.[47] He applauds Bultmann's rejection of Dilthey's view that the understanding of a text means construing it as a life-expression. On the contrary, Ricoeur states, it is not the author's life that governs understanding, but the essence of the meaning expressed in the text. Ricoeur cites Bultmann's definition of myth, which gives worldly form to what is beyond known and tangible reality, as setting him in total opposition to Ludwig Feuerbach. He likewise approves of Bultmann's demythologizing program, which, far from being opposed to kerygmatic interpretation, is its first application. In fact, the kerygmatic core of the original Christian preaching not merely requires but initiates and sets in motion the process of demythologizing.

At the same time, Ricoeur faults Bultmann for reflecting only on the "objectifying" myth and not on language as such, since whatever language replaces the myth itself requires interpretation. How could kerygma give rise to demythologizing if it did not initiate thought, if it were not both event and meaning, thus "objective" in a sense other than the mythical? Bultmann did not sufficiently think through the nonmythological core of the biblical statements, and by contrast the mythological statements themselves. This question, Ricoeur insists, is at the heart of post-Bultmannian hermeneutics.

Finally, though wholeheartedly agreeing that a text accomplishes its meaning only in personal appropriation, Ricoeur states that the New Testament scholar moves too rapidly to the moment of decision. The primary task of hermeneutics is not to bring about a decision in the reader, but to allow the matter of the text to unfold. At this point Ricoeur refers to Heidegger, for whom *understanding* is opposed to the activity of *finding oneself situated*. Rather, understanding addresses our own most possibilities and deciphers them in a situation we cannot project because we are already projected into it. In theological language, this means that "the kingdom of God is coming," that is to say, "it calls upon our own most possibilities, starting from the very meaning of this kingdom that does not come from us."[48] All in all, Ricoeur concludes, everything that opposed Bultmann to Feuerbach drew the Marburger closer to Kant. Myth for Bultmann was not, as for Feuerbach, the projection of the human into a fictitious beyond, but the representation in worldly form of what is beyond known and tangible reality. But he was

47. *Essays*, 49-72.
48. *From Text to Action*, 97.

complicit in Kant's division of the intelligible from the sensible world since he held that what was represented in this way still lay beyond.[49]

V. Convictions

A. The Thing of the Text

Ricoeur is committed to the proposition that the division between subject and object, fact and value, causality and teleology, a division long plaguing Western thought, is overcome in the understanding of language as constitutive of human existence. As he writes, "man is instituted by the word . . . by a language less spoken *by* man than *to* man."[50] How this occurs Ricoeur explains by way of his reference to "the thing" or "world" of the text. Ricoeur never tires of repeating that every text by its subject matter or by what it discloses through its referential power opens up a "world" of its own.[51] The meaning of a text is thus not behind it, but "in front of it." It is not something hidden but disclosed. For this reason, what needs to be understood in a story or narrative is not the person speaking behind it. The sense or reference of a text is expressive of a "world" and not another person.[52]

A text also speaks of the way by which I may orient myself in its world. But this event, this being invited into the "world" of the text, is not at my disposal; I am not master of it. The invitation to enter its world (and thus to experience a "new being") is prior to any willing or sense of obligation.[53] Ricoeur writes:

> The idea itself of announcement, of proclamation, of kerygma, presupposes . . . an *initiative on the part of meaning*, a *coming to us of meaning*, which *makes speech a partner* or correlate of existential decision. If the meaning of the text does not *already confront the reader*, how shall the act it announces not be reduced to a simple symbol of inner conversion?[54]

49. *Ibid.*, 95-97, 101; "Philosophical Hermeneutics and Theological Hermeneutics," 13; Ricoeur, *The Conflict of Interpretations*, 389-92, 394-97.

50. MacIntyre and Ricoeur, *The Religious Significance of Atheism*, 92; Reagan and Stewart, *The Philosophy of Paul Ricoeur*, 231, 237.

51. Reagan and Stewart, *The Philosophy of Paul Ricoeur*, 90-91, 139, 144; Reagan, *Paul Ricoeur, His Life and His Work*, 107; Ricoeur, "Philosophical Hermeneutics and Theological Hermeneutics," 95.

52. Ricoeur, *"Exégèse et Herméneutique,"* 53; Reagan and Stewart, *The Philosophy of Paul Ricoeur*, 145, 155.

53. *Ibid.*, 144; MacIntyre and Ricoeur, *The Religious Significance of Atheism*, 71-72, 79.

54. Ricoeur, *The Conflict of Interpretations*, 398; author's italics.

The pre-Socratics, says Ricoeur, had an appreciation for that reorientation or "shift of center" effected by the word, the *Logos*. And in the thought that I am not master of this speaking, of the text's invitation to enter its world, I find consolation and give thanks, thanks for the "gift" of language.[55]

The task of hermeneutics is thus to explicate this "world" in which I can dwell. If interpretation is not to be reduced to the mere analysis of structures, or if it is not to rush pell-mell toward facilitating self-understanding, it must unfold the world of the text. Of course, the "destiny of the text" is accomplished when the reader "reenacts" what it says, when, in Gadamer's terms, there is a "fusion of horizons," the merging of the world of the reader and the world of the text. But the world of the text and the way of orienting oneself in it need first to be displayed.[56]

To put this issue of the text is to depsychologize it, to rescue it from romanticism. But it also means to have done with the question concerning the text's "inspiration," since no privilege attaches to the invitation to enter its world. What is unique about biblical hermeneutics is its "thing," the world of its text. And herein lies its truth: not in its correspondence, not in answering to criteria of falsification or verification, but in its allowing its "world" to be, a world I may inhabit and in which I can project my optimal possibilities.[57]

B. The Function of the Text

When Ricoeur proceeds to indicate how or in what way the text projects its "world," he refers to its "poetic" dimension. It is the "poetic," defined as function, not as genre or mode, that has the power to disclose new ways of being. It is the "poetic" that restores participation in an order of things prior to our disposing of them as objects. Recognition of this function comprises the "semiotic approach," a technique totally distinct from the historical-critical method and originally applied in the area of fairy tales and folklore. It is this approach that assigns the primary expressions of biblical faith to the poetic function of language, for the biblical word projects a "world" with the power to make a break and create a new beginning.

At the heart of the "poetic" lies metaphor. Metaphor, the "transfer" of

55. MacIntyre and Ricoeur, *The Religious Significance of Atheism*, 90, 94.

56. Ricoeur, "Philosophical Hermeneutics and Theological Hermeneutics," 12; *From Text to Action*, 95; Reagan and Stewart, *The Philosophy of Paul Ricoeur*, 90-91, 145.

57. Crossan, *Paul Ricoeur on Biblical Hermeneutics*, 10; Reagan and Stewart, *The Philosophy of Paul Ricoeur*, 91; Ricoeur, "Philosophical Hermeneutics and Theological Hermeneutics," 14; *From Text to Action* 98; "Hermeneutic of the Idea of Revelation," 10.

reality according to a new model, is what gives the "poetic" its power. Metaphor generates in me an "imagination" by which I respond to the text as opening to me a "world" or a new being, an imagination prior to my deciding or choosing. Metaphor, or the symbol that makes possible its "transfer," is not a defective language, nor a mere provisional device to be replaced by a concept. On the contrary, it reveals "aspects of the ineluctable" — something that cannot be the object of biological, psychological, or sociological knowledge. It touches on the very essence of things. It articulates a domain of experience prior to understanding where consciousness of self is constituted at its lowest level. The most poetic language, or even the most sacred symbol, works with the same vocables as the most banal term in the dictionary. But a mystery nonetheless adheres to the "poetic" because it speaks about being. By way of this meditation, Ricoeur aims to recover the metaphor or the symbol for those for whom the "heremeneutics of suspicion" have led to a loss of faith and meaning.[58]

C. The Wager

Clearly, hermeneutics conceived in this fashion involves a wager — a concept reminiscent of Blaise Pascal.[59] By following the lead of the metaphor or symbol, the interpreter wagers on a better understanding of self. If such understanding occurs, the wager is to that extent verified. But its verification is not the satisfying of some philosophical notion of what is true. For the level of truth or certitude appropriate to this hermeneutics, Ricoeur uses the term "attestation," a middle ground between the *cogito* of Descartes and the perpetual suspicion of Marx, Nietzsche, or Freud. And although "attestation" is a much weaker claim than that of Descartes's sovereign *cogito*, and thus is always vulnerable, only the one who imagines philosophy to be free of presuppositions can object to it. At the same time, what is wagered can be submitted

58. Ricoeur, *The Symbolism of Evil*, 9, 18, 311-12; "Du Conflit à la Convergence des Methodes," 84; *The Conflict of Interpretations*, 77-78; MacIntyre and Riceour, *Paul Ricoeur on Biblical Hermeneutics*, 16; Ricouer, "Philosophical Hermeneutics and Theological Hermeneutics," 13, 20; "Hermeneutic of the Idea of Revelation," 9, 10; Paul Ricoeur, "The Bible and the Imagination," in *The Bible as a Document of the University*, ed. Hans-Dieter Betz (Chico, Calif.: Scholars Press, 1981), 53, 56; Ricoeur, *From Text to Action*, 95, 101; "Rhetoric-Poetics-Hermeneutics," 65; *Critique and Conviction*, 169.

59. See Blaise Pascal, *Pensées*, tr. with intro. A. J. Krailsheimer (New York: Penguin, 1966), 151: "Let us weigh up the gain and the loss involved in calling heads that God exists. Let us assess the two cases: if you win, you win everything, if you lose you lose nothing."

to a logic of probability. In this way Ricoeur's hermeneutics supports the historical-critical and structural approaches to Scripture.[60]

Intent on the distinction between philosophical and biblical hermeneutics, Ricoeur writes that the self achieved through entry into the "world" of the biblical text is not a crowning of the self of philosophical hermeneutics:

> the mode of the Christian life is a wager and a destiny . . . whoever assumes it is not entitled by his confession to remain in a defensive position or to take pride in a superiority toward all other types of existence. . . . The self in response here is responding precisely to *that* ensemble of symbols fixed by the biblical canon and developed by one or the other historical tradition grafted onto the Scriptures. . . .[61]

The self disclosed by the biblical "poetic" is thus a response to a discrete network of symbols within its canon. If the self of the biblical paradigm were in fact identical to the self in philosophical hermeneutics, it would lose its character as wager. In an excursus appended to his essay "Philosophical and Theological Hermeneutics," Ricoeur describes the nature of the "wager" from the biblical perspective. Writing that Christian faith appears to alternate between ideology and utopia, he states that it is rooted deeper than this struggle on the surface of history:

> As the Remembrance of some epoch-making events — the Exodus and the Resurrection — it shares something with the positive concept of ideology. As the Expectation of the Kingdom to come it shares something with the positive concept of utopia. . . . The root of faith is somewhere near that point where Expectation springs forth out of Memory. *But this, too, is not something that we may see and possess.* This *concealed* source *reveals itself only in its effects* at the level of the conflict between utopia and ideology.[62]

The journey is from text to metaphor to "generative imagination" to a "world" and its possibilities to its "attestation" to its probability, and overall the assumption, the presumption, the "wager" as to its certainty, weaker than the "truth" of a sovereign self but stronger than perpetual suspicion.

---

60. *The Symbolism of Evil*, 308, 355, 357; "Du Conflit à la Convergence des Methodes," 51; "Hermeneutic of the Idea of Revelation," 13; Reagan, *Paul Ricoeur: His Life and His Work*, 75-77.

61. "Le Sujet Convoque," 84.

62. "Philosophical Hermeneutics and Theological Hermeneutics," 28; authors' italics.

VI. Exegesis

A. Paul and the State

While it is true that Ricoeur's work gives greatest attention to the use of language in theory, he has not left his readers without illustration of its use. Due to the parallel interest in philosophy and theology, his writings contain as many references to biblical as to nonbiblical sources. In an early essay entitled "The State and Coercion," Ricoeur opens with the statement that Greek political thought abandoned the attempt to reconcile the patterns of love and justice, then turns to the New Testament, to Romans 13. In the midst of an appeal to love, the apostle Paul presents us with the magistrate or "authority." This leaves us with a problem, says Ricoeur, since it seems impossible that "authority" should be born of love. And while the apostle is aware that the two streams must converge, his use of the term "institution" (i.e., "authorities that exist have been instituted by God" [v. 1]) indicates that he finds no unity here. Further, Paul's linking the state to the wrath of God ("the authority is the servant of God to execute wrath" [v. 4]) only confirms the dilemma.

By way of solution, Ricoeur notes Paul's use of the "demonological myth" to illustrate the state's authority (it "bears the sword," etc.). He argues that only as we refuse to regard the myth as an "explanation" can we perceive the richness of its instruction. What the myth teaches is that an "internal dialectic" inheres in the "institution": its "order" is unstable and dangerous. Only the totally negative commandment "thou shalt not kill" can provide the working principle able to balance the ethics of love and the state. It is respect for life that provides the bridge between love and justice, ethics and politics.

Ricoeur's conclusion is that the "strictly logical duty" issuing from his reflection would be to become a conscientious objector. But faced with the question of whether or not he should risk his life that the state may survive plunges him into an "ethic of distress." On the other hand, the prospect of going to war to secure the state's survival plunges him into an "ethic of distress." The one action involves treason against the state, the other murder of the neighbor.[63]

---

63. Paul Ricoeur, *The State and Coercion* (Geneva: John Knox, 1957), 6-16.

B. The Symbolism of Evil

This volume represents Ricoeur's first venture into a philosophical analysis of symbolic language. It is also his most sustained theological work, containing hundreds of biblical references and their exposition. Opposing the notion that philosophy must avoid symbolic language or convert it into literal discourse, the volume is dedicated to the proposition that symbolism constitutes self-consciousness at its deepest level, that by interpreting the great symbols we aim at a "second naivete" and thus "hear" them again. "The symbol," in effect, "gives rise to thought."

The "thought" given rise to in this volume has to do with the symbols of defilement, sin, and guilt as expressing the human experience of evil. With *defilement* comes the experience of terror, dread of the impure, but also a scheme of rationalization linking defilement to suffering as cause to effect This first stage of "fault" Ricoeur finds reflected, for example, in Isaiah 6:5, 7. With *sin* comes the consciousness of having violated a personal bond, of the transgression of a "covenant" and its commands. This stage Ricoeur finds reflected in such passages as Exodus 20 or Amos 5:7, 21; 6:12. With *guilt* emerges consciousness of self, awareness of the "I" as over against deity, as expressed, for example, in Psalm 51. At each stage noting analogous symbols in nonbiblical sources, Ricoeur argues that each new experience with its symbols is charged with what precedes. The result is a "circular relation," the last symbol interpreting the first, and the first furnishing the last with its power. In each stage, Ricoeur notes a benefit as well as a deficit. For example, the world of defilement is anterior to any division between the ethical and physical, for which reason suffering can acquire the role of a symptom, eliminable through observing the proper ritual. But defilement as the cause of suffering is an absurdity in light of the innocence of a Job. In the world of sin, the category of being "before God" dominates and may eventuate in the concept of "pardon." But it does not yet succeed to the stage at which "wrath" is the obverse side of the "love" of God. Selfhood characterizes the stage of guilt, but guilt may also lead to a "scrupulousness" confining the God-man relation to that of a will that commands and one that obeys. The concept toward which this series of symbols tends is the paradox of the "servile" or captive free will.

For Ricoeur, the Adamic myth and the Pauline concept of justification mark the uniqueness of the biblical, Christian view of evil. In the "Adamic myth," evil does not, as with gnosticism, originate with creation, but rather with history, with an ancestor of the human race. With Paul "justice comes to a man," retrospection from which reveals the unity of the entire domain of evil. And, finally, the "Adamic myth" with its view of humankind as the author of evil, and the "tragic view" of Job according to which evil suffered is an injustice, are both transcended in the figure of the "Suffering Servant" who makes of suffering, of evil, an action capable of redemption.[64]

C. The Parables

Ricoeur notes the "radically profane" character of the parables of Jesus. Through them we are disoriented before being oriented. He also notes the element of extravagance attaching to the parables, an element that he describes as a "limit expression," that is, a use that shatters the ordinary function of narrative structure to the point where it becomes metaphor. Because of this, the parables allow no translation into conceptual language. This is hard to bear since our scientific training tends to use figures of speech only as devices to be replaced by concepts. Ricoeur insists that it is not enough to say that the parables say nothing directly about the kingdom of God. On the contrary, when the parables are taken together, they have more to say concerning God and God's kingdom than any rational theology. Finally, Ricoeur describes the parables as addressed first to our imagination rather than to our will.

In his exposition of the parable of the wicked husbandmen in Mark 12:1-2 and parallels, or in his interpretation of the parables in Matthew 13, Ricoeur states that the "extraordinary is like the ordinary." It is precisely the profane person (a man who sows seed, a woman who takes leaven, etc.) whom the parables describe — a surprising feature, since in the moment we expect the language of myth we encounter the language of our own history. As for extravagance, adverting to the parable of the wicked husbandmen Ricoeur asks, "What landowner, in effect, would be so foolish as to send his son after his servants had been killed?" Regarding the parables of the treasure and pearl he writes that the kingdom is not compared to "the man who" but to what happens in the story. That is, we are required to think *through* the metaphor, not *beyond* it; to reflect on a figure that is not metaphorical for the sake of rhetoric but for the sake of what it has to say. And what it has to say is manifest in the plot, the structure of the drama. From the plot three critical moments emerge: the Event, the Reversal, and the Decision (in the parable of the treasure and pearl, the finding, the selling, and the buying). The kingdom of God is likened to the chain of these three acts. It comes as Event, as gift; it

---

64. Ricoeur, *The Symbolism of Evil, passim;* see also *The Conflict of Interpretations,* 282-85; Reagan, *Paul Ricoeur: His Life and His Work,* 23-24; Reagan and Stewart, *The Philosophy of Paul Ricoeur,* 87.

occasions Reversal; it culminates in a Deciding or doing engendered by the Event and the Reversal. Each parable, Ricoeur states, develops or dramatizes one or the other of these three critical terms. In illustrating how the parables taken together have more to say than any rational argument, Ricoeur refers to the "great metaphor" encompassing the parable of the sower, with its "euphoric" course and accent on the word, and that of the husbandmen, with its "dysphoric" course and accent on the body or life of the son. The metaphor embracing the two is that the body must die in order for the word to grow. Translated into the "exchange" between the parables' actors and the actual narrator, Jesus is signifying the growth of his word as dependent upon the "diminution" of his body. When the parables are seen in this way, we will not be tempted to reduce them to mere didactic devices or moralizing allegories, but will allow their "poetic power" to be displayed in us, since "it is in the heart of our imagination that we let the Event happen (i.e., let the Kingdom come), before we may convert our heart and tighten our will."[65]

VII. Assessment

A. Linguistics and Text

In an earlier century a thinker such as Ricoeur would have been attacked for his schizophrenia, however "controlled," for his attempt to synthesize the philosophical and theological concerns. He himself appears anxious to legitimize his approach as a way between the "fanaticism of purity" and "eclectic compromise at any cost." His friends also seem eager to defend him by asserting that where others see a dichotomy he views the two areas in terms of a dialectic that transcends a "lazy eclecticism."[66]

Whether or not Ricoeur is anxious to explain himself, be it in face of the philosophical or the theological community or both, and whether or not sufficient reason exists for his friends to defend him, it is a fact that the philosophical climate, at least, has changed so radically as to render immaterial whatever anxiety or need for defense there may be. Since the turn of the twen-

---

65. Ricoeur, "Listening to the Parables: Once More Astonished" (a sermon preached in Rockefeller Chapel of the University of Chicago), *Christianity and Crisis* 34 (1975): 304-8 (1975); "Philosophical Hermeneutics and Theological Hermeneutics," 27; "The Bible and the Imagination," 52, 57-58, 62, 65, 69-70; Reagan, *Paul Ricoeur: His Life and His Work,* 239-45.

66. Crossan, *Paul Ricoeur on Biblical Hermeneutics,* 17; *Paul Ricoeur: His Life and His Work,* 99.

tieth century, the philosopher's passion has turned from metaphysics to linguistics. The names with which to conjure now are no longer those of Kant, Hegel, Comte, or Mill, but of Ferdinand de Saussure (1857-1913), N. S. Trubetskoy (1890-1938), Roman Jakobson (1896-1982), Benjamin Lee Whorf (1897-1941), Claude Levi-Strauss (1908-), Noam Chomsky (1928-), or Jacques Derrida (1930-). Semantics, semiotics, the examination of signs and symbols and their referents, extending to the investigation of lexemes, morphemes, sememes, phonemes — in short, language, speech, talk, has assumed first place on the agenda of philosophical inquiry.

This preoccupation with language has spawned the so-called structuralist, poststructuralist, or deconstructionist schools, each in its own way concentrating on language, whether as a system with a highly organized, sophisticated structure, or as a mental process, whether as founded in social structure, or as shaping perception and explainable by an invisible mechanism called "grammar." Whatever the approach or perspective, contemporary philosophical investigation begins with texts, with what is said, spoken, uttered, declared, declaimed, proclaimed, averred, or avowed. The utterance, then, the text is what legitimizes Ricoeur's interest in the two disciplines, since philosophy and theology both begin with the text.

Quite aside from the debate as to whether words or texts refer to entities outside themselves or merely to other words in the same sentence, for the contemporary thinker, thus also for Ricoeur, the text enjoys priority over the speaker or writer, over the hearer or reader. In a variation on that old line from Hamlet, "the text's the thing by which to capture the conscience of the king," a conscience, at least, whose call is conformable to the "thing of the text," to the new being it proffers.

But with all this assigning priority to the text, Ricoeur will not leap to construct a "theology of the word" in the manner of a Bultmann and his students that does not include a "long detour" through structural analysis. The fault with a theology of the word lies in its inattention to the word as having passed from speech to writing. For Ricoeur this transition is not a deprivation. He is not saddened at the gospel's assuming written form. Like Gadamer he may even refer to the written word as enjoying a kind of "eternity." His entire enterprise has been facilitated by that move from speech to writing. But precisely for that reason he insists on the impossibility of interpreting signs, symbols, or significations apart from a structural analysis of their forms, that is, on significations as deposited, handed down in written form.

B. Text over Interpreter

The text has preeminence over the interpreter. Ricoeur passionately rejects the figure of the Cartesian self-secure *cogito*. And he rejects the imperious "I" of the romantic who believes interpretation consists of a merger of the reader's self with that of the author. As if the ego in that *cogito*, the "self," were something sovereign and self-contained, without dependence on the other for its selfhood or consciousness. In his exposition of the "subject as called" Ricoeur describes the prophet as receiving a *soi*, a self, in confrontation with the God who is introduced as source and authentication of his calling and mission. There is no "I," no self, without a "Thou." And, as if it were possible for the interpreter to get behind the text to its "author," to a distinct and discrete self separate from and not identifiable with the text; as if there were an explicit and not an "implied" author.

Or, as if part of the reason why this cannot be done is that the interpreter is unable to come to the text free of bias, or, to use Ricoeur's term, "innocent." Interpretation is always under "suspicion" since there is always the possibility that the interpreter's prejudgment will impede the "world" of the text's coming to be. The phrase "hermeneutics of suspicion" has been carelessly bandied about. It is often pressed into the service of relativizing texts so that they may mean anything at all. Ricoeur is clear as to the necessity for taking a stand in interpretation, despite the lack of total certainty. If he were not, what he has to say about the "wager" would make no sense. With Ricoeur, the "hermeneutics of suspicion" consists in a "deconstruction" of the interpreter's prejudice. And here is where Marx, Nietzsche, and Freud, however hostile to religious faith, serve as "internal critique." They assist the interpreter to achieve the distance from self that understanding in light of the text requires. Taken in this sense, the "hermeneutics of suspicion" is an integral part of interpretation, and the critique of the three "adversaries" the portal through which any kind of mediation of faith must pass. In Ricoeur's words, "we are again going to use another kind of suspicion, but a suspicion with respect to ourselves."[67]

In this connection, Ricoeur has been highly complimentary of Bultmann's demythologizing program. To dissociate the "true" scandal of the cross from the "false scandal" of its cultural vehicle, to purify the gospel proclamation of its mythological vestments, is a perfectly legitimate enterprise. But Bultmann neglected critically to analyze "the existential reinterpretation" he had extracted from the myth. In a description of the task of the "hermeneut" Ricoeur lays down an axiom Bultmann had presumably avoided: "not

---

67. Reagan and Stewart, *The Philosophy of Paul Ricoeur*, 224.

simply to surrender before the standard of believable and unbelievable of his time, but also to question it."[68] Bultmann accepted the language and conceptuality of his day without subjecting it to the same analysis he had applied to the biblical mythology. Even the "post-Bultmannians" assumed they could harness Heidegger "as is" to the apostle Paul.

C. Text and Author

Ricoeur has not rejected the historical-critical method but attempted to weed out from it those three "illusions" of source, author, and addressee. But is not disallowing the "illusion of the author" excessive in light of the old "redaction-critical" discovery, that the writings of the New Testament plead for living, breathing persons who pursue a definite goal with their work?

No one can identify the author of the first Gospel, for example, by giving him a name or describing his workplace. But if his text should indicate that the arrival of the Baptist, rather than legitimizing the Old Testament word is in fact legitimized by it, and is thus the "creature" of that word, would such radical departure from the approach of his co-evangelists leave us altogether in the dark respecting him and his concern? Or if, as Ricoeur insists, "man is language," not only "as good as" but "*is* his word," why the need for a wedge between "man" and "word" in an "implied author"? Would it be a concession to the "historicism" endemic to historical-critical method to regard the text as the creation of an author whom we may not identify to the soul's satisfaction, but who has nevertheless left some clues to himself, some "lineaments" in what he has written? Is there not sufficient evidence of material as well as historical continuity between the intention of the text and that of its author? In Ricoeur's "correction" of the historical-critical approach, has the dialectic of the historical and the structural tended toward the old antinomy?

D. Wager and Transcendence

Recent scholarly research in America, particularly in the area of Jesus research, advertises its use of factual, empirical evidence open to confirmation by "neutral" observers. With all his summons to a hermeneutics of suspicion, to the dimension of "distantiation" required of self-understanding, Ricoeur is leagues away from encouraging neutrality in interpretation. He writes that

---

68. *Ibid.*

though the phenomenologist, say, may give the name of truth to internal coherence, it is truth without belief, truth "at a distance." At this level one may be curious but not concerned. To move beyond this intermediate state requires "passion," "risk," a "wager." Anxious or no in face of the charge of eclecticism, Ricoeur writes again and again that interpretation begins and ends in risk. Use of the term "risk" is deliberate since there is no final synthesis of faith and veracity or intellectual honesty. There is only the wager on the "available believable." But without the wager there is no understanding of the text. As he says:

> The Gospel will always be carried by an extraordinarily fragile testimony . . . the Cross *remains* a folly for the intelligent, a scandal for the wise. But at the same time a new structure of communication, a new discourse appears which is of cultural importance, and which happens through which one could call an "available believable." . . . Each epoch permits a believable and an unbelievable. So it is certain that the language in which "those things" have been spoken is folly; but, at the same time, it is folly which speaks into a certain available believable at a given time.[69]

Here we must add a word concerning the shaper of the "risk" or "wager" in Paul Ricoeur. In *Critique and Conviction,* he reflects on the death of Christ, the resurrection, and his own personal survival. First of all, he supports the "liberation" of the theology of the cross from its sacrificial interpretation. Second, he admits to being tempted, in Hegelian fashion, to understand the resurrection of Jesus as resurrection in his community. Resurrection, then, would consist in having a body other than a physical body, that is, an "historical body." Ricoeur asks, "Am I entirely unorthodox in thinking this?" Respecting the narratives of the empty tomb and the appearances he is prepared to admit they convey some theological sense, although it is buried within the images of the narrative. "I know nothing," he writes, "of the resurrection as an event. . . . Here, the entire empirical narrative appears to me to conceal rather than to give form to its theological sense." He nevertheless muses on the possibility of the empty tomb's signifying the gap between Jesus' death as elevation and his effective resurrection in the community, and on the appearances as meaning that the "spirit of Jesus" who offered his life for his friends now animates his disciples, transformed from deserters into an *ecclesia*. As to his own survival, Ricoeur writes that his position is in complete accord with his interpretation of the resurrection of Christ: life is stronger than death. It is extended horizontally in the other, the survivor, and (with a nod toward process theology) is

---

69. *Ibid.,* 220.

transcended vertically in the "memory of God." In this sense, Ricoeur adds, he holds his position to be Christian, however peripheral it may be respecting the dominant theologies. "Let God, at my death, do with me as he wills. I demand nothing, I demand no 'after.'"[70]

Which brings us to the matter of transcendence. One of Ricoeur's reviewers contrasts the French thinker with Immanuel Kant. He states that while Kant dreamed of a transcendence within the area of the practical, one could only "think of it" there. For Ricoeur, on the other hand, "practical activity is the place of the actual realization of the transcendental."[71] The quotation requires translation: where there is attention to the "world" of the text and the "new being" it proffers, there is transcendence. Not that transcendence is identified with attention to the text. Practical activity is the "place where" transcendence is realized; it is the setting of the scene for, but not the efficient cause of, transcendence. Recall Rudolf Bultmann's statement that while only God can create the "point of contact" (Anknüpfungspunkt) between the kerygma and its addressee, it is the task of the interpreter to set the scene for its occurrence in an intelligible proclamation.[72] Ricoeur, too, is at pains to distinguish the idea of transcendence or revelation from any "practical" or mental activity and can even write that "something secret" is its "limit-idea."[73] Still, the weld between text and transcendence is so strong that the "limit-idea" may easily be suppressed by a prejudice against texts with referents beyond themselves, and Ricoeur may be used to advocate positions he rejects. If, for example, understanding of the word "God" or "Christ" means to follow the "direction of the meaning" of the term, why could not its gravitational pull or the "horizon" it opens up simply be identified as symbol or metaphor? Ricoeur's statement regarding the revelation as "a feature of the biblical world proposed by the text"[74] is capable of more than one interpretation. Giving larger place to that "something secret" as the "limit-idea" of revelation may be a risk or wager not all Ricoeur's readers will allow.

A similar problem exists respecting Ricoeur's reference to "truth." Agreed, our model of truth needs correcting, it cannot be identified according to mathematical or logical models. But who is to prevent interpreting Ricoeur's statement regarding truth as a road to follow, as a becoming, to read that it equals "hermeneutical suspicion," structural analysis, or whatever else

70. Critique and Conviction, 152, 154, 158, 161.

71. Ricoeur and Jüngel, Metaphor, 19-20.

72. See Bultmann, Essays: Philosophical and Theological (New York: Macmillan, 1955), 135ff.

73. "Hermeneutic of the Idea of Revelation," 7.

74. Ibid., 10; From Text to Action, 96.

interpretation requires, and once more to overlook the necessity for a stance, a posture, a wager?[75]

E. Bless the Contradiction

To reprise, Ricoeur has not simply attempted a synthesis of conflicting ways by which to interpret a text. He has developed a theory by which those conflicting ways can all be embraced. He recognizes that the analysis of a text requires attention to its structure, and insists that any interpretation must go the often tiresome route of structure analysis. He also knows that no text is loosed from time or history, and contends that freeing historical-critical research of its illusions does not involve cutting the text loose from time and history. And he asserts that no interpretation of a text is without a "wager" since no absolute criterion exists for determining its rightness or wrongness. If the text is to be treated as it deserves, the structural, historical-critical, and the "existential" are all to be gathered up, and each allowed to play its role without assigning preeminence to one or the other.

And where does this gathering occur? Ricoeur answers: in the text itself, more, in a particular kind of text, a text able to engage the reader at a level where the normal, usual differences between texts and readers are overcome. That is, in a "poetic," in a text charged with symbolic, even mythical expression, for just such a text fires the imagination ahead of understanding, ahead of explaining, ahead of deciding for or against. Such a text, as Ricoeur sometimes writes, "elicits effort and desire" and ends in changing its reader. The term "poetic," of course, is not restricted to poetry. It involves a congeries of types charged with symbolic expression. Ricoeur's preoccupation with symbol, with sign or metaphor, has nothing of the aesthetic about it, but serves his conviction that it is this type of text that is able to engage its readers ahead of whatever divides them. He most often speaks of such a text as proposing a "world," a totality of meanings, a "global horizon" in which the reader can live.

From the perspective of the history of thought, Ricoeur's approach is an attempt to overcome the old dichotomy between subject and object, whether between the "I" and its world, as with Descartes, or between this world and the beyond, as with Kant, a division legitimized in the romanticist approach of a Dilthey or Schleiermacher.

But with all this merger of text and reader at a level beneath any dis-

75. Ricoeur, "Du Conflit à la Convergence des Methodes," 295.

tance between them, the initiative is, after all, with the text and its "world." The text "comes to" the reader; its "meaning" is present before the reader arrives at it. The text's "coming" and the reader's arrival may occur together, or, the word may function as a "crossroads" where something happens to us at the same time as we master it, but there would be no occurring together, no crossroads, if the text were not already there.

There is something breathtaking about the initiative Ricoeur assigns to the text and its world, something Augustinian, "predestinarian," but also reminiscent of Greek tragedy and its preoccupation with fate, with destiny — to say nothing of the early fascination with Karl Barth and the temptation to repress whatever the reader might bring to the text, thus to deny philosophy any *entre* to revelation.[76] Even Ricoeur's affinity for Marx, Nietzsche, and Freud, with their "hermeneutics of suspicion," served that repression. At any rate, that entire preoccupation with the reader, the interpreter, with the reader's world or the interpreter's assumptions that has marked interpretation in this country, and biblical interpretation above all — has all been stood on its head in the interest of overcoming the division between subject and object, text and interpreter, understanding and explanation, destiny and choice.

The weight of immanence assigned to the text, the word, to language, is just as breathtaking. For Ricoeur the uniqueness of the biblical word consists only (apparently) in the fact that a Name, "God" or "Christ," is its centrifugal force. Further, the "world" in front of the biblical text enjoys no privileged position (apparently) over against other worlds in front of other texts, for which reason opting for that world or its new being involves a "wager" or "risk." God, the "ineluctable," revelation, faith, desire, response and change — all occur with the text, so that the text is no longer a means *by which* or *through which* the one or the other is grasped or met or achieved. To that extent the structuralist argument still holds: there is no referent beyond the text or word itself, for the word itself is the revelation. It is the text, the word, the *logos* uncapitalized that has assumed the flesh the *Logos* capitalized once assumed in order to "dwell among us."

On the other hand, Ricoeur's preference for what he calls the "kerygmatic reading," a reading that makes more sense to him because it is centered on the symbolism of a cross, and thus gives the word "God" a "density" that the word "Being" does not contain,[77] that preference could come from something the text evokes, arouses, calls to mind, summons up, but which is not there, at least not immediately there, in the text itself — something become a

---

76. Ricoeur, *Critique and Conviction,* 150.
77. *From Text to Action,* 98.

"destiny" from years of choosing. After all, there is no "innocent" reading. But to the extent of that preference, the "logocentric," perhaps "Idealistic" argument still holds: there is a referent beyond to which the text points, a referent beyond the text itself.

To the question, What kind of faith deserves to survive the critique of Freud and Nietzsche? Ricoeur responds: "It would be a faith that wanders in the darkness. . . . This God does not protect me but delivers me up to the dangers of a life worthy of being called human. Is not this God the Crucified, the dying God . . . ?"[78] That would be a faith that the text itself and alone cannot give. And since it is Ricoeur's faith, it qualifies, if it does not downright contradict, his attempt at embracing all the conflicting views and methods and interpretations at some deeper level. But it is a blessed contradiction for all that.

---

78. MacIntyre and Ricoeur, *The Religious Significance of Atheism*, 88.

14

BREVARD CHILDS

Biblical Criticism under the Discipline of the Canon

I. The Postmodern Predicament of Academic Biblical Criticism[1]

If one were to choose a recent textbook that explains contemporary biblical criticism to beginning theological students in mainline denominations,[2] one could do no better than *To Each Its Own Meaning*, edited by Steven L. McKenzie and Stephen R. Haynes. This handy collection of essays covers the contemporary landscape on everything from source, form, and redaction criticism to more recent methods such as reader-response criticism and feminism. Fittingly for the textbook genre, the collection takes a positive approach to all positions. It affirms each method of criticism as a valid contribution to biblical studies. Competing methods represent not confusion but "diversity"

1. This section is in part adapted from Walter Sundberg, "The Social Effect of Biblical Criticism," in Craig Bartholomew, Colin Green, and Karl Möller, eds., *Renewing Biblical Interpretation* (Grand Rapids: Zondervan, 2000), 1:66-81.

2. The term "mainline" refers to a commuter train route running from downtown Philadelphia to the wealthy suburbs. It has become a sociological metaphor used to identify Protestant denominations that are largely white, affluent, and open to the secular influences of modern culture. Eight denominations are commonly cited as belonging to the mainline: American Baptist Churches in the USA, Christian Church (Disciples of Christ), Episcopal Church, Evangelical Lutheran Church in America, Presbyterian Church (USA), Reformed Church in America, United Church of Christ, and the United Methodist Church.

— a decided virtue in contemporary academia. The concern for diversity extends to the choice of contributors. The editors proudly describe the authors of the essays in terms of their personal identities: "Four are women and nine are men. Seven are Hebrew Bible/Old Testament scholars, and six work primarily in New Testament. Three are from Roman Catholic backgrounds, one is Jewish, and nine represent a variety of Protestant denominations." As if this were not enough, the editors employ age distinctions in their selection: "in the interest of balance, some younger scholars were assigned chapters on more traditional methods, while more established scholars were asked to write chapters on new methods."[3]

To some readers, especially of the older generation, this argument might appear overly scrupulous in its concern for inclusiveness. To many theological students born in the 1970s, however, it makes perfect sense. They have been raised under an educational philosophy that posits an essential connection between the "accidents" of gender, race, and ethnicity and the "substance" of ideas. "Diversity" has become an ethical imperative in the contemporary university. Its purveyors believe that it is best secured by attending to the physical characteristics and social circumstances of scholars. It teaches theological students to accept variety as a theological blessing.

In this intellectual milieu, it is impossible for a single school of thought to command theology. Powerful theological movements such as existentialism and neoorthodoxy may have inspired the first two generations of pastors and theologians in this century (a "generation" understood in its traditional definition of thirty-three years), but they have had only marginal impact on this third and last generation of the century. Even such notions as "Old Testament theology" and "New Testament theology" — let alone "biblical theology" — that dominated the theological curriculum in biblical studies into the early 1970s, have fallen on hard times. The Bible is now commonly understood to be the product of disparate communities of the past. For Scripture to be relevant, it must be allowed to speak in various ways to different communities of the present, each of which has its own legitimate needs. No single theology represents the voice of the past or the needs of the present. No religious community may claim privileged access to the content of the Bible. There are as many theological ideas as there are groups and individuals. To demand uniform opinion is wrong.

This situation means important changes for the discipline of biblical studies. Instead of seeking *the* proper method of biblical criticism that dis-

---

3. Steven L. McKenzie and Stephen R. Haynes, eds., *To Each Its Own Meaning* (Louisville: Westminster/John Knox, 1993), 5-6.

closes *the* meaning of a specific text, it is now commonly asserted that there is neither a proper method nor a single interpretation. Does this mean that there is "no king in Israel" and the people do "what is right in their own eyes" (Judg. 21:25)? Not quite. Scholars such as Stephen E. Fowl and L. Gregory Jones argue that common ground for debate among biblical scholars can be found. What determines biblical interpretation is the "interpretive interest" of the exegete and the community of discourse to which the exegete belongs. For example, if the opening chapters of Genesis are placed before "a physicist, a Marxist, a psychoanalyst, a Christian advocate of 'creation science' and an Augustinian Christian," what will happen? "The interpreters will only clarify and perhaps resolve their differences to the extent they can articulate more precisely what their interpretive aims are when they read the Bible."[4] Meaning is not merely a function of what works for the interpreter, but a "social activity" that "is subject to the political arrangements in which people interpret" and ideas are "confirmed, constrained, and determined."[5] Each interpreter is responsible to a specific political community with its values and strictures. "Thus there is no interpretive practice which is free of some kind of political presumptions. Hermeneutics is inevitably, though not restrictively, a "political discipline."[6] By examining the political arrangements that influence the interpreter, Fowl and Jones assert that different exegetical interests can be measured according to their social effect. The social effect of scholarly ideas is a criterion of judgment that everyone understands and accepts and thus can become the basis for creating common discourse concerning the Bible.

To propose a political approach to the analysis of biblical interpretation may appear undesirable to those who are committed to some form of religious orthodoxy. To politicize hermeneutics encourages a type of discourse that focuses more on the status of the people employing the Bible for their own purposes than what the Bible says. It is to enter the slippery world of "postmodernism" where the meaning of texts and authorial intent disappear behind the ideological commitments and even subjective whims of readers who make a text do what they want. This is always a problem for any community that reads the Bible as divine speech. But a political hermeneutic may be unavoidable in the present intellectual climate. The fact is that the contemporary university is divided into competing special interests in all fields, includ-

---

4. Stephen E. Fowl and Gregory L. Jones, eds., *Reading in Communion* (Grand Rapids: Eerdmans, 1991), 15-16.

5. *Ibid.*, 16-17.

6. *Ibid.*, 16.

ing religion. In these circumstances, academic debate tends to gravitate toward questions of ideology and social influence.

This state of affairs may provide, however, an opportunity for religious believers to gain a fresh hearing in the university. If it is recognized that there is no neutral ground for deciding the meaning of a biblical text, then no position can claim objective truth or scientific impartiality. All positions involve some form of faith stance and group allegiance that is open to political evaluation. This includes not only the believing biblical scholar but also the secular biblical critic whose ultimate commitment is to the ideal of unencumbered inquiry fostered by the Enlightenment worldview. In a postmodern intellectual climate, everything is up for grabs.

What does a political analysis of a secular biblical scholar teach us? It would appear that such a scholar, ensconced in a secular academic environment, is free to pursue intellectual curiosity wherever it might lead. One would think that this situation is ideally suited to serve the radical pluralism of contemporary biblical studies. In fact, however, the demand to publish and the desire to obtain tenure involve the academic exegete in a highly political context that operates with its own beliefs, taboos, and tests of loyalty. The scholar whose *Sitz-im-Leben* is the quest for a permanent job is pressured to conform to the conventional wisdom of colleagues and book editors. This usually means treating Scripture as one ancient text among others. Neither the biblical claim to unique revelation nor the Bible's supernaturalistic worldview may be assumed as a matter of intellectual judgment. The belief that the Bible validates the traditions of living religious communities or that it answers the spiritual needs of modern people (or postmodern people for that matter) is studiously ignored.

This reflects the political situation of the American university. Universities are largely divorced from religious ties and obligations. They are for the most part insulated from accountability to religious demands by the institutional safeguards of academic freedom and tenure. It is no wonder that people in religious communities are suspicious when their children go off to college. "'An empire of invisible forces operates within the educational realm to move university study of religion' toward a minimizing of what to the church is primary and an ignoring as irrelevant of any claims for biblical revelation or authority."[7]

Curiously enough, in the wild and wooly world of postmodern sensibility, the freedom that the university affords secular biblical scholars may be

---

7. James D. Smart, *The Past, the Present, and the Future of Biblical Theology* (Philadelphia: Westminster, 1979), 153. Smart is quoting the New Testament scholar Paul Minear.

coming to an end. In contemporary academic culture, especially in America, the canonical authority of the classics of Western literary culture is increasingly under attack. In such a context, biblical criticism in the tradition of the Enlightenment worldview, which remains largely beholden to historical-critical method, may be hard-pressed to provide an adequate account of its social utility for university life. Its inevitable tendency is to make the Bible an artifact of an ancient civilization instead of the guiding document of a living community. Biblical criticism thus becomes the investigation of what Jon D. Levenson calls "an exotic culture." This places the biblical critic in a predicament. The critic is "at a loss to explain why *this* exotic culture is to be preferred over others or, for that matter, over our familiar culture, whose need for attention seems obvious."[8] As Levenson observes, with an unblinking eye toward the actual, concrete situation of the majority of professional biblical scholars:

> In an era of multiculturalism and budgetary constraint, this [problem] inevitably entails explaining how the relocation of commitment from a traditional religious sphere can maintain a place of relative privilege for the study of the Bible. Should the answer substitute a cultural for a religious motivation and center on the importance of the Bible in Western civilization, then, in the current climate, a defense of the importance of the West, at least for American students, is imperative. This is, of course, ironic in light of the tendency of historical criticism to think of itself as transcending particularism and debunking claims of privilege.[9]

Levenson confronts contemporary biblical scholars with the unavoidable social fact of their existence. Whether they are willing to acknowledge it or not, the truth is that biblical scholarship's reason for being has been "the residual momentum of religious belief" in Western society. Without some form of the community of faith, biblical criticism in the Enlightenment tradition is without persuasive warrant. Biblical criticism is able to accomplish many things, but it cannot create the tradition that gives it life. If it is to retain its status as an academic enterprise, biblical criticism must, in some way, serve the religious communities that find their origin in Holy Scripture. The problem facing the Enlightenment tradition of criticism, then, in whatever particular form or method it takes, is the inability to explain effectively the religious significance of its work. What makes the Bible religiously convincing is its continuing relevance to succeeding ages as "useful for teaching, for reproof,

---

8. "The Bible: Unexamined Commitments of Criticism," *First Things* 30 (1993): 25.
9. *Ibid.*, 33.

for correction, and for training in righteousness" (2 Tim. 3:16). The exposition of this continuing relevance is vital to the task of biblical scholarship if such scholarship is to engage in the quest for truth. Success at expositing the Bible as a document of the past is indisputable. But what, finally, is the point of it? If biblical criticism does not find a way to relate itself to the religious community, it will become not simply "ancillary" but "parasitic."[10]

The predicament of the secular biblical critic, then, is that in the end he or she lacks a viable communal base (which is also its political base) that provides it with the energy and relevance to pursue biblical studies. One scholar who anticipated this contemporary predicament of the academic biblical critic, making a distinguished career of examining it and responding to it, is Brevard Childs.

II. Biography

Brevard S. Childs was born in Columbia, South Carolina, on 2 September 1923, to Richard Austin and Reaux (Jones) Childs. The home in which the family lived for approximately five years was owned by Childs's maternal grandfather, born in 1850, president of a Columbia bank, and dubbed "the last Confederate" by his son-in-law. Most of the mother's family are buried in the old graveyard of Columbia's Trinity Church. The parents of Richard and of Reaux came from English stock, with a mixture of French and Dutch, the one family of Methodist and the other of Episcopal persuasion. The Childses' home contains a variety of old family portraits, one of "Uncle Eben," presumed killed at the battle of Chicamauga, and the other of grandfather Jones, an officer in the Spanish-American War.

In the summer of 1929 the Childs family moved to Flushing, New York, where Richard was to take up a post on Wall Street ("some timing!" writes the son, in obvious allusion to the stock market crash). In Flushing, the Childses attended the local Episcopal Church, but when the father heard that the First Presbyterian Church of Flushing had a minister from the South, the family promptly joined, thus becoming Presbyterians "by accident." Brevard attended grammar school in Flushing, and high school at Bayside, an institution closer to home and from which he graduated in January 1941. He spent the next two years at Queens College in New York City. Following service in the United States army from 1943 to 1945, he returned to academic studies in 1946, and received his Bachelor and Master of Arts degrees at the University

10. *Ibid.*

of Michigan in the spring of 1947. In that year Childs entered upon theological study at Princeton Theological Seminary in Princeton, New Jersey, and upon graduation in 1950 began four years of doctoral work at Basel University in Switzerland, which included a winter semester at Heidelberg in 1951.

On 7 August 1954, Brevard married Ann Taylor, a student of Mt. Holyoke College, whom he had met at Basel during her junior year abroad. The couple moved immediately to Mission House in Franklin, Wisconsin, a missionary center of the Reformed Church in the United States founded by a colony of German emigrants. Four years later, in the fall of 1958, Childs took up teaching duties at the Divinity School of Yale University in New Haven, at which he served as Sterling Professor of Divinity until 2000, the year of his retirement.

Writing of his early and later years, Childs assigns greatest influence to his parents and his close family circle. Initially, the Presbyterian Church exerted considerable influence on the youthful scholar, since "it took [him] some years to get beyond Hodge and Warfield." If getting beyond strict Calvinistic thought did not occur all at once, it no doubt climaxed in his years at Princeton, from which he recalls only a few, largely negative influences. Childs further writes that while in Europe he learned much from Gerhard von Rad, celebrated Old Testament scholar at Heidelberg. Despite his four years at Basel, however, it was only upon returning home and beginning to teach that Childs had a serious encounter with its most noted theologian, Karl Barth, whose influence was felt much later and came largely through reading.

Childs, recipient of numerous awards and prizes, and his wife Ann make their home at Bethany, Connecticut, and Cambridge, England.

III. The Irritant

What has exercised Childs throughout his life is the separation between the descriptive and constructive elements of biblical interpretation, that is, the distance between "Biblical Theology" as a primarily historical task *and* subsequent theological reflection, a distance celebrated, for example, by Krister Stendahl in his article on "Biblical Theology" in *The Interpreter's Dictionary of the Bible*. There Stendahl wrote that the "first and crucial task of biblical theology" was to limit the original text to what it meant. This was the "new phenomenon in biblical studies," a "mature growth of the historical and critical study of the scriptures." The following makes clear to what extent Stendahl had separated the two tasks:

This descriptive task can be carried out by believer and agnostic alike. The believer has the advantage of automatic empathy with the believers in the text — but his faith constantly threatens to have him modernize the material. . . . The agnostic has the advantage of feeling no such temptations, but his power of empathy must be considerable. . . . The meaning for the present — in which the two interpreters are different — is not involved.[11]

Childs totally rejected the separation. In an article written for the journal *Interpretation,* he asks:

Does not theology need normative as well as descriptive categories in order to execute its task? . . . Can the theological task of a commentator be exhausted when he remains on the level of the witness? Is there not a responsibility to penetrate to the substance toward which the text points?[12]

In his first major piece, *Biblical Theology in Crisis,* Childs answers his own question: "To the extent that the use of the critical method sets up an iron curtain between the past and the present, it is an inadequate method for studying the Bible as the church's Scripture."[13] In his commentary on Exodus he gives the reason for his answer: "The rigid separation between the descriptive and constructive elements of exegesis strikes at the roots of the theological task of understanding the Bible."[14] Separation between the two tasks belonged to that "sterile impasse" which resulted from a setting of limits in the nineteenth century.

Childs acknowledged he was not alone in his irritation, but shared it with others such as James Smart, Floyd Filson, and his colleague Paul Minear. Minear, for example, had argued that a method designed to treat events of the "old age" according to the operation of the laws of that age was incapable of understanding biblical history; that the task of the biblical theologian was to study the biblical point of view with "eyes of faith," to be addressed by God himself in a "final, ever-repeated act of creation, judgment and redemption."[15] Childs states that the irritation, the prescription for its removal in the use of biblical criticism, coupled with a robust theological perspective, is a

---

11. "Biblical Theology," in *The Interpreter's Dictionary of the Bible* (Nashville: Abingdon, 1962), 1:422; see also 418 and 425.

12. "Interpretation in Faith," *Interpretation* 18 (1964): 433, 436.

13. *Biblical Theology in Crisis* (Philadelphia: Westminster, 1970), 141-42; see Childs's remarks concerning the Uppsala University faculty as well as of Stendahl, 26 and 79.

14. *The Book of Exodus* (Philadelphia: Westminster, 1974), xiii.

15. Childs, *Biblical Theology in Crisis,* 44.

peculiarly American phenomenon.[16] He later discovered, in encounter with theologians of Europe — some of whom he heard in his student days but ignored — that it is not unique. For example, in a 1969 symposium held at Yale on Barth's theology, Childs admitted he had been typical of most biblical scholars and had not taken Barth seriously, but that he had now had a change of heart. Perhaps that discovery, more than what Childs shares with others in America, encouraged him to attempt a new way to interpret the Bible.

IV. The Prescription

A. History and Theology

In his construction of a biblical theology, Childs seeks to remove the irritant. But in doing so, he does not merely pay lip service to the historical task. Rather, he asserts that the descriptive lies at the heart of the theological task; that the fundamental criticism of Luther's or Calvin's exegesis, or even of the exegesis of Karl Barth, is that they did not execute the descriptive task with sufficient precision.[17] In the volume on Exodus, he writes that serious theological exposition of the biblical text requires attention to the entire range of problems involving text and source criticism, syntax and grammar, history and geography. In his New Testament as Canon he affirms the entire set of procedures to which the biblical text must be subjected before it can be understood, procedures involving the determination of milieu, date, authorship, addressees, literary growth, and the like. His criticism of Paul Ricoeur and his disciples is that their understanding of the Bible as a deposit of metaphors containing inherent powers by which to interpret present experience irrespective of their source, and thus their concern to illuminate what lies "ahead" of rather than behind the text, displays little or no interest in the text's historical development.[18] For this reason, Childs's reference to the reader's "religious stance" as playing a legitimate role "after" the descriptive task has been attended to, when the reader chooses whether or not to identify with the perspective of the text he is studying,[19] is not intended to distance the religious from the descriptive task. A century earlier, Adolf Schlatter had asserted the legitimacy of a "methodological atheism," which in the interest of begetting pure, genuine observation tabled

---

16. *Ibid.,* 21.
17. "Interpretation in Faith," 438, 440.
18. *Introduction to the Old Testament as Scripture* (Philadelphia: Fortress, 1979), 77.
19. *Ibid.,* 72-73.

the question of God "for a time" *(nur zeitweilig)*. But to exclude the question of God altogether, wrote Schlatter, rendered science a caricature and led to polemic against rather than submission to its object.[20]

In that wedding of criticism to theological reflection, however, Childs leaves no doubt that he gives priority to theology. In the 1969 symposium, he cited with approval Barth's giving the lion's share to theological reflection.

> Barth came to the Bible, from the outset, from a confessional standpoint. He confessed that the Old and New Testaments were Scriptures of the Church, that they contained the prophetic and apostolic Witness, that this was the normative Witness, and that in this context (as the Church had received it) one remembered how the Church fathers and the Church had heard the Word, and yet waited in expectation that the Word of God would become alive through the Holy Spirit for them.[21]

Childs concedes that the attempt at combining criticism and reflection is fraught with risk, a risk that some of his critics suggest has landed him in the fundamentalist aversion to critical method. In a review of *Biblical Theology in Crisis,* J. A. Sanders hints at his latent "biblicism."[22] In a testy review of *Introduction to the Old Testament as Scripture,* James Barr refers to Childs's "deep disillusionment with historical study," an attitude "deeply welcome to conservative opinion." Childs, writes Barr, creates a vacuum into which reactionary notions naturally flow, since he removes "the extrinsic critical effect of modern biblical study which was the main obstacle to these convictions."[23] In a volume written in 1987, and covering "all" contemporary biblical theologies, Manfred Oeming refers to the "two phases" in Childs's biblical-theological sojourn, the first marked by attention to critical method, the second and latest by aversion to traditions-historical inquiry, or "dogmatic flight" from the difficulties of historical work. Oeming writes:

> In recent years, the rejection and criticism of historical criticism, long since widespread in evangelistic-evangelical circles, has received support from

20. *Atheistische Methoden in der Theologie,* ed. Helmut Burkhardt and Gerhard Maier (Wuppertal: Brockhaus, 1985), 38, 46.

21. David L. Dickermann, ed., *Karl Barth and the Future of Theology* (New Haven: Yale Divinity School Association, 1969), 33.

22. "Childs' position might easily sponsor a kind of biblicism of its own, which he himself regrets in the early Biblical Theology Movement," writes Sanders in a review of *Biblical Theology in Crisis* in *The Union Seminary Quarterly Review* 26 (1971): 303.

23. "Childs' *Introduction to the Old Testament as Scripture,*" *Journal for the Study of the Old Testament* 16 (May 1980): 15, 23.

well-known representatives of the exegetical science. Stuhlmacher [Prof. Peter Stuhlmacher of Tübingen University] and Childs are merely exponents of the discontent or helplessness abroad in wide circles toward the value and results of historical-critical work.[24]

According to Oeming, this aversion may root in "good old American respect for positivism." According to Childs, however, it is precisely the wedding of the descriptive and constructive tasks that preserves the integrity of the descriptive task. In fact, the whole point of emphasizing the canon is "to stress the historical nature of the biblical witness."[25] Later, in an introduction to volume two of the translation of Childs's *Biblical Theology* into German, Oeming states that he has revised his opinion of Childs's work as reflective of philosophical naiveté and historical empiricism.[26]

B. Canon as Locus

For Childs "canon" is the locus at which the descriptive and constructive aspects of interpretation combine, the term "canon" functioning as cipher for that process by which the church's sacred writings were formed and by which they exercise their roles in the life of each generation of believers. The choice of the term "process" is deliberate since "canon" denotes the interpretive activity of those who not merely seek to identify with the received tradition but also to appropriate its message. For this reason, the received tradition is structured so as to enable it to perform a role in the life of each generation. In this regard, Childs concedes to adherents of the "newer criticism" in English literature that an interpreter "can" use only the final stage of literature as a legitimate context. But he sees the final stage as culminating or gathering up, and thus including, each level of the tradition's collection and of the reflection upon it, since at each level the hearer or reader has been confronted with the power of the content of the tradition.[27]

For lack of attention to this idea, some of Childs's reviewers contend

24. *Gesamt biblische Theologien der Gegenwart* (Stuttgart: Kohlhammer, 1987), 215-16; see 195-96.

25. *Introduction to the Old Testament as Scripture*, 71.

26. Brevard Childs, *Die Theologie der einen Bibel*, tr. Manfred and Christine Oeming (Freiburg and Basel: Herder, 1994, 1996).

27. Childs, *Biblical Theology in Crisis*, 98; cf. Childs's response in *Journal for the Study of the Old Testament* 16 (1980): 52; Childs, *The New Testament as Canon*, 27; and Childs, *Old Testament Theology in a Canonical Context* (Philadelphia: Fortress, 1986), 11, 14.

that he focuses rigidly on the last stage of the process, that is, on the "final literary text" apart from its antecedents. James Sanders expresses hesitation at Childs's focusing so much on the "final literary text," adding that although the traditions attained stability at points along the way, they were nevertheless adapted to the needs of succeeding generations.[28] Another reviewer queries, "Why must one necessarily designate the final transmitted form of a biblical book as intentional?" adding that Childs's approach "shrinks" the biblical witness by restricting the scope of God's action in history.[29] Manfred Oeming saw in Gerhard Maier, ultraconservative head of Tübingen's Bengel House, a striking analogy to Childs, for whom "the obligatory norm can only be the present text, the text actually given into our hand."[30] Other reviewers simply set Childs down as one more redaction critic. The author of a review in the *Expository Times* writes that the term "canonical" adds nothing to the sense; that "we are within the field of redaction criticism, although Childs frequently distinguishes his approach from that."[31] Of the reviewers consulted, precious few catch the connotation of process. One is Rudolf Smend of Göttingen, whose theological sojourn bears striking resemblance to that of Childs and who writes: "Childs is far from restricting [canon] to the collection of Biblical books in their more or less present form. He uses it in large measure of the pre-history of these books."[32]

"Process" and nothing else explains Childs's preference for the Masoretic Text of the Old Testament, in which more than one critic believes he detects a chink in his armor.[33] Childs insists that the history of the Old Testament text participates in the canonical process. He asserts that the Masoretic Text is not the canonical text but rather the "vehicle for its recovery" — it gives access to the text "held in common by ongoing religious communities." Because taking the canon seriously means to establish the level of the biblical literature "in accordance with its historical stabilization by the Jewish community," this "mutilated MT text" has the priority due to its standing in that community.[34]

---

28. "Biblical Criticism and the Bible as Canon," *Union Seminary Quarterly Review* 32 (1977): 163.

29. *Journal for the Study of the Old Testament* 16 (1980): 168, 170.

30. *Gesamt biblische Theologien,* 217.

31. Review of *The New Testament as Canon* in *The Expository Times* 97 (1986): 99.

32. "Questions about the Importance of the Canon in the Old Testament Introduction," *Journal for the Study of the Old Testament* 16 (1980): 47-48.

33. R. E. Murphy, "The Old Testament as Scripture," *Journal for the Study of the Old Testament* 16 (1980): 41: "One fails to see why a later generation of the People of the Book should be pinned down to a doubtful, if not erroneous, form of the text as normative"; cf. James A. Sanders, *Horizons in Biblical Theology* 2 (1980): 187, 188.

34. Childs, *Introduction to the Old Testament as Scripture,* 100, 101, 104, 106.

Childs has never abandoned the term "process." In 1985 he wrote that the formation of the canon involved a series of decisions affecting the shape of the literature; in fact, such distinctions as Albert Sundberg and Theodore Swanson drew between "Scripture" and "canon" limited "canon" to the final stages of a long and complex process begun in the preexilic period.[35] This "final form" of the text has the lion's share of attention because the total process could only be perceived when it had reached its goal. It is this "final form" that reflects the entire history of the believing community's interaction with its traditions.[36] For this reason, methods that concentrate on the preliterary shape of the biblical traditions and whatever "situation-in-life" of the Jewish or Christian community that shape reflected come under attack in Childs's work. Of Traditions-Historical work on the Old Testament Childs writes: "To seek to give theological autonomy to a reconstructed Yahwist source apart from its present canonical context is to disregard the crucial theological intention of the tridents of the tradition, and to isolate a text's meaning from its reception."[37]

To all of this Childs refuses to attach the designation "method." He specifically avoids such terms as "canon criticism" or "canonical criticism" precisely because they suggest the formulation of a method to supplement or replace others of its kind. The term "canon" (without the article) does not suggest a new exegetical technique but rather a *context* from which the literature is to be understood and interpreted. Attention to this point could have saved his critics space and effort.[38]

V. Canon and Church

Essential to Childs's definition of "canon" is the fact of its reception by the church. For if "canon" is where the descriptive and constructive meet, the locus for that meeting is the church as recipient of the canon. This involves a certain restriction, that is, a restriction to a discrete collection recognized by the Christian community as sacred scripture. For although the church's

---

35. *Ibid.*, 58-59.

36. *Ibid.*, pp. 75-76; Childs, "Response to Reviewers," *Journal for the Study of the Old Testament* 16 (1980): 54.

37. *Old Testament Theology in a Canonical Context*, 11.

38. *Introduction to the Old Testament as Scripture*, 16. In "Response to Reviewers," Childs writes (53): "Some of the misunderstanding of parts of my book stems from replacing my broad use of the term with a much narrower, traditional usage, and thus missing the force of the argument."

"hearing of the text" may not be divorced from "that other community of faith which lives from the same Bible," or from the "countless other stances outside of any commitment to faith or tradition," it nonetheless gives priority to a particular corpus because it believes that corpus testifies to the transcendent reality to which it owes its life.[39] On the other hand, the church as context spells extension, for by its juxtaposing of both the Old and the New Testament, the church has created something that is not restricted to the one or the other. Childs writes:

> The formation of a canon of Scripture is a recognition of the need for a context, different from both Testaments, in which the Christian church continues to wrestle in every new age with the living God who continues to confront his people through the ancient testimony of the prophets and apostles.[40]

This concept of "canon" in "context" has one eminent consequence for interpretation. In the practice of "biblical theology" as it developed after the First World War, the exposition of the one Testament was carried out independently of the other. The works of Gerhard von Rad and Rudolf Bultmann are primary examples. For Childs, the church as the context of "canon," the place of meeting for the descriptive and the constructive, requires a relation between the Old and New Testaments, precisely because the church confesses that it encounters the transcendent reality to which it owes its life through the testimony of the apostles *and* the prophets.[41] Childs goes so far as to speak of the "ontological relation" or "ontological correspondence" between the two Testaments — both functioning as vehicles for the divine revelation.[42]

VI. Canon and Confession

Childs faults academic biblical criticism, including the so-called "Biblical Theology Movement," represented by such figures as G. Ernest Wright (1909-74), John Bright (1908-89), and Reginald Fuller, for assuming that one comes to the biblical text from a vantage point outside it, thus failing to take the text

39. Childs, *The Book of Exodus*, ix; Brevard Childs, *Biblical Theology of the Old and New Testaments* (Minneapolis: Augsburg-Fortress, 1993), 8.
40. *Biblical Theology in Crisis*, 113; see also 112.
41. *Ibid.*, 113, 159.
42. "Interpretation in Faith," 440, 442.

seriously in its "canonical form."[43] Childs sees nothing illegitimate in such activity. He writes:

> The role of the Bible is not being understood simply as a cultural expression of ancient peoples, but as a testimony pointing beyond itself to a divine reality to which it bears witness. To speak of the Bible now as scripture further extends this insight because it implies its continuing role for the church as a vehicle of God's will. Such an approach to the Bible is obviously confessional. Yet the Enlightenment's alternative proposal, which was to confine the Bible solely to the arena of human experience, is just as much a philosophical commitment. . . . The basic hermeneutical issue at stake turns on the fact that no modern biblical theology can function without some other conceptual framework.[44]

At the 1969 symposium, Childs referred to Barth's complaint that one could not get *behind* the text, could not get at Scripture from a context other than the "canonical," since there was no neutral position from which to begin and from which to move from neutrality to commitment.[45]

Thus, Childs insists, there is no unbridgeable chasm between "hard-nosed," critical exegesis and the "ecclesiastical form" assigned the sacred writings. In fact, "penetrating theological exegesis" is rare among those who share little or nothing of the faith reflected in the literature.[46] The preface to Childs's commentary on the book of Exodus is as succinct a statement as he gives anywhere respecting the descriptive and interpretive task as joined at the locus of "canon" within the "context" of the Church:

> The purpose of this commentary is unabashedly theological. Its concern is to understand Exodus as scripture of the church. The exegesis arises as a theological discipline within the context of the canon and is directed toward the community of faith which lives by its confession of Jesus Christ.[47]

VII. Nothing but the Text

Childs insists that the canonical approach, with its requirement that the interpreter share the faith reflected in the literature, does not divert attention

43. Childs, *Biblical Theology in Crisis*, 102.
44. *Biblical Theology of the Old and New Testaments*, 9, 42.
45. Dickermann, *Karl Barth and the Future of Theology*, 32.
46. Childs, *The New Testament as Canon*, 21, 39.
47. *The Book of Exodus*, ix.

from the text. On the contrary, the interpreter is bound to the text in strenuous fashion. This is because the biblical text is understood to reflect nothing less than transcendent reality. According to Childs, it is other schools of thought that have to answer for their methods. The fundamentalist and the liberal seek to ground biblical truth on propositions *apart from the text.* The proponent of "salvation history" searches for continuity between the Testaments in events *behind the text,* requiring a process of critical reconstruction to extract the theological data from the text.[48]

Childs expresses appreciation for the "experiential-expressive category" used by his colleague George Lindbeck to sketch the theory of religion held by Bernard Lonergan (1904-84). According to Lonergan (as interpreted by Lindbeck), the objectivizing of common core experiences in biblical religions is not merely a symbolizing of those experiences, but has its source in the revealed will of God, thus ensuring its status as norm. Childs uses the category "full of insight" to distinguish his position from the liberal model.[49]

Childs may entertain the greatest reservation toward the so-called literary approach. For example, in his reference to an exegesis free of dogmatics or of faith as capable of being "equally" stifling and superficial, he cites with obvious approval George Steiner's "devastating" review of *The Literary Guide to the Bible* edited by Robert Alter and Frank Kermode. In that review Steiner had written:

> The separation . . . between a theological-religious experience of Biblical texts and a literary one is radically factitious. It cannot work. This is to say that the plain question of divine inspiration . . . must be faced squarely and unflinchingly. . . . The author of Job . . . was not producing "literature." Nor were those who bore witness to the "darkness upon the earth" the evening of Good Friday. A literary elucidation of such texts is legitimate and can be helpful, but only . . . if it tells us that that which it omits is the essential.[50]

With this sentiment Childs is in full agreement. Or again, when colleague Lindbeck offers his own "cultural-linguistic" approach in opposition to that of Lonergan, which he describes as creating a nest of problems, he draws Childs's fire:

48. Childs, *Biblical Theology of the Old and New Testaments,* 17-18.

49. *The New Testament as Canon,* 543; see George Lindbeck, *The Nature of Doctrine* (Philadelphia: Westminster, 1984), 31-32.

50. George Steiner, "The Good Books," *Religion and Intellectual Life* 6 (1989): 15-16; see Childs, *Biblical Theology of the Old and New Testaments,* 12; see also Robert Alter and Frank Kermode, eds., *The Literary Guide to the Bible* (Boston: Harvard University Press, 1987).

The attempt of many literary critics to by-pass the problem of biblical reality and refuse to distinguish between the text and the reality of its subject matter severely cripples the theological enterprise of Biblical Theology. It is basic to Christian theology to reckon with an extra-biblical reality. . . . [Lindbeck's] proposal of the text creating its own world — some would call it fictive world — into which the reader is drawn has its origins far more in high church liturgical practice than from the Bible.[51]

But if it is the text and nothing but the text that mirrors the divine reality, no single text or cluster of texts may be assigned that function in preference to others. Again, Childs is adamant: to seek a relation between Old and New Testaments means to take seriously the church's confession of a *canon of Scripture,* thus to reject any appeal to a "canon within the canon."[52]

The rejection of a canon within the canon does not mean that all texts are treated on the same level, or that inherited tradition is uncritically appropriated. Childs states that it is precisely the function of "canonical shaping" to render the received material in "different critical ways."[53] Again, Childs's reviewers furnish contradictory appraisals. Norman Porteous questions whether Childs's critical handling of the biblical witness is compatible with his insistence on canonical authority, and Luke Timothy Johnson refers to his inability to "let go of the historical and engage the theological," while Hans Hübner concurs that ultimately Childs flees the problems of historical criticism.[54]

VIII. Assessment

A. Canon and Encounter with God

We have arrived at the heart of Childs's concern: to render transparent the reality reflected in the text. In each piece he has turned to print, Childs has recited, repeated, accented, trumpeted, elucidated, adumbrated this concern — as if it were some elusive thing his reader were chronically apt to miss or over-

51. *Biblical Theology of the Old and New Testaments,* 20-21; see Lindbeck, *The Nature of Doctrine,* 32ff.

52. *Biblical Theology in Crisis,* 159.

53. *The New Testament as Canon,* 41-42.

54. See N. W. Porteous, review of *Biblical Theology in Crisis, The Scottish Journal of Theology* 25 (1971): 494; Luke Timothy Johnson, review of the same volume in *Commonweal* 120 (1993): 21; see also Hans Hübner, *Biblische Theologie des Neuen Testaments* (Göttingen: Vandenhoeck & Ruprecht, 1990), 70 n. 172.

look. In midst of the bulk of criticism and analysis, of historical recollection and dogmatic reflection, of exegesis and interpretation, Childs's single theme is that of the canon as the vehicle to encounter God. From the beginning of his work, Childs has argued that the final task of exegesis is to seek to hear the word of God; that since the divine reality to which the Bible witnesses is not confined to the historical past, historical tools are inadequate to exhaust the material.[55] In *Biblical Theology in Crisis*, he asserts:

> The canon marks the area in which the modern issues of life and death are defined in terms of what God has done and is doing, and what he demands as a response from his people. . . . The God of the Bible is not a theological system, but a living and acting Lord, the one with whom we have to do — now. *We are confronted, not just with ancient witnesses, but with our God who is the Eternal Present.*[56]

In *The New Testament as Canon*, Childs argues: "The theological issue turns on the Christian church's claim for the integrity of *a special reading which interprets the Bible within an established theological context and toward a particular end, namely the discerning of the will of God.*"[57] Or again: "The canonical interpreter stands within the received tradition, and, fully conscious of his own time-conditionality as well as that of the scriptures, strives *critically to discern from its kerygmatic witness a way to God which overcomes the historical moorings of both text and reader.*"[58] In *Biblical Theology of Old and New Testaments*, Childs says: "A major thesis of this book is that this basic problem in Biblical Theology can only be resolved by *theological reflection which moves from a description of the biblical witnesses to the object toward which these witnesses point, that is, to their subject matter, substance, or res.*"[59] And again: "*Scripture . . . points beyond itself to the reality of God. The ability to render this reality is to enter the 'strange new world of the Bible.'*"[60]

Of course, making the "subject matter," the "substance," or *res* transparent was not a matter left to criticism. For if the text itself was not the "generative force of truth," then its hearing, exposition, or criticism required confirmation by that very reality it intended to reflect: "A canonical context includes not only the scope of the sacred literature, but the means by which

---

55. "Interpretation in Faith," 440, 443-44.
56. *Biblical Theology in Crisis*, 219; see also 101-2; author's italics.
57. *The New Testament as Canon*, p. 37; author's italics.
58. *Ibid.*, 51-52; author's italics.
59. *Biblical Theology of the Old and New Testaments*, 80; author's italics.
60. *Ibid.*, 721; italics mine.

the reader engages the scriptures, namely an expectation of understanding through the promise of the Spirit."[61] Again: "Through the Spirit the reality to which the text points . . . is made active in constantly fresh forms of application."[62] Thus, when Childs refers to the "process" by which the canon achieved its authoritative form, or speaks of the "historical and theological forces" at work in the canon's growth, he has more than immanence in mind. It is the Spirit of God that renders the Scripture medium of encounter with God in each new generation of faith. For this reason, there is no avenue to the Christ worshiped by the Christian church apart from the biblical testimony. And for this reason Childs approves James Sanders's broadening of the definition of canon to include a process, but opposes his explanation of the canon's growth as a search for identity in times of crisis. He challenges Walter Brueggemann's substitution of the interpreter for the text as the decisive tradent of the norm. And his quarrel with Peter Stuhlmacher of Tübingen has to do with the latter's substitution of the Old Testament's "vertical, existential dimension" for its construal as a "horizontal stream of tradition from the past," its witness limited to its effect on subsequent writers.[63] James Barr, like others, had argued that the "actual biblical period," not the later world of canonization, should be the interpretive basis.[64] In the parlance of the sixteenth century, there is something *schwärmerisch* or unhinged about these attempts to connect the normative to the existential or the interpretive, to the history of the tradition's effects, or to "the actual biblical period," presumably recoverable by means of historical science.

B. Forebears

Childs admitted that in his 1970 sketch of the problems of Biblical Theology he "had not thrown the net wide enough," that it had only slowly begun to dawn on him that everything turned on how the material was to be understood.[65] Just as slowly or gradually may have dawned the consciousness that others had been ahead of him moving toward the same goal. For example, Irenaeus had formulated a framework for interpretation that sought to join the church with the living voice of God according to the truth of its apostolic

61. Childs, *The New Testament as Canon*, 40.
62. Childs, *Biblical Theology of the Old and New Testaments*, 724.
63. *Ibid.*, 72 and 77; *Introduction to the Old Testament as Scripture*, 57.
64. "Childs' *Introduction to the Old Testament as Scripture*," *Journal for the Study of the Old Testament* 16 (1980): 14.
65. *Biblical Theology of the Old and New Testaments*, xv.

content. And Origen sought to relate the two Testaments theologically in terms of the selfsame divine reality that was its subject matter. Augustine understood the impact of the biblical message as evoking an existential dimension to faith. For Luther, the application of the gospel to the hearer was not an additional level of meaning, but an integral part of the one transforming word of the gospel. But of these "ancients" Childs seems to prefer Calvin as clearest:

> God, to instruct the church, not merely uses mute teachers but also opens his own most hallowed lips. Not only does he teach the elect to look upon a god, but also shows himself as the God upon whom they are to look. . . . God, the Artificer of the universe, is made manifest to us in Scripture. . . . The highest proof of Scripture derives in general from the fact that God in person speaks in it. . . . Above human judgment we affirm with utter certainty . . . that [Scripture] has flowed to us from the very mouth of God by the ministry of men.[66]

As for the "moderns," it is chiefly Barth with whom Childs stands together in the fight — as his reviewers are never slow to point out. In fact, writes Patrick Miller, Childs's indebtedness to Barth and the Reformers is even greater than his explicit references suggest. And Oeming stated that Childs's notion of the entire canon as the one, equally valid word of God within the one, unified community of faith is more suggestive of a piece of Barthian dogmatics than of any kind of tenable historical judgment.[67] In fact, Barth's exposition of Genesis in *Church Dogmatics* III/1 illustrates what Childs is after: the tendency always to "move down, to move through, and talk about the transparency," to confront the reality of the material in such a massive way as to confront God. In midst of his exegesis of the Genesis "saga" Barth writes:

> If we do not know the God of Israel, the Father of Jesus Christ, who is Himself Jesus Christ in concealment, how can we possibly understand the speaking and acting Subject of the biblical creation saga? How can we realize what it means that the reference here is to a real Creator and real creation? How can we differentiate between myth and saga, or between this saga and others? But to know this God, and in this way to realize the abso-

---

66. *Calvin's Institutes: A New Compend*, ed. Hugh T. Kerr (Louisville: Westminster, 1989), 28, 30, 31; Childs, *Biblical Theology of the Old and New Testaments*, 32, 35, 38, 44-46.

67. Patrick Miller, review of *Biblical Theology in Crisis*, *Journal of Biblical Literature* 90 (1971): 210; see Susan E. Schaeffer's review of *Biblical Theology of the Old and New Testaments* in *Lutheran Forum* 29 (1995), 58; Oeming, *Gesamt biblische Theologien*, 204.

lute uniqueness of the saga which speaks of Him, is to know Him as one's own God. . . .[68]

C. The Misapprehension

Once upon a time an entire generation sang requiem for an epoch in which the Bible was read objectively, loosed from the commitment for or against it. At that time, Adolf Schlatter had insisted that the act of thinking followed living, for which reason one's own life-situation had to be incorporated into the historical putting of the question. As far as Schlatter was concerned, that life-situation was given beforehand, in the context of the effects of the history of Jesus Christ.[69] Theology, wrote Rudolf Bultmann, required a mode appropriate to its object. It could not be carried on "out of curiosity" or for the purpose of earning a living, but as a "venture in which we ourselves are at risk." For if God was the object of faith and accessible only to it, then a science apart from or merely alongside faith saw neither God nor faith.[70] And Hans-Georg Gadamer, whose notion of "process" in the transmission of the tradition Manfred Oeming found "closely related" to that of Childs, had written:

> The gospel does not exist in order to be understood as a merely historical document, but to be taken in such a way that it exercises its saving effect. This implies that the text, whether law or gospel, if it is to be understood properly — i.e., according to the claim it makes — must be understood at every moment, in every concrete situation, in a new and different way. Understanding here is always application.[71]

This insistence on the Bible as requiring a decision on its behalf derived from the conviction that one encountered its "Object" — God — through it. And for that idea, the older generation of rebels had harked back to forebears to which Childs is making his appeal.

Now biblical research is being attempted as if that earthquake of the "teens" and "twenties" had never occurred. For this reason, almost all of

---

68. *Church Dogmatics*, ed. G. W. Bromiley and T. F. Torrance (Edinburgh: T&T Clark, 1956-77), III/1:92.

69. Cf. Ulrich Luck's introduction to Adolf Schlatter, *Zur Theologie des Neuen Testaments und zur Dogmatik*, Theologische Bücherei (Munich: Kaiser, 1969), 41:13, 17-19, 24-25.

70. Rudolf Bultmann, *What Is Theology?* tr. Roy A. Harrisville (Minneapolis: Fortress, 1998), 20, 22, 84, 102, 155, 160.

71. *Truth and Method*, tr. rev. by Joel Weisheimer and Donald G. Marshall (New York: Crossroad, 1990), 309.

Childs's critics have either misunderstood, half understood, or ignored, clumsily or artfully, what has persistently served as his primary concern. In what he may imagine to be a partial concession to Childs's program, Porteous writes that "one can readily agree that the Bible provides the classic and indispensable witness to God's concern and action."[72] Terence Fretheim summarizes Childs's position respecting the Bible as "most fundamentally a witness to God's word and action, supremely embodied in Jesus of Nazareth."[73] In his review, Sanders writes of Childs's call for a new Biblical Theology movement "on the basis of a biblical understanding of the ways one might contemporize the church's essential traditions." In another he describes canonical criticism as stressing the Bible's ontology as a "paradigm of God's work" from which we may construct paradigms for our own.[74] Johnson writes that Childs has not grasped that what theology engages is the living God "encountered in human experience."[75]

For Childs the Bible is more than a classic and indispensable witness to God's concern and action, however embodied; its understanding more than a contemporizing of the church's traditions; its ontology more than a paradigm, and more than a documenting of the human experience. For Childs the Bible, in the context of the church's confession, is the instrument of encounter with the living God. Sanders' statement to the effect that "Childs sees [the] canon as God's Word,"[76] though imprecise, is as close to Childs's primary concern as his reviewers will get.

What would it have cost his critics to take note of that goal which he has unswervingly sought to reach? How would such attention have spelled compromise? Or are the references to Childs's indebtedness to Barth, or the disclaimer that he had produced anything new,[77] a screening or a bowdlerizing of what in less discrete company would have been a forthright frontal attack: "This fellow believes that the Bible not merely talks about God, but actually mediates encounter with God, and has gone and attempted a scheme calculated to facilitate that encounter"? Why not simply characterize the notion as

72. Review of *Biblical Theology in Crisis* in *The Scottish Journal of Theology* 25 (1971): 494.

73. Review of *Biblical Theology of the Old and New Testaments* in *The Catholic Biblical Quarterly* 56 (1994): 326.

74. Review of *Biblical Theology in Crisis* in *Union Seminary Quarterly* 26 (1971): 304, and "Biblical Criticism," *Union Seminary Quarterly* 32 (1977): 164.

75. *Commonweal* 120 (1993): 21.

76. *Horizons in Biblical Theology* 2 (1980): 181.

77. Cf. Miller, *Journal of Biblical Literature* 90 (1971): 210; James Barr, *Journal for the Study of the Old Testament* 16 (1980): 12.

an absurdity? Fretheim may be the least squeamish in taking on Childs directly. He writes that Childs's formulations of the Bible's witness "so often reflect a world other than the one in which I live."[78] Fair enough. But life in the one world should not render impossible the apprehension of life in another. As a matter of fact, that "other world" has more than one inhabitant. One of the most provocative thinkers of the age speaks of the notion of a "spirit" in or "behind" the letter as a "relevant presumption." Just this presumption, he asserts, underwrites the concept of the "iconic," the belief that the icon is not so much a representation of the sacred person or scene as its "immediate manifestation," its "epiphany." And as for "canon," whatever mediates that immediacy or epiphany to the reader to the point of altering the "texture of consciousness" is "canonical."[79]

D. The Question of Method

Where the "guild" might have attacked is at the point of whether or not any construal in biblical interpretation can facilitate encounter with God. A previous generation was more generous in these matters. The fact that Barth disparaged critical method did not stop Schlatter and Bultmann from recognizing its capacity to at least set the scene for, if not actually to create, the encounter with God. Schlatter insisted that historical research, rather than putting faith in question, actually uncovered its effectiveness. And in his review of Barth's commentary on Romans, Bultmann has this to say:

> When in exegeting Romans I detect tensions and contradictions, places high and low; when I take pains to show how Paul is dependent on Jewish theology or popular Christianity. . . . I am not just carrying on historical-philological criticism, but am doing it from the viewpoint of *showing where and how the subject matter is expressed, in order to lay hold of the subject matter* which is greater even than Paul.[80]

Of course, for all his commitment to method, Schlatter was damned as a pietist whose faith in the Bible rendered him unfit for scientific work, and

78. *Catholic Biblical Quarterly* 56 (1994): 326.

79. *George Steiner: A Reader* (New York: Oxford University Press, 1984), 85, 91; see Steiner's *Real Presences* (Chicago: University of Chicago Press, 1989) with its advocacy of the "logocentric" view throughout, i.e., the view according to which words have referents beyond themselves.

80. Jürgen Moltmann, *Anfänge der dialektischen Theologie,* Theologische Bücherei (Munich: Kaiser, 1962-63), 17:141-42, author's italics.

Bultmann's method appeared to reduce the biblical text to one long, elongated, and pendulous disquisition on self-understanding, to the point where he was unable to speak of God apart from human existence.

It may be that Childs has erred in supposing that his theological method could render the divine reality transparent. It may be that the "guild's" preoccupation with perspectives, stances, postures, methods, and methodologies, the resulting, contemporary malaise, and the dizzying number and variety of solutions served up to us now are nothing but the tale of a pursuit of something that can never be caught. It may be that the passion and power of exposition can never be communicated, at least not to the point where "epiphany" occurs. It may be that exegesis, interpretation, is not a science, a *Wissenschaft* that allows some space to intuition or divination, but an art that uses rules only to fuel or focus its passion. George Steiner asks, "Can a logic of immanence account for the coming into being of the fact of meaningful form?" and he answers:

> A triple echo may be of help. The precept is in Augustine; the rephrasing is by Boehme; it is Coleridge who transcribes: "I warn all Inquirers into this hard point to *wait* — not only to plunge forward before the Word is *given* to them, but not even to paw the ground with impatience. For in a deep stillness only can this truth be apprehended." . . . There is no mysticism in this monition; only the elusive light of common sense.[81]

Isaiah Berlin (1909-97) echoes the sentiment in an essay on "political judgment." When we speak of statesmen, Berlin writes, we resort to metaphors; we speak of a good political eye, or nose, or ear — "a species of direct acquaintance" distinct from description, calculation or inference. Refuting Freud's dictum that while science cannot explain everything, nothing else does, Berlin stated that in ordinary life, those are Utopian who place excessive faith in laws and methods derived from alien fields, mostly from the natural sciences, and apply them with great confidence and somewhat mechanically.[82]

Childs is hardly unaware of any of this. In his response to reviewers in *Horizons in Biblical Theology* he includes a telling concession calculated to make liars of all who attack him for his rigidity:

> Slowly I began to realize that what made von Rad's work so illuminating was not his method as such, but the theological profundity of von Rad him-

---

81. *Real Presences*, 224.
82. Isaiah Berlin, "On Political Judgment," *The New York Review of Books* 43 (1996): 30.

self. The same observation holds true for Wolff and Zimmerli. I am convinced that no amount of methodological refinement will produce a quality of interpretation which that generation achieved whose faith in the God of Israel was hammered out in the challenge to meet the Nazi threat against the life of the church.[83]

Brevard Childs would scarcely apply the same observation to himself. The question, however, is whether or not anyone else in this generation has achieved what Childs has achieved by virtue of passionate commitment to the Scriptures as the instrument of encounter with the living God. Apart from that commitment, we are, as Steiner insisted, left only with immanence, deprived of whole dimensions of thought and creativity, indifferent to theology and metaphysics, dead to aesthetic creation and reception, and ultimately dead to God.

83. *Horizons in Biblical Theology,* 208.

15

Two Traditions of Historical Criticism

I. The Nagging Question

With the theologies of Paul Ricoeur and Brevard Childs, we have come to the end of our story. Both scholars are sufficiently contemporary to bring the theological conversation to the present.

Ricoeur is especially significant in that he provides a vantage point from which to consider the dizzying array of recent trends. Various forms of liberation theology, including feminist theology, apply a Marxist hermeneutic to the reading of the Bible. Ricoeur knows what it means to appropriate Marx, as well as other critics of Christianity such as Nietzsche and Freud, and has reflected on the hermeneutical consequences of such appropriation. Phenomenology, structuralism, and linguistic analysis seek to uncover enduring anthropological and mythic patterns of meaning that may be found within and beneath the biblical text. Ricoeur is a helpful guide, having been something of a twentieth-century pioneer in the use of these methods. Literary criticism concentrates attention on the received text of the Scriptures. Here again, Ricoeur is one of the masters of the craft.

Brevard Childs is himself responsible for a contemporary trend. Like literary criticism, canonical criticism attends to the received biblical text. The method has proven especially attractive to those who recognize the enormous cost of historical criticism to the life of the church and yet who refuse to abandon it. The Lutheran Carl Braaten speaks for many when he observes in a symposium on Bible and church sponsored by the Center for Catholic and Evangelical Theology:

Which hermeneutic is best qualified to understand the Scriptures? That of the autonomous scholar whose private ideological commitment is disguised as objective scientific research or that of a community of faithful memory that forthrightly acknowledges the Scriptures as its divinely inspired authority? Brevard Childs's "canonical method" of biblical interpretation includes the church as intrinsic to a hermeneutic of historical inquiry in search of the true subject matter of the Scriptures.[1]

As Braaten makes clear, the suspicion of historical criticism is not confined to those on the Evangelical Right in the church. There is a growing sense that the spiritual inadequacies of the method should no longer be accepted as the price of doing scholarly business. The nagging question is, What role will historical criticism play in the future of biblical theology? Certainly, the discipline will not disappear. It has accomplished too much for that to happen. It does seem evident, however, that, "the Enlightenment model of historical criticism has become increasingly problematic."[2]

II. The Enlightenment Tradition

Historical criticism in the Enlightenment tradition relies on rational, scientific investigation to reveal the content of Scripture. In its ideal form, this tradition believes that it is able to go beyond the reach of cultural presuppositions and philosophical commitments to establish the historical meaning of biblical texts once and for all. It is this tradition of scholarship that is being called into question.

We share this suspicion. By telling the story of the development of historical-critical method through an analysis of major figures who have engaged it and reflected theologically on its significance, we hope we have given this suspicion a firm foundation in the historical record itself. The fundamental lesson of the story we have told is this: no method of interpretation can transcend its cultural milieu. This means that no biblical critic can escape the reach of history to achieve true meaning by the use of reason and critical method. There is no "absolute moment" in which the interpreter of the Bible becomes the objective outsider who exercises disinterested awareness, uncovers the facts, and pronounces final judgment. Yet this was the primary assumption

---

1. Carl E. Braaten and Robert W. Jenson, eds., *Reclaiming the Bible for the Church* (Grand Rapids: Wm. B. Eerdmans, 1995), xi.

2. William Baird, "Biblical Criticism," in *The Anchor Bible Dictionary*, ed. David Noel Freedman (New York: Doubleday, 1992), 1:736.

that shaped the Enlightenment tradition of criticism from its origins in Spinoza and Reimarus through its development in liberal Protestantism in the work of Schleiermacher, Strauss, Baur, and Troeltsch.

Throughout our study, we have used history to expose the historical critics. Especially important to the character and shape of the Enlightenment tradition was the context in which the discipline of historical-critical method originated. In terms of its philosophical presuppositions, this origin is inextricably connected to the emergence of classical liberal politics, beginning in the seventeenth century, which created the Enlightenment worldview of Western culture.

It was in the seventeenth century, in the aftermath of one hundred years of bloody conflict from which no European nation was exempt, that the modern system of sovereign nation-states emerged and finally won complete ascendancy over institutional Christianity. Before that time, institutional Christianity had defined the worldview and much of the structure of European civilization. Europe was, as Ernst Troeltsch put it, "a Church-civilization, based on the belief in an absolute and immediate Divine revelation and the embodiment of this revelation in the Church as the organ of redemption and moral discipline." The political power inhering in this religious vision was enormous. The "Divine will" was conceived as "everywhere, immediately present, exactly recognizable, having as its organ an infallible institution."[3]

The Augustinian dogmatic tradition undergirded this vision theologically. It taught that human beings are corrupted by original sin and in need of control by the God-given authority of government and church. Government held the power of the sword to punish evildoers. The church held the keys to the kingdom. Behind government and church stood the mystery of the divine predestinating will that was believed to weave the chaos of world events into a web of necessity and design. Virtually nothing escaped this theological vision; if it did, it was labeled heresy.

While the Reformation assaulted the legal power of both prince and priest, it did not finally break them. As for the Augustinian dogmatic tradition that sustained church civilization, the Reformation meant, if anything, an intensification of its claims concerning predestination and a strict defense of its teaching on grace. "To say that Augustine exaggerates in speaking against heretics," said Luther at the beginning of the Reformation, "is to say that Augustine tells lies almost everywhere. This is contrary to common knowledge."[4] Politically, the effect of the Reformation — whatever its original intention — was

3. Ernst Troeltsch, *Protestantism and Progress* (Philadelphia: Fortress, 1986), 21.
4. *LW*, 31:9.

to divide both government and church, unleashing and arming the terrible force of religious passions. At the beginning of the Reformation, Erasmus prophesied that the ensuing conflict would compare to the ruthless battle of Achilles and Hector. He was right.

In order to survive, the European states sought to secure their political superiority over religion in the Peace of Westphalia (1648). The Glorious Revolution in England and the constitutional settlement (1688) were part of the same process. These settlements permitted the states of Europe to exercise Erastian dominance over rival confessions within their borders. The interest of nation-states in controlling doctrinal conflict was understood — at least by leading political theorists of the intellectual elite — in utilitarian fashion. They argued that the needs of the civil order transcended the commitment to absolute religious claims. If one were forced to choose between peace and dogmatic truth, peace was the rational choice. Since the Bible was the source of dogmatic truth, it too had to be made subordinate to political requirements. Historical-critical method became the means to accomplish this end. Historical criticism thus emerged in the exigencies of political crisis. It was a child of the Wars of Religion. Its hermeneutic of suspicion was tied to the demands of the new political philosophy.

Spinoza and Reimarus pursued the objectives of the new philosophy by attempting to go behind the text of the Bible to explicate its narrative exclusively as a story of political relationships. This fundamental move was grounded in the presupposition, taken from ancient Epicurean philosophy, that the essence of institutional religion is the priestly manipulation of the fear of the gods by means of dogma and ritual. Ruthlessly employing this presupposition in the examination of the "history" of the biblical text, Spinoza, Reimarus, and their followers sought to neutralize the authority of the Bible as revelation. They interpreted Scripture as the ideological account of a particular people of the ancient past whose religion and culture could be exhaustively explained by the discovery of mundane causes. They also claimed that traditional dogmatic exegesis of the Bible was driven by a nefarious purpose: to insure the political power of the ecclesiastical hierarchy. As an exercise in the manipulation of the fear of the gods, traditional exegesis was not a valid path to a genuine understanding of the biblical record. The figure of Jesus was usually exempted from this criticism and presented as a universal teacher of rational morality who was opposed to institutional religion.

In the classic form it took at the time of its emergence, the discipline of historical criticism projected the ideal of the independent, rational scholar, freed from the prejudicial ties to the *ancien régime* and the dominant religious community. Spinoza, the stateless cosmopolite hounded by Jew and

Christian alike, and Reimarus, the secret writer, wary of the fanaticism that underlies conventional opinion, have both come down to us as the heroes of the new historical criticism. They have inspired generations of scholars as examples of individualistic, prescient scholars, unencumbered by dogmatic commitments, who envisioned a more humane society. In one way or another, Schleiermacher, Baur, Troeltsch, and, most of all, Strauss conformed to this same image.

It is not surprising that biblical critics have been pictured this way. From the seventeenth to the nineteenth centuries, the imperative of intellectual integrity forced aspiring biblical scholars to oppose the fundamental claims of inherited Augustinian orthodoxy, especially as these claims were intertwined with the politics of throne and altar. The battle for freedom from the Bible was a fight against the ideological use of the Bible to support a governing elite. It was a battle for civic equality and individual rights. Against the orthodox assertions that human nature is corrupt, that salvation requires supernatural intervention, and that human fate is in the hands of an electing God, the Enlightenment tradition of historical criticism embraced the tenets of the emerging Enlightenment worldview. Humanity is perfectible. It is capable, solely by the light of reason, to bring about a new, just society. The dark, predestinating will of God is not the necessity of all things. On the contrary, the true context of human life and behavior is the divine bestowal of freedom. Freedom is the first and essential condition of the good life on earth. This means freedom of the mind from superstition, from the destructive force of religious passion, and freedom in the civil realm from the arbitrary oppression of political and ecclesiastical authorities. The Enlightenment worldview exalted reason over tradition. The academic scholar, as the self-chosen arbiter of all things reasonable, became the judge of all things religious.

These original impulses that gave rise to the Enlightenment tradition of historical criticism explain much of what has followed in the development of historical-critical method in liberal theology. From Spinoza through Troeltsch to much of contemporary scholarship that is tied to the university departments of religion, historical criticism has concentrated its effort to understand Scripture by attending to the period of biblical composition and searching for temporal causes to explain the dimensions of biblical faith. The "belief system" of the people of the Bible has been interpreted as the culture-bound effort, borne of contingent events, to comprehend the mystery of existence. The scholarly elite that examines this ancient effort at understanding assumes that it has the power *to go behind* religious claims to uncover their latent meaning and human motivation. It asserts its independence of dogma and ritual. It professes to have deeper knowledge of the Bible than religious communities that adhere to the authority of the Bible. In all of these tasks, the purveyors of the Enlightenment tradition of historical criticism seek to separate the "meaning" of the Bible from the "truth" to which they give their allegiance. This is precisely what Spinoza intended historical-critical method should do when he invented it. The method has conformed to his intentions.

Spinoza and Reimarus, to be later followed by David Friedrich Strauss, knew why historical criticism was relevant in their age. It was an agent of destruction whose purpose was to nullify the arbitrary political power of those who used the Bible to legitimate their authority. For good or for ill, this task was largely accomplished in the nineteenth century. This success did not necessarily entail the wholesale rejection of Christian faith. Beginning with Schleiermacher, we see the emergence of a liberally spirited Christian elite who conceived what John Stroup has called a "nonecclesiastical *Christentum*" that was ready to make peace with the Enlightenment.[5] By 1900 this group so dominated German academic life and the professional bureaucracy of the German state that liberal Protestantism was no longer a rebel against throne and altar, but a primary defender of a new establishment: a secularized middle class dedicated to the elevation of German culture in which religion was intellectualized and privatized, and for which Christian faith functioned as ideological support. Protestant students flocked to Germany from abroad to learn the new liberal theology. They carried back to their homelands the message and techniques of historical criticism, eagerly adapting them to the needs of progressive cultural factions within their own denominations and societies. Through trials and tribulations, wars and cultural changes, this liberal theology has been tenacious in its hold on the imagination of biblical scholars. It has been eminently successful in the fulfillment of its original mandate. For significant portions of the Christian intellectual elite in the West, Christianity has been made to conform to the tenets of the Enlightenment worldview.

Given this historical success — that is to say, given the fact that the old battle against "church civilization" has been won — what is the theological task of historical criticism today? Thousands of people spend long years training in the method and practice of historical criticism as their life's work. What is the purpose, especially in a society where the Bible has lost its influence for large portions of the cultural elite?

To begin to answer this question honestly, scholars in the Enlighten-

---

5. "The Idea of Theological Education at the University of Berlin: From Schleiermacher to Harnack," in *Schools of Thought in the Christian Tradition,* ed. Patrick Henry (Philadelphia: Fortress, 1984), 159. See also 157.

ment tradition need to examine not only the "meaning" of the Bible but the "truth" to which they pledge their intellectual loyalty. We have learned from the examples we have studied that what has functioned as truth for those who stand in the Enlightenment tradition has been the cultural assumptions that have dominated their social milieu. These assumptions too often have operated as uncritical criteria of judgment; indeed, they have served as the equivalent of "revelation." Whether it was deistic rational religion (Spinoza and Reimarus), romantic devotion to feeling (Schleiermacher), the Hegelian dialectic (Strauss and Baur), or the demands of historicism (Troeltsch), the Enlightenment tradition has been motivated by its need to make apology for its "faith" in the Enlightenment worldview. This faith has gone so deep that it has led its army of believers either to the wholesale rejection of biblical religion or the radical resymbolization of orthodox faith according to the demands of the prevailing culture. J. Gresham Machen was right. What we have in the Enlightenment tradition of criticism is nothing less than another religion that supplants biblical faith.

The chronic hostility of the Enlightenment tradition toward religious communities and their creeds and its need to impose its own faith in place of them is, in our view, the key factor that is responsible for the continuing suspicion of historical-critical method in the church, even among mainline denominations that train their clergy in its use. This factor, above all others, continues to fuel the war of the worldviews. This war has led today to what Luke Timothy Johnson calls "a crisis in pedagogy" concerning the teaching of the Bible that plagues biblical scholarship in the university. This crisis "has little to do with constraints imposed on scholars from the outside. It has much to do with the emptiness of biblical scholarship apart from communities for whom these ancient texts have real-life significance."[6]

III. The Augustinian Tradition

Historical criticism in the Enlightenment tradition, then, bears a problematical and tension-filled relation to the church. But this does not exhaust the possibilities of the method. There is also the story of historical criticism of the Bible in the Augustinian tradition. This tradition of scholarship began slowly in the confessional neopietist revival in the mid-nineteenth century when scholars such as von Hofmann, a student of Schleiermacher, took to heart the confessional protest against the cultural hegemony of Enlighten-

6. *The Real Jesus* (San Francisco: Harper, 1996), 75-76.

ment ideas in German university life and among the German Protestant clergy. The exercise of historical-critical method is necessary, said von Hofmann, but it must be in service to the church and its tradition. It is through the experience of rebirth in the grace of Jesus Christ that the believer practices the method with full integrity. Von Hofmann's allegiance to church and dogma did not entail an apology for throne and altar. Although his scheme of *Heilsgeschichte* might later be misused, especially in a demonic secularized form, his actual employment of it in his own theology was to reassure the believer in the knowledge of God's saving grace. The history of the church is a unique history within the parade of human events. It teaches not the fear of God and the authority of hierarchy, but the promise and fulfillment of God's word that brings about new life and the empowerment of God's people. Within this dogmatic affirmation, made by faith through the Holy Spirit, historical criticism of the Bible carries out its task.

In the view of Adolf Schlatter, it is impossible to claim scholarly objectivity in the interpretation of Scripture. This is because it is of the essence of the Bible to reach out across the ages to evoke faith or unbelief. The Bible seeks no middle ground. It challenges the entire cultural habitat, including the individual's place in it. The Bible thus affects the total person, mind and spirit, calling that person to decision. That interpretation involves the personal self may make the scholar who seeks the security and distance of the speculative mind-set distinctly uncomfortable. So be it. The responsible biblical scholar simply has to reckon with the fact that his or her fundamental presuppositions will be examined, including those inherited from the Enlightenment worldview. That the Bible can do this, and do it in unpredictable ways, arises from its inherent quality as the word of God.

J. Gresham Machen is a transitional figure in our story whose argument against liberal theology turns the tables on the Enlightenment tradition. Much of the force of that tradition had been its political critique of the orthodox use of the Bible. By the time Machen arrived on the scene, liberal theology itself enjoyed cultural hegemony and the privileges of establishment. It is the "fundamentalist" Machen who stands as a witness to the historical particularity of the gospel and the otherness of Jesus as a figure who does not conform to the anthropology and philosophy of the age. The external grounding of the Christian proclamation in the narrative integrity of the biblical record is the core of Machen's argument. The New Testament proclaims the Lordship of Jesus Christ. One may affirm this proclamation or deny it. What cannot be done is to transform it or resymbolize it into something else. To do so is an act of arbitrary subjectivity. Further, it is the unethical manipulation of the common understanding of inherited religious language that denies the perspicuity of Scripture. Historical criticism is no "science" if it ignores the "facts" of what the Bible says. The biblical narrative of creation, fall, incarnation, cross, and resurrection cannot be gotten behind in order to make something new. The true identity of Christianity is to be found in the public record of its creedal declarations.

Historical criticism pursued for the purpose of exposing *what the Bible says* is the hallmark of the work of Bultmann and Käsemann. They engaged in the vocation of biblical scholarship against the backdrop of two world wars, which led both of them to a harsh reappraisal of the Enlightenment worldview. Bultmann and Käsemann could each make radical assessments of biblical claims, testing the limits of orthodox faith. But there can be no doubt that in their work the exercise of historical-critical method is inextricably connected to the proclamation of the church filtered through confessional allegiance to the Bible as the word of God. Humanity is in bondage to the will. It is in rebellion against God. Salvation comes through the word of Christ alone and his cross. This word of God conforms the world to itself, not itself to the world. The word offers no temporal guarantees, but requires that human beings confront the exigencies of existence without false comfort or intellectual illusion. For all the criticism that Bultmann receives for his use of Heidegger, it must be remembered that what finally attracts Bultmann to existential philosophy is its articulation of the desperate plight of the human being who faces the reality of death without protection. This is Augustinian to the core. That is to say, it stands within the dominant religious tradition of Western Christendom. And his greatest student, Ernst Käsemann, is imbued with the same urgent sense of the wretchedness of the human condition. The answer to this wretchedness is the gospel of Jesus Christ. It calls the church into the world, not to undergird the power structure of a renewed "church civilization," but as the gathering of the faithful who hear the word and witness to God who wins back the world to himself through the cross.

What we learn from Bultmann (at least on occasion) and Käsemann (on all occasions) is that, when all is said and done, historical criticism of the Bible is never able to go beyond establishing the Easter-faith of the first disciples.[7] The "science" of historical-critical method establishes the "fact" that *the disciples* believed that Christ had been raised from the dead and that, therefore, *in their eyes,* his ministry of preaching and the sacrifice of his life were validated by the Lord almighty, creator of heaven and earth. Whatever our view of the resurrection, historical criticism tells us where the initiative in the

---

7. The following is adapted from Roy A. Harrisville, *His Hidden Grace* (New York and Nashville: Abingdon, 1965).

biblical narrative is laid and where, therefore, it *ought to be laid.* Historical criticism can rightfully point to the little verb *egerthe* ("he was raised") trumpeted in the first three Gospels as well as in the earliest of all Christian expressions of the *kerygma* (1 Cor. 15:3ff.), every one of which assigns the initiative in this act not to the disciples, not even to Jesus (the verb is in the passive!), but to God himself. It can insist that if we must believe in such a thing as a resurrection, we must do so without prince or priest or the authority of the tenured scholar. We must acknowledge it as an occurrence that is contingent on a particular person, place, and period, a contingency that reflects the freedom and sovereignty of the One whose will creates time and times in which faith becomes a possibility. And it can tell us that the reason we have Gospels, and the Bible itself, is that an obscure, ragtag group of followers, without pomp, ceremony, or cultic blessing, were convinced of this contingency and hence of its sovereignty, believed that the initiative lay with God and not with themselves, believed that God was there before they believed. It is here, in this fundamental conclusion to historical research, that historical criticism of the Bible serves the confession of faith.

For Paul Ricoeur the biblical text has preeminence over the interpreter. Whoever the interpreter is, he or she cannot rest assured in a self-secure Cartesian *cogito.* Modern humanity may have freed itself from the oppression of unexamined traditions. It may be justly proud that it calls into question political and economic arrangements. It may display enormous courage as it explores and uncovers unconscious motivation and desires of the human psyche. But it still must know that it cannot stand on its own and that it cannot act alone to remake the world anew detached from the divine. Humanity can live authentically and fully only if it seeks the wisdom of the Scriptures. The scriptures stand outside humanity and draw it to an understanding and wisdom that otherwise it would not have. To be sure, the Scriptures require human talent and industry to be understood. The various hermeneutical energies of complex linguistic investigation, the sustained thought of philosophy, the rigors of structural analysis, the poetical insights of myth and literature are all needed to unlock the riches hidden within its pages. The Bible partakes fully of the historical and psychic particularity of the world. But this particularity points to the universal. God and his Christ come through the Bible. At least this is "the wager" made by the believer who engages in the arduous task of biblical criticism. And when criticism is done in this way, it is a rich and rewarding enterprise.

For Brevard Childs, the spiritual impact of historical criticism must be a factor of the criticism itself. The books of the Bible belong first and foremost to the communities of faith in which they arose. These communities collected and organized these books intentionally as canon, shaping the way in which the books would be understood. These communities did so because they saw themselves not merely as historical and cultural entities, but as witnesses to God. In exploring the biblical canon, historical criticism uncovers, among other things, the effectiveness, wisdom, and theological profundity of this witness as it reaches from the past across to the present and shapes that present in a way that brings it before God and thus changes the way believers live in the world.

What this Augustinian tradition of historical criticism teaches is that, in principle, the rigorous, scientific examination of the Bible can neither destroy nor support faith. It is obligated, however, to point to faith. Historical criticism limits itself to a verification of the verifiable, to a demonstration of the demonstrable — facts, objectifiable history, occurrences, whatever can be known or ascertained by dint of sheer logic and mental effort. It does so in the acute awareness that it is itself subject to changing cultural conditions that exercise a profound influence on how it approaches the biblical record at any given time. Faith, on the other hand, is the appropriation of an event that includes not merely fact but its interpretation, not merely the historical but its significance, not merely occurrence but its meaning. This conjoining of the word of God and the word about God, one event to be believed and obeyed, occurs on every page of Holy Writ.

In Romans 4:25, for example, Paul not merely announces that Jesus was crucified and raised, but that he was "put to death *for our trespasses* and raised *for our justification.*" Biblical criticism deals with only the first half of this sentence, but *faith embraces the whole.* And by faith we mean the assent to the proclamation of the word of God as delivered by that historical particularity we know as the church of Jesus Christ. If faith embraced merely the half, the fact of death and resurrection, it would not be faith at all but mere assent to a proposition. But this means that faith's specific and peculiar character is derived from appropriation of the significance of the fact and not the fact itself.

The Reformers clearly understood that it is not the record of something that has taken place, however verifiable, but rather a witness to the meaning of what has taken place that offers itself to faith. Luther, in his exposition of the Gospels, never tired of emphasizing the insufficiency of a mere *fides historica,* that is, of a faith construed as an assent to brute facts. He thunders that even Satan can believe that Christ was born of a virgin and was laid in a crib at Bethlehem; even the damned believe this story. What is all-important is that the *vobis,* the "to you" in Luke 2:11 ("to you is born this day in the city of David a Savior") be received in faith, for whoever cannot believe that

Christ is born for him, for her, for that one Christ was born in vain.[8] Accordingly, Angelus Silesius (1624-77) put the Christmas word in this fashion: "Wär' Christus tausendmal in Bethlehem geboren und nicht in mir — ich wäre doch verloren" ("I were lost, were Christ a thousand times in Bethlehem born, and not in me"). "Faith does not signify merely the knowledge of the history . . . but signifies a faith which believes not merely the history but also the effect of the history," states the Augsburg Confession, Article 20.

If it is true that faith receives its character as faith from trust in the witness to the meaning of God's saving act in Christ, how can it be destroyed or supported by a study or criticism of that which in the final analysis does not constitute faith as faith? Insofar as historical-critical method brings us before this central truth of Christian existence, it is not the enemy of the church, but its austere teacher, even its friend.

8. *WA,* 27:492; see also 10/I:71.

Index of Names

341

Index of Scripture References